A WALK WITH JESUS

Enjoying the Company of Christ

This study of the life of Christ by R.C. Sproul is based on the gospel of Luke. It can be used in your daily devotional time, whether in individual or family devotions. Most of the chapters are short, and each is based on a particular section of Luke's gospel. These sections are indicated at the beginning of each chapter. Alternatively, the book can be read straight through.

Christian Focus Publications publishes biblically-accurate books for adults and children. The books in the adult range are published in three imprints.

Christian Heritage contains classic writings from the past.

Christian Focus contains popular works including biographies, commentaries, doctrine, and Christian living.

Mentor focuses on books written at a level suitable for Bible College and seminary students, pastors, and others; the imprint includes commentaries, doctrinal studies, examination of current issues, and church history.

For a free catalogue of all our titles, please write to
Christian Focus Publications,
Geanies House, Fearn,
Ross-shire, IV20 1TW, Great Britain

For details of our titles visit us on our web site
http://www.christianfocus.com

A WALK WITH JESUS

Enjoying the Company of Christ

R. C. Sproul

Christian Focus

ISBN 1 85792 2603

© R. C. Sproul
First published in 1999
by
Christian Focus Publications
Geanies House, Fearn,
Ross-shire, IV20 1TW, Great Britain

Cover design by Paz Design Group, 1320 Edgewater Road,
Suite 200, Salem, Oregon, 97305, USA
© Photo – Digital Stock 1999

Contents

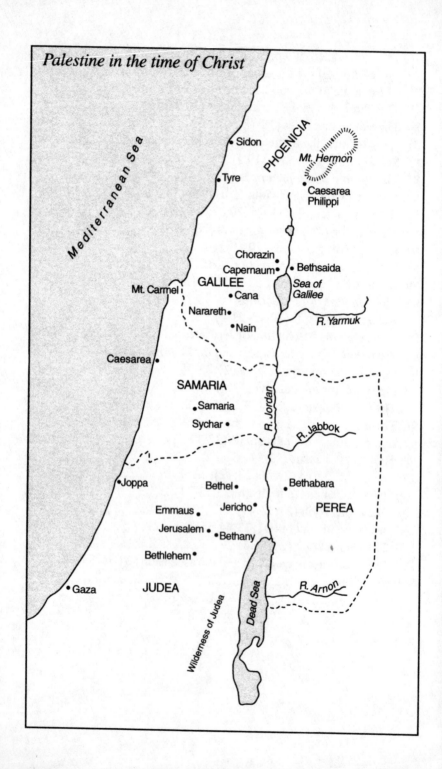

Palestine in the time of Christ

Mediterranean Sea

PHOENICIA

Mt. Hermon

Sidon

Tyre

Caesarea Philippi

Chorazin
Capernaum • • Bethsaida

GALILEE

Mt. Carmel

• Cana

Sea of Galilee

Nazareth

• Nain

R. Yarmuk

Caesarea •

SAMARIA

R. Jordan

• Samaria

Sychar •

R. Jabbok

• Joppa

Bethel •

• Bethabara

Emmaus •

Jericho •

PEREA

Jerusalem •

• Bethany

Bethlehem •

Dead Sea

R. Arnon

• Gaza

JUDEA

Wilderness of Judea

1. Introduction (Luke 1:1-4)

I am sure that every Christian has one gospel that stands out as his or her favourite. If I were forced to choose, I would have to select Luke's. I have studied and taught it in various settings. It seems that the more I read it, the more excited I get about it.

Why was Luke written?
At the outset of Luke (1:1-4) there is what is called the 'prologue'. It is very short, but contains a great deal of important information. In it Luke gives his reason for writing: 'so that you may know the certainty of the things you have been taught' (1:4). It is not as if he says, 'I realize other gospels have been written, but you can't trust them, so let me set the record straight!' Rather, he is attempting to fill out some of the bare details in the other gospels, in order to give a more comprehensive record.

He knows that others have already written about Jesus (1:1), but he seeks to give an 'orderly account' (1:3) of Jesus' life. The New American Standard Version translates as 'consecutive order'; however, that could be a bit misleading as it doesn't necessarily mean chronological order. The gospel writers were not as concerned with the exact sequence of events as we might be today. What Luke means is that he has arranged his gospel in a systematic, logical and readable structure. He does that so we can make sense of the patterns of Jesus' teaching and the movement of his life.

Luke refers to his sources as 'those who from the first were eyewitnesses and servants of the word' (1:2). This reference to 'eyewitnesses' reveals Luke as a historian. He approached his task in a manner customary to ancient historians and so was concerned about eyewitness testimony. For example, with regard to discovering the details of the birth of Jesus, we can imagine him going about Palestine, finding people who were there when Jesus was born: perhaps tracking down a surviving shepherd and asking him to recall the events of that night in the field

outside Bethlehem. Luke might have visited Mary and her
family, questioning and probing to get the information that
makes up the narrative. He had no interest in rumour or
speculation; he wanted eye-witness testimony.

Who was Luke?

The New Testament doesn't give us a comprehensive picture
or biography of Luke. However, we get hints from the New
Testament and the traditions of the early church that Luke was
the one identified by Paul as the beloved physician. His mastery
of language and artistry with words reveal that he was an
educated man. This was no rough-hewn fisherman, but a talented
wordsmith whose mastery of Greek resulted in writings of great
beauty. I think it is safe, therefore, to assume that the traditions
at this point have their roots in accurate history. The author of
this gospel was indeed Luke, the beloved physician and
companion of Paul.

Other traditions inform us that he lived until he was 84, but
he never married and so died childless. He was also said to be
an artist. Whether he was a painter of first rank remains a
speculative question, but that he was a word-artist is
indisputable. His gospel has a literary flow of singular beauty
that repeatedly impresses as we follow his narrative.

To whom did Luke write?

If we can answer that question it will give us insight as to why
the book was written. Luke's is the only gospel that is directly
addressed to a person, to someone named Theophilus (1:3).
There is a great deal of discussion surrounding this name, since
its meaning suggests it could be symbolic. It is made up of two
parts: *theo*, which comes from the Greek, *theos*, meaning God.
Then the word, *philaeo*, one of the New Testament words for
'love'. Put those two words together, *theos* and *phileo*, and we
discover that *Theophilus* means literally, 'one who is a lover of
God'. Hence, some have argued that Luke is simply addressing
his gospel to everyone who loves God. Everyone who loves

God then becomes, in symbolic terms, *Theophilus*.

Interesting and plausible as that theory is, I would not choose it. I think Luke was addressing this book to a specific person. We see that Theophilus is not merely addressed as 'Theophilus', but as 'most excellent Theophilus'. This term 'most excellent' was a common title in the ancient world for nobility. It was an official title for prominent persons of high social standing. Since it was also an ancient custom for authors to dedicate their work to a financial patron, who enabled them to publish their writings, I think Luke was aided in the preparation of his gospel by a wealthy person named Theophilus. Appropriately he addresses both his gospel and the book of Acts to him.

Characteristics of his gospel

It is interesting that Theophilus is not a Jewish, but a Greek name. One of the most clearly discernible things about Luke's account is that it was written primarily for Gentiles. Just as Matthew, with all his Old Testament references, is writing with Jews in mind, so Luke's concern is to communicate the gospel to those outside the Jewish community. It is not surprising that Paul's fellow missionary to non-Jews should write a gospel directed at Gentile nations. He is showing that the gospel is not merely for the Jew, but for all people. This theme of universality is seen repeatedly in the gospel. At the outset, when Luke gives the genealogy of Jesus, he differs from Matthew. Matthew only traces the lineage of Jesus to Abraham, but Luke goes all the way back to Adam. Matthew shows Jesus as one who came to redeem the Jewish people. Luke declares that Jesus came not only for the Jews, but for all mankind. This motif is woven through his gospel as Jesus meets non-Jews: Greeks, Syrophoenicians and others.

Luke's use of the name Theophilus also emphasises the historical setting of God's activity. It was common for late nineteenth century scholars to be sceptical about the trustworthiness of Luke and Acts. Luke was criticised as an historian. His accuracy on details of first century culture was questioned. However, the critics and sceptics have been embarrassed, as Luke's credibility has been successively vindicated. It seems that whenever archaeologists uncover a new Palestinian artefact, Luke's historical accuracy is upheld. One scholarly non-Christian rabbi thought Luke was the finest historian in the ancient world.

Luke had a concern not only for history and universality, but also for individuals, particularly women. One professor has described Luke's gospel as the *Ladies' Home Journal* of the Bible. We see Jesus ministering to women, talking and spending time with them. They were an important part of his entourage. Luke also gives special attention to children and the poor. Jesus cares for the poor and disreputable, as the Anointed One who came to preach the gospel to them.

Finally, Luke establishes the centre stage for the person and work of the Holy Spirit. He has been called the 'theologian of the Holy Spirit'. He ministered during the outpouring of Pentecostal power and what came from it. Luke emphasises the Holy Spirit in Jesus' ministry more sharply than the other gospels. His book is historical; about real people, places and predicaments, but it is also supernatural. Luke reveals the reality of the Spirit's power and presence as he is poured upon Jesus. He traces the Spirit of Christ in his public ministry: from his baptism to the cross; from his transfiguration to his resurrection; to the glorious portrait of Christ ascending into heaven.

2. Gabriel sent to Zechariah (Luke 1:5-25)

We might have expected Luke to start his account of the life of Jesus with his birth or the beginning of his public ministry. Instead Luke begins his record earlier, with the events surrounding the birth of John the Baptist.

At the outset Luke calls our attention to something important when he says those things took place 'in the time of Herod king of Judea'. These words convey a sense of foreboding. Israel was oppressed almost as badly in the days of Herod as they were under Pharaoh. They were under the tyranny of the Romans who had appointed Herod as a puppet king. 'Herod the Great' was ruthless and powerful. Although he was famous for accomplishments in architecture and building, particularly his completion of the rebuilding of the Jerusalem temple, he also murdered members of his own family, and he was the one responsible for the slaughter of the children at the announcement of the birth of Jesus. So Herod's name is infamous and Luke reminds us that the events he narrates took place in this dreadful period of history.

This was not a time of revival or religious zeal. Herod was not one who would call his people back to godliness. He was only interested in building monuments to himself. For him the temple was not a holy place where men could come to worship, but an enormous project for which he could take credit.

Sometimes when we read the Old Testament it seems as if God is performing countless miracles. As we read that concise record of biblical history, we sometimes get confused and lose sight of what reality was at a particular time. Have you ever considered that at this moment in Israel's history Israel had not heard from God through a prophet for 400 years? God had spoken through Moses, Abraham, David and the prophets right up to Malachi. Then there was silence – 400 years of silence from God. We have to include this important fact in our understanding of the historical setting before we will grasp what is happening in the events described in the first chapter of Luke.

Some people remembered the promises God made to their ancestors. They still celebrated the Passover and the other annual festivals, as well as many religious traditions. But after 400 years of waiting, many others had become secular. Luke introduces Zechariah, a priest, and his wife Elizabeth who had not turned away: 'both of them were upright in the sight of God, observing all the Lord's commandments and regulations blamelessly' (1:6).

The name Zechariah means, 'The Lord remembers'. The people had forgotten God's promises but there was a remnant who held firm. A priest, who had no prominent role in public life, lived up to his name and still believed in God. He was committed to the ancient promises and was married to a humble woman who believed them too.

Elizabeth's name means, 'My God is an oath'. Elizabeth herself had been born into a priestly family where, by God's providence, she was prepared for marriage to this godly man. I am sure that they had to encourage one another in times when people had forgotten God.

Here were two servants of God who believed the promises despite suffering one of the greatest disappointments that could befall a Jewish family: they had no children. No doubt they had prayed often about it, but by now they had probably forgotten those prayers, because of their age.

Then Luke records how a day of days came for Zechariah. Priests generally performed their duties in villages and towns. The greatest honour a priest could have was to serve in the temple. However, priests numbered in the thousands and to ensure the tasks were distributed fairly they were assigned by lot. Even then a priest would only serve in the temple once in his lifetime, and this once-in-a-lifetime opportunity fell on Zechariah in his old age (1:8-9).

Zechariah would have gone to the temple with both a joyful anticipation and a sense of fearfulness. He was going to enter the Holy Place to offer up prayers for the nation at the altar of incense. People gathered outside to see the priest when he came out after offering the prayers for the people, because they wanted to know if there was any sign that God had heard his pleas. As Zechariah's mind was fixed on the altar, 'an angel of the Lord appeared to him, standing at the right side of the altar of incense' (1:11).

Naturally Zechariah was terrified, but the angel's first words were, 'Do not be afraid ... your prayer has been heard' (1:13). The exact prayer is not mentioned, but it is unlikely that it was his prayer for a child. Rather, the prayer that has been answered is Zechariah's prayer at the altar for the redemption of Israel, for the Messiah. And because of that his wife will bear a special child who will fulfil a special task for the Lord, that of leading the return of the children of Israel to the faith of their fathers.

Zechariah would not have missed the fact that the angel was quoting from the book of Malachi, repeating the words of the last promise God made to Israel: 'See, I will send you the prophet Elijah before that great and dreadful day of the LORD comes. He will turn the hearts of the fathers to their children, and the hearts of the children to their fathers; or else I will come and strike the land with a curse' (Mal. 4:5-6).

The angel's announcement links the last promise of the Old Testament with the first promise of the New. Zechariah was given the message that he and his wife would be parents of the prophet who would announce the Messiah!

Zechariah had retained confidence in God's promises in an age of unbelief, but this promise is more than he can bear. He stumbles at it: 'How can I be sure of this? I am an old man and my wife is well on in years?' (1:18).

The angel replies simply, 'I am Gabriel. I stand in the presence of God.' Do you see the contrast? Zechariah shows his disbelief when he says,

Some categorise the biblical stories about angels as primitive superstition and mythology, despite the fact that angels are frequently mentioned in the Bible. Angels fulfil two main functions. First, they are messengers from God who announce important events. Second, they minister to God's people during great trials. It is no surprise then that at this time angels are much in evidence, announcing the birth of John and Jesus. This angel made an announcement to Zechariah that would change the course of history.

'I am an old man!' But the angel reminds Zechariah that he is speaking with the authority of God himself. He has come from God with his authority to make this announcement.

'Meanwhile, the people were waiting for Zechariah and wondering why he stayed so long in the temple.' They expected the priest's prayers to last a certain length of time, but too much time had passed and they were becoming apprehensive.

Eventually Zechariah came out, but he could not speak to them. They realised that he had seen a vision in the temple. The order of Luke's words is unusual for he says the people realised Zechariah had seen a vision before he made signs to them. The words seem to suggest that the people realised immediately. As soon as they saw his face they knew he had seen a vision. Perhaps as Zechariah walked out of the temple, he reflected the light of Gabriel's countenance, and the people knew he had been in the presence of a heavenly messenger.

After the days of his ministry in the temple were completed, he went home. No doubt he was eager to tell Elizabeth with signs and gestures of his extraordinary experience.

And Elizabeth became pregnant.

3. Gabriel visits Mary (Luke 1:26-38)

So much controversy rages over the place and function of Mary in the Christian religion. It is a point of contention between Roman Catholics and Protestants, and even between different divisions within those churches. But most Christians agree on the suitability of the title conferred upon Mary by the early church: 'Mother of God'. The title in the Greek language is *theotokos*. It did not call attention to her greatness, neither did it mean that Jesus derived his deity from her. It simply means that the child she bore is God incarnate. This woman had the most holy task of any woman in history.

How did Luke know of Mary's reaction to Gabriel's words? Where did he get his information? In the Introduction we saw that Luke was a careful historian who wanted to get his information from the earliest possible sources. Tradition teaches us that Luke got his information about these events from the lips of Mary herself. We can be confident that this record, although inspired by the Holy Ghost, was researched carefully.

In this passage Luke moves from Zechariah and Elizabeth, but continues to narrate the activities of Gabriel. He greets Mary with these words: 'Hail, favoured one. The Lord is with you.'

Mary's response, however, is very similar to Zechariah's when he met Gabriel. She was greatly troubled and wondered what sort of greeting this was. Gabriel's response again was, 'Do not be afraid, Mary.' His response is the most common negative prohibition that occurs in the New Testament. God knows that we are afraid to come too close to him or to those who remind us of his holiness.

Gabriel continues with a clear promise: 'You will be with child and give birth to a son, and you are to give him the name Jesus. He will be great and will be called the Son of the Most High. The Lord God will give him the throne of his father David, and he will reign over the house of Jacob forever; his kingdom will never end' (1:31-33). This is some message. Mary is astonished and asks the angel, 'How will this be since I am a virgin?'

The angel understood what Mary was asking. He answered, 'The Holy Spirit will come upon you, and the power of the Most High will over-shadow you. So the holy one to be born will be called the Son of God.' This child was not to be born by the normal biological process. He would go through the process of birth, being carried for a full term of pregnancy. Yet he was to differ from all humanity in that he did not have a human father. His conception occurred by the power of the Holy Spirit. This was a miracle in the strictest sense of all: it was an act that only God could bring to pass. God alone can bring something out of nothing; life out of death; fertility from a barren woman; a virgin birth.

Mary responds in words of submission, 'I am the Lord's servant. May it be to me as you have said.' There is no argument from Mary.

The second part of verse 38 has been given a special name in some theological circles. It is called 'Mary's *fiat*'. A *fiat* is a command. God created the world by divine *fiat*. Jesus raised

Lazarus from the dead by the sheer power of his fiat. So the word *fiat* is used to show that Mary is giving a commandment. Those who exalt Mary to a degree of importance beyond what Protestant churches would grant, believe Mary's *fiat* was necessary for Jesus to have been born.

Nothing could be further from the tone of Mary's words. Mary was not giving orders to the angel. She was saying, 'If this is what God wants, then I will do it.'

You may think that there could be nothing greater in all the world than to have an angel make an announcement like this to you. But can you imagine the awesome responsibility that was placed on Mary? Do you realise the price that this woman had to pay to become the mother of Christ? Later, we shall see the promise that goes with the birth of the Messiah is that a sword would pierce her own soul. Yet Mary says to God, 'If that is your will, then I'll do it.' The beginning of Jesus' life is marked by a mother who submits to the will of God. The end of Jesus' life is marked by the words: 'Not my will, but yours be done.'

> Of all the New Testament miracles the virgin birth of Jesus creates the most controversy. It is seen to be incredible by sceptics! At the turn of this century some scholars tried to find a way around it. They said the word *virgin*, if we look back to the Old Testament, could mean simply a young woman. They argued that the Bible never intended to teach a virgin birth in the first place. It is true that the word doesn't have to mean virgin, although that is its principal meaning. But even if the word virgin were not found in the text, how could we miss the concept, when Mary asks, 'How can I have a baby? I have never been with a man.'

4. Mary visits Elizabeth (Luke 1:39-56)

After the angel left Mary, she went to the house of Zechariah and greeted Elizabeth. As soon as Elizabeth heard Mary's greeting, Luke records that 'the baby leaped in her womb, and Elizabeth was filled with the Holy Spirit. In a loud voice she exclaimed: "Blessed are you among women, and blessed is the child you will bear!" ' As the angel greeted Mary, so does Elizabeth. 'But why am I so favoured, that the mother of my Lord should come to me?' she asks. Young Mary would normally have paid homage to Elizabeth, the older of the two; but Elizabeth recognises that she is in the presence of one whom God had highly favoured.

Two women are part of Luke's account of the life of Jesus: Elizabeth, old and barren; Mary, young and virginal. Both of them are to bear children; one to be the herald of the King; the other to be the King himself.

Mary's response to Gabriel's announcement and the words of Elizabeth is to praise the Lord. Mary's song, the *Magnificat*, is one of the most important hymns in the history of the church.

Mary sang from the deepest chamber of her soul. This is a prayer of prayers. What Mary says in this song of prayer is that from the depths of her being she wants God to be exalted. She is a model of adoration.

Great controversies have centred on the role of Mary in redemption. Some have argued that Mary was sinless. Interestingly, Thomas Aquinas came to the conclusion that Mary here confesses her sin. The mother of Christ confesses in the opening words her need of a Saviour. She recognised that her son was also her Saviour.

One of the reasons why Mary sings this song of praise is that she recognised something of great importance: God knew who she was. He noticed her. As a peasant of Nazareth she was not considered to be very important by anybody except her family. Yet God selected Mary to be the mother of Christ. So from the depths of her heart she cries out, 'My soul magnifies the Lord, for he has regarded the low estate of his handmaiden.'

And Mary said:
'My soul glorifies the Lord
    and my spirit rejoices in God my Saviour,
for he has been mindful
    of the humble state of his servant.
From now on all generations will call me blessed,
    for the Mighty One has done great things for me –
    holy is his name.
His mercy extends to those who fear him,
    from generation to generation.
He has performed mighty deeds with his arm;
    he has scattered those who are proud in their inmost
                                                                 thoughts.
He has brought down rulers from their thrones
    but has lifted up the humble.
He has filled the hungry with good things
    but has sent the rich away empty.
He has helped his servant Israel,
    remembering to be merciful
to Abraham and his descendants for ever,
    even as he said to our fathers' (Luke 1:46-55).

One unique thing about Luke's gospel is that he records
several songs inspired by the Holy Spirit. There were
several times in biblical history when the Holy Spirit
inspired people to sing, such as the songs of Moses, after
the children of Israel had been delivered from Pharaoh. It
seems that when God comes and gives his people a song,
it is to celebrate some victory that he has wrought. At this
point the greatest victory of all is still to come, when Christ
enters the world. It is interesting that the Bible promises,
that in heaven, God will give us a new song.

Mary experienced what every human being wants to experience: a sense of her dignity. She cried out in gratitude, words of prophecy: 'From now on all generations will call me blessed.' Two thousand years later Mary is still regarded as the most blessed woman in the history of the human race.

She goes on to praise the power of God. The God who promises to make the impossible possible is mighty. He does great things. Mary uses a frequent biblical image to describe God's might: she speaks of God's arm. The Psalmists often refer to the mighty arm of the Lord. The right arm of God has power that no human force can resist.

Imagine the pomp and circumstance of the emperors in the ancient world. They would march in procession and have slaves bearing their thrones along the way. As they were being carried along, the crowds would bow down to them. They were elevated on thrones in the air for people to admire the self-made gods. Then God would come and, with one tug of his wrist, emperors and kings of the ancient world crashed from their pedestals. This is what Mary says, 'He has brought down rulers from their thrones but has lifted up the humble.' She caught a glimpse of the future restoration of justice that would be inaugurated by the Prince of Righteousness. 'He has filled the hungry with good things but has sent the rich away empty.'

Towards the end of Mary's song we find the same motif we find later in Zechariah's song (Luke 1:67-79). She celebrates the God who remembers his covenant. Luke has an eye on history. He sees that the birth of Jesus does not happen in a vacuum, but 'in the fullness of time'. When Jesus is born, he is born after many promises from God. Covenants have been made between God and man. The promise that had been made to Adam, Noah, Abraham, Isaac and Jacob is now coming into fullness in space and time. 'He has helped his servant Israel, remembering to be merciful.'

Some Christian people seem only as zealous as the strength of the memory of their last religious experience. But there are times when we are called upon to live for Christ when we don't feel like it, when we don't have an overwhelming sense of his presence. Every Christian knows what it means to go through the 'dark night of the soul'. That is when we discover what our faith and memories are made of.

Even if you never experienced another blessing from God or sensed his presence again as long as you lived, you would have no justification to do anything but live each day in praise. You could do nothing but live in gratitude to God for what he has already done in your life. We easily forget, but we are fortunate that God does not forget. When he makes a promise, he keeps it. Mary understood that as she sang.

5. Birth of John (Luke 1:57-80)

In this passage our attention moves back again to the story of Elizabeth and Zechariah. Elizabeth has given birth to her son and all the relatives had gathered together to share in the rejoicing. Luke continues his narrative: 'On the eighth day they came to circumcise the child, and they were going to name him after his father Zechariah, but his mother spoke up and said, "No! He is to be called John" ' (1:59-60). The surprised relatives reply, 'There is no-one among your relatives who has that name.' Their astonishment increases when Zechariah himself writes in agreement that his name should be John. However, we recall that Gabriel declared in the temple that his name should be John.

Throughout the Bible names are often used to describe someone's personality. Jesus called Simon *Petros*, Peter, meaning stone or rock. Sometimes when a person's life was transformed their name would change: Abram became Abraham; Jacob, after he wrestled with God, became Israel; Saul became Paul.

There is a particular significance to the giving of names. Remember that when God created Adam and Eve, one of the first tasks he gave Adam was to name the animals. It was a symbolic gesture expressing the authority God gave him over all creatures. Similarly, in Israel, the act of naming a child was a demonstration of parental authority over the child. But in a few isolated incidents, God reserved that right for himself. On those rare occasions God said, 'I will name the child, because this child is under my authority and related to me in an extraordinary way.'

So when Gabriel announced to Elizabeth and Zechariah that they were going to have a baby, and what the name of that baby was to be, he was giving them a message they understood. He was saying, 'Your baby belongs to God. His name will be given by God himself. God has decreed his name shall be John.'

Zechariah had already been punished for his lack of faith and now God puts him to the test again. Everybody in the family wants to call the baby Zechariah, but Elizabeth refuses, so they go to the father. His answer is the same: his name shall be John. At that moment his punishment was over. He could speak again because he showed his submission to God, in relinquishing this child to his service.

We read that these events produced a sense of awe in all who witnessed them. They were reported throughout all the hill country of Judea. Everyone was asking, 'What manner of child shall this be?' They began to watch and remember. They saw 'the hand of the Lord was with him' as he grew up.

On this occasion Zechariah was also 'filled with the Holy Spirit and prophesied'. He sang in praise to God and in words of prophecy directed at his son. Again we find the themes of redemption, covenant and mercy. In verses 68 and 78 Zechariah uses the word 'come', which the New American Standard Version translates as 'visit', a significant word which would be easy to overlook. It has a rich history in the Old Testament for the people of Israel looked forward to those moments when God would visit his people. The Greek word that is used is *episkope*. The noun form of it is *episkopis* meaning 'bishop', somebody who looks at something intently. So a bishop is one who sees his people and who takes the time to visit them, particularly in their time of need.

There is a positive sense and a negative sense. The bishop in the ancient world was often like a general of the troops. He would come to the outpost not only to see how the troops were in times of crisis, but also in times of preparation to review the troops and see if they were in a proper state of preparedness. When God comes to visit us, for some it will be a surprise visit; they will not be ready for the bishop.

Zechariah, through the Spirit, understands that through these events – the birth of John and the announcement of Christ's birth – God is literally bishoping his people. God himself has come here.

Luke then tells us: 'And the child grew and became strong in spirit; and he lived in the desert until he appeared publicly to Israel' (1:80).

6. The birth of Jesus (Luke 2:1-7)

This part of Luke's narrative describes the most significant birth in the history of humanity. Notice that Luke the historian is very careful to give us the historical context in which Jesus was born. 'In those days Caesar Augustus issued a decree that a census should be taken of the entire Roman world. (This was the first census that took place while Quirinius was governor of Syria.) And everyone went to his own town to register' (2:1-3). This dimension of the narrative makes it quite different from all of the myths and fables that surround the religions of the ancient world. The Greek deities, for example, were never born and raised in real history.

But what was that historical context? Luke tells us that it was during the time that a decree had gone out to all the world from Caesar Augustus. He was one of the most important emperors in the history of the Roman empire, perhaps the most powerful human being before the day Jesus was born. Originally called Octavian, he had emerged as the chief ruler of Rome, and became the first man to be declared emperor of all of the Roman empire. He reigned from 30 BC to 14 AD, under the title Caesar Augustus – the august one. He began all kinds of building programmes and set up a massive system of centralized government, regulating commerce and trade. He strengthened the military and for his entire reign Rome was at peace. With

One of the most fascinating theological studies of our day has been the careful biblical examination of the concept of time. Oscar Cullmann has written a book called *Christ and Time*, and in it he analyses the biblical structure of time. He points out that two different Greek words in the New Testament are translated by our English word, *time*. But those two Greek words have dramatically different meanings. The most commonly found word, *chronos*, has come over into the English language. We use it in many ways: *chronometer*, a word for watch; *chronology*, a sequence of events in a historical manner; *chronicle*, sometimes used for newspapers. It refers to the normal passage of time, what we call *history*.

The other word translated as 'time' is *kairos*. It refers to a single significant moment in time, a moment that determines the future and destiny of all of history. In English we distinguish between that which is *historical* and that which is *historic*. Everything that happens is historical, but not everything is historic. The word *historic* describes moments of special significance; these could be called *kairotic* moments. In the Old Testament, such moments are the day of creation, the Exodus, the giving of the Law on Sinai, and so on. The death, resurrection, ascension and return of Jesus, too, are all moments in time for which the rest of time exists.

The New Testament uses the word, *pleroma,* to refer to the coming of Jesus. It is a single Greek word, but it is usually translated by the phrase 'fullness of time'. That fullness may be illustrated by a glass of water. If you fill a glass of water to the brim it is full, but that is not *pleroma*. When the fullness of *pleroma* takes place, the water flows over the edges. The world was absolutely ripe for the coming of Christ.

his leadership was born that famous period known as the *Pax Romana*, the peace of Rome. He did much to advance the culture of the Roman empire. Towards the end of his life he said, 'I found Rome bricks and I made it marble.' He distinguished himself as probably the greatest statesman of his time.

But there was a sad note from a religious perspective during the reign of Augustus, for it was then that religious worship of the emperor took hold and he took the title, *Dominus et Deus*: Lord and God. It was this title and allegiance to it that would produce grave crises in early church history, bringing Christians into severe trials and tribulations, because they refused to worship the emperor.

In the midst of consolidating his empire Caesar Augustus needed to conduct a census so that he could introduce a widespread taxation programme. To make it easier to implement, people were required to go back to the place of their birth, in order to register for the taxation. One of those who had to do this was a carpenter from Nazareth named Joseph. He did not want to leave his espoused bride to the ridicule and shame of those who were hostile to her, so he took her on an arduous journey, perhaps risking premature birth of her child, in order to fulfil his obligations to the state.

So it was that they went up from Galilee to Bethlehem, the city of David. Bethlehem had originally been called the city of war, and with the change of one letter, was renamed the city of bread and city of peace. It was in that small village that Christ was born. But notice, the only reason historically why Jesus was born in Bethlehem was because of this powerful imperial decree by Caesar Augustus.

It was no coincidence that this imperial decree of Caesar's happened to take place at this time, forcing them to make the journey to Bethlehem. Here is the most powerful emperor in the world acting out the decree of God himself. Caesar Augustus, in the final analysis, was but a pawn in the hands of the Lord God omnipotent. Remember how the prophet Micah had prophesied:

But you, Bethlehem Ephrathah,
> though you are small among the clans of Judah,
out of you will come for me
> one who will be ruler over Israel,
whose origins are from of old,
> from ancient times.   (Micah 5:2)

Micah said that the Messiah would be born in Bethlehem, and when it was God's time, it happened. Luke writes: 'While they were there, the time came for the baby to be born, and she gave birth to her firstborn, a son. She wrapped him in cloths and placed him in a manger, because there was no room for them in the inn' (2:6-7).

7. The shepherds (Luke 2:8-20)

Luke continues to describe the events surrounding the birth of Jesus. After announcing the birth in Bethlehem, he tells us about shepherds who were watching their flock nearby. Isn't it fascinating that when God chose to announce the birth of the Messiah to the world, he didn't inform the rich and powerful leaders of the day? Instead he chose to announce it to shepherds who were tending their flocks nearby. In all probability, the sheep they were tending were the ones that were to be used in the temple sacrifices.

The shepherds of Palestine were considered to be the lowest class of people. The nature of their calling prohibited them from frequent participation in the religious rituals of their day, and there were discriminating practices against them with respect to the law courts, for a shepherd was not permitted to give testimony. They were considered to be so unscrupulous and untrustworthy that their testimony was of little value. But although their contemporary society hated them, it seems that they held a special place in the heart of God.

I remember hearing a lecture entitled, *God's Love Affair with Shepherds*. It gave a remarkable overview of the entire history of redemption, showing the prominent role in biblical history that shepherds played. When God appeared in the burning bush to call a leader to bring forth the Exodus, he chose a man living in exile in the Midianite desert who was tending sheep – his name was Moses. When Israel became a nation, there came a time when a shepherd boy, David, was anointed king. Even if we go to the age of the prophets we find Amos, not a man of great stature, but a shepherd, whom God called into service for himself. Many prominent people in biblical history were called by God from the realm of the culturally insignificant, to be his servants. It was to such people that God sent the angel to announce the birth of the Messiah. Luke's narrative of this event is as follows: 'And there were shepherds living out in the fields nearby, keeping watch over their flocks at night. An angel of the Lord appeared to them, and the glory of the Lord shone around them, and they were terrified' (2:8-9). Like Zechariah in the temple they were paralyzed with fear, but again the angel says, 'Do not be afraid. I bring you good news of great joy that will be for all the people.' Here is the first record in the New Testament of the preaching of the gospel; the good news of great joy for all people.

Notice how personal the angel's message was: 'Today in the town of David a Saviour has been born *to you*; he is Christ the Lord' (2:11). The announcement was followed by directions to the shepherds: 'This will be a sign to you: You will find a baby wrapped in cloths and lying in a manger.' Bethlehem was not a large town. There were not many hotels, so consequently Joseph and Mary were turned away and had to find refuge in a place where Mary brought forth the baby and laid him in a manger. We tend to think of the birthplace of Jesus as perhaps being a stable with a crib made of wood. However, some of the earliest traditions indicate that the manger was in a cave.

Then suddenly there appeared 'a great company of the heavenly host', the angelic army of heaven. But this army that is often associated biblically with those who fight for God, are not declaring war, instead they are singing a song of peace: 'Glory to God in the highest, and on earth peace to men on whom his favour rests' (2:14). This announcement of peace on earth is not the *Pax Romana*, brought about by imperial decree. Nor is it the cessation of warfare between rival groups. This peace is the transcendent peace which brings an end to the conflict between men and God. To those who hear the message of the coming of the Messiah, the war is over. Peace has become incarnated in the Prince of Peace, who came to reconcile us with God.

When the angelic host returned to heaven, the shepherds resolved to go immediately to Bethlehem to find Mary and Joseph, and the baby in the manger. After seeing them, the shepherds became the first evangelists of the Christian church. Their testimony, although worthless in the law courts of the day, was valued by God. He entrusted to them the first human proclamation of the gospel of Jesus Christ. They heard the gospel; they came to Christ; they saw, believed and proclaimed. 'And all who heard it were amazed at what the shepherds said to them.... The shepherds returned, glorifying and praising God for all the things they had heard and seen, which were just as they had been told' (2:18, 20).

How did Luke know all these details concerning the birth of Jesus? Remember that he told his readers that he was going to set down a record based on eyewitness testimony. There is a clue to this problem in verse 19: 'But Mary treasured up all these things and pondered them in her heart.' It is very likely that Luke's source was Mary herself. He visited her and heard the details of what had happened in those early days. He discovered that they were not vague, far-removed memories, but they were etched into her consciousness for ever. She had pondered them as she nursed her child, nurtured him in youth, and watched the unfolding of his career as an adult.

8. The presentation of Jesus in the temple
(Luke 2:21-28)

The rite of purification (Luke 2:21-24)
Have you ever been so tired or so discouraged or so ill that you earnestly wanted to die, but were not allowed to?

Today, we are going to focus our attention on one of the earliest incidents of Jesus' life, the presentation of the infant Saviour in the temple.

> 'On the eighth day, when it was time to circumcise him, he was named Jesus, the name the angel had given him before he had been conceived. When the time of their purification according to the Law of Moses had been completed, Joseph and Mary took him to Jerusalem to present him to the Lord (as it is written in the Law of the Lord, 'Every firstborn male is to be consecrated to the Lord'), and to offer a sacrifice in keeping with what is said in the Law of the Lord: 'A pair of doves or two young pigeons' (2:21-24).

This brief passage of Luke's gospel gives us some insight into the course of the life of Jesus. From the very beginning of his life he was dedicated in every detail to the commandments of God. Even as a baby he was submitted by his parents to the minutest requirements of the Old Testament law, for in the life of Jesus we see one who is dedicated completely to fulfil every obligation that God laid upon his people. In Israel, eight days after giving birth it was mandatory for a woman to go to the temple for the rite of purification, for after childbirth a woman was considered to be ceremonially unclean. It was also a time to offer sacrifices. Sin-offerings were required, and normally the offerings that were made were two-fold. In the first place, a lamb was brought and sacrificed on the altar; and then an additional offering of a single pigeon or a turtledove was made, except in special circumstances. There was a provision in the law that was made especially for those who were very poor; instead of a sacrificial lamb and a pigeon or turtledove, they were allowed to substitute a second turtledove for the lamb, for the turtledove could be purchased cheaply. And so this text tells us something of the early poverty of Jesus' life, and of his humble background.

But not only was Jesus brought to the temple to undergo the rite of purification, he also was brought to be dedicated to the Lord. The Old Testament required of Jewish parents that the firstborn male child should be consecrated to God. Now, of course, many parents went through that procedure as a matter of custom and didn't take it seriously. But in this case, the child that was being dedicated had a special mission to fulfil as the one who was supremely dedicated to God.

The consolation of Israel (Luke 2:25-28)

There are many interesting characters in Luke's gospel, and one of my favourites is Simeon. Very little is known about him, but the sketchy profile that Luke gives us is loaded with significance. Simeon was righteous and devout. He was an old man, who had spent his life probably looking for the consolation of Israel. Isn't that an interesting phrase? 'The consolation of Israel.' The phrase is used in the Bible to call attention to the Jewish hope of the coming of the Messiah. Those Jews who have groaned in times of bondage, wept in times of exile, who now were oppressed under the heavy burden of the tyranny of Rome, looked to heaven for their release from suffering. You see, it is people who experience consistent grief, frustration and pain who want to be consoled.

We are also told that the Holy Spirit was upon him. The phraseology does not indicate a momentary appearance or manifestation of the Holy Spirit upon a man for mighty deeds, as we find sometimes in the Old Testament when the Spirit of the Lord came upon Samson, fell on Gideon, and other great leaders to enable them to perform mighty tasks. These were not lasting or abiding anointings of the Holy Spirit. But the context of this statement indicates that the Holy Spirit was abiding on Simeon. Simeon was especially singled out by God to be uniquely gifted by the Holy Spirit. Not only did he have the unique endowment of God's Spirit upon him, but God had given him a very special

I'm always glad when I see young people become zealous for the Christian faith and become filled with excitement about learning and studying and serving in this capacity or that in the life of the church. But I am also aware of the fact that the youthful exuberance of new Christians often dissipates as they confront a resisting world, a hostile environment. The obstacles and the difficulties that he encounters in his daily life often have a tendency to cool and temper the spirit of the young Christian. What really speaks to me is the old saint, the one who has kept the faith, who has fought the good fight of the faith, who has endured for decade after decade. It is no wonder to me that when the Bible calls us to postures of respect for people, that those who are singled out for honour include the elders who have been faithful, those people who have maintained devotion to God over a long period of time. Those are the people who deserve our utmost respect, and how easy it is for us to treat the elderly with contempt, as though their testimony, their track records, were insignificant.

revelation. We read in verse 26: 'It had been revealed to him by the Holy Spirit that he would not see death before he had seen the Lord's Christ.'

Luke does not tell us how Simeon received that revelation. All we know is, God privately told Simeon that before he died he would see the Messiah with his own eyes. I wonder how he handled that special information? I wonder if there were times that he doubted it? I wonder if he told any of his contemporaries that he had had a special revelation of this kind? What do you think would happen to you if God gave you a secret, a private message, and you told that to your friends? I think if you told too many of them you would learn very quickly to be quite selective in sharing that experience because most people would consider you a bit daft. When I think of Simeon, I think of this old saint, who spent his days in the temple. He would come into the temple each morning. He

would look around and the priest in the temple would say, 'What
are you doing, Simeon? What are you looking for?' Simeon
would say, 'Well, I just came today to check and see if the
Messiah was here.' He would be disappointed day after day after
day. But God had told him that he would see the Messiah and he
had waited and waited, and gone time after time after time,
presumably, to the temple, yet every time that he went, looking
for the Messiah, the Messiah was nowhere to be seen. The
promise was not fulfilled.

But then, one day, as was his custom, he came to the temple,
and we read that he came 'in the Spirit'. Luke tells us that when
the parents brought in the child Jesus, 'that they made concerning
him after the custom of the Law, then he (that is, Simeon)
received him into his arms and blessed God.' He saw a poverty-
stricken peasant couple, holding a baby which perhaps was still
adorned with swaddling cloths, but instantly, because of the gift
of the Holy Spirit, he recognized the Saviour.

9. Simeon and Anna (Luke 2:29-38)

Simeon's prophecy (Luke 2:29-35)
As Simeon saw the Christ-child, he burst into song under the
influence of the Holy Spirit, singing one of the earliest of all
Christian hymns:

> Sovereign Lord, as you promised,
>> you now dismiss your servant in peace.
> For my eyes have seen your salvation,
>> which you prepared in the sight of all people,
> a light of revelation to the Gentiles,
>> and for glory to your people Israel.   (Luke 2:29-32, NIV)

This song has become known as the *Nunc Dimittis*, after the
words of the early Latin translation.

Do you see what is behind the song? 'O Lord, I don't have to
watch this child grow up, I don't have to watch him talk with the
doctors in the temple as a lad of twelve years old; I don't have

to watch him multiply the fishes and the loaves to feed five thousand people to be convinced. I don't have to watch him walk on the water or turn the water into wine. I don't have to be on the Mount of Transfiguration. I don't have to be an eye-witness of the resurrection, or his ascension into heaven. I have seen all I need to see. Now, let me die in peace.' One glimpse of the Christ-child, and Simeon was ready to go home to God.

Simeon was faithful all along. But when the promise was fulfilled, he didn't run out into the street and say, 'I told you so! I told you so!' He didn't care for one minute that his reputation be vindicated. He just wanted to enter into his rest, to experience the peace that he had waited for so patiently.

There's another little detail in this song that is unusual. In the opening line, the word for 'Lord' is not the one usually used in the New Testament (*kyrios*). Instead it is a very unusual word, one used only infrequently for God: *despoteis*. This is the word from which we get the English word *despot*. It means one who has absolute power over someone. The word has a very negative connotation to us in the English language: a despot is one who rules by brute force and who exercises tyranny over people. That's not the point here in the New Testament. God is seen as having absolute authority over his servant, Simeon, and Simeon addresses God as his *despoteis*, indicating his total allegiance and total submission to the authority of God.

As he sang his song, we read that the parents of Jesus 'marvelled at what was said about him. Then Simeon blessed them, and said to Mary, his mother, "Behold, this child is destined to cause the falling and rising of many in Israel, and to be a sign that will be spoken against, so that the thoughts of many hearts will be revealed. And a sword will pierce your own soul also "' (2:33-35). Simeon, after he had taken the child in his arms and sung the *Nunc Dimittis*, then turned his attention to Mary and to Joseph, and under the inspiration of the Holy Spirit, uttered a very brief but significant prophecy. He said, 'Behold, this Child is appointed for the fall and rise of many in Israel.' A paradoxical statement. What did he mean? Did he mean that

Jesus, who would frequently be called a 'stumbling-stone' or a 'rock of offence', will be one that many people will come to for strength, to be elevated, to be established, to be set up, but others will trip over him and fall on their faces? The idea here as elsewhere in the New Testament is that with Christ there is no neutrality. When a person encounters Christ he is either for him or against him. He either trips over him, or is established by him, which fulfils, of course, the prophecy of Simeon.

Simeon said that Jesus would be 'a *sign* to be opposed'. The word for *sign* is a very strong word, and indicates a manifestation that is so visible, that is so clear, that no-one could miss it. It is a word that is often used in the New Testament for a miracle: for example, in John's gospel, when Jesus does a miracle John writes, 'And Jesus did this sign...'. It is the sign that bears witness to the identity of Christ, to his power, character and nature as the Son of God. It is a sign that will provoke hostility. People will speak against it.

Then the prophecy becomes much more poignant and personal, as there is a special word for Mary. It is a word of sadness, an ominous foreboding prophecy of the future. The gentle Simeon looked into her young face and said, 'And a sword will pierce even your own soul.' This can only refer to the passion of Christ. Mary was there when her son was crucified. The word for sword refers to a long sword: it could be called a spear. Think of Mary standing at the foot of the cross, when the centurion took a spear and put it into the side of her son. What did she feel? Obviously she didn't feel the cold blade of steel penetrate her own skin, but she felt it in her soul.

Anna's prophecy (Luke 2:36-38)

Following this solemn prophecy by Simeon, Luke gives a very brief account of an elderly woman who was also present:

> And there was a prophetess, Anna, the daughter of Phanuel, of the tribe of Asher. She was advanced in years, having lived with a husband seven years after her marriage, and then as a widow to the

age of eighty-four. And she never left the temple, serving night and day with fastings and prayers (2:36-37, NASB).

Anna is identified as a prophetess. That in itself makes her very unusual, for only on a handful of occasions throughout the Old Testament do we find the description of a prophetess, a woman gifted to speak the word of God to her people. It is also interesting that this woman is said to have been from the tribe of Asher, because Asher was one of the so-called ten 'lost tribes' of Israel. After the captivity in Babylon, the ten tribes, as tribal units, were pretty much lost from the scene, although there were individuals from them who still kept a record of their tribal lineage.

Luke tells us that she was very old and had spent the majority of her years in singular devotion to the things of God. She served God in the temple, day and night, with 'fastings and prayers'. It is interesting that Luke should describe her life of fasting and prayer as a life of service to God. Usually we think that service involves preaching, or teaching, or reaching out to the poor, the hungry or the imprisoned, all of which, of course, are forms of service and dedication to God. But this singular devotion of prayer and fasting can also be a ministry.

One of the most unusual people I have ever met was a gentleman I knew when I was a college professor. He was an elderly man, and had served for decades as a foreign missionary, until age and infirmity made it necessary for him to retire. He decided, however, that he still wanted to have a mission of service to God, and even though he was infirm and almost totally bedfast, he committed himself to working for Christ for eight hours a day. Those eight hours were spent in concentrated prayer. He couldn't walk; he couldn't give messages; he was almost blind and consequently couldn't write; all that he could do was to offer service to God through a ministry of prayer. What a saint he was! Whenever I spoke with him I couldn't help but think of the statement of James, that 'The effective prayer of a righteous man can accomplish much' (Jas. 5:16). And if there was anybody that I wanted to pray for me, it was this old, retired missionary, because he knew how to pray.

That's the kind of person Anna was, and like Simeon, she came into the temple. We read in verse 38: 'Coming up to them at that very moment, she gave thanks to God, and spoke about the child to all who were looking forward to the redemption of Jerusalem.' So, she, too, recognized in this baby the Messiah. For the phrase that she spoke to all who were 'looking for the redemption of Jerusalem' is very much like the one used of Simeon, who was looking for the 'consolation of Israel'. Both of those phrases mean the same thing. These were people who were looking for the Messiah. Anna was acquainted with that handful of people, God's remnant, who still believed, who still waited, who still hoped, for the coming of the Messiah, and she went and told them the good news that she had seen the Lord's Christ.

10. The childhood of Jesus (Luke 2:39-52)

The hidden years' (Luke 2:39-40)
Now Luke, at this point, does something rather uncharacteristic. Where the accounts of Jesus' life found in the other gospels can be brief and sketchy, Luke tends to fill in some of the gaps with a little more detail, as can be seen in the nativity narrative. He gives us more information about the birth of Jesus than any other writer. But at this stage in his narrative he skips over events that the other writers tell us about. For instance, there is no mention here about the visit of the Magi to the newborn Christ; there is no mention here of the slaughter of the innocents by Herod; there is nothing said of the flight into Egypt. For reasons known only to Luke, all he has to say about the first twelve years of our Lord's life is: 'And the child grew and became strong; he was filled with wisdom, and the grace of God was upon him' (2:40). Consequently, these years are usually called the 'hidden years' of Jesus. There is virtually nothing known of Jesus in his childhood, except that which can be reconstructed through deduction and speculation.

For example, we do know that Jesus was raised in Nazareth, that he was the child of a carpenter, and presumably he was careful to learn that trade, as it had significance for him later on in life. We also can assume that Jesus was careful to study the scriptures of the Old Testament and to fulfil the obligations of the synagogue and so on. But in terms of his activity there are no specific references before the age of twelve.

Luke, however, does tell us this much: 'And the child grew and became strong; he was filled with wisdom, and the grace of God was upon him' (2:40). We can imagine that the child Jesus, though he was a child, and not a superman, was the example of the new humanity. He was a child who was growing up uniquely

One of the interesting dimensions of church history is that, in addition to the books of the New Testament that are contained within the Canon, there are so-called 'apocryphal gospels' that appeared for the most part in the second century. These gospels were forgeries; they were spurious in content. If one were to take the time to read the Gospel of Thomas or the Gospel of Peter, for example, it would become immediately apparent that they are indeed fraudulent documents. The style and the content are not only incredible, but at times bizarre. Those who wrote these fraudulent gospels attempted to capture the public imagination by speculating freely on the early days of Jesus, about which the gospel writers were silent. One writer describes how Jesus, on one occasion, was lonely, and so he fashioned some doves out of clay, and said some magic words, and made the birds come to life to be his playmates. In another story Jesus was being tormented by some children, but he exercised his divine powers and zapped them. Of course, these stories always manifest a frivolous use of power, almost of the sort we would find in the comic book stories.

in at least one sense: he grew without the handicap of the power of original sin. He was the second Adam, who was like us in every respect except one: he was sinless. And that sinlessness not only means that Jesus never actively disobeyed the law of God, but also that he was born without the curse of Adam's seed, born without a corrupt human nature. And so he grew without the physical, mental and spiritual impediments of sin. And so it is natural to expect that he would be extraordinary as a human being even in his youth. It is not surprising, therefore, that Luke describes him as 'increasing in wisdom' for 'the grace of God was upon him'.

Jesus in the temple (Luke 2:41-52)
The only narrative that we have of Jesus in his youth is the well-known story of his visit to the temple in Jerusalem. The parents of Jesus went to Jerusalem to celebrate the Passover as was their custom. It was expected and, indeed, required of every male Jew, even from the provinces, to visit the Holy City to celebrate the greatest of all Old Testament feasts, the celebration of the Passover. And we read that Jesus was twelve years old. This has provoked some controversy. Some critics of the text say this is obviously a mistake; there would be no reason for Jesus' parents to take him to the temple then, because the custom in Israel was for the boy to come to the temple for the purpose of his bar-mitzvah, at the age of thirteen. This was the age at which the Jewish boy became a man, and went through the bar-mitzvah, which simply means 'son of the commandment', entering into the full measure of adult commitment to the covenant of Moses.

But research has shown that the critics have spoken too soon. It was customary in ancient Israel for boys to be taken to the temple a year or two in advance of their bar-mitzvah, so that they might become familiar with the operations of the temple and of the educational programmes of the rabbis there. It was almost like a trial run, a time of orientation, so that a child, when he did reach thirteen, would have had some preparation. So Jesus went to Jerusalem at twelve, perhaps for his initial orientation of the structures and customs of the temple.

After they had attended the feast and were returning home, unknown to Joseph and Mary, Jesus stayed behind in Jerusalem. As the pilgrims left Jerusalem, they travelled in their large family clans, by way of caravan. Luke writes that Mary and Joseph 'supposed him to be in the caravan, and went a day's journey, and they began looking for him among their relatives and acquaintances' (2:44, NASB). Usually, the women and the younger children would go at the front of the caravan, while the men and the older children would go in the rear. Now Jesus was at that age where he was in between the two groups. And it is very possible that Joseph thought Mary had him and Mary thought Joseph had him, or perhaps they thought that he was with the other members of the family – uncles, aunts or cousins.

When they discovered that Jesus was not with them, they were very distressed, and made their way back to Jerusalem. It is likely that they didn't begin their journey back immediately, but stayed overnight with the caravan, and left in the safety of the daylight. As they were one day out, it would take another day to return, and so it was on the third day that they were able to find their lost son. And when they found him, he was in the temple, sitting in the midst of the teachers, listening to them and asking them questions.

After the feast it was the custom for the theologians of Israel to remain there for a few days to have what they called 'theological disputations', in which they would share the latest ideas and insights into theology. The students of the rabbis would sit at their feet, for their learning process was very similar to that of Socrates and Plato at the Academy: it was through questions and answers. The students would ask the rabbi questions, and at times, as a teaching technique, the rabbi would return questions to the students. It was in that situation that Jesus was found, astonishing everybody with his unbelievable understanding and insight to these things, and all who saw him were amazed. And his mother said to him, 'Son, why have you treated us like this? Your father and I have been anxiously searching for you' (2:48).

Some have thought that Jesus was being irresponsible, perhaps even sinning, and that this would cast a shadow on the whole concept of his sinlessness. But if there was anything here it was a naïvety. Jesus assumed that his parents would understand and know what it was all about. He said, 'Why were you searching for me? Didn't you know that I had to be in my Father's house?' How significant that the first recorded words of Jesus are ones that go to the heart of his own destiny, to his vocation and calling as the Messiah. Here Jesus is consciously identifying himself as the Son of God, because it was his Father's house.

So the parents returned with Jesus to Nazareth, where he continued as a model child. Luke tells us that 'he went down to Nazareth with them and was obedient to them.... And Jesus grew in wisdom and stature, and in favour with God and men' (2:51-52). Jesus continued to grow, not as we do sometimes, from sinfulness to obedience, but he moved from faith to faith, from grace to grace, from strength to strength, from obedience to higher levels of obedience, because as he increased in his understanding and knowledge of what God had called him to do, he had a greater capacity for deeper levels of obedience. From a human perspective he remained for a season a carpenter's son. Piecing together the evidence from the rest of Scripture, we learn that Joseph died while Jesus was quite young. It would have been necessary, therefore, for Jesus to assume the role of the head of the house and the charge of the carpenter's shop. In all of these things he grew and grew, waiting for the beginning of his public ministry.

Luke again comments, 'But his mother treasured all these things in her heart' (2:51b). We can be sure that the record of this event in Jerusalem came to Luke from Mary herself, who had been watching and pondering as her child grew to maturity.

11. John the Baptist (Luke 3:1-6)

Luke's narrative moves on now to set the scene for the appearance of John the Baptist, the greatest prophet of the Old Testament. Yes, his history is written in the pages of the New Testament, but the period in which he worked and preached was still the Old Testament period. The New Testament, as a period of history, did not begin until Jesus inaugurated the new covenant and fulfilled the old. So John the Baptist was still living under the old structure. In fact, Jesus tells us that the law and the prophets reign *until* John, and the word *until* means up to and including John. Jesus said that none of the prophets were greater than John. We may have more information about some of the other prophets, but all of them shared a common responsibility: each wrote and spoke to foretell the coming Messiah. All except John; he was the herald of the King himself. He was the forerunner, uniquely endowed by God to usher in the age of the Messiah. The prophets of the old period dreamed of such a privilege, but to John it was a reality.

Luke gives his narrative of the appearance of John the Baptist a concrete, historical setting:

> Now in the fifteenth year of the reign of Tiberias Caesar, when Pontius Pilate was governor of Judaea, and Herod was tetrarch of Galilee, and his brother Philip was tetrarch of the region of Iturea and Trachonitis, and Lysanius was the tetrarch of Abilene, in the high priesthood of Annas and Caiaphas, the word of God came to John (3:1-2, NASB).

Both John and Jesus were born during the reign of the Emperor Caesar Augustus, the greatest statesman in the history of the Roman empire. In stark contrast to Caesar Augustus, however, the reign of Tiberias was characterized by extreme severity and cruelty. Augustus died in AD 14, and, as this was the fifteenth year of Caesar Tiberias' reign, we can assume that these events happened perhaps at the end of the year 28 or the beginning of the year 29.

We are also told that Pilate, who figures prominently in the

Passion of Jesus, was the ruler over Judea. Pilate's rule is strange because it was customary for Rome to install nationalist leaders to be their puppet rulers in conquered lands. When Jesus was born, for example, an Edomite/Jew was on the throne, even though he was responsible to Rome, and his name, of course, was Herod the Great. When Herod the Great grew old, and was deposed, however, his kingdom was divided among his sons, and these sons were called 'tetrarchs', which simply means a ruler over a fourth – a somewhat confusing idea because Herod the Great had only three sons. His son Archelaus was given that part of Palestine known as Judea in which Jerusalem is found. He was so bad and so wicked, that the people petitioned Rome to have him replaced by a Roman governor! The governor that was sent was an up-and-coming diplomat, by the name of Pontius Pilate. It is interesting also that in those days Palestine was a testing ground for young governors who had potential for the future. Because of the Jews' obstinate refusal to be Romanized, it was a difficult land to rule over and, therefore, was a great test. And there is a certain sense in which Pilate's entire future career was on the line with this appointment as governor of Judea.

Herod the tetrarch of Galilee is also mentioned in this first verse. He would be Herod Antipas, also a son of Herod the Great. He, too, figures prominently in New Testament literature. He is the one that Jesus calls 'that fox, Herod'. Herod the Great died in 4 BC, and Herod Antipas ruled over Galilee, the northern part of Palestine for thirty-five years, till he was deposed by the then-emperor Caligula for a very strange reason. He had enormous authority, power and riches, but he didn't like the title *tetrarch*. When he appealed to the emperor for the title of king, instead of receiving the title, he received banishment. He lost his kingdom over a title.

Two other interesting people are mentioned in the second verse: Annas and Caiaphas. These two men are described as being 'the high priest'. This begs the question whether Luke understands the workings of the temple in Jerusalem? If he did, surely he would know that the fundamental principle of the priestly system is that there is only one high priest at any given time? In this case, however, Annas had been the high priest for several years, but he got into trouble with Gratus, the Roman governor at that time. He deposed Annas, but Annas saw to it that his son-in-law, Caiaphas, was elevated to the role of high priest. And so Caiaphas was the official high priest when John the Baptist began his ministry, but Annas was still alive, and it is very clear from the biblical testimony that Annas was the power behind the priestly throne. This power is demonstrated later on during the trial of Jesus; Jesus was taken first to Annas and then to Caiaphas. The temple was under the control of two high priests – one who had been deposed and one who was now reigning officially – Annas and Caiaphas.

The voice of one crying in the wilderness (Luke 3:2-6)

We read in verse 2: 'the word of God came unto John the son of Zacharias in the wilderness' (NASB). Luke doesn't describe John's physical appearance in the detail we find in the other gospels; the strange garments made of camel-hair that John wore, and the strange diet of locusts and wild honey and so on. These descriptions make John seem like a wild man; he comes out of the wilderness, preaching a very strong and severe message of repentance. He is reminiscent of the Old Testament prophet Elijah, and the significance of this resemblance is something to which we will return later. But it is interesting that John comes from the wilderness, the traditional meeting-place between God and his people. The wilderness – a place of silence and loneliness – is often the place where God calls his people.

Luke writes:

And he came into all the district around the Jordan, preaching a baptism of repentance for the forgiveness of sins; as it is written in the book of the words of Isaiah the prophet,

'The voice of one crying in the wilderness,
"Make ready the way of the Lord,
Make his paths straight.

Every ravine shall be filled up,
And every mountain and hill shall be brought low;
And the crooked shall become straight,
And the rough roads smooth;
And all flesh shall see the Salvation of God.'" (3:3-6, NASB)

The word used for *crying* in the quote from Isaiah is not the word for soft weeping, but for *howling*. So the picture we get is of an energetic prophet crying out to the people of his day, to repent and be baptized.

Baptism was not unknown in the Old Testament, but it did have a specific function. Of the Old Testament rites of purification, of ceremonial cleansing, the most important was the practice of so-called *proselyte baptism*. This was reserved for Gentiles alone. If a Gentile wanted to become a Jew he had to do at least three things: he had to embrace the teachings of Judaism and make a confession to that effect; secondly, he had to undergo the rite of circumcision, to be singled out with the mark and sign of the covenant; and thirdly, he had to undergo the rite of proselyte baptism. Why? Because the Gentile, who was a stranger and foreigner to the covenant of God, was considered to be unclean. So before he could enter into the household of Israel, into the covenant of Moses, he had to be washed.

It follows, therefore, that we would expect John's announcement of the need to repent and be baptized to be directed at a Gentile congregation, but instead he does something that is both unique and scandalous to the nation. He came demanding that Jews be baptized. Unthinkable! Any Jew listening to him would have got the message, 'You are unclean!' John was addressing Jews, indeed, their religious leaders, as if they were Gentiles. The point is this: that a new era was about to start. The paths of Israel had become crooked. The religious leaders had become corrupt. The visible church of the day had become faithless. John is saying that the Messiah is ready to come, but the people are not ready. The people of God are unclean. If they want to meet the Messiah they will have to be cleansed first.

12. John's prophecy (Luke 3:7-15)

The day of the Lord is at hand (Luke 3:7-9)
'He therefore began saying to the multitudes who were going out
to be baptized by him, "You brood of vipers, who warned you
to flee from the wrath to come?"' (3:7, NASB). These are hardly
complimentary words! No wonder the ministry of John the
Baptist was short.

He continues: 'Therefore bring forth fruits in keeping with
repentance, and do not begin to say to yourselves, "We have
Abraham for our father", for I say to you that God is able from
these stones to raise up children to Abraham' (3:8, NASB). In
other words, he is warning them not to count on their traditions,
their birthright, the fact that they are descendants of Abraham,
for that is no guarantee that they are ready for the kingdom of
God. This great prophet is prophesying to his own people,
warning them that the day of the Lord is at hand. He is the herald
of the King, about to usher in a brand new age.

And then he says in verse 9: 'And also the axe is already laid
at the root of the trees; every tree, therefore, which does not bear
good fruit is cut down and thrown into the fire' (NASB). The
imagery here is not of a woodsman about to begin his task of
chopping down the tree. No, the imagery here is of a woodsman
who has already done the preliminary chopping; the axe is now
at the root, the very core of the tree. In my mind's eye I see a huge
tree that has been chipped away at, and is now beginning to
squeak as it totters back and forth, hanging by just one small
piece of pulp. And I see the woodsman raising his axe for the
final blow that will bring down the tree. John the Baptist's
message is that the kingdom is not far off in the future. The
Messiah is at the door; he is right at hand. The axe is laid at the
root of the tree. Any second and he will be here.

The people's response to John (Luke 3:10-15)
In Luke 3:10 we learn of the people's response to John's strident
call to repentance. 'And the multitudes were questioning him,

saying, "Then what shall we do?" And he would answer and say to them, "Let the man who has two tunics share with him who has none; and let him who has food do likewise"' (3:10-11, NASB). And so the prophet's first response sounds very much like the prophets of the Old Testament, showing concern for love, for charity, for a spirit of sacrifice, that those who had more than they needed should be moved with compassion towards those who are in want.

Luke continues: 'And some tax-gatherers also came to be baptized, and they said to him, "Teacher, what shall we do?" And he said to them, "Collect no more than what you have been ordered to" ' (vv. 12-13, NASB). To collect the taxes the Roman conquerors appointed local people from the rank and file of Israel herself, and these worked on a commission basis. They were assigned quotas of taxes that they had to raise and then they were paid on a percentage basis for meeting their quotas. Now some of them, of course, misused their power and authority as tax-gatherers, demanding of the helpless, the weak and the poor of the land more taxes than Rome herself required. And then of course, in their thieving fashion, the tax-collectors pocketed the difference. No wonder they were considered to be the worst kind of sinner. No wonder they were hated and despised by their own countrymen, for they were traitors, involved in exploitive treachery against their own fellow-countrymen.

However, the tax-gatherers also came and listened to John's preaching, and his admonition to them was simple: 'Collect no more than what you have been ordered to.' Notice John did not demand that they give up their particular occupation, but he did demand that they stop using their office as a means for extortion.

Luke goes on: 'And some soldiers were questioning him saying, "And what about us, what shall we do?" And he said to them, "Do not take money from anyone by force or accuse anyone falsely, and be content with your wages"' (3:14, NASB). Again, John the Baptist does not require that the soldiers cease being soldiers. In all probability the soldiers who were there were not fighters so much as functionaries of the local government to keep the peace. They were the enforcers of the tax-gatherers and again were not highly paid, and it would seem they took advantage of their protection and power as law-enforcement agents. John's words to them were, 'You are not to violate people with your authority. Nor are you to bring false accusations against people.' False accusations were customary in the graft and corruption of that day and still happen even in our own day, as several prominent cases have demonstrated. Of course, not all law-enforcement officers are like that, but it is a problem that goes with the territory. John also charged them to be content with their wages. Those who were not content with their wages were those who were most often tempted to make use of their power of extortion.

In verse 15 we read: 'The people were in a state of expectation and all were wondering in their hearts about John, as to whether he might be the Christ' (NASB). John was so strange; he had such a powerful message. He was so eloquent and the people were flocking to him. And the public mind was rife with rumour.

13. Preparing the way for Christ (Luke 3:16-20)

The rumours were flying about who John was, and many asked if he was, in fact, the Christ. Luke writes that: 'John answered and said to them all, "As for me, I baptize you with water; but One is coming who is mightier than I, and I am not fit to untie the thong of his sandals; he will baptize you with the Holy Spirit and fire"' (3:16, NASB). In this statement, John very clearly repudiates any notion that he was the Christ, but takes advantage of the question to bear witness to the one who is coming. This is John's destiny; this is his mission: to prepare the way for Christ. He points them to the one to come whose baptism is with the Holy Spirit and with fire. He will be mightier than John, and John declares that he is not even worthy to untie his sandals. That was really rather a radical statement for John to make. In those days, rabbis, teachers and religious leaders had disciples, as John the Baptist had disciples, as Jesus had disciples. And there were certain customs that governed the rules of behaviour of a student in the presence of his teacher, or a disciple in the presence of his rabbi. The disciple was not merely expected to learn from his rabbi, to be a humble student, but he was also expected to act in the capacity of the rabbi's servant. There was a rabbinic saying: 'Every service which a slave performs for his master shall a disciple do for his teacher, except the loosing of his sandal thongs.' The disciple performed the same services that a slave had to perform for his master with one notable exception, according to rabbinic tradition. The disciple was not required to untie the thong of the sandals of his rabbi; that was too humiliating, too beneath the dignity of a student who some day would take his own place as a rabbi. But here is John the Baptist, to whom all the rabbis are coming, who says: 'One is coming who is mightier than I, and I am not worthy to untie the thong of his sandals.'

It is interesting that the New Testament writers portray the coming of Jesus as a crisis experience, indeed as the most significant crisis of all of history. Ironically, the English word, *crisis*, comes from the Greek word, *croesus*, which means *judgment*. Much of the imagery of the advent of Christ centres on the warning that when Christ comes he comes not only to redeem mankind, but he comes to pronounce judgment. This is the judge of heaven and earth coming into world history, and his coming is the crisis by which all men will ultimately be judged. And therein lies the urgency of John's message. He is saying, 'The judge is at the door! The one before whom each one of you must stand and give an account for your life. He is coming now, but you are not ready! His winnowing-fork is in his hand and he will purge his floor. He will gather the wheat. And he will burn the chaff with fire unquenchable!' No wonder that John the Baptist's was a voice that had to be silenced. His preaching struck terror into the hearts of his contemporaries.

The voice that had to be silenced (Luke 3:17-20)

John continues his description of the coming one with these words: 'And this winnowing fork is in his hand to thoroughly clear his threshing floor, and to gather the wheat into his barn; but he will burn up the chaff with unquenchable fire' (3:17, NASB). The winnowing fork was the instrument used by farmers in the ancient world to divide the chaff from the wheat. The process was a simple one. The good kernels of wheat weighed more than the chaff and so the farmer would pile the wheat and chaff together on the threshing floor, and then, using this long fork-like tool, he would throw it all up into the air, and just the general movements of the air currents would be enough to do the job of separation for him as the lighter chaff would ride the air currents and be carried off to the side. Remember how John had used the image of the wood-cutter, saying that the Messiah is as close as an axe laid at the root of the tree? Now he carries this message further with the image of the farmer who isn't just thinking about coming into the threshing floor to divide the wheat from the chaff, instead his winnowing fork is in his hand. The moment of decision is now.

Luke continues:

> So with many other exhortations also he preached the gospel to the people. But when Herod the tetrarch was reproved by him on account of Herodias, his brother's wife, and on account of all the wicked things which Herod had done, he added this also to them all, that he locked John up in prison (3:18-20, NASB).

John the Baptist did not confine his preaching to Sabbath mornings at the synagogue. His preaching was public and was sharply critical of the power-structures of his age. He took on the religious authorities – the Sadducees and the Pharisees. He took on the military leaders. Then he took on the king, and publicly denounced him for his illicit marriage to his brother's wife, for in Jewish law, the act of marriage of Herod to Herodias was not only adultery, but was also considered to be incest. It was scandalous that the king, who in Old Testament days was supposed to be a model of devotion to God and of purity to the people, should carry on in this manner, taking advantage of his power and public position to disregard any kind of obedience to the laws of God. But John the Baptist rebuked him for it. No wonder the prophets of the Old Testament were killed, because their message was the message of criticism. The role of the prophet in Israel was to be the conscience of the nation, and here, when John the Baptist intruded into the conscience of Herod the tetrarch, he incurred the wrath of Herod's wife and of his daughter. This led to his imprisonment and ultimately to his death.

14. The baptism of Jesus (Luke 3:21-38)

Luke continues in verse 21 with a very important narrative: 'When all the people were being baptized, Jesus was baptized too. And while he was praying, heaven was opened, and the Holy Spirit descended on him in bodily form like a dove. And a voice came from heaven, "You are my Son, whom I love; with you I am well-pleased." ' This incident poses a bit of a puzzle: since John's baptism was a baptism indicating repentance of sin, and Jesus was sinless, why was Jesus baptized?

If you have struggled to make sense of this, let me tell you you are not alone. Many people in the church have struggled with that, but more significantly, we read in the accounts by Matthew and John that John the Baptist, himself, protested about it. When Jesus presented himself at the Jordan river for baptism, John said, 'Wait a minute! I can't baptise you; you should be baptising me!' But Jesus, in a sense, pulled rank and said, 'John, suffer it now. Let it be! For it must be done to fulfil all righteousness.' Jesus had a mission to perform and part of it was to fulfil all righteousness.

So what did Jesus mean by fulfilling all righteousness? As the Messiah, as the sin-bearer, it was incumbent upon him to fulfil the law of God in every detail. As sin-bearer, he had to enter into his people's indebtedness before God. He had to become one with them, entering into the sin of his people as the Lamb of God.

The standard response of any child who has ever been to Sunday school to the question: 'What did Jesus do for you?', is: 'He died on the cross for my sins.' We know that Jesus took the punishment that we deserve, but that is not all that he did to redeem us. Had he merely paid for the sins that we had committed, that in itself would have only wiped the record clean and put us back in a state of neutrality. It would have done nothing to earn entrance into the kingdom of God for us, for heaven requires not only that we be removed from our sins but also that we have a positive dimension of righteousness. What I am saying is this: it is as important to our redemption that Jesus lived, as it is that Jesus died. His atoning death had to be preceded by a life of perfect righteousness, fulfilling every command of the law. It was his meat and his drink to do the will of the Father. He said that not one jot or tittle of the law would pass away until all had been fulfilled. He set out to fulfil it. This was his mandate: it must needs be fulfilled, he said. John the Baptist might not understand why it was necessary for Jesus to be baptized, but Jesus knew that in order to fulfil all the requirements of the law, he had to be baptized.

Luke then calls our attention to another incident: when Jesus had been baptized and was praying, the heaven was opened and the Holy Spirit descended in bodily shape like a dove upon him, and a voice was heard coming from heaven which said, 'You are my Son, whom I love; with you I am well-pleased.' Some have argued that this was the point where Jesus received the Holy Spirit. But can we in all honesty think that one who was virgin-born, and amazed the teachers in the temple, was bereft of the Holy Spirit from his infancy through his adolescence up until the age of thirty? Of course not. Obviously the Holy Spirit was indwelling Christ in power from his very conception. But what happens here is the marking of the beginning of Jesus' public ministry. In a sense this is the ordination of the Messiah to his mission. The pouring out of the Holy Spirit is a new dimension given to the human Jesus to empower him for his Messianic task.

This empowering is accompanied by the heavens themselves

opening and God speaking, audibly, from heaven. Imagine that! We have the word of God written, but that word comes through the human agents of revelation, the prophets and the apostles. But here God speaks in his own voice from heaven, and this is the first occurrence of that in the New Testament. And he speaks to confirm the consecration of his Son to the task of Messiah.

In one sense, this is the message that God declares from heaven every time he speaks audibly in the New Testament. There are three occasions when that happens: here is the first one, and the second is at the Mount of Transfiguration when again, the heavens open and the voice is heard and God says, 'This is my beloved Son: hear him.' And then thirdly, just days before the crucifixion and perhaps during his last public message, Jesus says, 'My soul has become troubled; and what shall I say? "Father, save me from this hour"? But for this purpose I came to this hour. Father, glorify your name.' And then came a voice from heaven saying, 'I have both glorified it, and will glorify it again' (John 12:27-28, NASB). Three times God speaks, three times the heavens are opened and the voice of God is heard to declare the dignity and the glory of his unique Son.

This opening of the heavens to announce the coming of Christ, reflects a fulfilment of a prophetic hope that Isaiah had uttered many centuries before. 'Oh, that you wouldst rend the heavens and come down' (Isa. 64:1, NASB). Finally, God came down, and here the heavens are opened to bear witness to that, and the Holy Spirit is visible to Christ and to John.

Luke then concludes this third chapter of his gospel with Jesus' genealogy, his family tree: 'Now Jesus himself was about thirty years old when he began his ministry. He was the son, so it was thought, of Joseph, the son of Heli, the son of Matthat...' If we take the time to examine the genealogy given by Luke and compare it closely with the genealogy that Matthew gives us, we will find some discrepancies, as critical scholars have been quick to point out. Why does Matthew give one list and Luke another? Well, without getting too technical, there are different possible solutions to this. One of the most common is the idea that Matthew gives us the genealogy of Joseph, and Luke simply gives us the genealogy of Mary. Remember, Matthew was writing his gospel to Jews, and to them the most important issue is not the virgin birth, but whether Jesus is the legal descendant of David, for the Messiah must be of the lineage of David, and that lineage legally comes through Joseph.

When we read Luke's gospel, however, we find that Luke's preoccupation is not so much with Joseph, but with Mary, from whom he obviously got his early data and information. It is very possible that what Luke gives us is the family history of Mary, who also by virtue of her father, is a descendant of David, and that would solve the difficulties. There have been other solutions offered, namely, that what we have here is simply a line of those who are legitimate descendants of David who were eligible for the throne, versus those who were literal descendants of David, but that again raises technical problems.

Perhaps the most significant thing for our edification is where the genealogies stop. Matthew's genealogy stops with Abraham, and Abraham is considered the father of the Jewish nation, so again Matthew is showing the Jewish credentials of Christ. Luke, by verse 38, has taken us right back to Adam, who was the son of God. Luke is showing the universality of the mission of Christ. Jesus Christ is not just for the Jews, but for the Gentiles, for the Romans and the Greeks. Jesus is the new Adam, the author of the new humanity, the one who comes to redeem and to reconcile men from every tribe and nation, not merely giving himself as a ransom for the lost sheep of Israel, but pouring out himself as a substitute for the sinful children of Adam's race.

15. The temptation of Jesus (Luke 4:1-13)

Immediately following the experience of his baptism, Jesus was directed to the wilderness, to undergo temptation.

Comparisons between the tests of Adam and Jesus
In the history of the world two men have been placed on probation to pass a test at the hands of God: Adam and Jesus of

Nazareth. Before we consider the actual content of the test facing Jesus, I would like to consider this question: What was the difference between the test that Adam underwent in Paradise and the test Jesus experienced in the wilderness? There are several important differences that we can note in comparing and contrasting the two episodes. When Adam was tempted, he was in the midst of a beautiful paradise. Many Christians down through the centuries have found it beneficial to take time out from their daily lives to retreat to a beautiful mountain situation, for example. Contemplating and meditating on the beauty of creation inclines their hearts and thoughts to the things of God. What better place to be spiritually strong than paradise with the grandeur of its surroundings and the nearness of God. Jesus, on the other hand, was led into a lonely place, a wilderness. It was hardly a situation that is conducive to being strong in the Spirit and inclined towards obedience to God. So it is important that we understand that the site of Adam's temptation was more pleasant than that of Jesus.

But in addition to that, we also note that when Adam first encountered the temptation, he faced it with the companionship of his wife. When Jesus was tempted, it was in the context of solitude. Think of your own temptation experiences. Is it not easier to compromise your ethics when you are alone, when you are unknown? When Jesus was confronted by Satan, he was far away from recognition; there was no-one present to see what he would do. But not only that, Jesus was in the situation of loneliness. Søren Kierkegaard, the Danish philosopher, once said that loneliness is perhaps the most difficult of all human situations to endure for any length of time. It is understood that the supreme form of punishment, greater even than incarceration, is solitary confinement; to be forced to be utterly alone, totally cut off from any kind of human communication and fellowship. When Jesus Christ faced all of the forces of hell in an attempt to undermine his integrity, he was there alone.

A third difference between the two temptation experiences is the different physical states of Adam and Jesus. We know that

the paradise situation was a place where God had said to Adam
and Eve that they could eat freely of all of the fruits of the trees
of the garden. It was a gourmet's paradise. When Satan came to
Adam to test him, he tested him on a full stomach; he wasn't
undermined by physical pain or yearning. But Satan comes to
Jesus when he was greatly weakened in his humanness, without
food for forty days, without human fellowship for forty days,
and it was at that moment of weakness that Satan attacked.

We have looked at the differences between the temptation of
Adam and the temptation of Christ, but something that we often
miss when we look at these temptations is their similarity. To
uncover the similarity we need to understand the focal point of
the temptations. On the surface, we see that Jesus was tempted
to eat bread and to a frivolous use of miraculous powers.
Virtually every commentator you read on this passage argues
that Satan was trying to force Jesus to misuse his powers. Well,
that is part of it, but if we examine this text carefully we see that
the issue confronting Jesus was deeper than that, more basic,
more foundational. In fact, it is exactly the same temptation that
was brought before Adam and Eve. Satan is defined in the early
chapters of Genesis as the most subtle of all of the beasts of the
field, and we will see the subtlety of the temptation as we
examine the tests.

We read in verse 3: And the devil said unto him, 'If you are
the Son of God, command this stone that it be made bread.'
Think back to the account of the temptation of Adam and Eve in
the garden of Eden. What was at stake there? Remember how the
serpent came to Eve with a question. The question was simple:
'Has God said that you may not eat of any of the trees of the
garden?' Is that what God had said to Adam and Eve? He had
made a beautiful paradise, and planted trees loaded with fruit.
Did he then say, 'OK, look but don't touch'? Of course not, and
Satan knew that very well. Eve was quick to reply that the
restriction applied only to the tree in the middle of the garden.

Why did Satan ask a question that was so obviously false?
Remember the subtlety of the tempter. Jean-Paul Sartre, an

important existentialist philosopher, says that unless man is autonomous, he is not really free. Unless we are free to create our own values, our own norms, our own laws, then we are not really free, we are simply slaves to the divine sovereign. This was one of the arguments that Sartre brings forth against the existence of God. But do you see the subtlety there? The suggestion is that unless your freedom is limitless or absolute, then you are not really free at all. It is human nature to think that because there is one restriction that we are never allowed to do what we want.

Well, this was the suggestion Satan made to Eve. But then Satan moved away from that subtlety and made a direct assault on the integrity of the word of God. Eve had said that God had told them that if they ate of that tree they will surely die. Satan said, 'You will not die! But you will be as gods, knowing good and evil.' His words are a direct contradiction of the truth of what God had said. Jesus, in his discussion with the Pharisees, recorded in John, called Satan the father of lies, he was a liar *from the beginning*. It's obvious that Jesus is thinking of Satan's direct lie and contradiction of the truth of God in his statement to Eve. God had said one thing: 'If you eat you *will* die.' Satan comes along and says, 'If you eat you will *not* die.' Who is telling the truth? God, who is of the very essence of truth? Or Satan, the deceiver? Well, we know what happened. Adam and Eve believed Satan rather than God, and they fell, and the fall was dreadful.

What does that have to do with the temptation of Jesus? Remember that Jesus comes on the scene of history as the new Adam, the second representative of mankind. He faces the same kind of test, the same kind of temptation. Only instead of failing that test, he passes it.

Jesus is put to the test (Luke 4:3-13)
Satan begins his questioning of Jesus with the words: 'If you are the Son of God, tell this stone to become bread.' He doesn't say, '*Since* you are the Son of God ...' but he comes with an implied question: '*If* you are the Son of God ....' What was the last

message that Jesus had heard before the Spirit drove him into the wilderness? The heavens had opened and God had said: 'You are my Son, whom I love; with you I am well pleased.' Then the Spirit that he is anointed with in his baptism, drives him into the wilderness and it would seem that the Father left Jesus in isolation for forty days. There was no further communication; no vision of loveliness; no fellowship with the Father. Jesus was utterly alone for forty days. If it were me in the wilderness, I would be asking myself, 'Was I hearing things back there by the River Jordan? Is this any way for God the Father to be treating his Son?' Satan says, '*If* you are the Son of God ....' What is under attack here is not really the identity of Jesus, so much as the trustworthiness of the word of God.

How does Jesus respond? Jesus answered Satan, 'It is written, "Man shall not live on bread alone."' *It is written* was a phrase every Jew would recognize. 'It is written' does not simply mean that it is written down in the town hall, or in a paperback novel. The phrase has clear reference to the sacred scriptures of the Old Testament. Jesus could just as well have said: 'The Bible says.' Matthew gives us an extended version of Jesus' response: 'Man shall not live on bread alone, but by every word that proceeds out of the mouth of God' (Matt. 4:4, NASB). He is saying, in effect, 'Look, Satan, I'm not going to turn these stones into bread, because I don't need bread as much as I need the word of God. I live by the word of God; I trust the word of God. I may be hungry now, but my Father said I am his Son and I am going to live by that.'

Then we read:

> Then the devil led him up to a high place and showed him in an instant all the kingdoms of the world. And he said to him, 'I will give you all their authority and splendour, for it has been given to me, and I can give it to anyone I want to. So if you worship me, it will all be yours' (4:5-7).

How does Jesus respond? He replied, 'It is written, "Worship the Lord your God and serve him only."' Again Jesus replies

THE TEMPTATION OF JESUS

with 'It is written ...'. God alone is the One we are to serve and worship. To treat anyone else in this way is to violate the written word of God.

The devil led him to Jerusalem and had him stand on the highest point of the temple. 'If you are the Son of God,' he said, 'throw yourself down from here. For it is written,

"He will command His angels concerning you
   to guard you carefully;
they will bear you up in their hands,
   so that you will not strike your foot against a stone." '

Here we see the incredible subtlety of Satan. He says, 'So, you like to quote the Bible? I'll quote the Bible too. Doesn't the Bible say that he will give his angels charge over you? If you are the Messiah, if you are the Son of God, then let's see if the Bible is true – jump off the temple and see if the angels catch you.' But Jesus recognized right away that in spite of the fact that Satan was quoting Scripture at him, he was using a defective hermeneutic, that is, he was twisting and distorting the meaning and interpreting Scripture against Scripture itself. And Jesus said, 'It says: "Do not put the Lord your God to the test."' In other words, 'I'm not allowed to put God to the test; instead God is testing me.'

'When the devil had finished all this tempting, he left him until an opportune time' (4:13). Here we see the most significant difference between Jesus and Adam: Jesus believed God. Let me say it again. It is not simply that Jesus believed *in* God, but he *believed* God. He believed the word of God, and in the midst of this crisis, he trusted the truth of God's word. What happens when we are put to the test? More often than not we follow the example of Adam rather than the example of Christ. One of the greatest crises in the church today is the crisis of unbelief in the word of God. It is one thing to believe *in* God, it is another thing to *believe* God. Christ triumphed over Satan because he believed God. He trusted God, he put his life in the hands of God, and he was victorious.

The temptation narrative is a very important episode in the life of Jesus, but we would be remiss if we thought that this was the end of temptation for Jesus. At other times throughout Jesus' life and ministry Satan returns, sometimes speaking through Jesus' own disciples, as at Caesarea Philippi, suggesting alternate routes to the kingdom to the one that God had laid before him. We are told by Luke here that Satan left him *for now*. Jesus passed the test for that moment. But Satan departed for a season, to lie in wait, looking for a sign of weakness. But that weakness never came. Christ remained triumphant throughout.

In Matthew's account we are told that after Satan left, the angels appeared and ministered to Christ. He didn't have to jump off the temple; he didn't have to turn the stones into bread. As soon as he was victorious, God vindicated his word and sent help to his Son.

16. Jesus' public ministry begins (Luke 4:14-32)

Luke tells us in 4:14 that after Jesus endured the temptation in the wilderness, he returned in the power of the Spirit into Galilee and news about him spread through the whole countryside. And verse 15 says: 'He taught in their synagogues and everyone praised him.'

Jesus appears in the synagogue in Nazareth (Luke 4:14-19)
Imagine turning up at church one Sunday morning, only to discover that the guest preacher was Jesus himself. That happened regularly in a small town in Palestine: 'He went to Nazareth, where he had been brought up, and on the Sabbath day he went into the synagogue, as was his custom. And he stood up to read' (v. 16). This marks a very important moment in the public ministry of Christ. In fact, it is interesting that when Luke selects the material for his gospel, he moves directly from the temptation account to this appearance of Jesus in Nazareth. From the other gospel writers we know that Jesus had a ministry that was already significant in Judea before he moved into Galilee and came to Nazareth. Luke gives us only one verse on that. But now

Jesus is coming home. The people who saw him grow up are going to witness him in his public ministry for the very first time.

We read in verse 17: 'The scroll of the prophet Isaiah was handed to him.' We don't know why the scroll of Isaiah was chosen, whether this was the assigned text of the day, or whether Jesus had earlier suggested they use this text. In all probability Jesus himself had not selected the text, but had simply been invited to read it and then offer a sermon comment on it. 'Unrolling it he found the place where it is written:

'The Spirit of the Lord is on me,
    because he has anointed me
    to preach good news to the poor.
He has sent me to proclaim freedom for the prisoners,
    and recovery of sight for the blind,
to release the oppressed,
    to proclaim the year of the Lord's favour' (4:17-19).

That text is from Isaiah 61. It is a future prophecy that Isaiah had recorded centuries earlier, looking forward to the coming of the

Jesus was recognized by now as a *bona fide* rabbi. Frequently he is given the title 'Master' or 'Teacher'. The Greek word is *didaskolos* which is the New Testament equivalent to the Hebrew *rabbi*. To be recognized as a rabbi was to hold an extremely high position of honour. In our culture today we do not give such honour and homage to ministers and the like, although in certain places in Europe there is quite a degree of courtesy and respect shown to clergy and theologians. Rules of courtesy and protocol in the ancient Near East, however, dictated that a son must rise when his father entered the room, unless that son was a rabbi. If the son was a rabbi, then the custom was reversed and it was the duty of the father to stand in the presence of his son.

Jesus is accorded all of the rabbi's honour and respect in the synagogue. He is given the opportunity to preach the message of the day. 'He stood up to read.' When the scriptures were read in the synagogue, not only did the speaker stand, but everyone else stood for the reading of the Holy Scripture, as a mark of respect.

Messiah. And here is the Messiah, standing up in the synagogue, reading that prophecy to the people of his home town.

Jesus is rejected in his home town (Luke 4:20-32)
After Jesus reads the scroll, what happens? In verse 20 Luke says: 'Then he rolled up the scroll, gave it back to the attendant, and sat down. The eyes of everyone in the synagogue were fastened on him.' When I used to read that text, I imagined that Jesus went to the front of the congregation to read the scroll. Then, when he was finished, he turned around and handed back the scroll, went back to his pew and sat down. Probably that's how most of us would see it, because we read into the text our own customary understanding of how our religious observances and worship services are conducted. But that's not the way it was in the Jewish synagogue. The sermon was not given from a pulpit with the preacher standing, but rather the preacher sat at the front and usually the disciples, or the hearers, sat at his feet. So when Jesus sat down, he was taking the position of one about to give a message from the text that he had just read.

What Luke records of this sermon is perhaps only a brief synopsis, but I am not sure. Perhaps it was very short, but it was certainly one of the most dramatic and undoubtedly one of the most controversial sermons ever preached: 'he began by saying to them, "Today this Scripture is fulfilled in your hearing."' Now again, that is all Luke tells us of what Jesus said. He hints in the next verse that Jesus said other things, but this is the line he focuses upon. What a powerful statement! The people listening to him had watched him grow up. They heard him read a description of the mission of the Messiah, and then claim that this prophecy had been fulfilled in their hearing!

What was the response of the crowd? They were obviously very volatile; their opinions changed rapidly. Verse 22 says, 'All spoke well of him, and were amazed at the gracious words that came from his lips.' They were obviously impressed by Jesus' command of language, his articulation and style of exposition. But then they said, 'Isn't this Joseph's son?'

'Jesus said to them, "Surely you will quote this proverb to me: 'Physician, heal yourself! Do here in your home town what we heard that you did in Capernaum.' I tell you the truth,... no prophet is accepted in his home town"' (vv. 22-24). Jesus anticipated something very normal and basic to human nature: that the people who knew him, who had seen him carrying out the mundane tasks of carpentry and taking care of the family, who had rubbed shoulders with him in the market-place, at the well and at the synagogue, would not believe his claim to be the Messiah. Jesus reminded them that a prophet is never without honour except in his own home area.

After those words, however, he goes on to give the people of Nazareth a very important warning which explains why Luke selected this narrative to introduce Jesus' public ministry. Jesus says in verse 25

The word, Messiah, *messiach* in Hebrew, is translated by the Greek word *Christos*, which comes across into English as the word *Christ*. So often when we think of the name of Jesus we think that his name is Jesus Christ, but properly speaking his name would be Jesus of Nazareth, or Jesus bar Joseph – Jesus son of Joseph. The word *Christ* is actually a title that means *Messiah*, which in turn means One anointed by God for a special task. Therefore, anybody in the Old Testament who had a special anointing of God for a prophetic ministry or a priestly ministry or even a king who was anointed, was in a certain sense a messiah, an anointed one. But in Jewish theology the prophets taught of the coming day when not just *a* messiah would come, but *the Messiah*. One who was ultimately and uniquely endowed by the Holy Spirit and anointed of God for the special task of redeeming his people. It is that Messiah, that Christ, that is being described in this scroll of Isaiah. Jesus outlined the agenda of the Messiah, ending with, 'To proclaim the year of the Lord's favour.' In Jewish terminology, the 'year of the Lord's favour' meant the age of the Messiah.

(NASB): 'But I say to you in truth, there were many widows in Israel in the days of Elijah, when the sky was shut up for three years and six months, when a great famine came over all the land; and yet Elijah was sent to none of them, but only to Zarephath, in the land of Sidon, to a woman who was a widow.' Jesus is reminding them that when God chose a widow to be blessed by the ministry of Elijah, he chose a woman of Sidon, not a Jew, but a pagan Gentile.

Then he continues his illustration in verse 27 (NASB): 'And there were many lepers in Israel in the time of Elisha the prophet; and none of them was cleansed, but only Naaman the Syrian.' When Elisha was anointed of God and given supernatural powers, he did not heal the lepers of Israel. He healed a Syrian Gentile. Remember Luke's gospel was written to communicate the life of Christ and his benefits to a Gentile world, and his writing contains more of Jesus' statements about reaching out to the Gentiles than any other gospel writer. Here Jesus is calling attention to God's acts of mercy in the Old Testament to those outside of Israel.

What was the people's reaction? 'All the people in the synagogue were furious when they heard this. They got up, drove him out of the town, and took him to the brow of the hill on which the town was built, in order to throw him down the cliff' (4:28-29). They were so incensed that they cast him out of the synagogue and wanted to kill him.

This is the stone which the builders rejected. Jesus came to his own, but his own would not receive him. He came home to preach and first they were impressed, then they were incensed, and the congregation rose up in rejection of Christ. They sought to take his life, but miraculously he just walked through their midst and away from the town of Nazareth. It would seem from what we can discern from the rest of the New Testament that Jesus never set foot in Nazareth again.

If he preached in your church, would you marvel at the power and the grace of his speech? Would your soul be thrilled? Would you be hanging on every word that came out of his mouth? Or

would you be filled with fury and want to destroy him? Would
he be accepted or rejected by your congregation? Only you can
answer that question.

Then he went down to Capernaum, another town of Galilee.
There he taught on the Sabbath; and the townspeople were
amazed at his teaching, because his message had authority
(4:31-32). The people of Capernaum recognized the power of
his words and they did not seek to execute him.

17. Jesus' ministry of demon-exorcism (Luke 4:33-37)

Luke's narrative goes on now to record an encounter with a
demon-possessed man:

> And there was a man in the synagogue possessed by the spirit of
> an unclean demon, and he cried out with a loud voice, 'Ha! What
> do we have to do with you, Jesus of Nazareth? Have you come to
> destroy us? I know who you are – the Holy One of God!' And Jesus
> rebuked him, saying, 'Be quiet and come out of him!' And when
> the demon had thrown him down in their midst, he came out of him
> without doing him any harm' (4:33-35, NASB).

The New Testament has much to say about Jesus' work with
respect to demons. But this whole area has provoked all kinds of
questions for the modern interpreter of sacred Scripture. For
many years it seemed no-one in our culture took the New
Testament narratives about demons very seriously, but in the
past decade or so, there has been a renewal of interest in that
particular dimension of Christ's work as we have seen the rise
of all kinds of cultic and occultic practices in our society.

Some scholars have dismissed these biblical accounts as
being part of the simple superstitious, pre-scientific outlook of
first-century people. Rudolf Bultmann, a noted New Testament
scholar, for example, wrote that no-one can avail themselves of
the benefits of modern medicine and technology, and still
believe in a world inhabited by demons. But, in very sober terms,
the New Testament portrays Jesus as being involved in demon-

exorcism. Though it is retold for us in sober language, nevertheless there is an atmosphere of astonishment. This was not a commonplace happening, and there was quite a bit of consternation about it then even as there is now.

If we are going to take the New Testament seriously, however, we must accept that this is an integral part of the historical record. Dr. Berkouwer, one of the most noted European theologians of the twentieth century comments: 'There can be no theology without a demonology.' What he meant was simply that if we are going to gain our theology from the New Testament, we have to take seriously the whole perspective and view of the teachings of Christ.

Demon-exorcism is almost totally unheard of in Old Testament times, and rarely mentioned even in the New Testament after the gospels. But, while Jesus was on the earth, and was exercising his public ministry, there was a highly concentrated and intense time of confrontation with the powers of Satan. It seems as though all the forces of hell appeared in an attempt to undermine the ministry of Christ. The Bible tells us elsewhere that one of the most important tasks of Christ was to destroy the works of the devil. Therefore, we should not be surprised that he engages in mortal combat with the demonic realm.

Later on in his gospel Luke recounts Jesus' words on another occasion to those observing him: 'But if I cast out demons by the finger of God, then the Kingdom of God has come upon you' (11:20). Jesus, by these words, gives his interpretation of the significance of his own work at that point. Virtually all of the miracles of Jesus could be categorized – miracles of healing, miracles of nature, and so on – and all the classes of miracles were also performed by various individuals in the Old Testament. But the one category of miracle that we don't find in the Old Testament is the one at the heart of Jesus' ministry: the powerful exorcism of Satan. This was one of the clearest manifestations of the power of the kingdom of God on earth: that Jesus had authority over the satanic world.

The authority of Jesus (Luke 4:36-37)

What has one to believe in order to be redeemed? Suppose a person understood the message of the New Testament and believed that these things were in fact true. Would that be enough to redeem him? Well, according to James 2:19 that would only be enough to qualify the person to be a demon, because the demons understand the truth and they know that the truth is the truth, but they shudder before it, for they hate it. In order to be redeemed, there is another element of faith that one must have: not only must we recognize the true identity of Jesus, and grant that it is true, but we must *submit* to it. Recognizing it to be true is vitally important, but it is not enough, as we see in this passage from Luke. The demon recognized Jesus; he knew more about who Jesus was than all the people in the synagogue. He understood the identity of Jesus from an intellectual perspective, more than the disciples did. But the difference was that the demon hated Jesus. The demon was filled with repugnance in the presence of God. He was also frightened by the power that Jesus manifested, and asks: 'What are you doing here? Have you come to destroy us? We know that you are the Holy One of God.'

There are records in the first century of other people in rabbinic circles who at times were involved in exorcism. A few litanies of incantations that the exorcist would recite have survived, and these indicate that the exorcists hoped that there was some power in these incantations that would make the evil spirit leave the person whom he was tormenting. But Jesus doesn't have to resort to such practice of spells or incantations. Rather, he commands Satan on the basis of his own authority, rebuking him and telling him to leave. We see the satanic kingdom bowing before the authority of Christ.

Luke records the reaction of the onlookers: 'And amazement came upon them all, and they began discussing with one another saying, "What is this message? For with authority and power he commands the unclean spirits, and they come out." And the report about him was getting into every locality in the surrounding district' (4:36-37, NASB). Luke uses two words to describe this

activity of Jesus: authority and power. We know already that
people had earlier expressed amazement at the fact that Jesus did
not speak like the Pharisees or the scribes, but he spoke as one
having authority. The Greek word for authority is *exousia*, and
it is used frequently in the New Testament to describe the style
of Jesus' teaching and ministry. His teaching was different from
other rabbis. It was traditional for the rabbis to take pride in the
fact that they added nothing of their own to the orthodox
teachings that they taught. It was customary for the scribes, the
Pharisees and the rabbis to give their lesson and then cite the
earlier rabbinic authorities to substantiate their case or their
position. That is still very much the case with scholars today. If
you have ever read a scholarly book on any subject you may have
found working through the many technical footnotes in small
print a bit laborious. There are a number of reasons why
footnotes are used in scholarly literature. Firstly, they are used
to give credit to another author for the use of information from
his or her work. Secondly, they are used to give fuller explanation
of a point or a concept. Thirdly, perhaps their most important use
is to give evidence to the fact that the author has done his
homework and has read the best literature on the subject.

Jesus, however, didn't do it that way. For the most part, Jesus
gave his teaching from within himself and on the basis of his
own authority; and, so the Bible tells us, the kind of authority
that he had was not like the scribes and the Pharisees, but he
spoke as one having *exousia*.

This Greek word *exousia* is really a compound word. It has
a root and a prefix. The prefix is *ek*, and means simply *from* or
out of. *Ousia*, comes from the verb, *to be*, and means, *being*. It
is the word that the philosophers used for the concept of *essence*
or *substance*. Literally, what that word 'authority' means is that
Jesus' teaching came out of substance. Jesus wasn't just engaging
in superficial teaching, but there was a substance, a weightiness,
that was residing in him, and out of that he spoke.

Luke tells us that the word Jesus uses for exorcism, like his
teaching, is also a word of *exousia*, a word of authority, before

which even the demons must shudder and must obey. He says that his authority is accompanied by power. There are different words for power in the New Testament. The one used here is frequently used in conjunction with the work of the Holy Spirit. It is the Greek word *dunamis*, an overwhelming, transforming power. It comes into English in the word, *dynamite*: something of enormous, explosive power. The people were astonished when they saw the forces of hell trembling in the presence of Jesus for they recognized that when he spoke there was *exousia*, substantial authority, and there was *dunamis*, power.

18. Christ's healing power (Luke 4:38-44)

In Luke 4:38-39 we see another incidence of Jesus' healing power: 'Jesus left the synagogue and went to the home of Simon. Now Simon's mother-in-law was suffering from a high fever; and they asked Jesus to help her. So he bent over her and rebuked the fever, and it left her. She got up at once and began to wait on them.'

The way that Jesus handled the fever of Peter's mother-in-law was very unusual, certainly from a medical perspective. Jesus is requested to help her and so he rebukes the fever. Perhaps they expected that he would put his hands on her and pray that she would be healed but instead he spoke to the fever, almost as if the fever were capable of hearing. He rebuked it and the fever departed, and the woman was instantly restored to fulness of health.

This passage has played a role in controversies between Protestants and Roman Catholics with regard to the celibacy of the priesthood. Protestants have pointed out that this account refers to Simon Peter's wife, and if Peter was the first pope of the Roman Catholic church, what was he doing with a wife? In response, some have argued that Peter became pope only after his wife had died. Nevertheless, it is a passage that is called upon from time to time to stir up debate over that point. That obviously is not the reason why Luke includes it in the narrative; he is simply giving an example of the power of Christ to heal.

Luke continues in summary fashion: 'And while the sun was setting, all who had any sick with various diseases brought them to him; and laying his hands on every one of them, he was healing them. And demons also were coming out from many, crying out and saying, "You are the Son of God". And rebuking them, he would not allow them to speak, because they knew him to be the Christ' (4:40-41, NASB). Why did Jesus not want them to speak about who he was? This is what scholars refer to as the 'Messianic secret'.

'Messianic' refers to the concept of Jesus as the Messiah, and in one sense Jesus was very careful with that secret. Even though in his synagogue speech in Nazareth, he identifies himself as the one spoken of by Isaiah, nevertheless, he is very careful to unveil his identity gradually and in very select company. For some reason Jesus did not want it spread all over the land that he was the Messiah.

We can speculate as to why Jesus was so hush-hush about his identity. One of the most common speculations is that he was trying to develop a proper understanding among the people of Israel as to the true mission and identity of the Messiah, because he was constantly being confronted with popular misconceptions about the Messiahship. Think of the incident when he feeds the five thousand. Right away they want to crown him king! They want a political messiah, a royal messiah, someone who is going to bring fire down from heaven to destroy the Roman legions. So the people had really not understood that the Messiah would be a suffering Servant sent to die. Perhaps that is one of the main reasons that Jesus tried to keep a low profile at first with respect to this full identity.

Desire for privacy
'And when day came, he departed and went to a lonely place; and the multitudes were searching for him, and came to him, and tried to keep him from going away from them' (4:42, NASB). The people were reluctant to let Jesus go, but he withdrew from them. This was to be his practice again and again. Jesus, in his

humanity, as we are told on other occasions when he healed somebody, would feel the power go out of him. He would be spiritually, emotionally and physically drained by the giving of himself in this ministry of compassion. There were times when he simply had to flee from the multitude to get some rest, to get alone with God, to get away from the clamouring multitudes. When he gave them his attention, he gave it undividedly as we read in verse 40. But it was a costly thing for Jesus; strength was dissipated, power was drained from his body, and he would then, from time to time, go into a quiet place to be refreshed, to be filled. Privacy is one of man's most precious possessions. But the irony is that we rarely understand the value of our privacy until we lose it. Jesus, however, had to get alone. But the people came to him and pressed upon him, and said, 'Don't go!' They wanted to keep him there.

He responded to them by saying, 'I must preach the kingdom of God to the other cities also, for I was sent for this purpose' (4:43, NASB). In other words, he said, 'I would love to stay with you, but I have to go to the other cities because I have a mission to fulfil. It is my duty under God.' And so Luke tells us, 'And He kept on preaching, in the synagogues of Judea.'

19. Jesus calls the first disciples (Luke 5:1-11)

In Luke 5 we have one of the most strange and, I believe, fascinating narratives in Luke's gospel. Luke not only records the calling of the first group of disciples (also chronicled in the other gospels), but he gives us some additional information about that particular occasion.

In the presence of the Holy (Luke 5:1-7)

Jesus was preaching to a large crowd of people on the shore of the Lake of Gennesaret. He saw two boats out of which the fishermen had gone because they were washing their nets. Jesus got into Simon's boat, and asked him to put out a little way from the land. He sat down in the boat and began teaching them. When he had finished speaking, he said to Simon, 'Put out into the deep

water and let down you nets for a catch' (5:1-4, NASB). If there
is ever a time when Simon Peter, the rock of the church, exhibits
impatience or annoyance at his Master, it is here. He says to him,
'Master, we worked hard and caught nothing!' It is almost as if
Simon Peter is looking at Jesus and saying, 'Jesus, when you
speak to us about the things of God we hang on your every word.
But give us a little bit of credit! Maybe we are not great rabbis,
but we know about fishing. We've let down those nets a hundred
times and we can't even catch a minnow!' But Peter reluctantly
acquiesced to the command of Jesus, 'But, at your bidding I will let
down the nets.' It is as though Simon Peter is humouring Jesus.

What happens is remarkable, for they caught a huge multitude
of fish, to the point that their nets were breaking, and they had
to get their partners in the other boat to come and help them.
Even then the boats were so full of fish that they began to sink.
How did Peter react in the face of that miracle? I would have
thought that Peter, as a professional fisherman, would have been
eager to take Jesus on as a partner in the business! That's what
any enterprising businessman would have done if he found
someone who could do what Jesus did there. Instead of that,
however, Peter asks Jesus to leave: 'Depart from me, for I am a
sinful man, O Lord.' What an incredible response!

If we examine this passage carefully we see that there is a
kind of similarity between Peter's reaction to Jesus and the
reaction of the demons to Jesus. The demons recognized his
holiness and were terrified. When Simon Peter saw the awesome
power of Christ, he too was terrified, because he recognized
something of the majesty of Christ, the holiness of Christ, that
was showing through. Human beings are always terrified in the
presence of the Holy.

Man's fear of God's holiness (Luke 5:8-11)
Sigmund Freud says that humans invented religion because they
are afraid of the forces of nature, and so to seek some comfort
and solace from the forces of nature, they begin to invent deities.
I don't doubt that we have the capacity to do that, but if there is

anything that scares me more than hurricanes and earthquakes, it is the holiness of God. If our religion were an invention, born of fear, we would hardly be inclined to invent a holy God. We will see more of that concept being developed by Luke on other occasions throughout his narrative. Jesus made people uncomfortable.

It is significant that the people who became hostile to him, the ones who plotted his death and were most threatened by his presence, were the Pharisees and the Sadducees, those most noted for their manifestation of righteousness. They seemed to be so far ahead, so morally superior to everyone else, that they were looked up to as the moral paragons of the community. But when the incarnation of pure righteousness, unblemished holiness appeared, their righteousness just seemed as filthiness. Their holiness seemed as profanity. Their standard of excellence was totally eclipsed by the presence of the Son of God, and they despised him.

John Calvin, reflecting on the reaction of the Old Testament saints to the appearance of God in his holiness, said that men uniformly were filled with dread and terror. Isaiah in the temple, when he saw God high and lifted up and heard the seraphim singing, 'Holy, Holy, Holy', cried out in response, 'Woe is me! For I am undone. For I am a man of unclean lips' (Isa. 6:5). As soon as he saw real holiness, he was immediately aware of his own sinfulness. He not only discovered who God was, but he also discovered who he was.

As fascinated as people were by the power of Jesus, they were also terrified and intimidated by his righteousness. There was a certain sense in which sinful men simply could not abide the presence of the Son of God. He had to be removed. If he would not leave them, then sinful men would make sure that they would put him away, that they would drive him out, and if necessary, even kill him. These words were not spoken by a demon or an enemy of Jesus, but by Simon Peter, his own disciple; when he sees the identity of Jesus, he says, 'Depart from me, for I am a sinful man.' How many people still have that posture towards

Christ, still do everything they can to keep him at a distance, to keep him removed from their thoughts, because the very idea of Christ makes them uncomfortable. Holiness is scary, but oh, that all of us would understand the grace, mercy and compassion that is borne by that same Man of holiness who says to people whom he makes uncomfortable, 'Fear not! Peace be with you!'

Not only was Simon amazed, but Luke tells us that so were James and John, the sons of Zebedee, who were partners with Simon. But Jesus said to them, as he says to all of those who would come close, 'Don't be afraid; from now on you will catch men' (5:10). Then Luke comments: 'So they pulled their boats up on shore, left everything and followed him.' The call to discipleship was in the midst of a manifestation of holiness.

20. Jesus heals a man with leprosy (Luke 5:12-16)

In biblical times, to contract leprosy was not merely to suffer the ravages of a debilitating disease that affected one's body and brought disfiguration of its members, but perhaps even more important was what it meant to a person socially, emotionally and personally. Once a person was pronounced to be leprous, he was forced by law to remove himself from all contact with healthy individuals in his community. It meant a life of banishment, a life in abject exile, removed from family and employment. It was a truly miserable existence.

It is just such a person whom Luke describes here: 'While Jesus was in one of their towns, a man came along who was covered with leprosy. When he saw Jesus, he fell with his face to the ground and begged him, "Lord, if you are willing, you can make me clean"' (5:12). This is a pathetic record of a pathetic human being. Luke does not identify the particular city, though if we reconstruct this episode from the information in the other gospels, we can be fairly certain that this incident took place in or around Capernaum. Old Testament law prohibited any leper from entering into a city, to engage in discourse or any form of communication with the residents. So perhaps it was at the outskirts of the town that the leper besought Jesus for a cure, or perhaps this man, residing in the abysmal conditions of a leper colony, was so moved by the spirit of hope by the news of the ministry of Jesus, that he was willing to break the law to seek out Jesus.

Luke explains this man's illness in a bit more detail than the other gospel writers do, lending credence to the idea that Luke was a practising physician. Other gospels just describe the man as having leprosy, but Luke describes this man as being *full* of leprosy. It wasn't that the tips of his fingers or the edges of his ears had just begun to show the dreadful white marks of this disease, but the suggestion is that the disease was very advanced. When he saw Jesus, he fell on his face and implored him: 'Lord, if you are willing, you can make me clean.' What incredible words! He doesn't just come up to Jesus and negotiate with him for the price of a cure, nor does he come to him and say, 'Jesus, will you heal me?' or 'Can you heal me?' When we go to the doctor, we assume that the doctor certainly would heal us if he or she were able. We assume that it is the doctor's duty to do as much as he possibly can through the use of surgery or the medical treatments that he has at his disposal.

When this man went to Jesus, however, there was no question in his mind about the power of Christ. He bowed before the sovereignty of Christ. In pure humility, he said, 'Jesus I know that you can – will you?' This does not cast a shadow on Christ's posture about his willingness to pour out his mercy of healing to people who were in need. Everything we know about Christ would make him all the more willing to heal than any physician we have ever known, but again this man somehow recognized that he was in the presence of One whose power and authority far transcended anything he had ever encountered or even dreamed of encountering. In his posture of humility he said, 'Jesus, if you will, I know you can.'

Verse 13 tells us that Jesus 'reached out his hand and touched the man. "I am willing," he said. "Be clean." And immediately the leprosy left him.' One little verse, but it is packed with significance.

There is another aspect worth considering here. In Jewish society, the leper was a pariah, an outcast, an untouchable. The Pharisees of the day had developed a theory of salvation by discrimination. One must keep oneself from any contact with the sinners of the world, from the outcasts of the society. They were elitists, and would have no dealings with Samaritans, or tax collectors. They would certainly never come into physical contact with a leper. But part of Luke's concern is to demonstrate to the world that the Christ of the gospels is One who reaches out to touch the untouchable, to love the unlovable. Imagine the shock of the bystanders, when they saw Jesus stretch out his hand and touch a person who was full of leprosy. What are the means of the healing of Christ? The means of healing was the word of Christ; the same power by which the world was created; the same power that would bring Lazarus from the dead is the power demonstrated here. Instantly, the leper was healed.

In the ceremonial law of Israel, not only was it prohibited for a leper to come into the city limits, but even on the outskirts of the city he was required to either wear a bell around his neck or shout 'Unclean! Unclean!' to warn people, lest they be brought into contact with him. Evidently, the varieties of what was called leprosy in those days were highly contagious.

Most common forms of what is called leprosy today, more technically known as Hanson's Disease, on the whole are not contagious. But the particular diseases covered by the generic term, leprosy, in the Bible were highly contagious, and the hygiene rules forbade any form of human contact one to another. Not only was the leper forbidden to come near to someone who was whole, but the ceremonial law also forbade a whole person from touching a leper. Jesus breaks the ceremonial law in this encounter. Here is the lawgiver himself in the flesh, who on repeated occasions instructs the Pharisees that it is always lawful to do good, that the law is designed to heal and to protect, not to destroy. Thus it is permissible to help a person who is ill or dying on the Sabbath day even if it involves work. Jesus demonstrates here that that law forbidding touch may be transcended if it is for the purpose of bringing cleansing, wholeness and healing through the power of Christ.

What was the reaction? As soon as Jesus healed the man, 'He ordered him to tell no one, "But go and show yourself to the priest, and make an offering for your cleansing, just as Moses commanded, for a testimony to them"' (5:14). Jesus again is careful to conceal the full measure of his identity at this point in his ministry. He charges the man he has just healed not to tell anyone, but of course the secret is not to be totally kept, for there is one group of people who will obviously see the results of this work: the priests. Jesus, scrupulous to maintain the law, sent the man to the priest. In biblical times it was the priest's responsibility to look after the hygiene of the people. It was their job to ensure that the people kept every detail of the Levitical law. It was also their job to pronounce the diagnosis in the case of leprosy. Thus, when this man was healed, Jesus told him to return to the priest to have his healing verified and to make his offering. I am sure that when the man went through the required waiting period, to see whether or not he was truly cleansed of his disease, there was no anxiety, no fear, because he knew the power of the touch of Christ. The touch of Christ is as transforming of people's lives today as it was for that man who had been consigned to a leper colony, to the garbage dump of human society. That power is still in the world. People need to come to Christ today with the same attitude, with the same drive, with the same beseeching spirit of that leper who cried, 'Lord, if you are willing, you can make me clean.'

Miracles of Jesus in Luke

1. Casting out an unclean spirit in Capernaum   4:33-37

2. Healing Peter's mother-in-law in Capernaum   4:38-39

3. Healing the sick one evening in Capernaum   4:40-41

4. Draught of fish   5:1-11

5. Cleansing a leper   5:12-15

6. Healing a paralytic   5:18-26

7. Healing a man's withered hand   6:6-11

8. Healing a centurion's servant   7:1-10

9. Raising of a widow's son at Nain   7:11-16

10. Stilling the storm   8:22-25

11. Freeing the Gadarene from demon possession   8:26-39

12. Sending the demons into the swine   8:30-33

13. Raising Jairus' daughter   8:40-56

14. Healing the haemorrhaging woman   8:43-48

15. Feeding of the 5,000   9:10-17

16. Healing the epileptic boy   9:38-42

17. Curing a man who was blind and deaf   11:14

18. Healing the infirmed bent woman   13:11-17

19. Healing the man with dropsy   14:1-6

20. Cleansing the ten lepers   17:11-19

21. Giving blind Bartimaeus his sight   18:35-43

22. Healing a servant's ear   22:49-51

21. Jesus heals the paralytic (Luke 5:17-26)

Who has the authority to forgive sins in this world? That's an issue with which Jesus confronted the Pharisees.

Luke continues his narrative with an account of Christ's healing of the paralytic. The situation finds its initial setting in verse 17 in a teaching experience, where Christ is performing, not the role of the physician or the miracle-worker, but the role of the rabbi. He is teaching, and one would expect his own disciples to make up his audience, but his fame had become so widespread that he attracted the attention of the intellectuals. And Luke tells us that the Pharisees and the teachers of the law, the most highly skilled professional theologians of the day, were coming out of every town of Galilee and Judea, and Jerusalem, the intellectual centre of Israel. The leading theological minds of the day were gathered together to hear the teaching of Jesus.

And as this was taking place an interruption occurs:

> 'Some men came carrying a paralytic on a mat and tried to take him into the house to lay him before Jesus. When they could not find a way to do this because of the crowd, they went up on the roof and lowered him on his mat through the tiles into the middle of the crowd, right in front of Jesus' (5:18-19).

The earnestness of these friends shows us that getting close to Christ is not a casual thing for those who understand their need; they will stop at nothing to come to his presence.

The story continues in verse 20: 'When Jesus saw their faith, he said, "Friend, your sins are forgiven." ' Jesus makes this statement in the presence of the theologians who had come to check up on his theology. He could have said, 'Take up your bed and walk'; or 'Be healed'. He could even have said, 'Be cleansed', as he did to the leper. He didn't say anything about the leper's sins, but now he addresses this one who is paralysed, 'Friend, your sins are forgiven.'

We might speculate as to why he used this approach. We do know that unresolved guilt can in fact paralyse human beings, not just emotionally and psychologically, but physically too. It may be that this man had a deeply rooted guilt problem that was the cause of his paralysis. However, we must be careful here, because elsewhere in the New Testament Jesus makes it abundantly clear that you cannot always assume that a person's sickness is directly related to the degree of his sin. We don't want to draw any conclusions like that from the text. But obviously Jesus did notice a peculiar relationship here between his sin and his suffering.

So he says to him, 'Friend, your sins are forgiven.' At this the Pharisees and the teachers of the law 'began thinking to themselves, "Who is this fellow who speaks blasphemy? Who can forgive sins but God alone?" ' This was an axiom of Jewish theology that only God had the authority to forgive sins. You can see the outrage of the theologians when Jesus made this statement. They accused him instantly of blasphemy, for if only God can pronounce the forgiveness of sins, and Jesus is pronouncing the forgiveness of sins, this means that Jesus is claiming an authority and a power that belong only to God.

Jesus, however, 'knew what they were thinking and asked, "Why are you thinking these things in your hearts? Which is easier: to say, 'Your sins are forgiven,' or to say, 'Get up and walk'?" ' (5:22-23). What did Jesus mean by this? Many New Testament scholars have debated the meaning of this question, but without arriving at an agreement. But in verse 24, Jesus says that the reason he told the man, 'Your sins are forgiven,' is 'that you may know that the Son of Man has authority on earth to forgive sins'. Jesus took this opportunity not only to heal a paralysed man, but also to make an astounding declaration in the presence of the theological and intellectual community of Israel.

After this, Jesus says to the paralytic: ' "I tell you, get up, take your mat and go home." Immediately he rose up and went home, praising God. Jesus could have done it either way: he could have said, 'Your sins are forgiven' or 'Rise up and walk'. In the end, he does both. He declared himself to be the Son of Man, the One sent from heaven, who had been given all authority on heaven and earth, including the divine authority to forgive sins.

Jesus here uses a title for himself that is very important. Throughout the New Testament we find various titles being used for Jesus: Teacher, Lord, Christ, Son of Man, Son of God, Lion of Judah, and Master. The title that is used more often than any other in the New Testament is the title, Christ, or Messiah. The second most common title is this one, the Son of Man. Although it is used some 83 times in the New Testament, in all but about three of these occasions it is used by Jesus himself. It is far and away Jesus' preferred self-designation.

Why did Jesus call himself the Son of Man? It is tempting to make a quick judgment along these lines: When the Bible is talking about Jesus' divine nature it calls him the Son of God, and when it is talking about his human nature it calls him the Son of Man. Unfortunately it does not work out that way because there are times when the title 'son of God' has reference to people who are simply sons by virtue of obedience. The title, Son of Man, is not a humble reference by Jesus to his own humanity. Certainly it contains within it an allusion to Jesus' identification with us in our human situation. But it has its roots in the Old Testament, particularly in Daniel. In the vision that Daniel has into the very inner chambers of heaven we see the figure of the Son of Man. The Son of Man is sent to the world by the Ancient of Days, who is God. And the purpose for which the Son of Man is sent is to be the divine judge of all mankind. And so, far from being a humble self-designation of Jesus' earthly humanity, it indicates that Jesus is identifying himself with this heavenly being. Every rabbi there would have caught the inference. This is a radical statement of ultimate authority, that causes untold consternation among the Pharisees and the theologians present.

The man who was healed by the power of the Son of Man left that situation in a state of reverence, awe and adoration for God. The observers – the theologians, the jealous rabbis, the competitors of Christ, the Pharisees – left, charging Jesus with blasphemy. But one thing they all had in common: 'they were all seized with astonishment and began glorifying God; and they were all filled with fear, saying, "We have seen remarkable things today"' (5:26, NASB). Indeed they had. They had seen a man who had supernatural power because he carried with him supernatural authority.

The real issue in the Christian life is whether or not we see in Christ the authority of God himself. As the great high priest he has the authority to forgive our sins. If you are paralysed by guilt, take it to Christ – he has the authority to forgive you.

22. Jesus calls Levi (Luke 5:27-39)

When Jesus began his public ministry, even though his baptism was in the Jordan and his temptation was in the Judean wilderness, he returned to the north of Palestine and made his ministry base in the town of Capernaum, on the north-eastern edge of the Sea of Galilee. Many of the miracles of Christ and the teaching episodes of his ministry took place there. We can safely assume that the call of Levi took place near by the Sea of Galilee.

The first thing we learn about Levi is that he was a tax-gatherer. We have already seen that these people were one of the most despised classes in all of Israel – because they collected taxes from their own countrymen to be paid to the hated Roman conquerors.

When we consider the group of men that Jesus gathered around himself, it is almost impossible to believe that these people could get along with each other for five minutes. On the one hand, at least one, and probably two disciples, were Zealots; totally and passionately committed to the violent overthrow of the Roman government. Imagine these men sitting at the feet of Jesus, next to a tax-gatherer who had been employed by the hated Roman government. On the other hand, there were fishermen, such as James and John, who were added to the number by Christ, right along with Levi. One of the tax duties that Levi would have had was to receive daily payments, almost extortionary tax, from the men who fished in the Sea of Galilee. We can be fairly sure that James and John already knew Levi, and hated him as they had to pay their dues daily from their own catch of fish to this man.

The place for the receipt of custom monies (a tax on travel and commerce) meant that Levi conducted his business outside the city of Capernaum, making it possible to collect revenues from traders and marketers who were making their move from various points across the nation. An official who had the responsibility for a custom tax-booth received a very lucrative commission, and it is obvious that Levi had become a wealthy man. Though it was odious to his countrymen, nevertheless being a tax collector was extremely profitable for Levi.

Jesus' invitation to Levi is met with an astonishing response: 'Levi got up, left everything and followed him.' Levi presumably doesn't even close the account books. He gets up out of his chair, leaves his cash register, his ledger, his receipts, his lucrative business and began to follow Christ. That says something not only of the commitment of Levi, but it tells us something about the captivating power of Christ.

And then Levi 'held a great banquet for Jesus at his house, and a large crowd of tax-collectors and others were eating with them' (5:29). So the first thing he does for his new rabbi is to throw a party to which he invited all the other tax-gatherers. Isn't it interesting that when a man is called to discipleship by Christ he can't wait to tell his friends and associates of his new experience. So Levi throws a party, and invites the rest of his crowd to come and meet Jesus.

This party obviously attracted widespread attention because we read in verse 30: 'But the Pharisees and the teachers of the law who belonged to their sect complained to his disciples, "Why do you eat and drink with tax collectors and 'sinners'?" ' Now this is not an idle question. One of the prevailing ideas of the rabbis of Jesus' day was that of salvation by segregation. It was considered necessary to keep oneself set apart from anyone that was considered a sinner. If one kept oneself away from such people, somehow one would be able to avoid any kind of contamination, any kind of guilt by association. But Jesus comes and not only does he associate with the lepers, the outcasts, the sinners, but he goes to dinner at a house full of tax-gatherers. This enraged the Pharisees, but Jesus said: 'It is not those who are well who need a physician, but those who are sick.' There is no point in a doctor giving of his time visiting healthy people. A doctor's task is to take care of the sick. Jesus goes on to say: 'I have not come to call the righteous but sinners to repentance.' This is not to say that Jesus was regarding Pharisees as being righteous and not needing a physician, but they considered themselves

When Jesus saw Levi, he walked over to him and simply said, 'Follow me.' These words can be seen as an invitation to join the intimate group of disciples that surrounded Jesus during his earthly ministry, but there is a literalism involved in that command that is often overlooked. Jesus, as was the case with other rabbis in the ancient world, was what we call a 'peripatetic' teacher. He would move about the countryside with a group of students around him who would follow him wherever he went. As Jesus walked down the street or through the community, the disciples would walk along behind him, committing to memory the words he uttered. Thus a disciple was a person who joined himself to the company of a rabbi and was committed to mastering whatever it was that the rabbi could transmit to him by way of teaching. The word, *disciple,* is the word, *mathetes,* which means, simply, *learner.* A disciple of Christ is one who studies under Christ, who submits himself to the teaching of Jesus, who listens as the Master speaks, who seeks to understand what the Master is saying, and to emulate the response that the Master requires. The life of a disciple is one of service, study and obedience.

righteous, they didn't need a doctor for their souls, and they didn't want Jesus practising his trade on those who most needed it. The irony, of course, is that no-one needed it more than the Pharisees, but they missed the point.

But the Pharisees continued complaining: 'John's disciples often fast and pray, and so do the disciples of the Pharisees, but yours go on eating and drinking' (5:33). The Pharisees were as upset with John the Baptist as they were with Jesus, but here we see them holding up John's disciples in a favourable light, in an effort to turn Jesus against John, and John against Jesus.

Jesus' response to their criticism is fascinating: 'You cannot make the attendants of the bridegroom fast while the bridegroom is with them, can you? But the days will come, and when the bridegroom is taken away from them, then they will fast in those days' (5:34-35, NASB). Here is a very penetrating prophecy from Jesus. Before a wedding, you fast in preparation for the wedding feast. But once the bridegroom comes, the cake is cut, the food is brought out, the wine is served, it is a time of celebration. Jesus is saying: 'Some have been fasting all the time, waiting for the appearance of the Messiah. But when the Messiah is here, you don't fast! You celebrate! You feast!' And the Pharisees, I think, got the message of what Jesus was saying.

To these teachings in response to the Pharisees, he adds a very important short parable: 'No-one tears a piece from a new garment and puts it on an old garment; otherwise he will both tear the new, and the piece from the new will not match the old' (5:36, NASB). If you use new material to patch a hole in an old garment you have two problems. In the first place they don't match, and in the second place, the first time you wash it, the new piece of material shrinks and when it shrinks it rips away from the joint of the old garment, leaving a ragged hole.

And Jesus emphasizes these words with another parable: 'No-one puts new wine into old wineskins; otherwise the new wine will burst the skins, and it will be spilled out, and the skins will be ruined. But new wine must be put into fresh wineskins' (5:37-38, NASB). In the ancient world wineskins were made out of animal skins. People would carry their wine around in these wineskins and they would last for quite some time, but after a while the wineskins would stretch and would lose their elasticity. If you put brand new wine into those old skins, the wine, as it continued to ferment, would burst the skins, destroying both wineskin and wine. New wine has to go in new wineskins so there is room for the expansion of fermentation. Jesus is saying to the Pharisees that a new situation is breaking through, and they need to understand that some of their customs from the ancient days of fasting don't fit the presence of the Messiah on earth. They have to be

This incident raises the question of whether Christians today should be involved in fasting. In the ancient world, fasting was a very important religious exercise. For the day of Atonement, the Yom Kippur celebration in Israel, instituted in the book of Leviticus, people were called upon to fast. Fasting was also part of the routine of mourning, and was practised during times of national disaster and as a sign of personal repentance. During the Babylonian Exile, however, fasting, instead of being a voluntary exercise, was turned into a rigid obligation. From this point on into the inter-testamental period, it was believed that a person could accrue merit in the sight of God by practising fasting. So instead of doing it as a spiritual discipline, or as an expression of humility, dependence and devotion to God, it became a very formal externalistic type of piety. The prophets, of course, were very critical of this hypocrisy, as was Jesus. But at the same time we have to remember that he never repudiated the value of voluntary fasting as a spiritual discipline. It was a discipline that the disciples themselves would practise on other occasions. But in this instance Jesus was saying that the time was not right for fasting for it indicates mourning, sadness and catastrophe. But he gives an ominous warning that the day will come when the bridegroom shall be taken away from them and then they shall fast. This is a reference, obviously, to his coming crucifixion.

prepared for all of the new dimensions of authentic faith that he was setting before them.

Then he says, 'No-one after drinking old wine wishes for new; for he says the old is good enough.' The Pharisees are true to human nature. They weren't ready for change; they weren't ready for the newness of the kingdom of God. But Christ changes people; he will change you, unless you cling to the old. He stands before us with a call to discipleship, a call to a new life.

23. Lord of the Sabbath (Luke 6:1-11)

In these studies on Luke, we have seen that Jesus often experienced serious conflict with his contemporaries, particularly the theologians. Those who were most rigid in their application of the traditions of the rabbis were the ones who were often so infuriated by Jesus' conduct. This conflict between the traditions which had arisen in Jesus' day, with Jesus' own teaching and lifestyle, is very important to Luke as he explains the significance of Jesus' life and ministry.

The disciples pick some grain (Luke 6:1-5)
At the beginning of chapter 6, Luke records one of these conflicts. Jesus and his disciples are walking on the Sabbath day. They are obviously weary and hungry, and to avail themselves of food and nourishment, they went through someone's field. As they did so, the disciples plucked the tops of the stalks of grain, and rubbed them in their hands and ate the grain in that fashion, as was customary in those days. When the Pharisees saw this, they were greatly annoyed, and accused Jesus of doing something that was not lawful on the Sabbath day. One might suspect at the outset that the transgression of which Jesus is being accused, was stealing somebody else's grain, but this was not what the Pharisees had in mind. The Pharisees were very knowledgeable of the law of the Old Testament as well as the myriad laws that had been added by the tradition of the rabbis. The Old Testament makes explicit provision for the traveller to enter a field and help himself to this minuscule amount of grain that could be gathered

by hand. Jesus was not violating the Old Testament law.

The Pharisees, however, had something else in mind. They were concerned that Jesus, in order to get this nourishment from the grain, was involved in acts of harvesting, threshing and preparing the grain for eating. This is what is called 'theological nit-picking'. The Old Testament law, as such, did not forbid people from this simple act of preparing food for themselves. What the law forbade was working on the Sabbath day. Now that is a very general term. But the rabbis had prescriptions to interpret the law down to the finest detail. They had about a thousand laws which regulated what could and could not be done on the Sabbath day. The vast majority of those laws were not positive commandments in terms of what should be done on the Sabbath day, but they were negative prohibitions; statements of what was not allowed. The Bible certainly does have negative commandments, but the Pharisees weren't satisfied with that; they had to add to those prohibitions to the extent that life became terribly burdensome for people.

Jesus responds to their accusation that he is breaking the law by reminding them of an incident from Scripture: 'Have you not even read what David did when he was hungry, he and those who were with him, how he entered the house of God, and took and ate the consecrated bread, which is not lawful for any to eat but the priests alone, and gave it to his companions?' (6:3-4, NASB). Jesus responds with a rather embarrassing question for the Pharisees, a question that carries a sharp criticism: 'Are you men so ignorant of the word of God that you don't know what it plainly teaches? You have mastered the traditions of men, but you obviously have not mastered the word of God.' The incident to which Jesus is referring occurred in the Old Testament when Saul, the anointed king of Israel, was consumed by jealousy of David almost to the point of insanity. Saul began to pursue David with one thought in mind and that was to destroy him. David was forced to live as an outlaw. In the narrative of David's flight, we read how he, with a few of his men, came to the priest Abimelech. They were hungry and had nothing to eat, and the priest had compassion on them, but the only provision he could offer David in this state of weariness and flight was the consecrated bread that was used on the table of shew bread, which he did, and for which the Bible utters not the slightest hint of rebuke or admonition.

Jesus himself, by implication here, makes it perfectly plain that ceremony must always give way for the well-being of a person in need. Ceremony is important, and Jesus never minimizes its importance, but the ceremony is there for the benefit of people. Jesus elsewhere says that the Sabbath was made for man, not man for the Sabbath. But the rules and regulations of formalistic religion had developed into exacting traditions, that undermined the spirit of the law of the Sabbath day, that the Sabbath, instead of being a time of celebration, rest and contemplation of the riches and the majesty of God, had become a time of human oppression. And Jesus was going to put a stop to that.

In verse 5 Jesus makes one of the most radical statements of his earthly ministry: 'The Son of Man is Lord of the Sabbath.' Remember how earlier Jesus had handled the anger of the Pharisees when he healed the paralytic by pronouncing the forgiveness of sins. Jesus declared before his critics that as the Son of Man, the One who comes from heaven, he had the authority that they believed belonged to God alone. If there was any ambiguity in that claim, it vanished altogether in this statement that Jesus makes now. What is he saying? Who is the Lord of the Sabbath day? Well, who instituted the Sabbath in the first place? It didn't start with Moses on Mount Sinai, nor did it start with Abraham, nor even Noah. It is a law that God established at creation. In biblical theology the Sabbath law is called a 'creation ordinance' precisely because it was set down as part of God's law built into the creation. So therefore, since the Sabbath law is a creation mandate, what follows is that it is a mandate set down by the Creator. And who is the Lord of the Creation, but God himself? And when Jesus tells them he is doing this so that they might know that he is the Lord of the

Sabbath, he is claiming nothing less than the authority of the Creator of heaven and earth. Can you imagine the response of the Pharisees to that?

In Luke 6:1-5 the narrative shows Jesus' repudiation of the negative dimensions that had grown up in Sabbath-keeping among the Pharisees. But Luke goes on to relate another incident that stresses the positive dimension of Sabbath-keeping.

The man with the withered hand (Luke 6:6-11)

> On another Sabbath, he went into the synagogue and was teaching, and a man was there whose right hand was shrivelled. The Pharisees and the teachers of the law were looking for a reason to accuse Jesus, so they watched him closely to see if he would heal on the Sabbath (6:6-7).

Here we see Jesus performing the function of a rabbi, teaching in the synagogue. But in the midst of the people was a man with a withered arm. The scribes and the Pharisees watched Jesus intently, to see whether he would heal on the Sabbath day. There was another provision of rabbinical tradition that allowed medical attention to be administered, but only in a life-threatening situation. The Bible doesn't teach that, but the tradition did.

They wanted to see what Jesus was going to do with the man with the withered arm. He was suffering, but it was not a life or death situation. However, we read that 'Jesus knew what they were thinking and said to the man with the shrivelled hand, "Get up and stand in front of everyone." So he got up and stood there' (6:8). Jesus doesn't try to heal him in a covert manner, but knowing that the trap was set, makes it very clear what he is going to do: he invites the man to stand where everyone can see him. Before doing anything with the suffering man, Jesus asked the Pharisees: 'Is it lawful on the Sabbath to do good, or to do harm, to save a life, or to destroy it?' (v. 9, NASB). Masterful question. He looked around and nobody said a word.

Jesus was not going to let that suffering continue one moment more. 'He looked round at them all, and then said to the man,

"Stretch out your hand!" He did so, and his hand was completely restored. But they were furious, and began to discuss with one another what they might do to Jesus' (6:10-11). But Jesus had stopped their mouths before he even did the act, because the lesson that he was teaching them was that the Sabbath day is a perfectly appropriate time to do acts of mercy, to minister to the physical as well as to the spiritual needs of people. The Pharisees were unable to rejoice with the man who had been healed; their jealousy was so intense that they missed the presence of God, they missed the tenderness of Christ reaching out to heal a man. They missed the courage of Jesus who risked his own reputation and physical well-being before the fury of his contemporaries in order to bring wholeness to a wretched person.

24. The commissioning of the apostles
(Luke 6:12-16)

Luke begins this next section of the narrative by describing how Jesus 'went out to a mountainside to pray, and spent the night praying to God' (6:12).

What would be so pressing on his heart that he needed to wrestle in prayer for an entire night? Luke gives us the answer:

'When morning came, he called his disciples to him and chose twelve of them, whom he also designated apostles: Simon, whom he named Peter, his brother Andrew, James, John, Philip, Bartholomew, Matthew, Thomas, James son of Alphaeus, Simon who was called the Zealot; Judas son of James, and Judas Iscariot, who became a traitor' (6:13-16).

Now this is not the initial calling of the twelve. Luke has already told how Jesus called Simon and Levi, and in the other gospels we read how Jesus called the others also, and he did those individually. Jesus had far more disciples than twelve. On one occasion we are told he sent seventy of his disciples out on a particular preaching mission. From that larger group of disciples Jesus selects twelve, who would occupy an intimate place with him, and who, from this time forward, are not merely to be considered disciples, but are also commissioned as apostles.

The New Testament sometimes refers to the twelve as disciples, and at other times refers to them as apostles, leading some people to the conclusion that the word *disciple* means the same as the word *apostle* and vice versa. But that is not the case. Their meaning is quite different: the identity, or the job of an apostle is quite distinct from that of a disciple. We have seen that the Greek word for disciple, *mathetes*, means simply a *learner* or a *student*, one who attached himself to a rabbi to learn and serve. But there comes a point in the development of Jesus' disciples, when Jesus begins to train some of them for another task: to become apostles. The task of an apostle is a very special one. The word, taken from the Greek *apostolos*, comprises the

In the ancient world a person who functioned in the role of an apostle was usually a representative of a king or some important political ruler, who had the authority to speak on behalf of his ruler. He was usually serving in the function of an emissary, much as an ambassador would serve today. The apostle carried with him the authority of the one who sent him. Now that is crucial to understanding the role of the apostle in the New Testament. Jesus elsewhere said, when he sent out the apostles, 'Those who receive you, receive me. Those who will not receive you, do not receive me.' In fact, Paul says that the foundation of the church is the prophets and the apostles, with Christ being the chief cornerstone (Eph. 2:20). The church is established on the basis of the teaching of the apostles, not because they are special in and of themselves, but because it is through the apostles that we get the word of Christ. Sometimes people comment: 'I believe what Jesus said, but it is Paul that bothers me; I won't listen to the apostle Paul.' But, we don't know anything that Jesus ever said, except through the message of the apostles. Therefore when we try to put Jesus against Paul we are simply putting one apostle against another. An apostle speaks not on the basis of his own authority, but on the basis of the one who commissions him.

prefix, *apo*, which means, *out of*, or, *from*, and the root, *stelo*, meaning, *to send*. So an apostle, literally, is *one who is sent*.

The first apostle that we meet in the New Testament is not Peter, or Paul, or James, or John; it is Jesus himself. He defines his role as one who is sent by the Father. Remember how the Pharisees responded to that? 'We believe in God, we believe in the Father; it is you we repudiate.' Jesus' response was simple: 'If you repudiate me, by implication you must be repudiating the one who sent me.' The transfer of authority from the Father to the Son is, in turn, transferred to his own apostles, so they function in an absolutely unique role in the church. No minister in the church today has the authority of an apostle nor do any of the great theologians. All defer to the authority of the apostles, which resides in the fact that they were set apart and commissioned by Christ.

In verses 14-16 Luke gives us a list of those commissioned with apostolic authority. This list is found frequently in the New Testament, although the names aren't always the same. In every list, however, the name that is mentioned first is Simon Peter. Peter wasn't the first disciple to be called, but he heads every list in the New Testament because he certainly emerged as the leader of the twelve in the early church. It is also interesting, that the last one that is named in every list, is the one whom Jesus later said was a 'devil from the beginning', Judas Iscariot.

It was these twelve men that Jesus chose to be the New Testament counterpart to the twelve tribes of Israel. They were the men who not only were the disciples, but were commissioned as apostles, with the authority to speak the word of Christ. What happened to these men? The New Testament features some of them and others remain in relative obscurity. However, tradition tells us that virtually every one of them met a dreadful and violent death, except for John, who suffered other ignominies and humiliations before being banished as an old man to the Isle of Patmos. Tradition also says that Bartholomew was crucified, that Thomas was thrust through with a spear and killed, that Simon Zelotes, according to tradition, was crucified in the year

74 in Britain, and the rest of the disciples suffered various kinds
of martyrdom.

So we have the twelve men: one a traitor, eleven who
committed themselves to their lives' end, who sealed the
testimony of their faith in their own blood. These were the men
whom God gave to the Son after he wrestled in prayer all night.

25. Jesus addresses his disciples (Luke 6:17-21)

Luke's account of the famous Sermon on the Mount begins in
verse 17, and there are some startling differences between this
account and the more extensive version in Matthew's gospel.

Matthew tells us of a sermon that Jesus preached on a
mountain, but Luke says that Jesus came down and stood on a
level place. How do we resolve this discrepancy? Probably the
simplest way is to concentrate our attention on the possible site
of the sermon. The site most commonly held to be the place is
on a hillside outside of Capernaum, overlooking a valley. The
slopes are more or less stepped, and at various points there are
level places. Thus, it is possible to reconstruct this scene in a way
that reconciles the two texts; we could see Jesus at the pinnacle
of the hill, with his disciples, moving down towards a plateau,
perhaps midway down the mountain. So it is possible that
Matthew and Luke had the same site in mind.

Another possibility is that Luke and Matthew are describing
two different events. The content of the sermons is similar, but
by no means the same. It is quite usual for preachers to give the
same message more than once. We see this in the work of
contemporary theologians: their favourite themes are expounded
again and again, because these are the issues that concern them.
I am sure that it was as true for Jesus as for anyone else.

Another noticeable difference between the two accounts is
one of length. Matthew's record takes up three and a half
chapters, whereas Luke's does not even comprise a complete
chapter. Some of the material found in Matthew's is found on
other occasions in Luke's gospel. To explain this we need to
understand that these authors remembered or had access to the

recorded sayings of Jesus and, as was customary and completely appropriate in the ancient world, they arranged the material not necessarily chronologically but thematically and topically. This was in no way a violation of standards of truthfulness or of historical reliability, but simply a matter of editorial freedom.

Whatever the occasion, wherever the setting, the most important thing for us is the content of the message. We read in Luke's version that multitudes of people came to hear Jesus speak, and they came from as far north as Tyre and Sidon and as far south as Jerusalem. There were long journeys for people to make, but they came in great crowds. They came, not only to hear Jesus' teaching, but also to get close to him to seek relief from their diseases. Luke tells us that Jesus healed all those who came to him, 'for power was coming from him'.

The actual text of the sermon begins in verse 20. Of the three groups of people gathered there, the Twelve, the larger group of disciples and the vast multitudes, Jesus' words are addressed to his own disciples. In a sense he was addressing all believers. It is a message for Christians.

The first beatitude (Luke 6:20)

'Looking at his disciples, he said, "Blessed are you who are poor, for yours is the kingdom of God."' This is the first beatitude in Luke's version. These sayings are called Beatitudes because they follow a formula that begins with the pronouncement of bene-diction, where Christ says, 'Blessed are ....' This is a traditional formula that every Jew would understand, having its roots in the Old Testament prophets. One of the techniques that the prophets used to deliver the messages that God had given to them, was the device called the *oracle*. The oracles were of two types: positive and negative, what we call oracles of *weal*, or good news, and oracles of *woe*, or bad news. The positive oracle pronounced God's blessing upon the people for some particular virtue, and conversely, a negative oracle was prefaced by the word, *Woe!*

In Matthew's version of the first beatitude he includes a qualifier: 'Blessed are the poor *in spirit*, for theirs is the kingdom of God.' Luke doesn't have that qualifier. He just says 'Blessed are you who are poor.' That little *you* in there may make a distinction, because we might jump to the ill-advised conclusion that God is announcing his benediction indiscriminately on anyone who suffers from poverty. To understand what Jesus is driving at here we need to look at the biblical literature, particularly in the Old Testament. There have been those throughout history who have believed that there is a peculiar form of merit to be found in poverty and have trusted in their poverty rather than in Christ for salvation. That is a very dangerous thing to do.

It is possible to distinguish at least four different ways in which the Bible speaks about the poor. In the first instance, the Bible speaks about those who are poor because they are lazy. In Proverbs we see a very strong work ethic and severe chastisements from God against those who suffer from poverty as a result of their own neglect of labour. The biblical attitude towards such ones is one of judgment. But we cannot just jump to the conclusion that the only reason that people are poor is because they are lazy.

We see in the Old Testament a second category of the poor: those who are poor as a result of calamity, natural disaster, or some kind of sickness or debilitating disease. We call these people the handicapped or the victims of natural catastrophes. Take, for example, the farmer whose crop is wiped out by the drought. He has worked diligently, but because of natural circumstances his crop is destroyed and he is left destitute. Then there is the person who cannot make a living because he has suffered the ravaging effects of a disease. The Bible calls for particular concern, mercy and support for those who are poor as a result of calamity.

Then there is a third group of the poor: those who are poor because they are the victims of ruthless oppression at the hands of powerful tyrants. The Jewish nation itself was formed because the God of heaven and earth heard the groanings of this group of people who were enslaved in Egypt. God acted, saying, 'Let my people go!' There is a certain sense in which the heart of God beats for those who are poor because they have been victimized by unscrupulous and unjust oppressors.

The fourth category is a special one: these are the ones who are poor for righteousness' sake; those who forsake the material comforts of this world in order to seek a higher calling for the sake of the kingdom of God. There are countless people, servants of Christ, whose whole lives are a sacrifice of service to Christ. Some have foregone higher salaries, for example, in order to be servants of Christ. Those who suffer poverty for righteousness' sake are singled out for a particular blessing of God.

These four categories, however, identify the poor in material terms. But Matthew's qualifier would exclude all four of these, for he says 'Blessed are the poor *in spirit*'. What does he mean there? Obviously he means those who are not the arrogant, self-sufficient type. These are the people who look for their fulfilment in life upon the approval of God, and who see their own value as a reflection of the blessing of the King. It is this group of people that Jesus is addressing, It is remarkable that he says to them, 'yours is the kingdom of God'. Most of the beatitudes promise a future blessing. Jesus is saying that those who are poor towards this world, but rich towards God, right now enjoy a special privilege in God's kingdom.

The second beatitude (Luke 6:21)
Jesus continues: 'Blessed are you who hunger now, for you will be satisfied. Blessed are you who weep now, for you will laugh.'

The word, 'blessed', has been translated or transposed in some modern versions of the Bible by the word, 'happy'. But happiness and blessedness are two very different things. It is possible for a person to feel no happiness, but at the same time be in a state of blessedness. Jesus is saying that what we receive from this kind of loyalty to him is not the warm, fuzzy feeling that we equate with happiness, but a condition which is brought about by God Almighty. There is a profound difference.

Luke's setting of these statements differs markedly from that of Matthew, who writes: 'Blessed are those who hunger and thirst for righteousness, for they will be filled.' In Matthew's version again we see a spiritual hunger and thirst, a driving desire for the things of God. Jesus shows us where our priority should lie: 'But seek first his kingdom and his righteousness, and all these things will be given to you as well' (Matt. 6:33). Jesus wants people who have a burning desire for righteousness.

In Luke's setting, however, the emphasis is on the difference between *now* and *later*: 'Blessed are you who hunger *now*, for you shall be satisfied. Blessed are you who weep *now*, for you shall laugh.' Jesus is distinguishing between the way things are now and the way they will be when the kingdom of God is manifested and God's justice reigns supreme. A former student of mine wrote a poem entitled, *The Topsy-Turvy World*. Its theme was that we live in a topsy-turvy world, a world where righteousness is devalued, and where unrighteousness is exalted; where paupers ride on horseback, and princes walk in rags. That image has stuck in my mind because it reflects the difference between the outlooks in the world in which we live and the world in which Christ reigns. The attitude of our day is: 'Get it now! Never mind the eternal consequences of your present actions, you only go around once.' According to this view the Sermon on the Mount is nonsense, but if this is truth from God, then he is telling us to be wise, to think in eternal categories, and not to be slaves to the present. What happens right now, counts eternally, and this is the essence of the message that Jesus is giving here.

26. Christ's value system (Luke 6:22-26)

Beginning in Luke 6:22 Jesus gives us a very striking set of values: 'Blessed are you when men hate you, when they exclude you and insult you and reject your name as evil, because of the Son of Man.' Our culture's view is that happiness comes from popularity. We bend over backwards to find ways to get people to relate to us in a positive manner. How could it be a blessing to be hated, to be ostracized from the community? Jesus, however, is not indiscriminately pronouncing a blessing on anyone who is hated, or ostracized, or who suffers the reproach of mankind. He is specifically speaking to those who suffer such rejection for the sake of Christ.

Now, it is one thing to be rejected because we are ill-mannered or offensive to people. The Bible tells us that we are to seek to be at peace with all men, and to be the salt of the earth, kind, generous and friendly. But loyalty to Christ, devotion to him, will ultimately and inevitably bring some experience of the reproach of men. Christ promised that those who bore his name and who embraced his values would indeed suffer the same kind of humiliation and despising of men that was a normal part of his own existence. This statement, however, is not simply about loyalty to Jesus; it is a powerful statement about Jesus' own identity. Some people seek a compromise position between embracing Christ as the Son of God incarnate, and rejecting him out of hand as a lunatic. They view Jesus as nothing more than a great man, a wonderful teacher, whose lessons are of great value for the general ethical virtue of mankind. Some have even reduced the essence of the New Testament teaching to the Sermon on the Mount, seeing it as a good example of homespun moral wisdom. Such thinkers overlook the central fact that this address focuses its attention not merely on various moral maxims or ethical principles, but upon loyalty and devotion to Christ himself. The eternal destiny of people is determined by how they respond to him. He promises heaven to those who suffer for his sake, who remain loyal to him.

Jesus continues: 'Be glad in that day, and leap for joy; for behold, your reward is great in heaven; for in the same way their fathers used to treat the prophets' (6:23, NASB). Again this is an extraordinary admonition by Jesus. He doesn't say that if we suffer the reproach of men for his sake that we are to be patient because some day we will be able to rejoice about it. Jesus says the *very day* that we suffer that kind of reproach, the *very day* that we are victims of false witness and slander for Christ's sake, *that very day* we should rejoice. Jesus reminds his people that the prophets were treated in their own day in just the same way and their reward is also great.

From blessings to woes (Luke 6:24-26)
Continuing in verses 24 and 25 (NASB), Jesus changes from the *Beatitude* to the oracle of doom, using the formula of the *Woe*. He says, 'But woe to you who are rich, for you are receiving your comfort in full. Woe to you who are full, for you shall be hungry. Woe to you who laugh now, for you shall mourn and weep.' Again, it would be easy for us to jump to the conclusion that Jesus is pronouncing a judgment on anybody who enjoys prosperity. However, although he is warning people who are rich, he is warning a particular class of rich people. On another occasion he states how hard it is for those who have riches to enter into the kingdom of God. There is a peculiar temptation built in to prosperity; the prosperous can be self-sufficient; they can be given to arrogance and smugness, assuming that they can buy and sell anything, that they have no need of God. However, the Bible makes it very clear that prosperity in and of itself is not evil. Many of the great saints of Scripture were not only wealthy in spirit, but materially also: such as Abraham, Job, Joseph of Arimathea and Nicodemus. But if riches incline us towards that false sense of security, then indeed the worst curse a person could ever have would be to be overburdened with wealth. As Jesus warned, 'For what is a man profited if he shall gain the whole world, and lose his own soul?' (Matt. 16:26, AV). So Jesus pronounces woe upon people who are rich.

Then he goes on to say, 'Woe to you who laugh now.' Again, Jesus is not making an indiscriminate judgment upon laughter. As the Bible says, there is a time to laugh, there is a time to cry. Jesus himself manifested a good sense of humour. He is speaking here, however, about those who laugh with derision, who are laughing at people: 'Woe to you who laugh now, for you shall mourn and weep.'

'Woe to you who are full, for you shall be hungry' (6:25). Jesus is talking here about a different type of riches scenario, the scenario of the riches-to-rags. Again, it is a comment about value. This theme is found throughout the teaching of Jesus. If Jesus were here preaching to us, he would be asking us what our value-systems are, what we are putting our confidence in, where our hearts are, because there is a relationship between our hearts and our treasures. Jesus is saying that our hearts should be fixed on those things that cannot be destroyed or stolen. Our hearts should be fixed on those things of abiding and eternal value that no-one can take from us.

Christ continues his pronunciation of the oracle of doom: 'Woe to you, when all men speak well of you, for in the same way their fathers used to treat the false prophets' (6:26, NASB). Isn't this a strange statement of Jesus, that the curse of God hangs over those people who are too popular for their own good? This passage is on a collision course with the values of our culture, which teach us to seek popularity. There is nothing wrong in having people like us; there is nothing wrong in having a good reputation. The apostle Paul in Romans 12:18 says that we ought to be at peace with all men, as much as it is in our power, that we ought to have a good reputation. However, if *everybody* speaks well of you, watch out! In a sinful world there is only one way for all people to speak well of you, and that is if you are hypocritical, if you are compromising in your ethic, if you are taking a changing posture to suit the desires of those with whom you come in contact. A person of integrity and righteousness, on the other hand, is bound to alienate some in this world. Christ was the only perfect human being who ever lived, and yet he was hated by many of his contemporaries.

Jesus finishes this statement of woe by reminding his hearers that this is exactly what happened to the false prophets of Israel. The true prophets were objects of hatred – their message of repentance and holiness was scorned and resented, whereas the preaching of the false prophets was welcomed, for they told the people exactly what they wanted to hear. So, watch out if everybody speaks well of you!

27. Love your enemies (Luke 6:27-36)

The theme of the sermon changes now to human relationships with an ethic that is nothing less than astonishing. Jesus says, 'But I say to you who hear, love your enemies, do good to those who hate you' (6:27, NASB). So often when we hear the words of Christ and are comforted by his tender words of consolation, when our spirits are uplifted by the promises that he holds out for us for the future, it is easy for us to rejoice. But we are brought up short when we come face to face again with this radical ethic. On the surface it seems like Jesus is making a nonsense statement; surely he is asking the impossible when he says, 'Love your enemies.' An enemy, by definition, is somebody with whom we are experiencing estrangement, somebody who is against us, somebody whose hostility prevents us from responding warmly. How is it possible to love an enemy? How can we do it? In our culture we think of love in passive terms. Love is something over which we have no control. Love is something that happens to us, spontaneously – zing go the strings of our hearts. In New Testament categories, however, love is not something primarily that happens to us. Love, rather, is a duty, a requirement. Love has more to do with activity than it has to do with feeling. What Jesus is saying simply is this, 'Be loving to your enemies.' We may not be able to control how we feel about them, but we certainly can control what we do about those feelings. Jesus is saying here that the Christian ethic is not built upon retaliation, it is not given to vengeance. Yes, when we are injured and hurt we have every right to get down on our knees and ask God to vindicate us, to ask God for justice. But there is a great difference between seeking vindication and looking for vengeance.

The philosophy of retaliation is built into the fibre of our society. We don't just want to get even, we want to win, we want to conquer, we want to vanquish our enemies. But Jesus says, 'Be loving to your enemies.' That love sometimes can be very tough; that love may sometimes call forth for confrontation. Some years ago I witnessed this kind of love in action. A noted theologian was coming in for some criticism by a number of ministers. One minister in particular became very animated and upset and began to accuse this theologian of all sorts of wicked and hidden motives. The unfairness of the attack was evident to everyone in the room. How did this dignified theologian respond to this vicious attack? He didn't become red in the face, he didn't lash out in fury, he didn't retaliate in kind, but very softly he said to his assailant, 'Sir, you are slandering me.' With those quiet words of confrontation, the accuser recognized that he had indeed been guilty of a vicious assault. His response was immediate: he apologized and there was a complete change in his tone. It was a loving thing to do, not simply to absorb the comments in that situation, but to warn the man that he was injuring his own soul. So that is one way to love. It was one way of returning good for evil.

It is hard to return good actions for evil ones, and yet this is what the Christian is called to do: 'Do good to them which hate you,' Jesus said. It is easy to do good to those who love us, who hold us in high regard; but to be kind, generous and thoughtful to those whom we know despise us, requires all the grace that the human soul can bear.

Jesus goes on, 'Bless those who curse you, pray for those who mistreat you' (6:28, NASB). Now Jesus isn't asking us to do anything foolish here. He is not asking us to pray that our enemies would prosper above all people, or that they would have their way in everything they do. David, in his psalms, prayed some very difficult prayers; he asked that God would vindicate his saints and bring the wicked to ruin. He also declared, 'I hate my enemies with perfect hatred' (Psalm 139:22, NASB). A perfect hatred would seem to mean an unbridled hatred, a hatred that has no let up. But that is not what David meant. A perfect hatred is a hatred that has nothing but contempt for the wickedness of the perpetrator. It is a complete hatred, but, at the same time, it does not carry with it an ultimate desire for the total ruination of the soul of the evil-doer. Christ prayed for his own enemies. He didn't pray that they would be successful in their evil, but he prayed that their hearts would be changed, that they would be spared the final confrontation with the wrath of God, that they were moving towards. He prayed that their ways would be changed, that they may be redeemed.

Again, Jesus uses an illustration taken from daily life to underline this whole theology of the rejection of vengeance. 'Whoever hits you on the cheek, offer him the other also' (6:29, NASB). New Testament scholars differ in opinion as to how this text ought to be interpreted. Some say it ought to be taken literally. If somebody hits you on the jaw, instead of striking back, which would be the natural reaction, you are to offer the other side of your face to him as well. In Matthew's version the saying contains more detail. Matthew records Jesus' words as: 'Whoever slaps you on your right cheek, turn to him the other also' (5:39, NASB). Now for a right-handed person to strike someone on the right cheek, they would need to use the back of their hand. Possibly this action is significant: in the ancient world if you wanted to insult someone, to humiliate him publicly, you slapped him with the back of your hand on the opposite cheek. So perhaps what Jesus is putting forward here is not a response to physical violence, but a response to insult. If someone insults us, we are not to retaliate in kind; we are not to trade insult for insult. Christ is our example: he accepted the insults of the world and would not open his mouth; when the soldiers mocked him and humiliated him, he was as a sheep before his shearers, dumb. He spoke not a word in retaliation.

Jesus goes on to say that if someone takes away your cloak, you are to let him have your coat as well. The principle here is passive resistance to evil. It is not that we ought not to speak out against it, nor that we are supposed to run out and give our coat to every thief that comes down the street. But Jesus is saying something far more basic than that, something that is incorporated in the broader statement found in Deuteronomy: 'It is mine to avenge, I will repay' (32:35, NASB). So often that statement is seriously misunderstood, for, vengeance, as such, is seen by many as evil. But God says that innocent people will be vindicated, that victims of evil will be avenged, and that vengeance will be a perfect vengeance, because God himself will do it. We are not to take vengeance into our own hands. It is a mark of a saint that he follows Christ at this level.

Continuing his list of sayings that are all a part of his radical ethic of love and of kindness, Jesus says, 'Give to every one that asks of you, and whoever takes away what is yours, do not demand it back again' (6:30, NASB). Imagine what would happen if we had to give something to every person we ever met who asked of us. It would soon get around that our attitudes to charity was very extreme.

As a young pastor, I worked in a very depressed area. On one occasion our house was full of derelicts who were seeking a place to stay for the night. Then there was a knock at the door; it was another man down on his luck and obviously inebriated. He asked if I could put him up for the night. It seemed that the word had got around that this young pastor would let anybody come and sleep in his house that asked for it. I found out that there are practical problems in carrying out some of these statements in the Sermon on the Mount with absolute precision. It is important, when we read these short pithy statements of Jesus, these aphorisms, where he sets out very weighty principles in universal terms, to be careful to read them in the light of the whole of Jesus' teaching, for sometimes these statements are qualified elsewhere in the Bible.

For example, in Matthew 18:19, Jesus says: 'I tell you that if two of you on earth agree about anything you ask for, it will be done for you by my Father in heaven.' Consider the consequences of taking that statement at face value. I am sure that we could find two Christians who would agree that there should be no more sickness in the world, or no more wars, or that everyone repent of their sins and stop sinning. But if we agreed on those things and asked God, would we really expect God to change all of the predictions that he has given in his word about these matters, just to suit those two or three who agree? Obviously that general statement concerning agreement between Christians is to be understood in light of the rest of the Bible's teaching about prayer.

In Luke 6:30 Jesus is saying that the spirit that is to characterize the Christian in the kingdom of God, is willingness to give. Sacrificial giving is the mark of the Christian. But of course, there are limits that our own wisdom must give to us.

In the next verse we find the saying known as the Golden Rule: 'And just as you want people to treat you,' or, in more popular terms: 'Do unto others as you would have them do unto you.' It is called the Golden Rule, not by Jesus, nor by Luke, but by the church, because they see in this particular aphorism the essence of the entire sermon. Surprisingly, the Golden Rule was not new with Jesus. It was a principle that had a lengthy tradition among the Jews, although it was normally stated in a negative rather than in a positive sense. For example, Hillel, perhaps the greatest rabbi of Judaism, once said, 'What is hateful to you, do not do to your neighbour. That is the whole Torah, while the rest is the commentary thereof.' Jesus puts a positive twist to the saying by simply stating, 'Treat people as you would have them treat you.' This profound rule is one way we know whether or not we are behaving in an appropriate way towards our fellow man. If everyone in the world were to apply this one law, how different society would be.

In verses 32-34 Jesus demonstrates ways in which we can live by this Golden Rule. 'And if you love those who love you, what credit is that to you? For even sinners do the same. And if you lend to those from whom you expect to receive, what credit is that to you? Even sinners lend to sinners, in order to receive back the same amount' (6:32-34, NASB). Even sinners can return good for good, love for love; but Jesus is calling us to a higher ethic than that. He is calling us to an ethic of love to those who hate us, and doing good to those who do not do good to us. There is some question over the meaning of this verb, *palpizo*, here translated 'expecting nothing'. Sometimes it is used to mean 'to despair of', so Jesus is saying, 'Lend to people and not be despairing about it.' The reason why we lend and give assistance is not that we want to get some kind of return. This passage does not prohibit the granting of loans with a view towards a substantial return, but the point Jesus is making is that we should be willing to reach out and help such people, not despairing of them; to provide assistance not for our own personal gain, but out of a sense of compassion and concern for those who are in need.

If we act in this manner, Jesus said, 'And your reward shall be great, and you will be sons of the Most High, for He Himself is kind to ungrateful and evil men' (6:35, NASB). Being children of the highest means that you will be imitating God because this is the way God operates. God is kind to people who are unthankful; God is kind to the evil. He gives all kinds of benefit at times, even to those who are most wickedly in opposition and rebellion to him.

So we are to be imitators of God himself, and if that is not clear in verse 35, it is in verse 36: 'Be merciful, just as your Father is merciful' (NASB). We talk a lot about character, integrity and righteousness, but what is the ultimate guide for a virtuous character? The thing that we need to learn, perhaps more than anything else in our Christian lives, is who God is. We need to understand the character of God because all theology, all ethics, are nothing more and nothing less than a reflection of the character of God. We are to be merciful – that should be part of our character – because it is part of the character of God.

28. A warning against judging others
(Luke 6:37-42)

Verse 37 of Luke 6 is possibly the most well known verse in the New Testament for those who are outside of the kingdom: 'And do not judge and you will not be judged; and do not condemn, and you will not be condemned; pardon and you will be pardoned' (NASB). They may have never read the Bible, but they know it says, 'Do not judge.' One of the chief objections that the world brings against Christians is that Christians are hypocritical and judgmental. Certainly that may be true of some of us, but I think that this passage is quite often seriously misunderstood, for there are different kinds of judgment.

For a start, the New Testament speaks of a judgment that is condemnatory, that flows out of a spirit of arrogance and self-righteousness that has nothing to do with the Spirit of Christ. There is that kind of precipitous consigning of other people to hell, which the God of the Bible hates. We are never to be involved in that kind of judgmental spirit.

But there is another kind of judgment which we may refer to not as a judgment of condemnation, but rather as a judgment of discernment or evaluation. A New Testament Christian is not called to be naïve; the New Testament Christian is called to be alert to the power and the reality of evil that is all around us. We are to be able to discern between a righteous deed and a wicked one; to be alert to actions that are contrary to the teaching of Christ. We are to be able to recognize evil and to call it what it is, evil. But when we do that, so often the response is, 'Who are you to judge me?' And then the verse is quoted: 'Judge not, lest ye be judged.'

Jesus is talking here about an attitude, a mind-set that is sometimes found within the church to the church's embarrassment, a mind-set of contentiousness, a mind-set of criticism, that God does not enjoy. The basic posture that we are to have towards the world is that of charity that covers a multitude of sins. God has not called us to be the policemen of society, but to discern the difference between good and evil, and there is a time and place for the church to exercise prophetic criticism, not only to its own members, but to the world as well. But a negative spirit we are to resist with all of our mind.

Again, we have to be careful about taking these general principles found in verse 37 too far. Suppose a person was living a life of violent opposition to God, but, recognizing that there were many like him, his attitude was not only to approve of his own wicked conduct, but to approve of everybody else's sin as well. In fact, this is one of the characteristics of fallen man, not only to approve sin in himself, but also to encourage others to sin. Imagine such a person standing before God on the judgment day and saying, 'Your book says that if I don't condemn anybody you are not going to condemn me, so I can do whatever I want so long as I don't condemn anybody else.' That is not the point of what Jesus is saying here. He is speaking to an attitude of the heart and of the mind; if we flee from a condemnatory attitude, the return benefit to us will be a removal of condemnation.

In the Lord's Prayer, we pray, 'Forgive us our trespasses as we forgive those who trespass against us.' It is a terrifying thing to say before God because if God does indeed forgive us as we forgive those who sin against us, we may be in serious trouble. However, if we have a forgiving spirit, we will be more and more receiving of the forgiveness of God. But not only the forgiveness of God. If we are willing to forgive our fellow human beings, it is likely that we will receive a good deal of forgiveness from them also. If we are free of a condemnatory spirit, we will receive less condemnation from men. So, it is not just God who treats us according to how we behave.

In a similar vein verse 38 (NASB) enjoins us: 'Give and it will be given to you; good measure, pressed down, shaken together, running over, they will pour into your lap.' Again, it is not just that God will give to you, but that men will return these things to you. How is that return going to come? To explain this, Jesus borrows an illustration from the agricultural world, of the gathering of the wheat into bushels, perhaps preparing it for market. It is very important that the person who is buying wheat should not be cheated of the full amount, so to make sure that the full volume of the container is met, the wheat was taken by a good measure, a proper measurement, it was pressed down and shaken together, to make sure that every empty space in the bushel was filled, and then running over. Thus, it is an abundance of the measure that shall be returned to you if you give. If we are giving people, we will tend to attract giving people to us. If you find that people are always taking from you, what does that say about you personally? The psychologists tell us that there is a sense in which we dictate how other people respond to us. It isn't true in every circumstance, but as a general truth we tend to send out the signals and the message to people how we expect to be treated, who consequently treat us in that manner.

Again, Jesus repeats this principle that he has been stressing in his sermon: 'For by your standard of measure it will be measured to you in return' (6:38b). All of this is but commentary on the Golden Rule: 'And just as you want people to treat you, treat them in the same way.'

The blind leading the blind (Luke 6:39-42)

At this point in the sermon Jesus interjects a short parable to teach his disciples an important point. 'A blind man cannot guide a blind man, can he? Will they not both fall into a pit?' This illustration conjours up the rather humorous image of one blind man presuming to lead another blind man. Neither can see the way, so the obvious end of such a venture is destruction as both fall into the ditch. Jesus, of course, is not making fun of handicapped people, nor is he speaking lightly here, but he is trying to illustrate an extremely important point for all of us. Throughout his sermon Jesus is concerned that people have a proper understanding of the things of God, and is frequently critical of the bad style of leadership that was being given to the people of Israel from their so-called spiritual leaders, the Pharisees and the scribes. Here Jesus is likening these leaders of the people to blind men who presume to lead others.

Jesus, on another occasion, says of himself: 'I am the way, and the truth, and the life' (John 14:6). He sets his teaching up as that beacon of light that shows the pathway to people who want to find eternal life. There is a sense in which everyone is called to make a decision and to make a choice over who will guide them. Will we follow people who know where they are going? Or are we content to follow people who are wandering around aimlessly, blind to their destinies. This reminds me of a story in *Alice in Wonderland*. Alice came to a fork in the road, and she hesitated, not knowing which way to turn. She saw the Cheshire Cat sitting there and grinning at her. It asked her what the matter was, and she replied: 'I don't know which turn I should follow. I don't know whether to go to the left or to the right. Can you help me?' The Cheshire Cat said, 'That depends on where you are going.' Alice said, 'I don't know.' And the cat grinned and said. 'Then it doesn't matter.'

It is a tragic thing to have no idea where you are going. We often feel that sense of aimlessness, of being without direction, of not knowing exactly what we are about with our lives. But how much more tragic it is if we secure for ourselves leaders who don't know where they are going. But Christ knew where he was going, and he called people to follow him.

He goes on to say: 'A pupil is not above his teacher; but everyone, after he has been fully trained, will be like his teacher' (6:40, NASB). A disciple cannot lead the teacher; the teacher leads the disciple. It is a very simple statement, but so often we want to be in the position of leadership even with respect to Christ, forgetting who we are and who he is.

Jesus, once again, turns his criticism on the Pharisees: 'And why do you look at the speck that is in your brother's eye, but do not notice the log that is in your own eye?' (6:41, NASB). It is so easy to become a critic of other people, and the Pharisees, of course, were fond of exercising criticism, pointing out the faults of those around them. But they were blind to their own shortcomings, they were blind to their own sin, and in many cases their sin was greater than the sins of others that they were so quick to point out. So Jesus said to them: '... how can you say to your brother, "Brother, let me take out the speck that is in your eye," when you yourself do not see the log that is in your own eye? You hypocrite, first take the log out of your own eye, and then you will see clearly to take out the speck that is in your brother's eye' (6:42, NASB). The principle here is that criticism must start at home. We should be our own chief critics, not in a negative, destructive sense, but we should be more concerned about reforming our own lives, than we are about getting everybody else to change. It is tempting, isn't it, to think that all that is wrong with the world is found in other people, and if they would all just change, then everything would be fine and we would be happy. What we want is for people to accommodate us, rather than for us to change to be able to live in harmony with other people. There is probably no place where this is more obvious and more evident than in the common and typical situation of marriage counselling, when an estranged couple comes to the pastor or counsellor. So often the great desire of each individual is that somehow the counsellor will convince the other partner to do the changing, rather than to take that responsibility upon oneself. But Jesus' principle is this: let's start with improving our own lives before we attempt to help others with their problems.

29. A pattern for living (Luke 6:43-49)

Jesus then goes on to tell two stories which illustrate how we should live. The first concerns fruit trees and the second a wise and a foolish builder.

A tree is known by its fruit (Luke 6:43-45)

> 'For there is no good tree which produces bad fruit; nor on the other hand, a bad tree which produces good fruit. For each tree is known by its own fruit. For men do not gather figs from thorns, nor do they pick grapes from a briar bush. A good man out of the good treasure of his heart brings forth what is good; and an evil man out of the evil treasure brings forth what is evil; for his mouth speaks from that which fills his heart' (NASB).

Sometimes the teaching of Jesus is so simple that we miss its profundity. This illustration, drawn from life, is so simple: You don't get oranges from apple trees. But obviously what Christ is getting at here is that righteousness is not a peripheral thing. This was the mistake that the Pharisees made. They concentrated on rituals, external rites, behavioural patterns, superficial matters, to the extent that they neglected the heavier matters of the law. They neglected to get the pursuit of righteousness down into the core of their being.

If you want to see how much this teaching of Jesus has been misunderstood, ask of people if they believe that mankind is basically good or basically evil? I have asked that question many times and every time the overwhelming majority of people respond by saying that mankind is basically good. They are quick to point out that yes, there is sin, there is wickedness, there is evil. Nobody is perfect. But basically, down at the root of man's being, there is goodness, untarnished and unpolluted. Sin, in this view, is just a tangential matter, something that is accidental to our nature, not its very essence. This spirit has characterized our society for a long time; all we have to do to overcome the evil that we find in human society is to achieve a higher level of education. Sin is seen simply as a matter of not knowing better, not something that proceeds from the core of our being. That intellectual giant, Socrates, taught this sort of thing. He was convinced that wickedness or evil was simply a matter of ignorance. Hence his earnest pursuit of knowledge and his gadfly method of running around Athens provoking people to thoughtful discussions, trying to get them to stimulate their minds, to dig more deeply, so that they could get great knowledge, and with that greater knowledge would come goodness and the end of evil.

So, really, Socrates and others like him believe that sin is just a matter of making mistakes, that we just don't know any better. But Jesus is saying that sin comes from the very centre of our being. It comes from the heart. It is our nature to sin. Let me say it in another way which I think is consistent with the New Testament teaching: we are not sinners because we sin, rather we sin because we are sinners. That is, in our fallen human nature, committing sin is doing what comes naturally, not according to our original nature, but according to our fallen nature.

We need to be very careful about this view because so often in our culture we define goodness and evil not by the standards that God provides for us, but by doing an evaluation and a statistical analysis of what the behavioural patterns of people happen to be. For example, if we see a hundred people out of a hundred practising a certain thing, we are swayed by the statistical evidence and conclude that it is normal to do this thing, and if it is normal, it is human, and if it is human, it is good. This is what I call statistical morality, whereby the good is determined by the normal; what ought to be is determined by what is. Isn't that a topsy-turvy way to examine ethics? I mean, how deeply would we have to think about that to see the folly of it? How many people do you know who have ever lied? Have you ever lied? Diogenes in the ancient world walked through Athens with his lamp searching for an honest man; he never found one who was totally and completely honest. Every man, at some point in his life, has violated God's canons of truthfulness. Do we therefore come to the conclusion that it is a good thing to lie? I hope not, but you see, what Jesus is saying is that what is commonplace could be a manifestation of a corrupt nature.

Jesus says that it is a question of dealing with the core of the tree. The fruit does not corrupt itself, but corrupt fruit comes out of the corrupt core of the tree. 'The good man out of the good treasure of his heart brings forth what is good; and the evil man out of the evil treasure of his heart brings forth what is evil.' So, if we are seeking reformation in our lives, we can't approach it as if it were simply a superficial thing, an external matter, for it is our hearts that need attention. We need to get down to the very deepest level of our being, and consider the disposition of our hearts. Are our hearts disposed towards God, or are our hearts set against him? Do you rejoice when God is honoured? Do you enjoy the worship of God? Does your spirit thrill in a posture of adoration and reverence? Or are you indifferent to the things of God? Is the character of God something about which you have no interest whatsoever? Perhaps not only indifferent, but maybe even hostile towards the character of God? If you feel that way sometimes, just how deep are those feelings? Do they come from the surface, or are they coming out of the very depths of your being? If they come out of the depths of your heart, then I urge you to seek the presence of Christ. To seek him with all your heart, because you do not have the ability within yourself to change your nature; only God can do that.

Build your house on the rock (Luke 6:46-49)

In verse 46 Christ asks a very important question: 'Why do you call me, "Lord, Lord," and do not do what I say?' Matthew, in his fuller record of this section, says that many will come on the last day and say to Jesus, 'Lord, Lord, did we not do this in your name, and did we not do that in your name?' And Jesus will look at them and say, 'I never knew you. Away from me, you evildoers' (Matt. 7:22-23). The repetition of the address, 'Lord, Lord,' is a Hebrew method of communicating intimacy. It is only on rare occasions that we find the form of personal address repeated like this in Scripture. At certain times in the Old Testament people are addressed by the repeated form: God speaking to Abraham when he is about to sacrifice Isaac (Gen. 22:11); encouraging Jacob in his old age to take the trip to Egypt (Gen. 46:2); calling Samuel in the night (1 Sam. 3:10); calling Moses from the burning bush (Exod. 3:4), and so on. This form of address also occurs from time to time in the New Testament (for example, Luke 10:41; 13:34; 22:31). We also find it in the record of what is perhaps the most pathetic moment in human history; the Son cries out in his agony on the cross to his Father: '*Eli, Eli, lama sabachthani*? that is to say, My God, my God, why have you forsaken me?' (Matt. 27:46).

Jesus' point is that some don't simply acknowledge him as Lord, but they say, 'Lord, Lord.' The pretence is one of intimacy. People pretend to have a deep personal relationship with Christ, but the test of that is seen in the fruit of one's life. Jesus said 'Whoever has my commands and obeys them, he is the one who loves me' (John 14:21). And conversely, he says, 'Why do you call me, "Lord, Lord," and do not do what I say?'

'I will show you what he is like who comes to me and hears my words and puts them into practice' (6:47). Jesus wants people who not only hear him, but who obey him. Interestingly, in the New Testament, the verb 'to obey' comes from the same Greek root as the word 'to hear'. *Akouein* means 'to hear', and put a prefix on it: *hyperkouein*, and it means 'to obey'. And so, literally, 'to obey' means *hyper*-hearing, or really hearing. Jesus does not want people just to hear his voice, he wants them to do the things that they hear.

To show what such a person is like, Jesus gives a very vivid picture:

> ... he is like a man building a house, who dug deep and laid a foundation upon the rock; and when a flood rose, the torrent burst against that house and could not shake it, because it had been well built. But the one who has heard, and has not acted accordingly, is like a man who built a house upon the ground without any foundations; and the torrent burst against it and immediately it collapsed, and the ruin of that house was great (6:48-49, NASB).

Anybody can make a superficial response by saying, 'Lord, Lord.' But the genuine Christian life is a life that is lived by sinking deeply into the foundational principles of Christ, learning of Christ there, studying Christ there.

The person who hears Christ and puts into practice what he hears, becomes like that person who builds his house upon the rock. It is not enough simply to be titillated by the beauty of the Sermon on the Mount. This sermon was never given for the purpose of eloquence or for the purpose of entertainment. The Sermon on the Mount was an act in history where God incarnate revealed a pattern of living that provides stability in the midst of chaos, that provides character and strength when everyone else is falling apart. It gives the key to developing the kind of tree that produces good fruit, abiding fruit, fruit that doesn't corrupt at first exposure of trouble.

The Sermon on the Mount is addressed not simply to our ears, but to our hearts, to the end that we, when we meet Christ, might say, 'Lord, Lord,' and He will say, 'I know you, I know you by name. Come, my beloved, inherit the kingdom which my Father has prepared for you from the foundation of the world.'

30. The centurion's display of faith (Luke 7:1-10)

On numerous occasions in the New Testament, when Jesus speaks, the reaction of the people is one of amazement, but there are very few times when Jesus was amazed by what someone else said. Today, we are going to look at one of those incidents.

Having completed the Sermon on the Mount, Jesus continued his public ministry.

> When Jesus had finished saying all this in the hearing of the people, he entered Capernaum. There a centurion's servant, whom his master valued highly, was sick and about to die. The centurion heard of Jesus and sent some elders of the Jews to him, asking him to come and heal his servant. When they came to Jesus, they pleaded earnestly with him, 'This man deserves to have you do this, because he loves our nation and has built our synagogue.'

This is an interesting introduction to the account of Jesus' healing of the centurion's servant. A centurion was a soldier, who was in charge of a hundred men. It wasn't the highest military office; it was a kind of mid-range office, something akin to the rank of captain. This centurion had a servant, and it is obvious that the centurion cared very deeply for his servant: his attitude to him is not one of patronizing contempt, but love. He was upset when he discovered that the servant was sick, even to the point of death.

The centurion had never met Jesus. He had never heard him speak. He only knew of Jesus' reputation. But when he heard of Jesus he sent the elders of the Jews, the rulers of the religious community, to him. This Gentile Roman centurion, whose servant was dying, heard of Jesus' reputation, but knowing that Jesus is Jewish, he suspects perhaps that this Jewish preacher would not be interested in reaching out to help a Gentile soldier. So, to get the attention of Jesus, he goes first of all to the leaders of the Jewish community, and begs them to intercede on his behalf and see if it would be possible for Jesus to come and minister to his desperately ill servant.

As we think of this incident, it is helpful to remind ourselves

that one of Luke's great concerns in writing this book is to
demonstrate that Christ's ministry was not only to the Jews, but
was meant for the Gentiles as well. So Luke's account includes
many encounters that took place between Jesus and Gentiles.
And here of course is a most fascinating one. But, in order for the
meeting to take place, the elders of the Jewish nation came and
interceded for the centurion. Now that, in itself, is strange. There
was no love between the Jews and their foreign oppressors.
What kind of a man was this centurion, that he had friends
among the Jews? We could conclude that the soldier simply
ordered the Jews to intercede on his behalf, but as Luke tells the
story, the centurion wasn't present when the Jewish elders came
to Jesus, and so they had no reason to praise him unless they
really meant it. But that is exactly what they did. They came to
Jesus and they begged him, on behalf of the centurion, to come
and to heal the servant. Why? 'For he loves our nation, and has
built our synagogue.' Here is an occupying soldier who, instead
of holding this small Mediterranean country in contempt, actually
loved the Jewish nation. He was not a native of Israel, but he had
come to love the land and the people there, and he became so
much involved in their affairs that he built a synagogue for them.

So we are told in verse 6 that Jesus went with them. 'And
when he was already not far from the house, the centurion sent
friends, saying to him, "Lord, do not trouble yourself, for I do not
deserve to have you come under my roof."' What's going on
here? First of all, the centurion was greatly agitated, begging the
elders to get Jesus to come and take care of his servant. But when
Jesus accedes to the request, he is met by friends of the centurion
with a message which seems to contradict the earlier message.
The earlier message was, 'Please come!' The message is now,
'Don't trouble yourself!' Our expectation is that the friends will
say to Jesus that he is too late, the servant has died. It would seem
the centurion was feeling guilty about bothering Jesus. He was
torn between his own sense of unworthiness and his great fear
for the life of his beloved servant.

However, he doesn't ask Jesus to go away, but instead says

something quite remarkable: 'But say the word, and my servant will be healed.' You don't have to come to the house; you don't have to touch my servant. Just where you are, right now, say the word, that is all that it will take.

What an incredible statement of faith! The centurion explains his words for he says (v.8): 'For I myself am a man under authority, with soldiers under me. I tell this one, "Go!" and he goes; and that one, "Come!" and he comes. I say to my servant, "Do this!" and he does it.' Now the centurion is not boasting to Jesus of his high rank in the Roman army. He is not deliberately showing off his power and influence. Rather, he is being completely humble in making his request before Christ, but he is saying to Jesus that he understands authority, for he himself is under authority. Remember that the centurion's office is one of mid-rank. Therefore, he in turn was under the authority of those above him. He understands the nature of authority. He knew it was not necessary for Jesus to enter the house. All he needed to do was say the word!

Here was a man who had stood before generals, maybe even the emperor of Rome, who knew somehow that in Christ he was dealing with One who exercised consummate lordship.

Jesus was astonished by the faith and understanding that he found in this man. He had not been born and raised in the shadow of the synagogue, he had not been steeped in the literature of the Old Testament, he had not known intimately the oracles of God found in the prophets. He was a stranger to the covenant, a foreigner, an alien to the Old Testament world. But he understood authority, and he understood that Jesus had it. He understood that Jesus had a kind of authority that gave him the ability to have power over life and over death. This same Jesus who would reveal himself later on, after his resurrection, in the book of the Apocalypse with words like these: 'I am the Alpha and Omega' (Rev. 1:8). 'I have the keys of hell and death' (Rev. 1:18). He has the power, the authority over life itself.

The multitudes were amazed at Jesus, because they saw wonderful power, they heard profound wisdom and insight coming out of his mouth; but not one was able to penetrate the authority of Christ as this centurion did. He understood the thing that escaped the religious leaders of Jesus' day; the obvious manifestation of God incarnate, which took place in the midst of people that were blind to it, was recognized by a Gentile.

Jesus turned to the people who were following him and said, 'I have not found such great faith even in Israel.' When the centurion's friends returned to the house they found that the servant had indeed been healed. Luke does not tell us whether Jesus spoke the words the centurion asked for, but in Matthew's account of the incident Jesus did, in fact, say the word: 'Go! It will be done just as you believed it would!' (Matt. 8:13).

Luke's concern, however, is not simply to tell us another story about the miraculous healing power of Jesus, so it is not surprising that Luke skips over the very words of healing. He tells us that the work was finished, but he uncharacteristically eliminates some of the details, because his emphasis here is not on the healing of the servant, but on the attitude of the centurion, who comes before Christ, recognizing who he is, and approaches him in a proper spirit of humility. 'Lord, I do not deserve to have you come under my roof.'

Later in Luke Jesus tells a parable of two men who went up to the temple to pray, one a tax-gatherer, and one a Pharisee. The first a miserable, hated scoundrel; the other a religious leader. The Pharisee lifted his head up to heaven and said, 'God, I thank thee, that I am not as other men are, extortioners, unjust, adulterers, or even as this publican' (Luke 18:11, AV). There is a smug, self-satisfaction in his words as he thanks God. The publican, on the other hand could not even raise his head to heaven, but looking at his feet, he beat upon his breast, and said, 'God, be merciful to me a sinner.' Jesus comments that it was the latter man who returned to his house, justified. There is no hope for justification until one is ready to humble himself before God.

The Scriptures tell us in many ways that God gives grace to the humble. God's ear is in tune to the cries of the humble, but we are also told that he resists the proud, he brings down the arrogant from their lofty perches. Pride has devastating effects; it has destroyed churches, kingdoms and people. We have all seen it, and there is no profession or calling that is immune from its ravaging power. One can become so full of self-importance, that before he even knows it, his personality is engulfed by the kind of pride that God hates and works to bring down.

The centurion in this account had much to be proud of. He was a man who had achieved a significant rank and had standing in the community. How easy it would have been for him to command Jesus to attend to his sick servant. Instead, however, he humbled himself and Christ came to his home.

Is pride keeping Christ away from your home? Is pride a barrier to your recognizing the authority that is invested in him? Do you try to manipulate God, as if he were obliged to obey your commandments? Or do you recognize his authority, humbling yourself before him, crying on your knees that he is King of Kings and Lord of Lords?

Jesus said, 'Not even in Israel have I found such great faith.' May he find that kind of faith in your house.

31. Jesus raises a widow's son (Luke 7:11-16)

Following Luke's narrative of Christ's healing of the centurion's servant, we read: 'Soon afterward, Jesus went to a town called Nain, and his disciples and a large crowd went along with him. As he approached the town gate, a dead person was being carried out – the only son of his mother, and she was a widow. And a large crowd from the town was with her.' Luke begins this narrative of the encounter of Jesus with the widow of Nain by telling us that Jesus was continuing his itinerant preaching and teaching, moving around the regions of Galilee from Capernaum outward. His travels brought him to the village of Nain. This is the only time that this village is mentioned in the Bible. But what happened here, in this place, was exceedingly important for the ministry of Jesus.

The dead man in question was the only son of a widow, and Luke is keen to show something of the moving spirit of

The funeral procession was underway as Jesus approached. It was the custom in the ancient world, particularly among the Jews, to wrap the corpse in a cloth shroud and carry it in procession on a litter. It was also customary in the ancient world to hire professional mourners. Even in the case of a very poor person, so rabbinic tradition tells us, at least two people playing flutes, and one professional wailing woman were expected to accompany the funeral procession. But in this case Luke tells that the multitude surrounding the bier was great, for obviously the woman and her plight had provoked the compassion of a great multitude of people from the community.

compassion that characterizes Jesus in his earthly ministry. Luke describes how this woman was in profound grief: not only was she about to bury her only son, but this also meant there was no-one to carry on her family name, and as a widow, she was left without a male family member to give her support and protection. A widow in the ancient world was so much more dependent on her sons for her support than a woman in similar circumstances would be in our culture.

When Jesus saw her, he had compassion on her and said to her, 'Do not weep.' His first move was to go and speak to the grief-stricken widow. Unlike the incident where the centurion sent friends to Jesus to beseech him to do something for the ill servant, on this occasion there is no record of either the woman herself or anyone else calling her desperate plight to his attention. But Jesus, on his own initiative, beholding the woman in her sorrow, goes out of his way to speak to her. His words were words of comfort.

Verse 14 says something significant that we could easily miss: 'Then he went up and touched the coffin, and those carrying it stood still.' In the ancient world and particularly in the Jewish culture, it was considered unlawful from the viewpoint of ceremony to touch a corpse. To come in contact with a dead body was to risk personal defilement that would require a very rigorous procedure of ritual cleansing. But here Jesus violates the ceremony. He does this on several occasions in Scripture, never violating, of course, the moral law of the Old Testament, but using this as an occasion to say something to his contemporaries of the importance of life over ceremony. For we know that the Pharisees in the ancient community had made the opposite evaluation, at times regarding ritualistic ceremony as being more important than life and the exercise of mercy.

So Jesus touched the bier, and, speaking directly to the corpse, said, 'Young man, I say to you, arise!' And verse 15 says: 'And the dead man sat up, and began to speak.' The dead man did not simply move, which could be attributed to some kind of involuntary muscular reaction. No, the corpse sat up and began to speak. Then we are told that 'Jesus gave him back to his mother'. Can you imagine the response of this woman?

This is one of three records in the New Testament of Jesus' raising someone from the dead. The other two incidents concern Lazarus and Jairus' daughter. Here it was done, not to make a spectacular display of Jesus' power, but as an expression of Jesus' compassion for a widow. Widows and orphans were two groups of people that God singled out as deserving of special consideration by the church. Jesus' compassion went out to this woman who had experienced the grief of losing a husband, of having lost the deepest and most intimate type of human fellowship that a person can enjoy, but with at least the continuing and abiding joy of her only son. When her son died, it was almost too much for the woman to bear. It is a very poignant, human experience.

But then a strange visitor came into town and did something that was not only unexpected, but beyond belief. Sometimes we think that people in the ancient world found it easier to accept the miraculous. They may have had their sorcerers and magicians and all kinds of strange things, but no sorcerer of Egypt, no magician of Persia, could go to the cemetery or to the funeral procession and raise somebody from the dead. The people in the first century who witnessed this event were no less astonished than people would be if it happened in our society today.

Having witnessed this miracle, 'fear gripped them all, and they began glorifying God' (verse 16). Can you imagine the hush that fell over this multitude as they witnessed the dead man sit up and begin to speak? They were terrified, but at least these people had the good sense to glorify God. That was a quick reaction. What would you think? How would you have reacted? We all understand that there are certain things that even magicians can't pull off. Certain things belong to a type of phenomenon that only God can bring about, such as bringing something out of nothing, or bringing life out of death. So this multitude, not particularly trained in science and certainly not particularly trained in theology, when they saw this event unfold before them, the only conclusion they could come to, and they came to it instantly, was that this is a work of God: 'and they began glorifying God, saying, "A great prophet has arisen among us."'

Indeed, a great prophet had been raised in their midst. But notice that this wasn't enough to convince the people that God was there or that Jesus was God. They certainly recognized that this was a work that only God could accomplish, but they had a historical reference at that point. There were very rare, isolated instances in the Old Testament where people had been raised from the dead by the power of God, through the prophets. And so here, when they see somebody raising somebody from the dead, the immediate inference they make is that this man must be a great prophet. Indeed he was a prophet, but more than a prophet.

But let's finish what the people said: 'God has visited his people.' What a beautiful statement! God has visited his people. That's how the contemporaries of Jesus understood this act of mercy. The idea of God visiting his people is something that had its roots planted very deeply in the Old Testament. The prophets had said on several occasions that in the last days, God would visit his people. Think back to the early songs at the beginning of the book of Luke, sung by Mary, Zechariah, Simeon and others. In those songs, more than once, there was the statement that God, in the coming of this baby, was visiting his people.

As we saw in an earlier study the word for visit is the word from which we get the English word *episcopal*. An episcopal church is one governed by bishops. A bishop can be compared to a shepherd with his flock. He knows when his people are hurting; he knows when there is pain in his congregation. The bishop or pastor is to bring something of the presence of Christ into the place of need, because, in the Bible, the supreme example of the bishop is God. Christ, incidentally, is given that title by the author of Hebrews, who refers to Jesus as the bishop of our souls, the One who looks after us. He has been raised to the right hand of God where he serves as our great high priest, but in that priestly ministry, Jesus is still watching over us.

Jesus exercises the classic role of the bishop when he passes through the village called Nain. He visits a woman in the midst of her grief; and he visits the funeral and he visits the dead man and brings him back to life. In this act the people recognized not simply the visit of an itinerant preacher, nor even of just a great prophet; the people understood that this represented the visitation of God.

Christ has promised that he will continue to be the bishop of your soul, and there is a very real sense in which, if you are in need this day and go to him in prayer, by his Spirit, he will visit with you. That's the kind of God we have. Our God is a God who is alert to the cries of those who mourn, and who promises to bring comfort and, ultimately, to wipe away every tear from our eyes. We may not be quick to visit God, but God is willing to visit with us.

32. Jesus and John the Baptist (Luke 7:17-30)

Have you ever been plagued with doubts about whether or not Jesus was really the Messiah? It may surprise you to know that one of his closest friends and highest promoters obviously struggled with doubts himself.

After the miraculous raising from the dead of the widow of Nain's son, we read: 'This report concerning [Jesus] went out over all Judea, and in all the surrounding district. The disciples of John reported to him about all these things' (7:17-18, NASB). We noted in an earlier study that Jesus was not the only person in biblical times that had disciples; John the Baptist, who was the forerunner of Christ, also had disciples, some of whom later became disciples of Jesus.

Reports about Jesus' ministry were taken to John as he was languishing in prison, presumably awaiting his own execution. John then sent a rather strange message to Jesus: 'Calling two of them, he sent them to the Lord to ask, 'Are you the one who was to come, or should we expect someone else?' (7:18-19). This is John the Baptist speaking, the one who publicly declared Christ as the One who was to come, as the One whose shoes John was not worthy to untie, who baptized Jesus and inaugurated Jesus' public ministry, who was consecrated in his mother's womb by the Holy Spirit to be the prophet to herald the coming of the King and the kingdom of God. Imagine how Jesus felt to have this question raised by John the Baptist, the one whose testimony was so vital to his own ministry. But the question John raises is one that many people are still asking: was Jesus the One who was to come (that is, the appointed Messiah) or should we look somewhere else?

What in the world provoked such an inquiry from John the Baptist? Was he going through a crisis of faith? Was he becoming a bit impatient for Jesus to make a more spectacular move? Perhaps John himself had misunderstandings of the role and the character of the Messiah. Perhaps John, like the multitudes, was expecting a radical overthrow of the Roman government. These are merely speculations. It is difficult to know for sure. Some have suggested that John, with his character, and strength of faith, wouldn't have surrendered to moments of doubt; that this was a way of strengthening the faith of his disciples, so that they could hear Jesus' own answer to the question. That's a possibility, but I doubt it is the real reason. John the Baptist had been prepared of God for a dynamic ministry of preparation for the announcing of the kingdom of God, then all of a sudden he is taken out of the action and is thrown into a prison cell. He is suffering from isolation. He is in abject misery. Surely he would have been asking questions. What am I doing in this prison? When is Jesus going to make his move? How can Jesus allow the power of Herod to be greater than his, that I as a prophet, should be left here alone?

So the question comes. And Luke writes: 'At that very time Jesus cured many who had diseases, sicknesses and evil spirits, and gave sight to many who were blind. So he replied to the messengers, 'Go back and report to John what you have seen and heard: The blind receive sight, the lame walk, those who have leprosy are cured, the deaf hear, the dead are raised, and the good news is preached to the poor' (7:21-22). These words are very reminiscent of the passage from Isaiah 61 that Jesus read in the synagogue in Nazareth, a passage that speaks of the role, the duty and the activity of the Messiah who was to come. Remember how, after the text was read, Jesus gave a very brief sermon, declaring to the congregation, 'Today, this Scripture has been fulfilled in your hearing.' That bold declaration earned him the unmitigated wrath of his hearers. They didn't miss the point; they understood that Jesus was saying that he was the fulfilment of Isaiah's predictions of the coming Messiah. Here in this text, when Jesus returns the message to John the Baptist, he sends in the message a clue that John, being steeped in the Old Testament, would certainly not overlook. John would get the message. Jesus doesn't give a direct answer. He just says, 'Tell John what I am doing. Tell John to remember what the Scriptures say.'

Then Jesus adds something to the message to his dear friend, John: 'Blessed is the man who does not fall away on account of me' (7:23). Do you like to keep your religious affections a secret, particularly from your friends who are not enamoured by Christ? Is there a sense in which Jesus, though you embrace him as your Redeemer, is still a bit offensive to you? There are many, many people who struggle with that. But Jesus said, 'Blessed is the man who does not fall away on account of me.'

Something very human is going on here in this narrative. To have a loyal friend, someone on whom you can count in a time of crisis, is a great privilege. There are very few people in this world who are so loyal to other people, and care that deeply, that they will stand beside them in the worst moments of human crisis, particularly if it involves a personal risk to do so. John's life was on the line. He would eventually be beheaded because of his faithfulness to the mission that God had given him. But Jesus pronounced a blessing on those who would not stumble over him, on those who would remain loyal to him in the midst of their doubts and in the midst of difficult circumstances.

There is something very important in this exchange between Jesus and the disciples of John. How would you feel if a close friend and supporter sent a message to you which said, 'I am not really sure whether you are who I thought you were. Should I look for somebody else?' The normal human reaction would be to retaliate with criticism about the other person. But not Jesus. Jesus takes this occasion, after answering the enquiry of John, to give public testimony to his own endorsement of the greatness of John the Baptist. Jesus understood the agony of the attack of the enemy on John; Jesus understood what loneliness and solitude could do; Jesus understood that John the Baptist was perhaps a bit impatient for Jesus to get on with his Messianic agenda. He also understood that John was not a cowardly weakling who blew hot and cold with every wind of public opinion. So he said to the people gathered round him, 'What did you go out into the desert to see? A reed swayed by the wind? If not, what did you go out to see? A man dressed in fine clothes? No, those who wear expensive clothes and indulge in luxury are in palaces. But what did you go out to see? A prophet? Yes, I tell you, and more than a prophet' (7:24-26). Jesus says in verse 27: 'This is the one about whom it is written: "I will send my messenger ahead of you, who will prepare your way before you." ' Here Jesus identifies John the Baptist with the prophet who was to come before the Messiah, as predicted in the book of Malachi. John is not just *any* prophet; he is *the* prophet that the whole Jewish community had been waiting for to announce the breakthrough of the kingdom of God.

If those words were not a high enough praise for John the Baptist, Jesus goes on to say: 'I tell you, among those born of women, there is no-one greater than John' (7:28). He doesn't say that John is the greatest prophet, but that there is none greater. He puts him on a level with the great prophets of the ancient world – Elijah, Isaiah, Jeremiah, Ezekiel, Daniel. Then comes that enigmatic statement that we considered earlier in this study of Luke: 'yet the one who is least in the kingdom of God is greater than he.' Although John the Baptist exercised the highest role of any prophet in history, still he lived and died on the other side of the cross, the resurrection and the ascension. John died before Jesus inaugurated the kingdom of God. You and I live after the beginning of that kingdom. We live in an age when Jesus is not simply a peasant preacher in Palestine, but he sits exalted at the right hand of God, reigning as the King of kings.

How did the people respond? 'And when all the people and the tax-gatherers heard this, they acknowledged God's justice, having been baptized with the baptism of John. But the Pharisees and the lawyers rejected God's purpose for themselves, not having been baptized by John' (7:29-30, NASB). Those people who submitted to John's baptism, who acknowledged their need to be cleansed, were those who recognized the just call of God to them to repent. It was the Pharisees and other religious leaders who steadfastly refused to submit to the baptism of John the Baptist, assuming that they were far too righteous to need to be cleansed in the river by this wild fanatic from the wilderness.

But the tax-gatherers and the simple people were not so puffed up with pride that they failed to recognize that God had the right to call them to repentance. These people understood the justness of God's demand, and they humbly acquiesced unto it. By their actions they justified God; they showed by their own attitude that God was justified in requiring their repentance. So here again we find the conflict between pride and grace. If any one is to be justified in the presence of God that person must first recognize that God is just in demanding that we need a Saviour, that we come to that Saviour for our justification. The one who seeks to justify himself on the basis of his own righteousness is like the lawyers and Pharisees who refused to admit that they needed to be cleansed.

One of the most difficult things in the world is to accept grace. Our natural desire when we sin is to make up for our own sins. 'Let other people cling to a Saviour, but not me, I'll never need it, I'll never grovel in the dust.' If those are your thoughts, ask yourself if God really is being unjust by requiring of you that you humble yourself? May I suggest that it is not God who is unjust, and God does not need to be justified. We need to be justified, and we come to him for cleansing.

33. Jesus describes the people of his generation (Luke 7:31-35)

In verse 32 we come across a very fascinating saying of Jesus. In the previous verse Luke records Jesus asking, 'To what shall I compare the men of this generation, and what are they like?' He then answers his question by quoting the words of a popular children's saying of his day: 'They are like children who sit in the market place and call to one another, and they say, "We played the flute for you, and you did not dance; we sang a dirge, and you did not weep"' (7:31-32, NASB). This is one of those rare occasions where the New Testament draws on a saying from the popular culture of its day. As the children played with each other in the street, there would always be one who would be difficult to please, and the expression that the children used in this situation was this expression that Jesus cited. It probably means this: that a child comes along and wants to join in but he is glum, and so the children try to cheer him up by playing their pipes and singing a cheerful song and yet this sourpuss won't enter into the game and won't even crack a smile. So the children try to accommodate themselves to the one who is out of step by singing a mournful dirge but even then the child who is playing hard to get won't participate in the weeping ceremony.

Jesus, therefore, was likening this generation to an obstinate and stubborn child who is always going against the rest of the group. He goes on to show this obstinacy by comparing their responses to himself and to John the Baptist: 'For John the Baptist has come eating no bread and drinking no wine; and they say, "He has a demon!" The Son of Man has come eating and drinking; and you say. "Behold, a gluttonous man, and a drunkard, a friend of tax-gatherers, and sinners!"' (7:33-34, NASB).

Do you see what Jesus is saying? Some people just will not be pleased. John came in austerity, with a rigid, disciplined asceticism. They didn't like that, and condemned his behaviour as demonic. Jesus, on the other hand, participated in the social life of the people, rubbing shoulders with tax collectors and going to feasts, parties, and so on. They didn't like that either, and called him a glutton and wine-bibber. Worst of all, they accused him of associating with sinners.

To understand this section it is helpful to keep in mind Luke's concern in his gospel to dispel the heretical notion of the Pharisees that redemption comes through segregation, by keeping yourself aloof from people who were known to be sinful. This idea of salvation or redemption by segregation is blasted into smithereens by Jesus, who goes out of his way to reach out to the lost of his generation.

Jesus concludes this little rebuke with the words: 'But wisdom is vindicated by her children.' A wise course of action is shown to be wise, not necessarily in the planning stage when things are somewhat questionable, but by the fruit that it bears. As the Old Testament Wisdom literature tells us, there is a time to sing, there is a time to dance, there is a time to weep, there is a time to mourn. There are times when associating with the needy and the lost, even to the point of participating in their feast, is an appropriate course of action for a man or woman of God. There are also times when withdrawing from society into seclusion and rigorous discipline is also appropriate. Jesus says that wisdom shows the appropriateness of John the Baptist's peculiar behaviour and it also shows the appropriateness of Jesus' form of social activity.

The word *dikiaisoune* which the New American Standard Version translates as 'vindicated' is translated by the Authorized Version as 'justified'. Now, obviously we are not to interpret this to mean that wisdom is brought to a reconciled relationship with God, but rather that wisdom is shown to be genuine or authentic by the fruit that it brings to bear, which is what is indicated by the New International Version's rendering, 'proved right'. This distinction is very significant for our understanding of Scripture with respect to the idea of justification. Many have struggled to reconcile Paul's clear teaching in Romans of justification by faith alone with James' saying 'by works a man is justified, and not by faith only' (Jas. 2:24). This apparent contradiction can be dealt with, however, if we recognize that in the New Testament, the word for justification can be used in more than one way.

In its theological sense it describes how we are made right in the presence of God, and that is what Paul is talking about in Romans. But it can also mean to vindicate something. For example, James' main interest in the second chapter of his book is to answer the question: 'How do we know if a person's profession of faith is genuine?' Anyone can say that they have faith, but James points out that faith without works is dead; a deadly faith that couldn't save anybody. Then he shows, using Abraham as his example, how obedience demonstrated that Abraham's faith was genuine. So Abraham is justified by his works, not in the sight of God – God knew whether or not his faith was real – but in the sight of man.

We see that the concept of justification is used in the New Testament apart from the doctrine of justification, and this verse in Luke is a case in point. Wisdom is justified or shown to be authentic by the fruit that it brings to bear.

34. A sinful woman anoints Jesus (Luke 7:36-43)

Verse 36 indicates a shift in the narrative with the introduction
of a new story, but Luke is still concerned to show Jesus'
dealings with the Pharisees.

> Now one of the Pharisees invited Jesus to have dinner with him, so
> he went to the Pharisee's house and reclined at the table. When a
> woman who had lived a sinful life in that town learned that Jesus
> was eating at the Pharisee's house, she brought an alabaster jar of
> perfume, and as she stood behind him at his feet weeping, she
> began to wet his feet with her tears. Then she wiped them with her
> hair, kissed them and poured perfume on them (7:36-38).

This beautiful story has some interesting parallels with the
record of the anointing of Jesus in the last week of his life that
we find in the other gospels. But scholars, in general, are agreed
that certain elements in the narrative set it apart from the other
story, and that this is a different account, a different person, on
a different occasion.

Jesus has been invited to dinner at a Pharisee's house. Luke
records that there was an unexpected visitor at this dinner; a
'woman in the city who was a sinner', in other words, a
prostitute. Somehow she had some knowledge of Jesus, perhaps
she had encountered Jesus already on another occasion, because
Luke tells us that when this woman heard that Jesus was eating
at the Pharisee's house, she came in bringing an alabaster vial of
perfume.

In the ancient world, it was customary for people to come in
and spectate at large dinner-parties especially those held by
somebody of dignity, or respect, or social status. It was
unthinkable, however, to come in off the street, unannounced,
uninvited, to a dinner-party being held by a Pharisee. For a
prostitute to do that was absolutely outrageous. This woman
knew that she would provoke a scene, but she was desperate to
get close to Christ, and ignoring protocol, she came right into the
Pharisee's house, bringing with her an alabaster vial of perfume.

It was not unusual for women in the ancient world to have a bottle of perfume tied around their neck, that they could use on special occasions. The Authorized Version describes this as 'ointment', a misleading description. What this woman was carrying was not a thick, pasty ointment, but a very costly type of perfumed oil.

We read that when she came in, she stood at his feet, behind him, weeping. It was customary for those attending feasts to eat in a reclined position, leaning on their elbows, heads at the table and feet stretched away from the table. If Jesus had assumed this position along with the rest of the guests, his feet would be horizontal to the ground and it would be very easy for this woman to get at him from behind.

Luke then recounts this tender story for us. The woman began to cry, and while she was crying, she began to wash Jesus' feet with her tears. Then she stooped over, and wiped away the tears with her long hair, and kissed his feet, and anointed them with the costly perfume. It was considered a disgrace for a Jewish woman to unbind her hair in a public situation, but in order to dry Jesus' feet this is what she must have done. In so doing she was humiliating herself in the presence of everyone there, but obviously, she didn't care about that as long as she could make this extravagant display of affection and love for Christ. So she wiped away the tears with her hair and then kissed his feet, which was the sign of abject humiliation and servitude before the feet of a rabbi. Then she anointed Jesus' feet with this very precious oil.

The Pharisee, on witnessing this extravagant display of love, 'said to himself, "If this man were a prophet, he would know who is touching him and what kind of woman she is – that she is a sinner"' (7:39). Although he didn't speak out loud, Jesus knew what he was thinking, and he answered him, 'Simon (that is, Simon the Pharisee), I have something to say to you.' Jesus then tells a parable, concerning a creditor who had two debtors; one owed five hundred denarii, and the other fifty. Neither was able to pay him back, so he forgave them both. Then Jesus asked this

question, 'Which of them therefore will love him more?'
Interesting question. Simon answered and said, 'I suppose the
one whom he forgave more.' Jesus replied, 'You have judged
correctly.' This Pharisee answers Jesus' question with the
preface, 'I suppose ....' You can almost hear the acid in his voice,
as if it is beneath his dignity to answer such a simple question.
But Jesus is making a very important point, one that is made
elsewhere in the New Testament, that the person who has been
forgiven much, loves much.

The Pharisee's problem was that he had so hardened his heart
against sinful people, that he had lost his capacity to rejoice at
the repentance of a sinner. He was so caught up in his own self-
righteousness, that he couldn't bear the fact that some people
were being forgiven. This attitude still surfaces in the church
today. When someone who has committed a grievous sin then
responds with deep, deep repentance, some people oppose their
repentance because of jealousy or spite. They have no sense of
joy or mercy in the restoration of the lost. But Jesus understood
that the more sin this woman had committed, the more grace she
needed. The more grace she received, the more love she felt.

My whole experience of conversion to Christianity was
indeed just that, an experience of forgiveness. The more we
understand how great our own forgiveness has been, the more
spontaneous our love for Christ should be. That is why it is
important from time to time to remember the day of our
salvation; to remember who we are, and to remember that all we
have and all we enjoy is the result of the mercy of God. If we can
grasp that point, then our obedience will be motivated not by a
sense of duty, but by gratitude and a love that flows out of a heart
that has known forgiveness.

35. Jesus rebukes Simon the Pharisee
(Luke 7:44-50)

Luke's record of this incident at Simon the Pharisee's house, continues in verse 44:

> Then he turned toward the woman and said to Simon, 'Do you see this woman? I came into your house. You did not give me any water for my feet, but she wet my feet with her tears and wiped them with her hair. You did not give me a kiss, but this woman, from the time I entered, has not stopped kissing my feet. You did not put oil on my head, but she has poured perfume on my feet. Therefore, I tell you, her many sins have been forgiven – for she loved much. But he who has been forgiven little loves little' (7:44-47).

To this Pharisee who has been so critical of Jesus' behaviour, Jesus says, 'Do you see this woman?' Well, obviously he saw the woman, in fact, it was the sight of the woman that had upset him. But Jesus uses her and her activity to illustrate a very important point to the narrow-minded Pharisee. He reminds the Pharisee of the things that the Pharisee left undone in his behaviour towards Jesus, his invited guest. In the ancient world, to invite somebody for dinner was a very important social act of hospitality, and there were clearly defined rules surrounding it. The terrain of Palestine was dusty and dirty, and as people didn't have the kind of footwear we are accustomed to in our culture, bare feet or sandals being the norm, their feet would become caked with dirt and dust. Therefore, before entering someone's house, it was customary to be offered a basin in which you could wash your feet. But for some reason, the Pharisee made no provision for Jesus to have his feet cleansed. Neither did he greet him with the customary kiss. As is still the custom in many parts of the world, upon being greeted by your host you would exchange a kiss on the cheek and on each side of the head. A further amenity that the Pharisee suspended was that of supplying his guest with olive oil. Travelling for any distance would result in the hair also becoming encrusted with dust, so the olive oil was given to allow the guest to freshen up after being out in the hot sun and dusty streets.

These acts of inhospitality show the lack of love the Pharisee felt for Jesus, and stand in strong contrast to the demonstrative behaviour of the woman about whom the Pharisee objects. The rudeness of his behaviour prompts us to ask why he had invited Jesus to his house in the first place. It was obvious that he was not a disciple of Jesus, nor was he attracted to what he had seen and heard of Jesus. Reading between the lines, this Pharisee had invited Jesus to his house simply because he was looking for an opportunity to trap him or interrogate him.

Jesus then gets to the crux of the lesson he wants to teach the Pharisee: 'For this reason I say to you, her sins, which are many, have been forgiven, for she loved much; but he who is forgiven little, loves little' (7:47, NASB). Again, we have that principle of the correlation which exists between an understanding of one's forgiveness, and a response of love that follows from it.

That little word 'for' in the phrase '*for* she loved much' can be misleading. It suggests that the reason why she was forgiven was because she loved so much, and that God was moved to forgive her as a kind of reward for her loving attitude. But that would be a serious misunderstanding of this text, and would see forgiveness as the result of some kind of good work or charity on the part of the woman. However, it is clear from the rest of the text that what Jesus is saying is that he knows this woman has been forgiven of much, because how else can you account for the fact that she loves so much. It is not that she is forgiven because she loves, but rather she loves because she has been forgiven.

Love is at the heart of the Christian faith: love for God out of which comes an abundance of love and compassion for others. The apostle Paul writes, 'If I give all I possess to the poor and surrender my body to the flames, but have not love, I gain nothing' (1 Cor. 13:3). This was the Pharisee's problem: he had no love in his heart because he didn't know what it meant to be forgiven: Jesus said, 'he who is forgiven little, loves little'. I am sure that the Pharisee didn't miss the point.

If you have but slightly experienced the forgiveness of God, is that because your sins are slight? Or is the slightness of your experience of forgiveness a reflection of the degree or measure of your repentance? If you have experienced the forgiveness of Christ, in equal measure to the reality of your sin, then you have been forgiven much, because our sins have indeed been many, and so we are candidates to be great lovers of Christ, if we would but experience his forgiveness.

Jesus then speaks directly to the woman, saying simply, 'Your sins are forgiven.' No-one ever heard any more important words than those this woman heard that day in the house of Simon the Pharisee. Every demeaning, dishonest and immoral act that this woman of the city, this prostitute, had committed, was totally cleansed from her record when the Son of God said, 'Your sins are forgiven.'

The rest of the spectators who were also attending the meal began to ask themselves, 'Who is this man who even forgives sins?' (7:49). Forgiveness of sins was regarded by the Jew as being uniquely a divine prerogative. Only God had the authority to forgive sins. But here is Jesus declaring that this woman has forgiveness for her sins. So they raised the question, 'Who does he think he is that he can forgive sins?' Jesus apparently ignores their hostility and rivets his attention on this woman who doesn't care how many other people there are in the room, all she wants is the blessing of Christ, and her mind is on that and on that alone. Jesus says to her: 'Your faith has saved you; go in peace' (7:50).

This woman was sophisticated, worldly, rich enough to afford expensive perfume, but the one thing she didn't have was peace – for only Christ can bring peace to the heart of a human being.

Do you know peace? Or are you experiencing conflict within yourself and with other people and with God? Paul writes: 'Therefore, since we have been justified through faith, we have peace with God' (Rom. 5:1, NIV). The peace which we have with God once we come to the cross, is not a guarded truce where our next offence will cause God to rattle the sword afresh. No, it is an abiding peace, a peace that passes understanding. So here is a woman who had no peace for years, and, at the house of Simon the Pharisee, she anoints the feet of Jesus Christ, and he turns to her, and pronounces her forgiven. And his last words to the woman are, 'Your faith has saved you.' It was Christ who saved her, but in one sense it can be said also that her faith saved her, for faith was the instrument that brought her to Christ. Christ is the Saviour, not our faith.

36. Parables: he that has ears, let him hear (Luke 8:1-4)

Chapter 8 begins with a transitional verse, moving us into a new dimension of the teaching and preaching ministry of Jesus. 'After this, Jesus travelled about from one town and village to another, proclaiming the good news of the kingdom of God. The Twelve were with him' (8:1). The New King James' Version is interesting here for it says that Jesus was 'preaching and *showing* the glad tidings of the kingdom'. His ministry was not simply verbal, but he attended his preaching with demonstrations of the power of the intrusion and the presence of the kingdom of God.

In verse 4, we read: 'While a large crowd was gathering and people were coming to Jesus from town after town, he told this parable.' Jesus' teaching style is distinguished by the fact that it is frequently interspersed with this form of teaching that we call the *parable*. In fact, so often does Jesus speak in parables that on one occasion, using hyperbole, the New Testament indicated that he spoke in nothing but parables. But that was a purposeful exaggeration, to indicate the importance of the parable style to the teaching method of Jesus. He is the only one in all of the New Testament who ever uses the parable. Nowhere in the epistles, for example, do we find an example of the use of the parable.

Jesus was not the only person, however, that ever taught in parables. In the rabbinic tradition, other teachers had used this form, and they can be found in the Old Testament, though very rarely. One famous example relates to that episode in David's life when he had wilfully committed his sinful act with Bathsheba and then arranged that her husband should be killed in battle, that

'And also some women, who had been healed of evil spirits and sicknesses: Mary called Magdalene, from whom seven demons had gone out, and Joanna the wife of Chuza, Herod's steward, and Susanna and many others who were contributing to their support out of their private means' (8:2-3, NASB). Luke is careful to point out that the entourage of Jesus included certain women. We have noticed previously that Luke pays more attention to the women who were involved in the ministry of Jesus than any other of the New Testament writers. We are very fortunate to have this portrait of Jesus' close relationship with women, and the fact that he treated them with respect, honour and dignity, in a way that was quite unusual in the first century.

A few of those women are mentioned here by name. First is Mary, usually referred to simply as Mary Magdalene. She is described here as a woman out of whom had gone seven devils. In church history, and in the history of Christian art and literature, Mary Magdalene has functioned as the almost prototypal symbol of the fallen woman who was rescued from her corrupt life by the ministry of Christ. This fallenness is usually specified as being a kind of prostitution. But nowhere in the New Testament are we ever told or is it ever even suggested that Mary Magdalene was involved in prostitution. All we are told is that she had this affliction of demonic possession from which she had been redeemed.

The second woman to be mentioned is the wife of Chuza, Herod's steward, a man who had a position of considerable authority and power and presumably wealth. Joanna is mentioned one other time in the New Testament, again by Luke, right at the end of his gospel, because she was one of the women who came to the garden tomb and discovered the absence of the body of Christ. She was one of the first to report the resurrection of Jesus to the disciples. There are many commentators who believe that Joanna was married to the nobleman whose son was healed by Jesus (John 4:43-54).

The third woman to be mentioned is Susanna. Nothing is said about her identity, or what she did, what her function was, what her relationship was to the Christian community. All we have is her name. We are told of many others who ministered to Jesus from their own private means.

he might possess this woman. David was visited by Nathan, a prophet, who, in a parable, told of a very rich man, who owned many flocks of sheep and whose possessions were innumerable. There was one poor shepherd in the land who possessed but one lamb, his proudest possession. Nathan's parable continues to tell how the wealthy and powerful man came and stole the poor shepherd's lamb. When Nathan told the story, David was angered and enraged that such a thing could take place in his kingdom. 'Where is that man?' he demanded. Nathan stung David with some devastating words: 'You are the man.'

Now that particular use of the parable to confront David with his own sinfulness, shows how the parable functioned from time to time. The parable in Jesus' teaching was often used as a means of debate, as a means of expressing a point in the midst of controversy. He would tell a simple story in the presence of the Pharisees or the Sadducees, and would lead his opponents on till they would have to agree to the sheer simplicity of the story as it unfolded until they had got to the point of no return. Jesus used parables to drive home his point, in a way that was inescapable. For example, dealing with those who were adopting a posture of adversity towards people that they disapproved of, like the Samaritans, Jesus asked what it meant to love one's neighbour? The people replied with the question, 'Who is my neighbour?' Jesus responds by telling the simple story of the man who falls among thieves, and is helped by the Good Samaritan. Jesus ends his story with a rhetorical question: 'Who was the neighbour here?' Jesus shows the answer to the question in unmistakable fashion, by telling the story.

That is what a parable is. It is basically a story that is told not for its entertainment value, but to teach a truth, or to communicate a moral lesson. The word 'parable' itself comes from the Greek word *parabole*. The prefix is *para* and means *alongside of* or *accompanying with*. We think of *para*medics who assist the physicians in their activity, for example. This prefix is attached to the very simple root *baleio*, which means 'to throw'. Literally, a parable is something that is thrown alongside something else.

142

A Walk With Jesus

That is, Jesus gives a body of teaching that at times is abstract, and so alongside of it he gives a parable.

Why does Jesus speak in parables? There is no easy answer to that question. In fact, it has engendered considerable controversy in Christian scholarship. The superficial answer would seem to be that he does it to illustrate his point. Jesus is a great story-teller. One commentator points out that the stories we heard in our childhood are easy to remember. They have an ability to grasp our attention. Jesus' parables are rather like those stories. A basic rule of communication is, *illustrate*. It is the illustration that takes the message home. So when we look at the parables of Jesus it is tempting to interpret them merely as illustrations. However, there are questions about that, questions that are raised by some very difficult statements in the text itself. In verse 9 the disciples, having heard the parable, ask Jesus, 'What might this parable be?' From this question we can deduce, firstly, that the meaning of the parable was not immediately apparent, even to the disciples. Jesus goes on in verse 10 (NASB) to say, 'To you it has been granted to know the mysteries of the kingdom of God, but to the rest it is in parables; in order that seeing they may not see, and hearing they may not understand.'

There is a sense in which the parable has to be understood as a two-edged sword. On the one hand, it is given to clarify the difficult and the obscure, but on the other, there is an enigmatic element. The original hearers of Jesus did not have the benefit of 2,000 years of reflection, nor did they have the benefit of hearing Jesus' teaching in the light of the knowledge of the cross, resurrection and ascension. When we read these things we are already aware of who it is who is speaking. But some contemporaries of Jesus were befuddled by the parables. He deliberately cloaked his message in riddles, but not because he wanted to confuse people who genuinely wanted to hear what he was saying. As an illustrative device to clarify a point, parables were very useful to those eager to penetrate the content and meaning of the message that Jesus is proclaiming. But not everybody wanted to. There were those who listened to him, not because they wanted to hear a word from God, but because they wanted to trap him in his words, to find some way to bring him to trial and to destroy him. The parables confused them.

There is one more preliminary point that we need to be aware of before we consider this important parable of the sower. In the early centuries of the church, it was the custom to treat the parables of Jesus as allegories. Now an allegory is a particular type of symbolism where every single point of the story had some kind of hidden, esoteric significance. The allegory is almost a symbolic code. The most famous of all allegories is Bunyan's *Pilgrim's Progress*, where each person illustrates in symbolic ways the pilgrimage of the Christian life and the pitfalls that exist along the way. Jesus himself interprets some of the parables in allegorical fashion. In fact, the parable of the sower is treated this way. However, applying the method of allegorical interpretation to all the parables of Jesus will land you in deep trouble! Most New Testament commentators will say, therefore, that the basic point of a parable is simply this: to communicate one central point. Now, that is not always the case. There are times when we have this complicated allegorical style, but the safe way to approach it is this: don't treat a parable as an allegory unless the New Testament itself does.

For those who have ears to hear, the parable is there alongside the message of Jesus, to excite, to illustrate, to enlighten us that we might know the hidden things, the secrets of the kingdom of God.

Parables of Jesus in Luke

1. Lamp under a basket	8:16-17; 11:33-36
2. Wise man builds on a rock	6:47-49
Foolish man builds on sand	
3. New cloth on an old garment	5:36
4. New wine in old wineskins	5:37-38
5. The creditor and two debtors	7:41-43
6. The sower	8:4-15
7. The good Samaritan	10:30-37
8. A friend in need	11:5-13
9. The rich fool	12:16-21
10. The faithful and evil servants	12:35-40
11. The faithful and wise steward	12:42-48
12. The barren fig tree	13:6-9
13. The mustard seed	13:18-19
14. The leaven	13:20-21
15. The great supper	14:16-24
16. Building a tower	14:25-35
A king making war	
17. The lost sheep	15:3-7
18. The lost coin	15:8-10
19. The lost son	15:11-32
20. The unjust steward	16:1-13
21. The rich man and Lazarus	16:19-31
22. Unprofitable servants	17:7-10
23. The persistent widow	18:1-8
24. The Pharisee and the tax collector	18:9-14
25. The minas	19:11-27
26. The wicked vinedressers	20:9-19
27. The fig tree	21:29-33

37. The parable of the sower (Luke 8:5-15)

This parable is repeated in the other synoptic gospels, and it is obviously very important. It begins like this:

> A farmer went out to sow his seed. As he was scattering the seed, some fell along the path; it was trampled on, and the birds of the air ate it up. Some fell on rock, and when it came up, the plants withered because they had no moisture. Other seed fell among thorns, which grew up with it and choked the plants. Still other seed fell on good soil. It came up and yielded a crop, a hundred times more than was sown' (8:5-8).

Luke omits a word at the beginning that Mark includes in his version. Mark writes that Jesus began by using the word, 'Listen!' In his proclaiming of the kingdom of God, particularly when he did it through use of the parables, our Lord emphasized how important it was to pay close attention to his words. Jesus said, 'Listen!' and at the end of the parable he said, 'He that has ears to hear, let him hear!' Obviously Jesus considered the content of this parable to be of great importance to his audience.

On first hearing, the story he tells sounds rather strange. It would seem to be a story of a very careless farmer, who throws his seed willy-nilly to the winds, and some of it falls on the road, some on stony ground, some in a briar patch and thorns. What a wasteful use of seed. To understand what is happening here, we have to look at the sowing used in ancient Palestine, and in many parts of the world even to this day. One didn't go out and plough the field, and then, once the furrows had been carefully measured, go and deposit the seeds in the ploughed ground. On the contrary, the seed was sown first, and then the plough was brought across the land, ploughing it into the soil. Just by looking at the land, the farmer would not have been able to tell what lay below the top soil. He wouldn't worry about throwing seed among thorns, because these weeds would be ploughed under, and would not be a problem to the cultivation of the crop. Paths crossed the land that was cultivated; some were well-trodden, and would not break easily under the plough.

Sometimes the plough would strike stone just below the surface, and that would be the shallow ground of which Jesus speaks in this parable. So Jesus is not recounting a story about a foolish farmer. Rather he is describing a very typical farming procedure.

This is one of those rare occasions where Jesus not only tells the parable, but goes on to give its interpretation. 'This is the meaning of the parable: The seed is the word of God.' We have seen that it is dangerous to interpret all the parables of Jesus allegorically, but on this occasion Jesus does attach allegoric significance to elements of the story, beginning with the seed. The seed represents the word of God.

Now think of it for a moment. The word of God is preached indiscriminately, in a sense. Right now, as I comment on these words of Jesus, which I believe to be nothing less than the very word of God, I don't know you, I don't know your circumstances, I don't know how you will respond to the words of Jesus. You may be utterly disinterested, or you may be keenly interested to understand what Jesus of Nazareth taught, and receptive to his words. This message, these words, will be perceived differently by different people. Jesus said that's the way it is with the word of God.

Then he goes on to explain: 'Those along the path are the ones who hear, and then the devil comes and takes away the word from their hearts, so that they may not believe and be saved' (8:12). Notice that it is not that these people have heard the word of God and believed it, and then been robbed of their faith. No, before they have even had a chance to embrace the word Satan is there to rob them.

Then Jesus talks about the next group. He says, 'Those on the rock are the ones who receive the word with joy when they hear it, but they have no root. They believe for a while, but in the time of testing they fall away' (8:13). Jesus, here, is talking about people who, when they hear the word of God, get all excited and respond positively with great joy and excitement. They join a church, buy a Bible, attend a prayer group, and tell everybody about their conversion. Then some weeks later they have rejected it all. I don't believe that is an authentic conversion. It is possible to become emotionally drawn to Christianity, to become excited over what you hear about Christ, without it really taking hold of your soul. I know of a woman who, when she first read that verse, was terrified. She didn't know in the first weeks of her conversion what type of person she was – whether her conversion was genuine or not. She has spent the last fifteen years making sure that the word of God was settled in her heart. Christ said that he who endures to the end will be saved.

Jesus turned his attention to the seed that fell among thorns: 'The seed that fell among thorns stands for those who hear, but as they go on their way they are choked by life's worries, riches and pleasures, and they do not mature' (8:14). Some people who become involved in the Christian faith get side-tracked by the materialistic pursuits of this world, seeking creature comforts, a career, vocation, marriage, whatever it is, and they leave their first love. Now this may be a description of people who are in the kingdom by the skin of their teeth, who are unproductive Christians. But it is impossible to be a totally unproductive Christian. If there is no fruit at all in your life, it is clear that there is no faith in your life, for if there is any true, justifying faith in your heart, there will be fruit. It is more likely that this is a person who made a good start, enquiring about the things of God, but then found everything else in life far more important than finding out who God is. They bring no fruit to maturity.

Then Jesus said, 'But the seed on good soil stands for those with a noble and good heart, who hear the word, retain it, and by persevering produce a crop' (8:15). God has so prepared the hearts of some people that when they hear the word of God, they latch onto it wholeheartedly. They listen intently to it. They hold on to it. It germinates, life begins to sprout from it, fruit begins to blossom, and fruit is brought forth, with patience. No farmer has ever produced a bumper crop impatiently. No farmer can ever just throw the seed in the ground and expect fruit to be there present in abundance that same afternoon. It is easy to grow weeds, but, if you want a good crop, that can only come through careful preparation, careful cultivation, and then through patient waiting for the earth to be watered, for the sun to shine, for photosynthesis to take place, bringing together that beautiful, exciting, enchanting experience of the growth of life. It is true not only in the agricultural world, but it is true in the spiritual world as well.

What kind of ground does God find in your heart? Has the word of God taken hold in your life? Is there an indication of real fruit coming forth as you patiently wait for the harvest day, as you nurture it with more words from God? What Christ wants from his people is fruit; fruit that comes from a heart that is committed to him.

38. The parable of a candle in a vessel
(Luke 8:16-18)

Jesus continues to instruct his disciples, here using a very short parable. 'No-one lights a lamp and hides it in a jar or puts it under a bed. Instead, he puts it on a stand, so that those who come in can see the light' (8:16). Here again is one of those brief little figures of speech that Jesus uses to drive home a point, so simple and so direct that it would be very difficult to miss it. He describes a rather ridiculous scenario of somebody taking a lamp and, having lit it, taking great pains to obscure the light. We are not accustomed these days to illuminating our homes by candlelight or oil lamps except sometimes on special occasions; a romantic meal, or when we go out for dinner perhaps. But normally we use the modern conveniences that electricity provides for us. Most of us, however, will have experienced temporary power cuts where, for one reason or another, the supply of electricity is stopped. Sometimes without warning our homes are thrown into darkness, and we scrabble about in the dark to find candles to light the rooms. Candlelight is not very powerful compared to electric illumination, but when things are plunged into total darkness, we welcome whatever light we can get from the candle. No-one in this situation would light a candle and then put it under a bed, or place a pot over the top! Rather, he would try to find the place to set the candle where it gives maximum illumination to the room.

Jesus, however, is not interested in teaching us how to light a house; he is giving a spiritual lesson. He is saying how foolish it would be to take light that is designed to illumine a dark area and then conceal that light. Frequently the New Testament uses the image of light to refer to the appearance of Christ himself. He is the Light of the world. He charges his followers and his disciples to be children of light and says to them that they are the light of the world. Now if you are a follower of Christ, then that means that part of your ministry as a Christian is to be a torch-bearer, to be a light to a world that is plunged in darkness.

Some of us, however, are very reluctant to let that light shine. From time to time, and in a somewhat humorous vein, we hear talk of 'secret service' Christians, people who do everything in their power not to let anyone else know that they are in fact a disciple of Christ. Because to be known as a Christian in a secular society is to invite a certain amount of scorn and at times hostility, and many of us flinch from the reactions of people that are negative towards allegiance to Christ. Yet this is one of those occasions where we don't have to wrestle through the agonizing difficulties of a complex ethical decision. Our duty is absolutely clear. Christ tells us we *must* make that light shine; that we must let it be visible and that it would be a betrayal of him, nothing less than treason to our Lord, to obscure the light that he has ignited within us and among us. There is a little pamphlet that circles the Christian community which asks the somewhat provocative question: If you were charged in a law court of being a Christian, would there be enough evidence to convict you? Well, Christ tells us plainly that we are to put that light that he has given us on a lampstand so that all who enter may benefit from that light.

He goes on to say in verse 17 something that could strike

terror to our hearts: 'For there is nothing hidden that will not be disclosed, and nothing concealed that will not be known or brought out into the open.' This is not the only occasion in which Jesus speaks like this. Frequently, throughout the New Testament, Jesus says that in the Last Judgment, every idle word will come into account. All of the mysteries and secrets of this world will be revealed. This will be the day of final exposure. Of course, those whose lives are hid in Christ will indeed be covered and not subjected to humiliating embarrassment, for their sins have been forgiven and hid in Christ. But for those who harbour a covert, secret, sinful life for which they are impenitent, those secrets will be made manifest. 'Nothing is secret,' said Jesus, 'that shall not become known.'

The expression, 'a skeleton in the closet', is a figurative way of referring to things that we have done in our lives, that we are embarrassed by and ashamed of and would rather nobody knew about. We are very careful to whom we confess our secret sins, and in some cases, we confess them not at all. But we must be clear that nothing is secret from God.

We have a God who is omniscient, but his attitude towards us is not that of a prison warden, watching us lest we make a false move. Nor is he trying to behave like a transcendent policeman to spy on us. However, we cannot avoid the fact that God knows us completely, inside and out. He knows every deed that we have ever committed; he knows every thought that has gone through our minds.

Jesus concludes this warning, saying: 'Therefore consider carefully how you listen. Whoever has will be given more; whoever does not have, even what he thinks he has will be taken from him' (8:18). Jesus is warning us here to be careful what we are listening to, and to whom we are paying attention. Again he is talking about opening our ears to the words of Christ. Take heed! Be careful that you hear.

There is a further point hinted at here in this little saying of Jesus, that is a frequent motif in his teaching, and that is this: that with Christ, and with the words of Christ, there is no

It is interesting to speculate as to how God will expose all of
these secret things and the hidden, covert dimensions of our
personalities in that last day. One brilliant student I taught,
said to me once, that he, too, wondered how God would reveal
the secrets of our hearts on the last day. He was becoming
increasingly amazed at the capacity of the human brain to store
data and information, and gave a lengthy and complicated
description of how the brain works, saying to me that there is
no impression, no experience, no word that we ever hear, no
sight that we ever perceive, that is not recorded somewhere in
the inner chambers of our brain. The brain is a massively
complex computer with a storage capacity that is nothing short
of incredible. And he said, 'You know, I kind of envision it
this way, that on the last day God is not going to bring in
witnesses to speak against us, but he is simply going to unplug
our brains and run them through his own gigantic computer
and play back messages whereby our own brains will reveal to
us the storage data of our own experience and every word we
have ever spoken, every deed we have ever done, will be
confessed by our own brain cells. It will be all a matter of
absolute record.'

Now, of course, that is all speculation, but the man was
saying something that was important, and that is that we cannot
erase the reality of the deeds that we have committed. We
cannot blot out, as Lady Macbeth sought so desperately to do,
the blemishes upon our soul. But we try; we try to hide them,
we try to keep them concealed from people. It is not that we
are supposed to stand naked before the world and confess every
one of our sins before all mankind. No. But we are to reveal
those things and confess those things to God, knowing that if
we don't, that God will himself expose us. 'For nothing is
hidden,' says Jesus, 'that shall not become evident; nor
anything secret that shall not be known and come to light.'

neutrality. You either respond and move from faith to faith, from grace to grace, from life to life. Or you move in a negative direction from darkness to darkness, from unbelief to unbelief, from death to death. Jesus is saying that's the way it is. Where the word of God has taken root in a person's heart, that person begins to be nurtured; more and more is given to those who are open to the things of God. But to those who are closed, whatever semblance of benefit of the things of God that person has, they are going to lose it. God does not give his gifts to be played with. This is a very sober warning from Christ.

How do you handle your secrets? What do the secrets that you seek to conceal from other people signify to you about your life? Are those things hid in Christ? Or will they be exposed by Christ? Those are the only options a human being has: to hide himself in Christ, or to be exposed.

39. Jesus' ministry of teaching and working miracles continues (Luke 8:19-25)

Jesus' mother and brothers (Luke 8:19-21)

> Now Jesus' mother and brothers came to see him, but they were not able to get near him because of the crowd. Someone told him, 'Your mother and brothers are standing outside, wanting to see you.' He replied, 'My mother and brothers are those who hear God's word and put it into practice' (8:19-21).

This passage reads as if Jesus is almost impolite with respect to his mother and the members of his immediate family. Certainly, there is carried in this answer to his mother and to his brothers a rebuke that cannot be denied. Mary and his brothers were trying to get at him perhaps because they were concerned that he was over-extending himself. Remember Mary was human; she cared about her son, she saw him give himself away tirelessly, and she worried about him from time to time. And here was Jesus, in the midst of a very important dimension of his mission that his heavenly Father has sent him on, when suddenly he was interrupted by a well-intentioned mother, but one who is missing the point.

Jesus' reply to those who are concerned that his mother and brothers want to see him, is this: 'My mother and brothers are those who hear God's word and put it into practice.' Now Jesus is not suggesting that his mother did not hear the word of God or was opposed to the word of God. Everything that Scripture tells us would be to the contrary; Mary herself was a devout believer and she was not only the mother of Christ, but a disciple of Christ, totally committed to him as her own Messiah. There is every evidence that later, after his resurrection, the brothers of Jesus were also committed; at least James and probably Jude) became church leaders. But what Jesus does is to latch on to the opportunity afforded by this particular human situation to make a point that is very important. He says, 'My mother and brothers are those who hear God's word and put it into practice.'

There is an idea circulating in our culture – everybody believes in the fatherhood of God and the brotherhood of man, as if, by virtue of our natural birth in this world, we are the children of God. In one sense, the Bible does speak of us as God's offspring, inasmuch as he is the Creator of all human beings. But in the New Testament there is a special sense in which Christ speaks of the family of God. Christ is the only-begotten Son of God and the only way one becomes a child of God in the New Testament sense is by adoption. It is only those who are led by the Spirit of God who are the sons of God. And Jesus qualifies that even more carefully here. This family is not defined by biology, by blood-lines, by nature. It is defined by grace. 'My mother and brothers are those who hear God's word and put it into practice.'

Jesus calms the storm (Luke 8:22-25)

The narrative continues with an event that took place in a boat, during a storm at sea. It is a simple narrative: Jesus and his disciples were going to move from one side of the lake to the other. The lake that is in view here is the Sea of Galilee, a very large body of water. It is several miles long and a few miles across, and it would take some time to cross from one side to the other. As they sailed, Jesus fell asleep, and as he was sleeping a storm blew up. Now the men who were with Jesus on this occasion were professional fishermen, seasoned veterans who knew every nook and cranny of this body of water. They had been out on it hundreds of times, but they were also aware of the treacherous storm patterns that could occur from time to time without any warning. The Sea of Galilee is located in a basin that is surrounded by mountains. Situated as it is, the lake is subject to some unusual topographical phenomena. A violent wind can blow up suddenly, moving across the landscape and through the valleys that become wind-tunnels, compressing the air so that it comes swooshing across the lake without any warning, turning that calm and gentle body of water into a raging, tumultuous fury. Many people have lost their lives as a direct result of these storms on the Sea of Galilee.

In this narrative Jesus lies down in the back of the boat and goes to sleep. When the storm comes and the sea is raging, Jesus remains asleep. How can anybody stay asleep in the midst of that kind of upheaval in a boat? It would have been filling with water, as well as being buffeted by the waves and by the wind. Some have suggested that Jesus' ability to sleep through this storm indicates the placid tranquillity that Jesus enjoyed in his inner spirit, because he was not a man who suffered from anxiety. Being without sin, Jesus enjoyed a kind of inner peace that is unknown to fallen human beings. Another, perhaps less speculative interpretation, is that Jesus was just very tired. Repeatedly in the course of Jesus' ministry he felt the strength leave him, the power go out of him; he was constantly living on the edge of exhaustion. He may have been the God-Man, but he had a human nature that was given to weariness just like ours. Jesus could have been so exhausted that nothing would rouse him from the sleep that he was enjoying.

But it certainly roused the disciples: they were terrified and so they came to him, and woke him up, crying, 'Master, Master, we're going to drown!' Jesus got up, and, with the data that we get from the other gospel writers, what he did was to address the sea and the wind directly, using the form of command: 'Peace! Be still!' Instantly, the forces of nature submitted in obedience to the voice of their Creator. We are told on countless occasions in the New Testament, that Jesus is the one by whom the universe was made. He is the Creator of heaven and earth, and all of the forces of nature are underneath his authority. Here we see complete and abrupt submission to the authority of Jesus.

Imagine the reaction of the disciples to witnessing that kind of power and authority over nature. Jesus turned to them and asked the question, 'Where is your faith?' As if to say, 'Don't you know who's with you in the boat? How can you be petrified and worried for your life when the Lord of Life is with you?' One of the common objections to the Christian religion comes from the arena of psychology: it claims that human beings have a very deep fear of the impersonal forces of nature that threaten us; the ravaging power of micro-organisms that can invade our body and kill us; the unexpected visitations of natural catastrophe such as earthquakes, floods and fires. Freud speculated that as early man did not have control of these violent forces of nature, he began to sacralize nature, to invent deities that lived within the storm, and eventually from this process evolved the idea of a transcendent God who had power over all of the forces of nature. Freud discussed how we learn to deal with the threats to our well-being that come from other human beings. If somebody is angry with us, there are different methods we can try to assuage that anger: we can bargain with them, we can plead with them, we can reason with them. But how do you negotiate with a tornado? How do you reason with a flood? So Freud deduces that man, out of his fear of nature, invents a God who controls these things. You can't talk to the tornado, but you can reason with God; you can beg him for mercy.

The reason I like this story of Jesus calming the storm so much is that here we have an example of those forces of nature terrifying these seasoned veterans of the sea. Freud was certainly right at this point: man can be terrified by nature. But, what happens here is that after the threat posed by the forces of nature has been removed, the disciples became even more afraid! Why? Because they knew they were in the presence of the Holy One. That was Freud's mistake. He knew that we are afraid of impersonal non-holy things, but there is nothing more terrifying to man than the personal Holy God. And that's what the disciples were beholding in the boat.

'In fear and amazement they asked one another, "Who is this?"' (8:25). How would you answer that? What kind of man was Jesus? It is part of our nature to typecast people. This labelling is not necessarily a bad thing, because there are different kinds of people, and we use these categories as a convenience, a kind of shorthand to help us know how to relate to people. What category would you put Jesus in? He breaks the mould, there is no category. He is utterly and completely unique. Yes, he shares with us some common dimensions of our humanity, but he didn't sin, and there is nothing more commonplace to human behaviour than sin. Not only that, but he brought life out of death, and he exercised an authority that no human being would ever dare to presume. Here we have a clear example of what scholars call *sui generis*, something that is in a class by itself. That is why Jesus can't be put in the same category as other great religious teachers or prophets or founders of world religion. It is an insult to mention Jesus Christ in the same breath as Gautama Buddha, who was enlightened, perhaps. He was himself an atheist, he didn't claim to be God. Neither did Mohammed, although he had some profound insights. Other philosophers have had profound insights, too. But did Mohammed ever command the seas? Could Gautama Buddha raise the dead? Was Confucius without sin in his life? We have to create a different category, a singular genus, when we speak of Jesus of Nazareth. There was never a human being like him. The disciples were properly and very reasonably in a state of awestruck reverence.

Here we have One who is intrinsically worthy of our devotion. He is Emmanuel, God with us, and this incident illustrates it. What kind of a man is Jesus? Implicit in the question of the disciples is the answer that yes, he is a man, but he is more than a man. He is God Incarnate, God, who has authority over your life. How do you respond to him?

40. Healing of a demon-possessed man (Luke 8:26-39)

They sailed to the region of the Gerasenes, which is across the lake from Galilee. When Jesus stepped ashore, he was met by a demon-possessed man from the town. For a long time this man had not worn clothes or lived in a house, but had lived in the tombs. When he saw Jesus, he cried out and fell at his feet, shouting at the top of his voice, 'What do you want with me, Jesus, Son of the Most High God? I beg you, don't torture me!' (8:26-28).

This remarkable story of Christ's encounter with the demon-possessed man is not only found in Luke's gospel, but there are versions of it in the gospels of Mark and Matthew as well. Its setting is somewhere near the Sea of Galilee, and scholars agree it probably took place in a little town called Gergasa, which today is called Kirsa, on the south-eastern shore of the Sea of Galilee.

Jesus came into this region and was met by a man who had been possessed by demons for quite some time, and who is described as being naked. Nudity was scrupulously forbidden in Old Testament law and the modesty of Jewish apparel reflected that. To be stripped of one's garments was to be placed in a state of total humiliation and disgrace. Yet this man was apparently so demented and out of control that he ran around without any physical covering.

This man didn't live in a house, he lived among the tombs. The south-eastern shore was very rocky and barren and there were areas there that we know in ancient times were used for tombs. It was here that Jesus came across this man. On seeing Jesus, he cried out and then fell to the ground, asking: 'What do you want with me, Jesus, Son of the Most High God? I beg you, don't torture me!' Obviously it is the demons that are speaking here. It is fascinating to note that the demons had no difficulty whatsoever in recognizing the identity of Jesus. His Messianic nature was veiled to many, and even for some of his intimate disciples there was a growing awareness, at best, of the full measure of who Jesus was. But the demonic world recognized immediately the presence of the Son of God, and were terrified. Not only do they recognize his identity, they also recognize his authority over them, and they are terrified that Jesus might exercise his power to subject them to fitting punishment.

Matthew's version includes an interesting addition: '... torment me not *before the time*.' The New Testament, as we saw in an earlier study, uses two quite distinct words for *time*: *chronos*, the normal moment-by-moment passage of time, and *kairos*, a specific instant in time that is of peculiar significance, of great importance for history. The Greek concept of *kairos*, or the chairotic moment, is a moment that takes place in the context of *chronos*, or in the general passage of time. The Bible features again and again the importance of chairotic moments, those moments in history where God breaks into space and time, and performs an act of supreme significance for all of history: the Exodus, the giving of the Law, the birth of Jesus, the resurrection, and so on. All these are chairotic moments.

When the demons say, 'Don't torment us before the time!', the word used in Matthew's gospel, is the word, *kairos*, which points us to the fact that the demonic world itself is aware that at some future point their destiny is sealed. They know that at the time of judgment, God is going to subject them to relentless torment for their unmitigated evil. When Jesus appears in this incident, the demons are terrified that they are going to have to submit themselves to that kind of torment before the time. They thought they had more time to enjoy their activity of tormenting human beings and intensifying the amount of evil in this world. The narrative continues:

> For Jesus had commanded the evil spirit to come out of the man. Many times it had seized him, and though he was chained hand and foot and kept under guard, he had broken his chains and had been driven by the demon into solitary places. Jesus asked him, 'What is your name?' 'Legion,' he replied, because many demons had gone into him (8:29-30).

Often in Scripture, where conflict is involved, even in encounters between God and man, the revealing of one's name is significant. By revealing the name, that person or demon is acknowledging his submission to the one who demands it. We see this in the account of Jacob's night-time wrestle with the angel. He demanded that the angel tell him his name and the angel refused, and instead the angel renamed Jacob 'Israel', because he had struggled with God. So Jesus demands: 'What is your name?' Immediately the demons submit by naming themselves.

The demons continued to entreat Jesus, trying to bargain with him to minimize their punishment. In verse 31 they beg him not to command them to go into the abyss (seen as the abode of the demons, particularly to the time when Satan and his angels will be consigned to everlasting torment and punishment by being sent there).

The gospel writers record that Jesus doesn't send them into the abyss, instead he sends them into a herd of swine, as a lesser penalty. Here we see an example of Jesus acceding to the request of the powers of hell. How do we understand that? Those words, *before the time*, from Matthew's account are significant here. Although Jesus had unbelievable power over the demonic world and the authority to command these evil spirits to depart from the man, there is a sense in which Jesus did not have the authority at this moment to send these demons to hell, because that day, that chairotic point in redemptive history, has already been established by the Father. The Father has appointed a time when the final punishment of the demonic world will be realized and the Son of God respects that appointed time.

It is important to remember that God is the Lord of history, and the times that he has fixed from the foundation of the world are irrevocable. There is a time established for the final judgment and consignment of the demons to hell, there is a time for the appearing of the new heaven and the new earth. It is comforting to know that the God we worship is not at the mercy of the vicissitudes of history, but that he himself is the Lord of history, knowing the end from the beginning and that whatsoever he decrees to come to pass will indeed come to pass. That's why it is impossible for a Christian, in any ultimate sense, to be a pessimist. Though the world is filled with sorrows and pain, we are not in despair because we know that our destiny is in the hands of the One who is sovereign over space and time.

Luke continues: 'A large herd of pigs was feeding there on the hillside. The demons begged Jesus to let them go into them, and he gave them permission. When the demons came out of the man, they went into the pigs, and the herd rushed down the steep bank into the lake and was drowned' (8:32-33).

Critics of this account raise some further points. The first is regarding the presence of a herd of swine when pork was prohibited to Jewish people. However, this portion of the land was heavily inhabited by Gentiles. Caesarea and other towns were used as resort areas for people from Rome and elsewhere, and there were settlements in this region round the Sea of Galilee of non-Jewish people.

The second point regards this apparent need for the demons to inhabit some kind of physical receptacle. It seems to be, if we can reconstruct from the sketchy information that we have, biblically, of the nature of these evil spirits, that they do have a strong desire to inhabit some kind of concrete vessel of animate life. In any case, they could not stay in the man because Jesus was redeeming him – could they at least not go into the swine?

The third point regards the fate of the swine, who drowned themselves in the lake (verse 33). Some critics are very harsh in their judgment of Jesus here. Isn't this an example of cruelty to animals? This has been used more than once in an attempt to prove that Jesus was not in fact sinless. However, it is important to remember the order of creation; the created order is made by God to be a support system to man. Man is the crowning act of God's creation, he is given dominion over the world. The pig is the servant of the man, not the man the servant of the pig. If these demons must inhabit some place at this particular point in redemptive history, it is nothing less than a totally redemptive act on Christ's part to release the man of this infestation of the demonic world, even at the cost of a herd of swine.

> When those tending the pigs saw what had happened, they ran off and reported this in the town and countryside, and the people went out to see what had happened. When they came to Jesus, they found the man from whom the demons had gone out, sitting at Jesus' feet, dressed and in his right mind; and they were afraid (8:34-35).

The swineherders were obviously concerned about their swine, and would have been greatly distressed, but when they came back to the site, what did they find? They found this man, whom perhaps they had seen on other occasions running around naked through the tombs, demented, now sitting at the feet of Jesus, clothed and in his right mind. This is what the restoration of humanity is all about.

But then, once more, we see people's fear in the face of Jesus' power and holiness:

> Those who had seen it told the people how the demon-possessed man had been cured. Then all the people of the region of the Gerasenes asked Jesus to leave them, because they were overcome with fear. So he got into the boat and left (8:36-37).

When Jesus reveals his power and holiness, people are afraid. But one man wasn't: one man's fears were removed and he sat in his right mind at the feet of Christ.

This restored man begged Jesus to allow him to stay with him, but Jesus sent him away, with this order: 'Return home and tell how much God has done for you.' It was perfectly natural for this man who had known unbelievable torment, after being released of this torment by the work of Christ, to want to stay with Jesus. But Jesus gave him a mission immediately, sending him to his own home, that he might have a ministry there, telling of the great things God had done for him.

41. Jairus' daughter and a sick woman (Luke 8:40-56)

Now when Jesus returned, a crowd welcomed him, for they were all expecting him. Then a man named Jairus, a ruler of the synagogue, came and fell at Jesus' feet, pleading with him to come to his house because his only daughter, a girl of about twelve, was dying.

As Jesus was on his way, the crowds almost crushed him. And a woman was there who had been subject to bleeding for twelve years, but no-one could heal her. She came up behind him and touched the edge of his cloak, and immediately her bleeding stopped.

'Who touched me?' Jesus asked.

When they all denied it, Peter said, 'Master, the people are crowding and pressing against you.'

But Jesus said, 'Someone touched me; I know that power has gone out from me' (8:41-46).

Jairus was a man of prestige and respect within the community, but he had a desperate problem. His only daughter was dying. And this man, who obviously had heard of the ministry of Christ, came to him. He didn't enter into a negotiation with Jesus as a peer, as he might well have done; after all, he was a man of some status. He didn't demand that Jesus come and look at his daughter. No, this man in desperation for his daughter's life, rushed to Jesus and threw himself on the ground before Christ, begging him to come to his house. There would have been many people who heard the request that Jairus had made. As Jesus turned and moved away with this man, they were surrounded by a jostling crowd of people eager to witness another miracle.

At this point, Luke interjects a story within a story. He tells of another person who was present that day, a woman who was suffering from a pathetic ailment: she had been haemorrhaging for twelve years. There is a kind of irony here. On the one hand this man had had nothing but joy for twelve years through the delight that his daughter had brought to him. But, for the same period of time, this other woman has had unrelenting agony. She had been so plagued by this problem that she had spent her life-savings upon physicians, without being healed. This woman was desperate. Not only was she suffering from a physical malady, but, under the sanctions of the Levitical law, the fact that it was a haemorrhage meant she had been ceremonially unclean for twelve years. She was a pariah to the synagogue, to the community, to her family, because of this unclean malady.

As Jesus was moving rapidly in the direction of Jairus' home, this desperate woman forced her way through the crowd and touched the border of his garment. She didn't prostrate herself in front of him; she didn't beseech him to stop and help her. All she wanted was to get close, to touch the hem of the Master's garment. Instantly the haemorrhaging stopped. Twelve years of constant agony were over in an instant, by one touch of the hem of the robe of Christ. Immediately, Jesus asked out loud, 'Who touched me?' Everybody denied it. Peter, in his inimitable impetuous spirit, said, 'What is the matter with you, Jesus? Can't you see that every time you take a step you are jostled and bumped? And you are asking us who touched you! How are we supposed to know who touched you?'

But Jesus maintained his patience and simply says, 'Someone touched me; I know that power has gone out from me' (8:46). He knew that somebody had touched him in an unusual way because he felt the power going out of him. 'Then the woman, seeing that she could not go unnoticed, came trembling and fell at his feet. In the presence of all the people, she told why she had touched him and how she had been instantly healed. Then he said to her, "Daughter, your faith has healed you. Go in peace"' (8:47-48). In that moment of contact between a broken woman and the healing Christ, Jesus stopped to notice what everyone else around had overlooked. That woman didn't have the courage to come and talk to Jesus. She thought that she was too insignificant to require the direct and immediate attention of Christ. But here is Jesus Christ, on his way to raise somebody from the dead, followed by multitudes of people eager to witness this extraordinary act, and in the midst of it all, he stops to give his undivided attention to this poor, humble woman. Here we see the compassion and concern of God for the smallest individual in the world. Nobody is unimportant, but the dignity of your personality is worth the touch of Christ.

In this eighth chapter of Luke's gospel we find two very contrasting commands given by Jesus to people he has healed miraculously. In the case of the miracle that Jesus performs for the demon-possessed man, he instructs him to go home and tell everyone in his city the great things that God has done for him. But, when he heals Jairus's daughter, Jesus commands them to tell nobody. Again, we see that mysterious dimension of Jesus' public ministry which the scholars call the Messianic Secret; those occasions when Jesus cautions people from spreading abroad the stories of his power, indiscriminately. Perhaps it was safe to tell the stories around the Gentile areas of the Gerasenes, but here in a heavily Jewish community Jesus is very careful not to reveal the full measure of his identity until his moment of glory is at hand according to the time schedule of his Father.

Imagine what happened to the woman's soul, never mind her body, when Jesus did speak to her. He looked at her; he didn't say her name, but he called her, 'Daughter', and said to her, 'Daughter, your faith has healed you. Go in peace.' With these few words the woman recovered her health and her dignity because she had been noticed and ministered to by God incarnate.

Verse 49 continues: 'While Jesus was still speaking, someone came from the house of Jairus, the synagogue ruler. "Your daughter is dead," he said. "Don't bother the teacher any more"' (8:49). Imagine what Jairus was thinking. Obviously he had feelings like anybody else; I am sure he was glad that this woman had been healed, but who could blame him for thinking, 'If only Jesus hadn't taken the time to heal this woman, he would have made it to my house and maybe saved my daughter. But now it is too late! There is nothing he can do now.' 'Hearing this, Jesus said to Jairus, "Don't be afraid; just believe, and she will be healed." ' And he continued to his destination.

When Jesus got to the house he allowed only the girl's parents and Peter, James and John to enter. The hired mourners were inside sobbing and wailing, but Jesus said to them, 'Stop wailing. She is not dead but asleep.' Some read into verse 52 the idea that death for the Christian is only sleeping, but that is not the point that Jesus is making. Others claim that Jesus had noticed that the young girl was not really dead, but was comatose: her vital signs were not immediately apparent, and in the panic it was assumed that the girl had died. But that is not the force of the text either. Jesus is not denying that this girl had really died; what he is denying is that death was final. Their weeping and wailing turned to bitter laughter and scorn. Jesus responded to their laughter by making them absent themselves from the room.

Then he turned his attention to the daughter of Jairus, and he took her by the hand. Again, in defiance of the ceremonial laws forbidding a person to touch a corpse, he takes her tenderly by the hand, saying, 'My child, get up!' Her spirit came again and she got up straightway. He didn't just bring her back from death to a semi-comatose state; no, she was able to get up from her bed and Jesus called for food to be brought for her. When a patient starts asking for food that is a sign that real healing is taking place. The first thing Jairus' daughter wants is something to eat. 'Her parents were astonished, but he ordered them not to tell anyone what had happened' (8:56).

42. Jesus commissions the twelve (Luke 9:1-11)

When Jesus had called the Twelve together, he gave them power and authority to drive out all demons and to cure diseases, and he sent them out to preach the kingdom of God and to heal the sick. He told them: 'Take nothing for the journey – no staff, no bag, no bread, no money, no extra tunic. Whatever house you enter, stay there until you leave that town. If people do not welcome you, shake the dust off your feet when you leave their town, as a testimony against them.' So they set out and went from village to village, preaching the gospel and healing people everywhere (9:1-6).

This short passage introduces an element into the narrative of the relationship between Christ and his church that is very important. In Study 24, we saw that Jesus prayed all night before selecting from a larger group of disciples, twelve who were to function not only as disciples, but apostles as well. Even though the twelve apostles were first disciples, the terms do not mean the same thing. A disciple means a learner, a follower of a rabbinic teacher, whereas an apostle is a person who has been delegated specific authority to represent the one who sends that person on a mission. Here we see the apostolic mission sanctioned by Jesus. He called his twelve apostles together, to commission them and to endow them with power and authority to carry out a specific mission.

We read that he gave them power and authority over all demons and to cure diseases. The disciples, as human beings, even as students of the great Rabbi, did not possess power to perform miracles, nor did they have the authority over the demonic world. But now what Jesus is doing is delegating authority. He is transferring authority to the twelve.

The text says that he sent them to preach the kingdom of God. Now the verb that is used there comes from the word, *apostelo,* from which we get the word, *apostle*, one who is sent forth. In this sending upon the mission, Jesus, before he sends them out in his name, gives to them power (*dunamis*) and

This was the great question with the apostle Paul. Some challenged his apostolic authority, because there was more than one qualification under normal circumstances for apostleship. First of all, one would have to have been a student of Jesus, a disciple; secondly, one would have to have witnessed the resurrection; and third and foremostly, one must have had a direct and immediate call from Jesus Christ. The problem with Paul was that he had not been a disciple during Jesus' earthly ministry. His encounter with Jesus came after his death and resurrection, and so there were some who didn't acknowledge the apostolic authority of Paul. That is why the New Testament records on several occasions the call of Paul by the risen Christ, who made a special appearance to him, and his commissioning for his apostolic mission.

Is it, therefore, possible for there to be apostles operating in the church today? Well, if we answer that question by the criteria established in the New Testament, the only answer we can give is, 'No'. Paul, however, qualified by a direct and immediate call of Christ, so isn't it conceivable that somebody today could have a vision of the risen Christ and that Christ could commission that person to be an apostle? Although Paul did not meet all three criteria established by the New Testament, he did fulfil two of the most important principles, namely, that he was an eye-witness to the resurrection of Christ and was a recipient of a direct and immediate call by Jesus. But even those two vitally important facts did not stand alone. Before Paul began his apostolic ministry he was sent for confirmation by the rest of the apostles, whose credentials were not in question at all. They embraced Paul as being an authentic apostle.

authority (*exousia*). The power he gave them was explosive, awesome and mighty. It was that same power that Jesus used to heal people and to perform miraculous feats. He gave that power to his apostles.

But not only did he give them power, he also gave them authority, the authority that was given to him by the Father. This is why the church for centuries has made a distinction between apostolic authority and lesser human authorities in the church. Only those who are chosen, selected and empowered by Christ himself are considered apostles.

In verse 2 we read that Jesus sent them out to preach the kingdom of God and to heal the sick; their mission was both prophetic and priestly. Preaching is not held in high regard in many places in this day and age. The New Testament tells us that it is through the foolishness of preaching that God has ordained to save the world. It is God, and here God in Christ, ordaining the pre-eminence of preaching in the mission of the church. He didn't send them to preach the opinions of men, or mere concern for societal reform, but he sent them to preach of a divine and supernatural kingdom, the kingdom of God.

He sent them with some rather strange instructions for this mission: 'Take nothing for the journey – no staff, no bag, no bread, no money, no extra tunic.' This verse highlights one of the problems we have in seeking a harmony between the gospels, for in Mark's account we read that Jesus told them to 'take nothing for the journey, except a staff ...' (Mark 6:8). So what *did* Jesus say: don't take a staff or take only one staff? Many commentators get around the problem, however, by interpreting Jesus' words to mean: 'Take one staff but no more.' In the ancient world, when a traveller prepared for a lengthy journey, he would take provisions for future settlement, just as we do if we go away for any length of time. But the point that Jesus is making here is 'travel light'. His is a mission marked by a sense of urgency.

Jesus instructions continue in verse 5: 'If people do not welcome you, shake the dust off your feet when you leave their town, as a testimony against them.' In other words, he is warning them not to pour all of their energy into people who are not really prepared to listen: the harvest is ripe, so they must concentrate on when there is a hearing. In fact, the dignity of their mission was so high, that if, after they had invited people to become partakers of the kingdom of God, they were hostile, the apostles were to shake off the dust of that city from their feet as a symbol and move on.

They did as he commanded and set off on a theological and spiritual blitzkrieg, preaching the gospel and healing everywhere.

In verse 7 Luke records a strange response: 'Now Herod the tetrarch heard about all that was going on. And he was perplexed, because some were saying that John had been raised from the dead, others that Elijah had appeared, and still others that one of the prophets of long ago had come back to life.' Herod was more than perplexed, he was beside himself. It is one thing to imagine the impact that Jesus made when he, by himself, preached and taught and healed. But now that ministry had been magnified; twelve other people doing the same thing, under his authority. Rumours

It is of crucial importance to recognize that the apostles were established in one generation. Their authority and the continuity of their authority that lasts down to this day is found in the fulfilment of their commission to set down in writing the apostolic authority in the New Testament. That is why we should be cautious when people claim to believe what Jesus says, but refuse to submit to the authority of Paul. In rejecting the authority of an apostle, you are rejecting the authority of the One who sent that apostle in the first place. So we cannot have Christ without Paul, or Paul without Christ. This was a very sharp issue in the second century, with the advent of the heretical cult known as the Gnostics, who tried to supplant the authoritative position of the apostles in the Christian community. They claimed private revelations that exceeded those of the apostles. They claimed to believe in God and to believe in Christ but not to believe in the apostles. Irenaeus, the great church leader, gave them a simple answer. 'If you reject the authority of the apostles, you reject the authority of the One who sent them, namely Jesus, and if you reject Jesus, you reject the authority of the One who sent him, namely God.' All Irenaeus was doing was echoing the very argument that Jesus used against the Pharisees (as John's gospel so clearly records for us), when they stated that they believed in God, but would not accept Jesus.

were rife: some said that John had risen from the dead. Can you imagine how that haunted Herod the Tetrarch? 'But Herod said, "I beheaded John. Who, then, is this I hear such things about?" And he tried to see him' (9:9). I don't think he wanted to see him out of a spiritual need. I think he was terrified. But he wanted to look into this.

These words strike a rather ominous note: even though Jesus' ministry was provoking enormous applause and excitement, nevertheless the storm clouds were beginning to gather. Herod the Tetrarch is beginning to get upset and that is going to lead to grim consequences for Jesus and for his disciples in the not-too-distant future.

How important it is to recognize that we are under apostolic authority; that the words of the apostles, the teaching of the apostles is nothing less than the teaching of Christ. We ought never to neglect the authority and the power of the apostolic word.

43. The miracle of the feeding of the 5,000 (Luke 9:12-17)

In all four gospels we find records of the incident when Jesus Christ took five loaves of bread and two fish and fed five thousand people. Luke's account begins in verse 12:

> Late in the afternoon the Twelve came to him and said, 'Send the crowd away so they can go to the surrounding villages and countryside and find food and lodging, because we are in a remote place here.'
> He replied, 'You give them something to eat.'
> They answered, 'We have only five loaves of bread and two fish – unless we go and buy food for all this crowd.' (About five thousand men were there.)
> But he said to his disciples, 'Have them sit down in groups of about fifty each.' The disciples did so, and everybody sat down. Taking the five loaves and the two fish and looking up to heaven,

he gave thanks and broke them. Then he gave them to the disciples to set before the people. They all ate and were satisfied, and the disciples picked up twelve basketfuls of broken pieces that were left over (9:12-17).

What an incredible story! This is the only miraculous event that is recorded by all four gospel writers. Those who are critical of the trustworthiness of the biblical record are embarrassed by the unified testimony to this event. This is perhaps the most well-attested, eye-witness account of any miracle that Jesus ever performed during his earthly ministry.

Let's look at the story as it proceeds. The opening phrase: 'the day began to decline' suggests that this is very late in the day. However, in the Jewish custom, once noon had arrived, it was the expression to say that the day was beginning to decline. In a desert area where the sun is exceedingly hot, people are concerned about shelter, food and water in the heat of the afternoon. Concerned for the wellbeing of this vast multitude, the disciples suggest to Jesus that he send them away so that they will have time enough to go to the towns and get the necessary provisions. But Jesus said simply, 'You give them something to eat!' We can detect a mild sense of annoyance among the disciples when Jesus makes this suggestion, for they replied that all they had was five loaves and two fish, unless, of course, they were to go and buy meat for all of them. Of course, this suggestion was absurd: where would the disciples get provisions to feed five thousand people? The towns that were round about were small towns, and would not be prepared to feed a multitude. But Jesus persists, and asks his disciples to make the people sit down in groups of fifty. Reading between the lines, maybe the disciples saw that look in Jesus' eye and remembered the other miraculous things he had done. So they didn't argue, but did as he asked.

'Taking the five loaves and the two fish and looking up to heaven, he gave thanks and broke them' as was customary before eating a meal. Perhaps when the people saw Jesus with this handful of loaves and a couple of fish, saying a mealtime blessing, they thought he was going to give them some kind of symbolic teaching, calling attention to these fish and bread in a demonstrative way. After all, Jesus, on more than one occasion, did call attention to the daily provisions of people as a symbolic meaning of his whole ministry. In John's gospel, for example, Jesus said, 'I am the bread of life.' But here he doesn't just bless the food and then use it as an illustration; instead, he gives the fishes and the bread to his disciples to set before the multitudes.

Luke goes on to write how everyone was able to eat their fill. However, not only was there enough to satisfy the hunger of five thousand people, but there were also twelve baskets of scraps left over. Even when the five thousand people were filled, there was more food left than Jesus had to start with.

How do we account for it? There are three possibilities; either we have here a *bona fide* miracle, an event that only God could do, or else we have a fraudulent account by the writers, or perhaps we simply haven't understood it. Perhaps more than any other account in the New Testament, because of its degree of attestation, this story caused untold misery to the school of theology known as nineteenth-century liberalism. Its basic tenets included outright denial of any kind of supernatural intervention in this world by God. There was no real historical belief in a virgin birth, or an atoning death, or a resurrection of the body from the tomb, and all of the miracles of Jesus were dismissed as being unhistorical and, in fact, impossible. They are fairy tales, not to be believed by the sophisticated people of this day and age. Rudolf Bultmann, a neo-liberal of our own day, has stated that the twentieth-century person cannot listen to the radio and make use of other modern electronic gadgets and utilize contemporary forms of medicine and still believe in a world that is inhabited by demons and angels and miracles and that sort of thing. They just don't fit in the modern worldview.

The emergence of liberalism in the nineteenth century created a crisis for the church, which for nineteen hundred years had rested on the confession of faith that God was in Christ, that the supernatural came into the natural world, and that the story of his life is filled with accounts of miracles. There have always been sceptics and unbelievers throughout history that have challenged the supernatural claims of Jesus, but the sad phenomenon of nineteenth-century liberalism is that this challenge against the substance of the biblical record about Jesus came from *inside* the church. For liberals, what is essential to the Christian religion is not the supernatural or the miraculous, but ethics. The Christian religion is chiefly concerned with improving the lot of mankind; communicating to each other the importance of honesty, mercy, charity and compassion, and so on.

These scholars were anxious not to dismiss the Bible as having no relevance, so there were widespread attempts among nineteenth-century thinkers to reinterpret these stories in a way that would be meaningful to those still interested in the institutional church and the ethical core of Jesus' teaching.

I grew up in a situation where the miracles of Christ were considerably down-played and the emphasis was on human-itarian activities. Our pastor, a very learned and persuasive man, told us that we had to understand these miracle stories by way of reinterpretation. For example, at the wedding feast of Cana, nothing miraculous happened, no water was turned into wine, but rather Jesus had the men fill up the pitchers with water and give water to the guests; after all, isn't water the best wine to drink? So that story was set as a parable. Jesus wanted to teach people the ultimate value of water as a much richer and more enjoyable kind of wine, than the kind that has destructive capacities for intoxication, and so on. The feeding of the five thousand, too, has received its share of alternative explanations. For example, one theory was this: what took place was not a miracle – Jesus did not proliferate the loaves and pieces of fish to feed over five thousand people; rather he had the disciples go through the crowd to find people who were willing to share what they had with those who had brought nothing. Therefore, the real miracle here was not a supernatural event in space and time; it was an ethical miracle. Jesus had everybody share their lunch. Well, if that's the point, it was missed completely by four gospel writers.

But Jesus of Nazareth took five loaves of bread and two fish and fed over five thousand people to capacity and had twelve baskets of provisions left over afterwards. What does that tell you about him? Jesus did something here that only God has the power to do.

44. Peter's confession of Christ (Luke 9:18-22)

Luke picks up the thread of the narrative beyond the feeding of the five thousand with the following words: 'Once when Jesus was praying in private and his disciples were with him, he asked them, "Who do the crowds say I am?" ' This is an introduction to one of the most important episodes in the life of Jesus. Again it is Matthew who gives us a more complete exposition and detailed account of what happened on that occasion. Before examining the substance of the question that Jesus raises, it is worth commenting on the difference between Luke's version and Matthew's. Luke reports this incident immediately following the account of the feeding of the five thousand. If we examine the other gospels, however, we know that many other significant events took place in the life and ministry of Jesus between the feeding of the five thousand and Peter's confession. Why does Luke place it immediately on the heels of the feeding of the five thousand? There are two answers, at least. In the first place, the writers of the gospels did not always arrange their material chronologically: sometimes their concern was more topical. Notice that Luke does not say that it happened the day after the feeding of the five thousand; this would make his historical credibility suspect. Rather he prefaces it by saying simply that it came to pass. There is an editorial break here. Remember that each of the gospel writers had a specific audience to whom they were writing, and specific concerns to communicate to those people. And that is one of the reasons

Even today there are many opinions as to who Jesus is. It seems everybody has a favourite aspect of Jesus' personality and ministry that they would like to claim as an ally for their particular movement. The theologians and historians of the church have said that the question of Christology (that is, our understanding of the person and work of Christ), has been a major issue in four centuries in church history, and those centuries are the fourth century, which brought to us the Council of Nicaea and the Nicene Creed; the fifth century which culminated in the great historic Council of Chalcedon, and again in the nineteenth century and the twentieth century. So that the issue of the identity of Jesus is a paramount question for the church today in a way that has been paralleled perhaps only at three other periods in the history of the church. We are in a crisis of our understanding of who Jesus really was, and are still living out the results of the attack against the New Testament and against a supernatural understanding of Jesus that was so forcibly wrought upon the church in the nineteenth century.

Liberal theology tried to reshape and recast the image of Jesus, not so much as a supernatural being, but as a man of profound wisdom and insight. The Jesus of nineteenth-century liberalism was a Jesus who was recast as the supreme ethical teacher.

Then came the philosophy called Existentialism. Existentialists had the same problem; they didn't believe in a supernatural Jesus, so what did they do with Jesus? They put forth Jesus as the supreme model of existential man, the greatest existential hero that has ever lived. It seems that as philosophical schools change, Jesus becomes a chameleon, whose identity is shaped and reshaped to suit. Now that should warn us that there can be a difference between the Jesus of fact, and the Jesus of human opinion. We must be careful not to allow our own prejudice to determine who Jesus really was. Most people, although they don't believe in the deity of Christ, are willing to say something kind about Jesus – he was a great teacher, or prophet or whatever. Such are eager to be considered Christian. Some dictionaries define a Christian as anyone who is civilized, as opposed to one who is savage or uncivilized. So people still want to be associated with the good reputation of Jesus, without wanting all of the liabilities of being called a member of the church or of the classical Christian tradition.

why Luke includes information that Matthew doesn't, and so on.

But there is also another dimension – each of these writers had certain production limits imposed upon them as they set forth their narratives. If you have ever written a book or an essay as part of a course, you will know that space restrictions limit what you can say. You may not be able to say everything that you want to say, so you have to select what incidents to include. Well, that was true in New Testament days as well, because these documents were written on parchment, and the parchment was expensive. It was not easy to come by, and so an author had to organize his material in a way that would allow him to maximize the space that he had. Thus Luke gives us only a brief account of this important question, and so we need to draw on Matthew, to fill in some of the gaps.

Jesus had now withdrawn from his ministry to the crowds and was in prayer. The disciples were with him, and Jesus asks them a question: 'Who do the crowds say I am?' They replied, 'Some say John the Baptist; others say Elijah; and still others, that one of the prophets of long ago has come back to life.' There was no agreement as to who Jesus was. They don't know who he is, but they do recognize that he is extraordinary. The public has recognized that Jesus is at least a prophet.

Then Jesus turns his attention to the disciples, the intimate group of followers who were with him day in and day out, listening to his every word, entering into the privacy of his prayer discourse with the Father. Jesus said to them, 'But what about you? Who do you say I am?' (9:20). Peter responds saying: 'The Christ of God', or as Matthew records it, 'You are the Christ, the Son of the living God' (Matt. 16:16). That's how Peter viewed it: we think you are the Christ, the *Christos*, the *anointed one*, the promised *Messiah*.

Well, was Peter's answer just another human opinion? Was it just an impulsive response revealing Peter's great admiration and enthusiasm for his Master? Not according to both Matthew and Luke's accounts, for as soon as Peter says, 'You are the

Christ, the Son of the living God', Jesus responds immediately, 'Blessed are you, Simon son of Jonah' (Matt. 16:17). Jesus then explains why Peter is blessed, 'for this was not revealed to you by man, but my Father in heaven.' Simon's words were not a matter simply of human conjecture; they were the result of divine revelation.

Then Jesus extended the blessing: 'And I also say to you that you are Peter, and upon this rock I will build my church' (Matt. 16:18). And indeed, the church of Jesus Christ was built on the confession that Jesus is the Christ, the One sent from God to be our Redeemer.

Luke records, however, that Jesus then said something very strange: he 'strictly warned them not to tell this to anyone' (Luke 9:21). Here is another example, perhaps the purest example, of the Messianic Secret. After the resurrection, the commission of the church is to tell the whole world that Jesus is the Messiah; but in contrast, at this point in redemptive history, he tells them to keep it secret. In the account of the feeding of the five thousand – and perhaps that is why Luke records Peter's confession so close to that great miracle – the people wanted to make Jesus a political king. They didn't understand the character of what it meant to be the Messiah of God, and even the disciples didn't understand it.

Not even Peter, the beneficiary of divine revelation, understood, as is plainly shown by his response to Jesus' next words. Having identified himself with the Messiah, Jesus said: 'The Son of Man must suffer many things and be rejected by the elders, chief priests and teachers of the law, and he must be killed and on the third day be raised to life' (verse 22). These words left Peter not only incredulous, but on the verge of rage, as we see in Matthew 16:22. Our Messiah is a glorious king who comes in power to vanquish our enemies. It can't be that our Messiah will suffer and be put to death! But, no sooner does Peter raise that objection than Jesus turns to him and rebukes him saying, 'Get behind me, Satan!' The Son of God has pronounced the supreme blessing upon his disciple, Peter, then moments later he says, 'Get behind me, Satan!' Think back to the temptation of Jesus in the wilderness (study 15), Satan came to him, to entice him to be the Messiah without going the way of suffering and death. At that time, when Jesus triumphed and Satan departed, we remember that ominous statement: that Satan left him for a season. And come back he does as we see here, at Caesarea Philippi, agitating Jesus through the mouth of Jesus' boldest disciple. From the same lips of the man who has just declared that Jesus is the Christ, Jesus listens to the one who would deny his vocation of suffering. But Jesus recognizes it instantly. This was an attack from the father of lies, seeking to direct Jesus from his ministry. It was for this that he came. The Son of man must suffer these things. He must be delivered up, betrayed, be killed, be offered as a sacrifice. That is what it means to be the Christ, the Messiah.

If the Christ to whom you are responding is a Christ without suffering, without atonement, without incarnation, a Christ who is not Messiah, he is not the biblical Christ. I urge you to come to a clear, focused understanding of the true identity of Jesus, who is the Christ of God.

45. The cross that is made for every Christian
(Luke 9:23-27)

Jesus, having announced the necessity of his suffering and death, now broadens this mission to include his followers: 'If anyone would come after me, he must deny himself and take up his cross daily and follow me' (9:23). To follow Christ involves a kind of self-denial. Jesus is not talking about rigorous practices of asceticism whereby we deny ourselves a comfortable bed, or three meals a day, although we may be called upon to do that from time to time, but he is talking about something beyond that. He is talking about a cross that is made for every Christian.

There are few passages in the New Testament as misunderstood and abused as this particular passage. How many times have you heard people say, 'I have a cross to bear', and that cross is the unemployment of the husband, or a debilitating illness, or an undisciplined child, and so on. The concept of bearing one's cross has become a way of describing any form of suffering that we are called upon to endure. But that is not what Jesus is referring to here. He is not referring to what we may call common forms of suffering, the kind that afflicts Christian and non-Christian alike, and has no bearing on a person's commitment to Christ. What Jesus is saying here is that when we take the name Christian, and openly identify ourselves with Christ, we must be ready not only to bear the normal suffering that life brings, but to share in the particular suffering of Christ.

Countless times in the epistles, we find the promise that God has stored up for his people great joy, great glory, and that on the day of the consummation of the kingdom of God, all of Christ's people will share in the inheritance that God has given his Son. But there is a catch, isn't there? Unless we are willing to participate in the humiliation of Christ, we cannot participate in his exaltation.

In fact, the supreme mark of membership of the New Testament church is the sacrament of baptism. Baptism, among other things, is a symbol of our being ingrafted into Christ; a symbol of our being cleansed of our sins; a symbol of our new birth and so on. It is the sign of our burial with Christ, of our participation in his death and in his resurrection.

In the letter to the Colossians, Paul pointed to his own sufferings as an example of filling up that which is lacking in the suffering of Christ. That could be misunderstood to mean that there was something deficient about the passion of Jesus, that needs to be supplemented by the suffering of the saints. As if we could add anything of merit to the perfect sacrifice that Jesus offered once for all. Even Paul, with all of his greatness, couldn't add an ounce of merit to the perfect merit of Jesus. What Paul was getting at, however, is that there is a sense in which the church is the continuing incarnation, that we, the disciples, are not above our Master, that if Christ was hated in the world, we must be willing to be so too. We cannot just identify with his triumph of resurrection; we must be willing to bear the cross.

Some people have seen this statement as an anachronism. Jesus was talking to his disciples before he was crucified, so isn't this a clear example of a later editorial addition to the text? However, the cross was an extremely well-known symbol to the Jew, before Jesus was crucified. There was not a man among the disciples who had not seen at least one person arrested by a band of Roman soldiers and made to carry his own cross to the place of execution.

Then Jesus goes on to say: ' For whoever wants to save his life will lose it, but whoever loses his life for me will save it' (9:24). We can talk about religion in terms of ecclesiastical liturgy or the peaceful private practice of our devotions, but the real issue is where do you stand when the moment of truth comes, when your life or reputation is at stake? The altar of heaven is filled with the disembodied spirits of the saints, or the martyred dead, who have refused to compromise their loyalty to Christ, and who have paid with their lives. They wait for the day of their vindication, when Christ will appear before them, to crown them with a crown of righteousness.

There are also those, however, who when the moment of truth came, fled, and embraced the world: who saved their skins, and lost their inheritance in the kingdom. Jesus amplifies the statement: 'What good is it for a man to gain the whole world, and yet lose or forfeit his very self?' What point would there be in gaining the whole world, if the price tag was our soul? Yet that price is paid, day in and day out, by countless multitudes of people, who will exchange their birthright of heaven, for a moment's pleasure, or for more status, more power, more money, or whatever. I am not opposed to money or the things that money can buy, but if that is the main pursuit of my life and it costs me my soul, that's foolish business. It adds up to a total loss, a nett zero on the balance sheet, when all is said and done. There are certain things that no money or power can ever purchase for us. That is why you find rich men sobbing at the side of a grave. When the moment of truth comes, they realize they don't have the pearl of great price, the thing that is worth more than all the kingdoms of this world.

Jesus then puts this another way: 'If anyone is ashamed of me and my words, the Son of Man will be ashamed of him when he comes in his glory and in the glory of the Father and of the holy angels' (9:26). We all like to have affirmation. We are all sensitive to how other people respond to us. Nobody wants to be ridiculed or scorned. Yet every Christian experiences these things if he lets his faith be known. Every Christian at one point or another becomes a fool in the sight of the world. But imagine what it would be like if God appeared with his Son standing next to him, and surrounded by the court of the heavenly host of angels. How would you feel if they looked at you and were ashamed to be associated with you? Jesus makes it very clear that if we are ashamed of him before the world, then he will be ashamed of us in the presence of God the Father. Those words have to be burned into our minds. I would far rather put up with the scorn, rejection and shame of the whole world, for my whole life, than to have Jesus ashamed of me before the Father for five seconds.

Jesus concludes this narrative by saying: 'I tell you the truth, some who are standing here will not taste death before they see the kingdom of God' (9:27). That has bothered scholars! Did Jesus expect the finalization, the consummate conclusion of his kingdom in his own lifetime or during the lifetime of his disciples? No! Because the fact of the matter is that those very people that Jesus was talking about did not taste of death until they saw the kingdom of God. It doesn't specify at what point they saw it; but there were plenty of incidents where the kingdom of God broke through in visible force: the transfiguration, the day of the resurrection, the ascension, and so on. These happenings made it clear to his own disciples that what they were counting on was indeed a reality, and they could afford not to be ashamed to be called followers of Christ.

46. The glory of Christ (Luke 9:28-45)

The most dramatic unveiling of the glory of Christ took place on the Mount of Transfiguration. The probable site of this extraordinary event is Mount Hermon, situated a short distance from Caesarea Philippi. However, a rival location is Mount Tabor, to the south of Nazareth. This event was witnessed by three of the disciples – Peter, James and John.

> About eight days after Jesus said this, he took Peter, John and James with him and went up onto a mountain to pray. As he was praying, the appearance of his face changed, and his clothes became as bright as a flash of lightning. Two men, Moses and Elijah, appeared in glorious splendour, talking with Jesus. They spoke about his departure, which he was about to bring to fulfilment at Jerusalem (9:28-31).

To get a full idea of what occurred on the Mount of Transfiguration we need to refer to each of the writers of the synoptic gospels.

Both Luke and Matthew record that the face of Jesus *shone very brightly*. Matthew compares the face of Jesus to the brightness of the sun; Luke says the appearance of his face changed. What the disciples saw in the face of Jesus was the same kind of light that blinded Paul on the road to Damascus.

Further, *his clothes became very white*. Matthew says they were 'white as the light' (17:2). Mark says 'dazzling white, whiter than anyone in the world could bleach them' (9:3). Luke says 'as bright as a flash of lightning' (9:29). The source of the light that shone through Jesus' clothes was not external, it came from within himself, for he is truly God.

Luke also comments on the topic of conversation between Jesus and the two heavenly visitors, Moses and Elijah: 'They spoke about his departure [his death], which he was about to bring to fulfilment at Jerusalem' (Luke 9:30-31). This is in marked contrast to the disciples who did not understand what they were talking about.

There are several reasons as to why Moses and Elijah

appeared here. One is that both these men had unusual departures at the end of their time on earth. Moses was buried by God and Elijah was taken up to heaven in a whirlwind. But a more important reason is the roles they had. Moses was the mediator of the Old Covenant; it was through him that the law was given by God to Israel. Elijah was one of the most important of the Old Testament prophets. Moses and Elijah together represent the Law and the Prophets. The main purpose of the Law and the Prophets was to prepare the way for the coming of the Messiah.

Because of his sin Moses was prevented from entering the Promised Land along with the children of Israel (Deut. 34:1-4). But, in a far more wonderful way, he did get there. Many hundreds of years later he stood within the Promised Land and spoke personally with the Messiah.

Peter, nevertheless, felt he should say something. Noting that Moses and Elijah were leaving, he suggested, 'Master, it is good for us to be here. Let us put up three shelters – one for you, one for Moses and one for Elijah' (Luke 9:33). He did not understand what he was saying. It seems he wanted the experience of glory to continue, for Jesus not to go to the cross.

Although there is no record that Jesus answered Peter's request, the Father did speak. As the cloud of glory descended onto the mountain, the Father spoke from within the cloud and said: 'This is my Son, whom I have chosen; listen to him.' Matthew tells us that when the disciples heard the voice of God they fell on the ground, terrified. It was then that Jesus spoke to them and said, 'Get up. Don't be afraid' (Matt. 17:6-7).

When the disciples looked up they saw that the supernatural glory had gone, that Moses and Elijah had gone. Only Jesus was there. However, he said to them: 'Don't tell anyone what you have seen, until the Son of Man has been raised from the dead' (Matt. 17:9).

When they came down the mountain they were met by a crowd. They were told by a man in the crowd that the other disciples had not been able to deliver his son from demonic attacks. The situation described here illustrated the unbelief that marks people because of their sin (Luke 9:41). However, in his grace Jesus cast the demon out of the boy.

The crowd was very impressed by Jesus' power over the evil spirits. But Jesus warned his disciples not to be deluded by this apparent popularity: 'Listen carefully to what I am about to tell you: The Son of Man is going to be betrayed into the hands of men' (9:44). Again he referred to his approaching death. Sadly the disciples did not understand what he meant. What had been the subject of the conversation between Jesus and the heavenly visitors on the Mount of Transfiguration was beyond the ability of the disciples to understand at this stage. But after the resurrection and ascension of Jesus, when the Holy Spirit would have come, they would understand.

47. Who is the greatest? (Luke 9:46-50)

There is a sense in which each of us wants to have significance, to have the respect of other people, to do something truly great. The disciples were no different, and after being in the presence of Jesus, and inspired by his greatness, at times they quarrelled among themselves about the right to be closer to Jesus.

Luke records one such occasion:

> An argument started among the disciples as to which of them would be the greatest. Jesus, knowing their thoughts, took a little child and had him stand beside him. Then he said to them, 'Whoever welcomes this little child in my name welcomes me; and whoever welcomes me welcomes the one who sent me. For he who is least among you all – he is the greatest' (9:46-48).

Jesus' response was to teach his own disciples a powerful lesson in humility and in service. The first action that he did in order to communicate this truth to his friends, was to call a little child to him. It is one thing to be an ambassador for Christ to the great and powerful, but it is another thing to give of our time to a child, who is not great in the sight of this world. Nevertheless each child is important and has value in God's sight. What Jesus is saying is that when we take time for the child, it is as though we were doing it to him.

Then he adds something equally important, for he says, 'Whoever welcomes me welcomes the one who sent me.' You may remember that we have run into this concept before, when we looked at what it meant to be an apostle. So there is a line of continuity here, where Jesus is saying that if we really receive God, then we must receive the one whom God sends, and the one whom God sent into the world is Christ. If we receive Christ, then we must receive the ones that he sent into the world, namely, his apostles. So he is quick to add this thought to the broader concept of receiving the child in his name.

Then he said, 'For he who is least among you all – he is the greatest.' Quite simply, what our Lord is teaching is that greatness is measured in God's eyes by service, obedience and humility. We measure greatness in this world by power, wealth, achievement and talent. I am sure there will be many surprises when we reach heaven and discover whom God has elevated to the higher levels of privilege in his kingdom.

Then we read that John answered and said, 'Master, we saw a man driving out demons in your name and we tried to stop him, because he is not one of us' (9:49). John is upset; he has seen an exorcist casting out demons and doing it in the name of Jesus. He was not one of the disciples, however, and John obviously considers him to be a fraud who has no right to be ministering to people in the name of Jesus. How ironic that this report comes right after the episode where the disciples themselves had failed in their efforts to heal a possessed person. Now here is one who is not even one of the inner circle who is doing it.

'Do not stop him,' Jesus said, 'for whoever is not against you is for you' (9:50). This sounds like a contradiction of Jesus' words in Matthew: 'He that is not with me is against me' (Matt. 12:30). Can we make sense of both of these sayings?

In terms of the external ministry of the church, those who

are not pitting themselves in direct and overt opposition to the ministry of Christ's church, by virtue of the fact that they are not an obstacle, are indirectly a help. Here is a man who is involved in exorcism and in doing it he is promoting the ministry of Jesus. Whatever else the man understood, he understood that if there was any power to relieve people from demonic oppression it was associated with the power of Jesus Christ. The man was not undermining the ministry of Jesus. He was not against him; in fact, he was for him.

Conversely, it was in the context of a person's personal commitment that Jesus said, 'He that is not with me is against me.' Jesus is saying here that there is no point of neutral ground. One is either for Christ, or he is against Christ. You cannot remain neutral. So with these two statements we have to distinguish between one's commitment to Christ, and one's resistance to the work of his church and of his followers.

48. The hostility of the Samaritans (Luke 9:51-56)

We read on in verse 51 that, 'As the time approached for him to be taken up to heaven, Jesus resolutely set out for Jerusalem.' Jesus and his disciples had had several discussions about Jesus' future, about his Messianic vocation, about the fact that he, the same one who was transfigured in glory, must be delivered into enemy hands and suffer death. Jesus knew that that humiliation and suffering was to take place in Jerusalem, that he could not avoid his destiny, that the mission laid upon him by the Father was the cross. Now, he begins to move from Galilee to Jerusalem. There is still a long teaching ministry ahead, and he stops at several places along the way, but there is no question about his destiny.

As we read in verse 52, he 'sent messengers on ahead, who went into a Samaritan village to get things ready for him'. In those days, of course, it was customary for hospitality to be given to travellers along the way, but not many travelled in such a large band as Jesus did, and sometimes Jesus would come with the multitudes clamouring along beside him, with his disciples, not only the twelve, but the seventy, following in his path. When that entourage entered a little village, it was more than such a village could cope with; there were not enough inns, there was not enough food. So it was Jesus' custom to send a handful of his disciples on ahead to prepare the villages for his arrival so that things would be in order when he came.

On another occasion when Jesus went from Jerusalem to Galilee and from Galilee to Jerusalem, we are told by John that to do so Jesus had to go through Samaria. Galilee is in the north of Palestine, and Jerusalem is in the south, and in between the two was Samaritan territory. Now, the Samaritans were those who had intermarried with the pagans during the inter-testamental period, and had corrupted the purity of the Jewish faith. They were half-breeds both biologically and theologically, and a great hostility emerged between them and the Jews.

Jesus was now ready to move through Samaria, so he sends his disciples on ahead as usual, but we read in verse 53 that the Samaritans 'did not welcome him, because he was heading for Jerusalem'. Already Jesus was known in Samaria, and had some followers among the Samaritans. Why then this reluctance to receive him now? They had noticed that Jesus' face was set towards Jerusalem. This raised the contentious issue of the location of the central sanctuary. Jesus, in heading for Jerusalem, was saying that was where the sanctuary was, whereas the Samaritans worshipped God at Mount Gerizim. They hated the Holy City and for Jesus to head for Jerusalem was a slap in the face for the Samaritans, and so they didn't want to receive him as a guest along his way.

When the disciples, James and John, saw this, they were outraged by this lack of common hospitality among the Samaritans, and they said: 'Lord, do you want us to call fire down from heaven to destroy them?' They were probably thinking back to that great contest that Elijah the prophet had with the false prophets of Baal on Mount Carmel, when Elijah prayed and brought down fire from heaven. The disciples are so angry that Jesus has been insulted, that they are ready to go to war with the Samaritans. Jesus had to rebuke his disciples, for in their zeal they were ready to compromise the very essence of the ministry of Christ. Jesus didn't make a big stir in the middle of the Samaritan village, but quietly went on to the next town. What a great loss for the Samaritan village, to miss that opportunity for the visitation of God incarnate in their midst. There was a judgment implied in that, that Jesus chose another village. They missed out on their salvation, but Jesus gave them another chance; he did not call down fire from heaven.

It would be easy to draw the conclusion from this text that God is not concerned whatsoever to exercise judgment. In a sense, the disciples were thinking theologically when they wanted to call down fire on unbelievers, because they were students of the Old Testament. They had also heard Jesus say time after time that there was going to be a day of judgment and that fire would come down from heaven upon those who resisted Christ. So it is not that Jesus is saying that there never will be a judgment; but his present mission was not to bring the world to final judgment, but to redemption. The day of woe will indeed come, but the difference between God and the disciples is the difference between a God who is slow to anger, who is patient, gracious and long-suffering, and sinful disciples who were quick to anger, impatient and short-suffering. They were ready to bring swift and sudden destruction to the first act of disloyalty to Jesus.

49. Looking to the future (Luke 9:57-62)

'As they were walking along the road, a man said to him, "I will follow you wherever you go" ' (9:57). How many times have you heard people say that? 'Where he leads me, I will follow, even to the ends of the earth.' It is easy to say when we are filled with excitement and joy, and are thrilled with the benefits of God's grace, but when the moment of testing comes, it is not an easy thing to say. Jesus sobered the man, for he said to him, 'Foxes have holes and birds of the air have nests, but the Son of Man has no place to lay his head.' Jesus says to this man, 'If you want to follow me, you leave security behind. I don't even have a home. I don't know where my next meal is coming from. I don't know where my house is. If you are prepared to follow me, then you have to be willing to pay the price of not having a place to lay your head.' Jesus made that comment to people who wanted to follow him while he was making the journey to Jerusalem. He was going to die. If they wanted to follow him, they would have to leave their security behind.

Verse 59 continues: 'He said to another man, "Follow me." But the man replied, "Lord, first let me go and bury my father."' I don't know whether or not his father's corpse was lying at home; if it was, the son would most probably have been at the funeral, because it was his obligation to be there. Perhaps the man had a father who was close to death, and he was saying to Jesus that he would rather wait until his father was dead and buried before leaving all to follow Jesus. Jesus' reply to this is one of the most difficult sayings that ever comes out of his mouth. It sounds utterly insensitive and rude: 'Let the dead bury their own dead, but you go and proclaim the kingdom of God' (9:60). I don't think that Jesus was being insensitive. He obviously saw that this man was procrastinating and did not understand the urgency of the mission that Christ was on. To the Jew, one of the most important duties is to give a proper burial to their departed relatives, and under normal circumstances it would have been immoral for that man to abandon his father at the time of the funeral. But Jesus is showing by his words that what was happening, this mission in redemptive history, going to the cross in Jerusalem, was so urgent, that it supersedes even the normal importance of the burial customs of our cultures. There is no time to bury the dead. Right now the kingdom of God is at stake. Right now there is a war going on between the prince of this world and the Son of God and the outcome is going to be determined in Jerusalem. Right now in terms of redemptive history nothing else matters. Let the dead bury the dead. Now Jesus was not setting down here a standard for all times, that we are always supposed to neglect our dead and wounded. No, he said, 'Right now, the kingdom of God is at stake and there is only one place you can be and that is at the front line of the kingdom.'

'Still another said, "I will follow you, Lord; but first let me go back and say goodbye to my family"' (9:61). What more reasonable response could there be? 'I will follow you for the rest of my life, but all I want is fifteen minutes to go home and tell my family where I'll be.' And Jesus said, No! 'No-one who puts his hand to the plough and looks back is fit for service in the kingdom of God' (9:62). When you put your hand to the plough your vision can only be forward, to the future, never mind the past.

Many golden opportunities for the work of Christ in this world have been stifled and choked and killed because people could not keep their eyes off the past: 'Well, we always did it this way ...,' or, 'Here's what we did yesterday, why can't we do it ....?' Jesus told them to forget about yesterday. The future is where our eyes ought to be. The mission that he has given us is to go forward. Look toward Jerusalem. Jesus' face was set. He refused to look back.

What happens when a farmer, who is ploughing a field, keeps turning around to look at what he has just ploughed? Can you imagine what the furrows would look like? They would zig-zag across the field. It would be as if a drunken man was in charge of that plough, and where he thought he planted peas, cucumbers would come up. Jesus said, 'If you want to plough, if you want to have a harvest, you have got to plough a straight line.' And so it is with the kingdom of God. All those who would have God, who would press on to that kingdom, must have their eyes fixed on Christ, on his kingdom and on his future.

50. Jesus sends out the seventy-two disciples (Luke 10:1-16)

Just as chapter 9 began with Jesus sending out the twelve disciples on a special venture of ministry, chapter 10 also begins with Jesus sending out disciples, this time seventy-two in number. 'After this the Lord appointed seventy-two others and sent them two by two ahead of him to every town and place where he was about to go.' The twelve disciples represented the inner circle of students who followed after Jesus, but he had gathered a large multitude of adherents and, on this occasion, he appointed seventy of them for a specific task.

We have been following Jesus' journey from Galilee down through Samaria and into Jerusalem. This entire journey has been taking place in the midst of a great spirit of urgency, and here Jesus emphasizes again the urgency of the hour, by selecting seventy disciples for a special mission. He sent them out two by two, perhaps for mutual support or safety, or perhaps to fulfil the Old Testament principle that a witness's testimony is confirmed by the report of another witness. This apparently takes place in the last six months of Jesus' life.

Luke doesn't tell us exactly where these seventy-two were sent, but the conjecture is that they journeyed on the east side of the Jordan, to make sure that all of the cities there were covered with the preaching and the proclamation of the coming of the kingdom of God. There are also some hints that the cities to which they were sent were not centres of devotion, but cities which have been infiltrated by pagan ideas.

'The harvest is plentiful, but the workers are few. Ask the Lord of the harvest, therefore, to send out workers into his harvest field' (10:2). This theme of a harvest that is ripe is one that we find in the teaching of Jesus. The harvest comes through the providence of God and through his power, and yet those who are his children have not been prepared to participate in the harvest. Jesus instructs his disciples to pray that the Lord of the harvest would send labourers into his harvest. This is God's harvest, and all of those who participate in this task know the joy of working in the kingdom of God.

The charge goes on: 'Go! I am sending you out like lambs among wolves.' This statement by Jesus may give us an indication as to why the labourers are few. In many parts of the world today, working in the church is very safe, but to go out where the fields are ripe to harvest, to the mission field, for example, or into a hostile society, is to risk one's life, or one's resources. Jesus himself is the good shepherd, and elsewhere teaches that the shepherd is willing to lay down his life for his sheep. But here Jesus says to his disciples that he is sending them out as lambs to the wolves. Jesus himself is a lamb prepared for slaughter, and any Christian who is willing to follow after Christ must be prepared to suffer.

On more than one occasion Jesus says that those who follow after him will certainly know persecution, tribulation and suffering in the world. The Christian is called to live at peace with all men as far as possible. We are not to add to the offence of the gospel, our own abrasive personalities or lack of sensitivity. Some Christians seem to feel that the only measure of their loyalty as a disciple, is how much hostility they can stir up among people. Obviously we must avoid that kind of distortion of the New Testament teaching.

Yet, on the other hand, true disciples will inevitably encounter a hostile world, the ravenous wolves that Jesus speaks of. To understand this, we have to go back to the basic sinful disposition of the human heart to the things of God. The Scriptures make it quite clear that man by nature is not neutral with respect to God, nor does he have a deep affection and yearning disposition to hear of the things of God. Rather, natural man, we are told, is at enmity with God, is hostile towards the holiness of God and his person.

Christians, therefore, ought not to be surprised when that same hostility that is directed against God, and was directed against Christ, overflows and is poured out against Christians, particularly those involved in outreach. Think of the apostle

JESUS SENDS OUT THE SEVENTY-TWO DISCIPLES

Paul, or Saul as he was called then, who was filled with
animosity towards Christians, and went from home to home,
taking Christians into prison. Then, as he was travelling on a
desert road to Damascus, he was thrown from his horse and
was blinded by a brilliant light that encompassed all who were
there, and Christ in his glory appeared to him, calling in a loud
voice, 'Saul, Saul, why do you persecute *me*?' Not, 'why do
you persecute *Christians*?' but 'Why do you persecute *me*?'
Why did Jesus say that? Perhaps it was because of the close
relationship between the church as his body and himself, or
perhaps it was because Jesus recognized that the reason for the
hostility is that to the world the Christian represents humanity's
most hated enemy, God himself.

Where mission activity is to be done, spiritual warfare will
take place, and the commander-in-chief must send his troops
into battle, knowing that the opposition is strong. Jesus said, 'I
am sending you out like lambs among wolves.' Then he goes
on: 'Do not take a purse or bag or sandals; and do not greet
anyone on the road. When you enter a house, first say, "Peace
to this house." If a man of peace is there, your peace will rest on
him; if not, it will return to you.' These instructions follow
closely to the instructions given to the twelve at the beginning
of chapter 9. Again the instruction is to do without any excess
baggage, as this mission is of such urgency, that it is to be done
with speed. The urgency is so great, in fact, that Jesus even
calls them to ignore custom: 'Greet no-one on the way.' It
doesn't mean that the seventy were called to be curt and impolite,
refusing to greet people they met, but according to eastern
custom, if you met somebody on the way it was considered
polite to spend a lengthy time in chatting about the weather and
so on. Jesus calls on his disciples to dispense with those
formalities: there is no time for trivia.

Then he charges them, when they go into a house, to give
the classic greeting of 'Shalom': 'Peace be unto this house.'
But they are not to waste time on the homes that have no peace
in them, instead they are to let that peace return to them and get

on with their ministry. In verse 7 he says, 'Stay in that house, eating and drinking whatever they give you, for the worker deserves his wages. Do not move around from house to house.' If they find a house where they are afforded hospitality, they are to stay there and establish a headquarters. This was Jesus' way: when he came to Jerusalem his headquarters were at the home of Mary and Martha and Lazarus in Bethany. Jesus tells the disciples not to feel guilty about enjoying hospitality, for it was expected that the friends of the kingdom would give the necessary support base to keep the labourers strong for their task.

Some of the homes in the trans-Jordan may not have kept the strict dietary rules of Jewish custom. But Jesus told his disciples, 'Stay in that house, eating and drinking whatever they give you' (10:7). The implication here is that they are not to worry about what they eat. The task is too urgent to worry about ceremonial matters. This statement is made again in verse 8.

Verse 9 stresses again the urgency of this mission: this is not the mandate given to the church of all ages, but it applies to those crucial weeks that elapsed between Jesus' departure from Galilee and his arrival at the cross. This is a pregnant time in redemptive history, calling for the uttermost forms of urgency. Now the kingdom of God is about to break through. It has come near to the people, and the moment of crisis is upon the world, hence this peculiar sense of urgency.

However, whilst the urgency of that hour may not continue in the same dimension and the same intensity as at that particular moment in church history, nevertheless there is an urgency that abides. The church is still called to proclaim the advent of the kingdom of God.

Woe to those who will not listen (Luke 10:10-16)
Jesus goes on to say: 'When you enter a town and are welcomed, eat what is set before you. Heal the sick who are there and tell them, "The kingdom of God is near you." But when you enter a town and are not welcomed, go into its streets and say, "Even

the dust of your town that sticks to our feet we wipe off against you. Yet be sure of this: The kingdom of God is near." ' The dust on their sandals is to be a testimony against the people who do not listen and they are to proclaim to them that the kingdom of God had come near them, but they would not embrace it. Then Jesus follows with this solemn statement: 'I tell you, it will be more bearable on that day for Sodom than for that town.' It is tempting to think that every place is the same, that people are the same all over the world, and that it is just a matter of who is most vocal in a given community as to whether or not that town is open to the proclamation of Christ. But that's just not the way it is. There are certain places where the concentration of hostility to God is far more intense than in other areas, and Jesus recognized that. Some places where the disciples would go would respond favourably, but other places would manifest only hostility. Jesus draws a comparison with Sodom, that city which represents the quintessence of wickedness in the Old Testament, which was destroyed by divine judgment. Those towns and villages that reject their ministry will face a greater judgment on the day of judgment than the inhabitants of Sodom.

Then Jesus recites the oracle of doom against such towns, using the literary form of the oracle that the prophets used in the Old Testament: 'Woe to you, Korazin! Woe to you, Bethsaida! For if the miracles that were performed in you had been performed in Tyre and Sidon, they would have repented long ago, sitting in sackcloth and ashes' (10:13). We have considerable information on Jesus' ministry around Bethsaida, but there is not a single mention in the gospels of Jesus doing anything in Korazin, and yet here the woe is pronounced upon it, which leaves us to conclude that Jesus did have a ministry there. This serves to emphasize that not everything that Jesus did is recorded in the gospels. But evidently mighty works had been performed in Korazin and the people had not responded. And again he makes a comparative evaluation; had Tyre and Sidon seen the things that these cities had seen, they would have repented long ago. 'But it will be more bearable for Tyre and Sidon at the judgment than for you' (10:14).

Then he speaks of Capernaum which was his headquarters in Galilee, and where many of his deeds were done: 'And you, Capernaum, will you be lifted up to the skies? No, you will go down to the depths.' Again, we see the urgency of the task: to those who respond, there is life eternal, but to those who repudiate the kingdom of Christ, there is judgment. Jesus then continues: 'He who listens to you listens to me; he who rejects you rejects me; but he who rejects me rejects the him who sent me' (10:16). So committed is Christ to his disciples, so closely does he identify with them, that to abuse a disciple of Christ is seen by God as an abuse of Christ himself.

51. A time of rejoicing (Luke 10:17-24)

In this section we see a contrast between the mission of the seventy-two and the earlier mission of the twelve; the twelve ran into demonic powers over which they had no control. On this occasion, however, the seventy come back filled with excitement: Luke writes: 'The seventy-two returned with joy and said, "Lord, even the demons submit to us in your name." He replied, "I saw Satan fall like lightning from heaven." ' (10:17-18). Jesus doesn't say whether this vision of Satan was in his own mind, or whether it was simply his way of characterizing the impact of the mission against the forces of hell. One thing, however, is clear: with this breakthrough of the kingdom of God, Satan falls from his pedestal of power.

Jesus continues speaking to his disciples: ' I have given you authority to trample on snakes and scorpions and to overcome all the power of the enemy; nothing will harm you' (10:19). In the desolate wilderness area of Judea and in trans-Jordan lived snakes, spiders, scorpions and some varieties of wild birds. Jesus likens the power of being able to move through the wilderness, to the spiritual power of encountering the forces of hell. Traditionally the serpent is the symbol of Satan himself. In the very first proclamation of the gospel in Genesis 3, God said that he would put enmity between the seed of the serpent and the seed of the woman: 'He will crush your head, and you will strike his heel' (Gen. 3:15). Most commentators see that as a cryptic reference to the coming Messiah, who would pay with his own life, but yet in so doing he would crush the head of the serpent. Now that one who will crush the head of the serpent fully and finally, grants his disciples the power to tread on the serpent and on the scorpion, and over all the power of the enemy. That is the power of the kingdom of God. There is no possible way that the enemies of the Christian faith can ever prevail over the kingdom of God.

Jesus acknowledges the disciples' joy at seeing the power of Satan subjected to them as they used the name of Christ. But then Jesus tells them: 'However, do not rejoice that the spirits submit to you, but rejoice that your names are written in heaven' (10:20). There is a power that comes with redemption; there is the gift of the indwelling of the Holy Spirit, the dynamite of God's kingdom that is given to everyone who is truly converted to Christ. It can become an exciting thing to have this new power within your life, yet Jesus says this should not be the cause of our celebration. Rather, we should rejoice because our names are written in heaven. That is the greatest gift we will ever receive in our lifetime.

This allusion to names being written down would be clearly understood by his contemporaries, as it was customary when a child was born, for its family to have the name of that child registered as being a part of the family. When someone enters into the kingdom of God his name is inscribed on the register of the kingdom of heaven. If you are in Christ your name is written down in the Lamb's book of life.

We are told something of the joy of the disciples, but we are also told that Jesus rejoiced. The writers of the gospels tell us that Jesus was sorrowful, that he was filled with grief from time to time, but this verse (verse 21) is the only place where we are told Jesus rejoiced. Obviously there would have been many occasions when Jesus manifested joy, but this is the only one recorded for us. The sending of the seventy was a triumphant occasion, the results were positive, the disciples came back filled with enthusiasm. And Jesus was grateful for the success of this missionary enterprise.

Perhaps someone reading this is engaged right now in the missionary enterprise of the church. I urge any such people to take courage and comfort from the knowledge that, although much of your work goes unnoticed, such activity done for the sake of Christ brings not just satisfaction, but joy to your Lord. On this occasion, Jesus was so moved by his pleasure in the ministry of the saints, that he turned to the Father and prayed in the Spirit, saying, 'I praise you, Father, Lord of heaven and earth, because you have hidden these things from the wise and learned, and revealed them to little children. Yes, Father, for this was your good pleasure' (10:21). This passage has been misconstrued to mean that Jesus was saying that the gospel has been given to the uneducated and hidden from the educated, but that is not the point. Rather it means those who are babes in their spirit, who have an open heart, who are eager to hear the will of the Father, who hang on every word that is proclaimed, Jesus is glad that those enjoy the fruits of these gifts, rather than the proud of this world, who have no time for humbling themselves before their Father.

Then Jesus goes on to say, 'All things have been committed to me by my Father.' He is saying this in conjunction with what he has just experienced. The gift of the victory of the welcoming of the people, and the hearing of the gospel, is something that the Father has given to the Son. The only reason you are in the kingdom of God today is that you were a gift from the Father to the Son, so that the Son might see the travail of his soul and be satisfied. For 'all things', said Jesus, 'have been committed to me by my Father. No-one knows who the Son is except the Father, and no-one knows who the Father is except the Son and those to whom the Son chooses to reveal him.' Notice Jesus is not saying that no-one knows that there is a God, for the

Scriptures make it plain that God has not left himself without a witness. The heavens declare the glory of God, and Paul tells us in Romans 1 that the invisible things of God are clearly seen and perceived through the things that are made, so that all men have some awareness of the existence of God. What Jesus is speaking of here, however, is that no-one knows God intimately; no-one knows the inner character of the divine mind, save Jesus. When the New Testament speaks of knowledge it uses the Greek word *gnosis*. Sometimes it is used to refer to an external form of knowledge about something, but more frequently it is used of a knowledge of intimacy.

Jesus is remarking that people say they know the Father but reject the Son, but it can't be done: 'No-one knows who the Son is except the Father, and no-one knows who the Father is except the Son and those to whom the Son chooses to reveal him' (10:22). We don't know anything intimately about God: we know that God *is*, we can study nature and know something of his power, his justice, his eternality, and so on, but we don't know the character of God intimately, save through Christ. For Christ reveals the Father to us.

Just a few verses earlier Jesus cursed the unrepentant: 'Woe to you, Korazin! Woe to you, Bethsaida!' But now he pronounces the benediction on his own disciples, 'Blessed are the eyes that see what you see. For I tell you that many prophets and kings wanted to see what you see but did not see it, and to hear what you hear but did not hear it' (10:23-24). Wouldn't Abraham have rejoiced to see the feeding of the five thousand! Wouldn't Moses have enjoyed listening to the Sermon on the Mount! Wouldn't Elijah have delighted to watch Jesus turn water into wine! Wouldn't King Solomon in all his splendour have been willing to part with his riches for the opportunity of witnessing Jesus raise Jairus' daughter from the dead! Do you ever yearn to have been there, to see what the disciples saw? They were indeed blessed. But there will come a time when we will see him face to face, we will hear him with our ears, and that blessing will be ours and his joy will be fulfilled in us.

52. The parable of the Good Samaritan
(Luke 10:25-37)

In this section Luke records for us the encounter between Jesus and a penetratingly brilliant lawyer. 'On one occasion an expert in the law stood up to test Jesus. "Teacher," he asked, "what must I do to inherit eternal life?" ' This question is similar to the one posed by the rich young ruler that is recorded elsewhere in Scripture, and there is nothing unusual in that. Teachers and theologians are asked the same basic questions again and again, so it is not surprising that a question as central to the understanding of Jesus' ministry as this question of eternal life, should be asked by more than one person.

The lawyer, here, was obviously trying to trip Jesus up, as was common among his enemies, by asking difficult questions to see how Jesus would handle them. Jesus' response to the question is similar to one he gives elsewhere. Christ spoke regularly about eternal life, but he also reminded the people repeatedly of their obligations to fulfil the Law of the Old Testament. We see this in his dealings with the rich young ruler, whom he directs to the ten commandments. Similarly, in this incident Jesus directed the attention of the lawyer to the Law, not to the ten commandments this time, but to the summary of the whole Law found in the Great Commandment.

'What is written in the Law?' he replied. 'How do you read it?' Now this was a perfectly appropriate question to ask a lawyer, for this man was not a barrister or attorney in the secular sense, but rather one who was an expert in biblical law. Therefore, it was a strange question for him to ask of Jesus, as Jesus indicates in his reply: 'What is written in the Law?'

The lawyer is the one who is being questioned now and he gives the proper answer. 'He answered: "Love the Lord your God with all your heart and with all your soul and with all your strength and with all your mind" ; and, "Love your neighbor as yourself." "You have answered correctly," Jesus replied. "Do this and you will live" ' (10:27-28). It seems like a very simple question and answer session, doesn't it? All that is required of you to live eternally is to love the Lord your God with all of your heart, and so on. What could be more simple? But think about it, for a moment. There is no-one, not one person, who has kept the force of this commandment for the last five minutes, let alone for their entire lives. For to say that you love God with all of your mind, and all of your soul, and all of your strength, and all of your heart, really is to say that you never sin, because it would be impossible to sin if you loved God in this way.

Imagine, if you will, that someone did actually succeed in loving God with all his heart, strength, soul and mind. Even then, he would still be only half-way home, because he would still have to fulfil the second part of the Great Commandment: Love your neighbour as yourself. That, at times, is even more difficult than to love God, for God is altogether lovely. There is no just reason for us not to love God, but there are plenty of reasons why we would find it difficult to love all of our neighbours as much as we love ourselves.

But at least the lawyer provides the right answer, theoretically. However it is one thing to recite the answer; it is another thing to do it. 'Do this,' said Jesus, 'and you will live.'

Verse 29 is pivotal in this text: 'But he wanted to justify himself, so he asked Jesus, "And who is my neighbour?"' This man wanted to show himself to be righteous on his own, without any need of assistance of divine grace, so again he tries to trick Jesus by asking another question. This was not an honest question, the lawyer was just trying to press Jesus in order to win the debate, and also to justify himself because he is already beginning to feel the pressure of Jesus' comments.

Jesus' response to this second question was to take this opportunity to teach the lawyer by way of a parable.

'In reply Jesus said: "A man was going down from Jerusalem to Jericho, when he fell into the hands of robbers. They stripped him of his clothes, beat him and went away, leaving him half dead."' It is only a few miles from Jerusalem to Jericho, but the road goes through some of the roughest, most barren and desolate terrain on the face of the earth. It was an area notorious for thieves who preyed on travellers making the trip from Jerusalem to Jericho. Many of the people making this journey would have been religious leaders, as Jericho was a town inhabited in the main by priests and Levites, and since they had much activity to engage in in Jerusalem, they frequently made the journey back and forth.

Most of them were judicious enough to travel in larger groups so as to discourage thievery, but sometimes it was necessary for an individual to go alone. This was the case in the story Jesus told; a man travelling on his own was robbed, stripped and left for dead. The life expectancy of a person in this situation was not great. If further injury did not come by robbers, the elements would be enough to kill a wounded, naked person very quickly.

Then we read in verse 31: 'A priest happened to be going down the same road, and when he saw the man, he passed by on the other side.' The priest was in a hurry, and didn't want to get involved. But he made a mockery of his priesthood by his actions. 'So too, a Levite, when he came to the place and saw him, passed by on the other side.' In both instances, religious workers see the injured man. They looked, looked away, and went around him. 'But a Samaritan, as he travelled, came where the man was; and when he saw him, he took pity on him.' All three of the travellers saw the wounded man, but only the Samaritan had compassion on him.

Jesus goes on to show that the Samaritan's compassion was not simply a feeling, but was authentic, for real compassion calls forth action. We read in verse 34, that the Samaritan 'went to him and bandaged his wounds, pouring on oil and wine. Then he put the man on his own donkey, brought him to an inn and took care of him'. He bound up his wounds, and used the provisions he had made for his own trip, to minister to the painful wounds of this man. Then he set him on his own beast of burden, and took him to an inn to care for him. Then, 'The next day he took out two silver coins and gave them to the innkeeper. "Look after him," he said, "and when I return, I will reimburse you for any extra expense you may have"' (10:35).

There is more to this story than a simple explanation of what it means to love one's neighbour. Remember this story was given in response to the question, 'Who is my neighbour?' Now it was no accident that the one who ministered to the wounded Jew was a Samaritan. The Samaritans were a group with whom the Jews had no dealings, who were considered outside of the purity of the faith in Israel. And in Jewish oral tradition, in the Halakah, it is specifically

There is a popular distortion of Christianity that teaches the universal fatherhood of God and the universal brotherhood of man. However, the central meaning of brotherhood and fatherhood in the New Testament refers to those who are the adopted children of God. The Bible does not teach a universal brotherhood of man, but it does teach a universal neighbourhood of man. I am required to love each human being as much as I love myself. No wonder we fall under the weight of the demands of this law. You might be thinking, 'Nobody loves anybody as much as they love themselves, and nobody loves God with their whole heart, mind, soul and strength, so why should we be exercised about our neighbours?' But the point is, that is the standard by which we will be judged. God's requirements do not change simply because there is universal disobedience to them. We can take no comfort from the fact that none of us keep the law. In fact, we should be terrified by the fact that God calls it the Great Commandment. Therefore, in the logic of the New Testament, the Great Transgression would be a failure to love God with all our heart, strength, and soul, and the failure to love our neighbour as much as ourselves. That's the great transgression. That's why we are all exposed to the wrath of God. That's why if we try to redeem ourselves through keeping the law we will be lost for ever. That's why we need Jesus. It is only by his righteousness, that we will ever stand in the presence of God.

stated that the neighbour of the Jew is the Jew, that non-Israelites are not considered neighbours. Jesus was up against a deeply entrenched tradition that distorted the meaning of the Great Commandment. Jesus cut across that human tradition and restored the original meaning of the Great Commandment that God gave through Moses. The neighbourhood in which we are called to serve goes beyond the boundaries. It doesn't end, it encompasses the globe. All people are my neighbours.

So Jesus ends, 'Which of these three do you think proved to be a neighbour to the man who fell into the robbers' hands?' The lawyer replied, 'The one who showed mercy toward him.' And Jesus said to him, 'Go and do likewise.'

53. Jesus visits Martha and Mary (Luke 10:38-42)

> As Jesus and his disciples were on their way, he came to a village where a woman named Martha opened her home to him. She had a sister called Mary, who sat at the Lord's feet listening to what he said. But Martha was distracted by all the preparations that had to be made. She came to him and asked, 'Lord, don't you care that my sister has left me to do the work by myself? Tell her to help me!'
>
> 'Martha, Martha,' the Lord answered, 'you are worried and upset about many things, but only one thing is needed. Mary has chosen what is better, and it will not be taken away from her.'

This brief passage has a very poignant meaning. Jesus made more than one short visit to Jerusalem during those last six months, and his base it would seem was normally in the home of Lazarus, and his sisters, Mary and Martha, in the little village of Bethany near the Mount of Olives. On this occasion Martha is exercised because Mary has left domestic responsibilities to give her attention to the words of Jesus, leaving Martha to take care of all of the tasks. When Martha complains of this to Jesus, he rebukes her. But what is interesting is not so much the content of that rebuke, but how he addresses Martha. He looks at her and he says, 'Martha, Martha.'

This form of address, as we have already seen (study 29), is a literary form used to denote intimacy. It is one thing to address a person by their first name, but to repeat it is to use a Jewish form of affection and intimacy. This episode with Martha is in contrast to the previous instance of this form of address found in Luke 6:46. There, as we saw, Jesus was giving a stern warning to people who, on the Day of Judgment, will address him as 'Lord, Lord', pretending to know him, pretending to have profound affection for him. And Jesus will say, 'I never knew you, depart from me, ye that work iniquity' (Matt. 7:23, AV).

But Jesus does know Martha, and he has affection for her, and so when he speaks, his rebuke is couched in the most intimate terms of affection: 'Martha, Martha, you are worried and bothered about many things; but only a few things are necessary, really only one, for Mary has chosen the good part.' Remember this occurred during that six-month period when Jesus was working to a timetable of supreme urgency, and the normal domestic duties were set aside. Mary had an opportunity to hear words of life from the lips of Jesus; that was more important than taking care of the dishes. Martha should have dropped everything too. Press into the kingdom of God, that's the message that Jesus is bringing here.

This is the time to make the seeking of the kingdom of God the main business of our lives. We cannot afford to be casual about it, for what Christ requires is a headlong commitment, a commitment of abandonment to be at the feet of Christ. 'But one thing is needful:' said Jesus, 'and Mary hath chosen that good part, which shall not be taken away from her' (10:42, AV). What she has chosen, she will possess for ever. No-one can take it away from her. When the word of God is yours, it is yours for ever. My prayer is that on that last day, when Christ looks at you, he will recognize you and will repeat your name, saying, 'Come, my beloved, inherit the kingdom which my Father has prepared for you from the foundation of the world.' It is intimacy that we want, it is intimacy that we need, in the presence of Christ.

54. Lord, teach us to pray (Luke 11:1-2a)

This is a very important section of Luke's gospel. We read: 'One day Jesus was praying in a certain place. When he finished, one of his disciples said to him, "Lord, teach us to pray, just as John taught his disciples." ' That's a fascinating request, isn't it? Why did they ask for this, and not, say, for the ability to perform miracles or answer difficult theological questions?

These men were sensitive enough to notice that Jesus' power was not something that could be learned in three easy lessons. They understood that there was a connecting link between the awesome power that Jesus manifested, and the intense prayer-life to which he gave himself. The disciples were familiar with Jesus' habit of withdrawing from time to time to go off into a desolate place and spend long periods with his Father. They made the connection in their minds between the intimacy of Jesus' prayer-life and the power of his ministry. That is a ministry secret, for if you look not only at the ministry of Jesus, but at the ministry of Luther or Calvin or Augustine or any of the great Christians through the ages, you see this connecting link; those who are powerful in ministry are those who are also earnest in prayer. They know the source of their power.

They say to Jesus, 'Teach us how to pray.' Perhaps in an attempt to persuade Jesus to do it, they remind him that this is what John the Baptist did. John the Baptist also had disciples and he took great care to instruct them on the art of praying, because that's what it is: praying is an art. Prayer is not something that comes naturally. No-one is born a good pray-er, for there is nothing more repugnant to fallen man, to natural man, than to spend time alone with God. It is not our natural disposition to seek time alone with God. That can only come when we are redeemed, restored to fellowship with God and reconciled to him through Christ. Then we desire a great degree of intimacy; that's when we long to be able to converse with God and commune with him in a rich and majestic way. Is it not a common concern and yearning of Christians to be more accomplished in their prayer-life?

When you become familiar with the teaching of Jesus, and you see some of the strange twists and turns that he takes with his thinking and his style of teaching, after a while you are not so surprised when he gives a strange answer to questions. But here's one that always puzzles me. I would have thought that Jesus, in response to their request, would have instructed them to immerse themselves in the psalms, to meditate on them day and night, because they are the most majestic prayers ever recorded, prayers that are themselves inspired by the Holy Spirit. If you want to know how to adore God, read David's words as he cries out, 'O Lord, our Lord, how majestic is your name in all the earth!' If you want to know how to make supplication, how to make prayers of confession, read Psalm 51. If you look at the great saints of the ages you will see that the words of the psalms come out in their prayers time after time. God's words become their words as they speak to their God.

But that's not what Jesus did. Why? Perhaps because the disciples, who would have been familiar already with the psalms, had noticed there was a difference between the power of the prayers of David and the efficacy of the prayers of Jesus, and they wanted that something more.

It is not just a question of learning, they wanted to know what was appropriate for their prayers. What should they say to God? What is the proper form of respect? What is the proper form of reverence? What kinds of things are appropriate to request of God? What should be the priorities in prayer? To answer all of those questions in summary manner, Jesus sets before them a model prayer, containing the appropriate form of address, the proper concerns, and so on. But we are not simply supposed to memorize this prayer. We are called to analyse it, so that it can instruct us as to how to pray. For we want to be able to pray in a way that is pleasing to God and powerful for his church.

In a sense, what Jesus says in this passage was of life and death significance for him, for it contained some words that his opponents would seize upon to charge him with blasphemy, a charge that would eventually bring about his death. It is so commonplace for each one of us today, that we hardly notice the significance of it at all. The radical part of the prayer comes at the very beginning, when Jesus tells them to address God as 'Father'. Now the vast majority of Christians, when they pray, address God as Father. This is something that we take for granted. But at this point in history, when the prayer was first uttered, it was an innovation of the most radical sort.

In the Old Testament literature and other Jewish literature of antiquity, there are prescribed prayers that were to be offered to God on a daily basis. But not once do we have a single example of a Jew addressing God in the personal form of address that Jesus uses here. Yet, when we come to the prayers of Jesus, on every occasion, except one, Jesus addresses God by the personal form of address, 'My Father'. The exception is his cry from the cross: 'My God, my God, why have you forsaken me?', quoting from Psalm 22.

This radical departure from custom was not missed by Jesus' contemporaries. The Pharisees were infuriated by Jesus' claim to an intimate filial relationship with God. So angry were his opponents that they accused him of blasphemy, for in calling God his Father, he was making himself equal with God (John 5:18).

But here on this occasion, Jesus transfers this privilege to his disciples; they, too, are to address God as Father. They have been adopted into the family of God, and by the Spirit, and through the authorization of Jesus, can now come to God, the Maker of heaven and earth, and address him as Father.

55. The priorities of prayer (Luke 11:2b-4)

Jesus' next concern was to teach his disciples the priorities of prayer. He tells us what petitions to bring before our heavenly Father. The first petition is this: we should pray, 'Hallowed be your name'. Top of the list of Christ's priorities of prayer is that the name of God would be hallowed, would be treated as holy. Where the name of God is honoured, God is honoured.

How can a person respect and worship God, and yet use his name flippantly, or as an expression of cursing? The protection of the sanctity of the name of God comes at the beginning of the ten laws of Israel. 'You shall not take the name of the Lord your God in vain.' For God will not hold one guiltless who transgresses that order of respect and of reverence. It is impious, irreverent and blasphemous to play loosely with the name of God. And yet the world does it daily. Jesus was aware of this great problem and said, in effect, 'When you pray, let your first prayer be, "Hallowed be your name." That people may respect the name of God, that they may, in turn, respect him.'

The second petition of the Lord's Prayer is 'Your kingdom come'. God already reigns in heaven, his kingship is manifest to the angels and to those who are there, but the prayer of Jesus is that the reign of God would be recognized, embraced and obeyed on this planet, in the same degree that it exists in heaven. Christ's last mandate to his church before he departed this world was 'You shall be my witnesses.' We are to bear witness to the kingship of Christ, that people in this world would bow before him. For the world, in the final analysis, is not a democracy, but a kingdom. God owns the earth, and reigns over it. He has appointed Jesus as the king of the earth. His kingdom has been established, but the world still exists in rebellion against the appointed king. As Jesus said, 'Pray that that kingdom will be as manifest on the earth, as it is in heaven.'

Only when you have made those two petitions, that God's name would be holy and that God's kingdom would be made visible, can you then begin to pray for your daily needs: 'Give us each day our daily bread.' The daily allotment of bread was the basic nourishment of the people in the ancient Near East, and so Jesus is saying that we should come to God our Father and ask him to give us those daily provisions that we need to live.

We are to be concerned with interpersonal relationships; our relationship with God and our relationship with our fellow men. We ask for God to forgive us our sins. We need to do this daily, to keep close accounts with God. As we continue to sin, we need to continue to come before him, asking for his forgiveness so that we may experience the freshness and the newness of his mercy and of his healing each day.

'Forgive us our sins, for we also forgive everyone who sins against us.' That's an unusual petition to make, asking God to forgive us in the same measure that we are willing to forgive other people. God requires that we confess our sins. But once we confess, God immediately bestows his forgiveness; he does not hold those sins against us any more. By the same token, when someone sins against us and asks our forgiveness, we are not to withhold it for a single second, once that sin has been confessed, and repented of.

Luke's abbreviated form of the Lord's Prayer ends with Jesus' words 'And lead us not into temptation.' Now this is a strange petition, as it seems to suggest that God might lead us into temptation. James tells us in his epistle, that no-one is tempted of God, but rather the temptation comes from within our own sinful disposition (James 1:13-14).

The problem here is that the word 'temptation' is capable of different meanings in the New Testament. There is that temptation which comes from within us, as James points out. God never plants evil enticements in the human heart in order to lead them into sinning. But there is also such a thing as an external temptation, when, for example, someone, usually the devil, tries to persuade us to participate in something ungodly. Or as Satan came to Jesus to tempt him in the wilderness. There was no evil in the heart of Christ, but there was plenty of evil lurking outside of Christ in the person of Satan.

The third kind of temptation is when God tempts people, in the sense of putting them to the test. Remember it was the devil who tempted Jesus to sin, but it was the Holy Spirit that sent Christ into the wilderness for the purpose of being tested by Satan. And from time to time in the Bible we read of God putting people to the test: Adam and Eve, Abraham and Job, are some examples.

The Authorized Version rendering, 'deliver us from evil', is more accurately translated as 'deliver us from the one who is evil'. It is a prayer for deliverance from the power of Satan. Jesus is saying here that we should ask the Father not to direct us, as he did our Master, into that place of testing, not to leave us exposed to the unbridled attacks of the enemy, for we are not confident that we have the strength to withstand that kind of assault on our souls.

But if we are to believe anything in the teaching of Jesus, we must take seriously the fact that we are involved, not only with those visible forces and powers that seek to seduce us, but also in cosmic warfare of an invisible sort.

Paul instructs us in Ephesians to 'put on the whole armour of God'. Why? 'For our struggle is not against flesh and blood, but against the rulers, against the authorities, against the powers of this dark world, and against the spiritual forces of evil in the heavenly realms' (6:12). And so we are to pray for protection and deliverance from the power of Satan.

56. Perseverence in prayer (Luke 11:5-13)

Following Jesus' teaching on how we should pray, he then goes on to tell the disciples a parable to illustrate the effectiveness of prayer.

> Then he said to them, 'Suppose one of you has a friend, and he goes to him at midnight and says, "Friend, lend me three loaves of bread, because a friend of mine on a journey has come to me, and I have nothing to set before him."
> Then the one inside answers, "Don't bother me. The door is already locked, and my children are with me in bed. I can't get up and give you anything." I tell you, though he will not get up and give him the bread because he is his friend, yet because of the man's boldness he will get up and give him as much as he needs (11:5-8).

In the ancient Near East people retired early, and midnight was a most unusual hour to be knocking on your neighbour's door. However, the man who goes to knock on his neighbour's door has first heard a knock on his own door. A journeying friend has dropped in on him unexpectedly. Because of the intensity of the heat of day, it was common for pilgrims to travel in the cool of the night, and it was not impolite or discourteous to knock on the door of a friend late at night to seek lodging in the midst of a perilous journey. Hospitality is of great importance, not only in the Bible, and among the Jewish people, but in the whole Mid and Near Eastern culture where there is a long tradition of extending hospitality to the stranger or the traveller.

Jesus is setting forth here a story that is designed to illustrate a point. The people would know that it was unthinkable that a friend would refuse to open his door, even at midnight. Jesus said, 'I tell you, though he will not get up and give him the bread because he is his friend, yet because of the man's boldness he will get up and give him as much as he needs.' In the first place we would expect the man to get up out of bed to meet the needs of his next door neighbour or of his friend, but Jesus is saying, even if that won't do it, surely the man will finally get up because the first man is so persistent.

Jesus is telling us that when we pray, we are to do so persistently, not casually. We are to pray like we mean it. He goes on to say: 'Ask and it will be given to you; seek and you will find; knock and the door will be opened to you' (11:9) Here is one of our Lord's most encouraging statements of invitation for his people to pray. Elsewhere we read, 'You have not, because you ask not' (Jas. 4:2). Consider the riches we have lost from our Father's house because we have simply failed to ask for them. So often our prayers are so nebulous, so general.

Those kinds of prayers hardly encourage us to come back for other prayers. It is the person who prays specifically who has the blessed experience of seeing prayers answered, and this encourages more specific prayer.

Jesus says that if we ask, we shall receive, and if we seek, we shall find, and so on. He illustrates his point further by making a comparison with earthly requests that children bring to their parents. 'Which of you fathers, if your son asks for a fish, will give him a snake instead? Or if he asks for an egg, will give him a scorpion? If you then, though you are evil, know how to give good gifts to your children, how much more will your Father in heaven give the Holy Spirit to those who ask him!' (11:11-13). What kind of diabolical father would smile at his hungry child and say, 'Here is an egg, my son,' and then hand the boy a scorpion? Such a father would be a disgrace to the community. Jesus is making the point that even fallen, corrupt, earthly people know how to give good gifts to their children, so how much more will our heavenly Father, who doesn't know how to be evil, give good gifts when we ask him? How much more is he willing to give the Holy Spirit to those that ask? Have you ever asked God for the Holy Spirit? You may have asked him for bread; for success; for healing, perhaps; but he also invites you to ask him for the Holy Spirit.

57. The lord of the flies (Luke 11:14-26)

In verses 14-16, Luke describes another confrontation between Jesus and the demonic world, a clash between the Prince of Peace and the prince of this world: 'Jesus was driving out a demon that was mute. When the demon left, the man who had been mute spoke, and the crowd was amazed. But some of them said, "By Beelzebub, the prince of demons, he is driving out demons." Others tested him by asking for a sign from heaven.'

Here was a person suffering from demonic possession that made him unable to speak. When Jesus healed this man and liberated him from the forces which held him, instead of the people rejoicing, some began to accuse Jesus of being in league with Beelzebub. Beelzebub is one of the New Testament titles for Satan, who is the chief authority in power over the demonic kingdom. Originally, the word was Beelzebul, meaning the Lord of the Court, or the Lord of the Place, a person who has authority over a certain domain. In the New Testament, repeatedly we are informed that it is Satan who has control over this world, hence the title, Beelzebul. But then, perhaps as an attempt to demean this enemy of God, in Jewish tradition the name was changed to *Beelzebub*, which means, literally, the Lord of the Flies.

Not only were some accusing Jesus of working his miracles through the power of Satan, but there were others in the same group who tempted him, seeking from him a sign from heaven. The crowd had just seen a sign from heaven, but they wanted something even clearer to prove that Jesus was from heaven and not from hell. Jesus responds by going right to the heart of the issue: 'Any kingdom divided against itself will be ruined, and a house divided against itself will fall. If Satan is divided against himself, how can his kingdom stand?' (11:17-18).

One of the oldest strategies of warfare is to divide the enemy. A nation preoccupied with internal disputes is weakened and made vulnerable to attack from without. Every general knows it, every competitor knows it, and Jesus draws the attention of his critics to it. If Satan has control of this world, and has possessed this poor man and made him unable to speak, why would he then empower Jesus to redeem him?

Jesus now presses the point home a little more sharply, because there were those in the Jewish community who were also practising the healing rite of exorcism, trying to overcome the rule of Satan over the people. After showing the foolishness of suggesting that Satan would work against himself, he challenges them to think consistently; the same charges they are levelling against him, would have to be levelled against them, too. 'Now if I drive out demons by Beelzebub, by whom do your followers drive them out?' (11:19). Of course, they didn't want to say that they were doing it by the power of Satan, because that would reveal their wickedness. If they claimed to be doing it by the power of God, Jesus would ask how they knew. They would say that only God would do this. The only inference one could draw was that Christ was not on the side of Satan.

Then Jesus continues: 'But if I drive out demons by the finger of God, then the kingdom of God has come to you' (11:20). We have seen already how in Jewish tradition the phrase 'the finger of God' is a title used for the Holy Spirit. Thus Jesus was saying simply, 'If you see me casting out Satan, not by an evil spirit, not by the Lord of the Flies, but by the Holy Spirit, by the Lord of truth and by the power of God, then you know that the kingdom of God has come upon you.'

With his next breath Jesus gives an illustration of what is happening in the spiritual realm: 'When a strong man, fully armed, guards his own house, his possessions are safe. But when someone stronger attacks and overpowers him, he takes away the armour in which the man trusted and divides up the spoils' (11:21-22).

What is Jesus talking about? He is not simply giving us a lesson on battlefield tactics. Who is the man who guards his homestead? It is the prince of this world, who has had the armour and the strength to ward off any victory, who has had his way with this man and made him dumb. But suddenly somebody stronger than the prince of this world appeared, the Son of God, and he stripped the strong man of his armour. Jesus is describing his own victory over Satan. Christ is the Victor, the one who is stronger than the prince of this world.

The Scriptures warn us repeatedly against Satan, describing him as a roaring lion seeking whom he will to devour. He masquerades as an angel of light, deceptive, seductive, enticing us to fall. The image of Satan as a roaring lion is an image of strength. We are certainly no match for a lion. We are no match for Satan. Yet the Scriptures tell us that if we resist Satan, he will flee from us. This roaring lion, growling and intimidating everybody, will turn tail and flee, if we resist him as God teaches us to. Jesus says to his people: '... the one who is in you is greater than the one who is in the world' (1 John 4:4). We are weak, Satan is stronger, but Jesus is strongest, and if we have the power of Christ within us, by the Holy Spirit, then that power is stronger than the power that is in the world and the power that is in Satan. That is why we must have the Spirit, and we must put on the armour of God in order to resist the devil.

Then Jesus adds: 'He who is not with me is against me, and

he who does not gather with me, scatters' (verse 23). There is
no neutrality. Not everyone who is an unbeliever is demon-
possessed, but all unbelievers are under the influence of Satan.
Augustine mused on that passage centuries ago, and described
graphically what he understood to be the meaning of it. He said
that we are like donkeys, and we have a rider on our back. That
rider is either Satan or Christ. Everyone is in either one camp or
the other.

What does your life reveal about where your allegiance lies?
Are you loyal to Christ, or have you tried to stand on neutral
ground? Well, according to Jesus, there is no such place. If you
are not for him, then you stand on the side of Satan. I urge you
to stand with Christ, that he may be for you Christ the Victor.

Jesus continues:

> When an evil spirit comes out of a man, it goes through arid places
> seeking rest and does not find it. Then it says, 'I will return to the
> house I left.' When it arrives, it finds the house swept clean and
> put in order. Then it goes and takes seven other spirits more wicked
> than itself, and they go in and live there. And the final condition
> of that man is worse than the first (11:24-26).

He had exorcized the demon from within the man, but is that
enough to redeem the man? Is that enough to get him into the
kingdom of God? You see, to get into the kingdom of God it is
not enough simply to be rid of the influence of Satan for a season.
If a person is exorcized of a demon, and has nothing good to
replace it, he may think that he can continue to live his life on
the basis of his own strength, that he doesn't need to look to
God for assistance, he doesn't need to have the Holy Spirit.
There is a vacuum in his heart. Jesus described the fate of such
a person, in these verses. The demon returns, bringing seven of
his diabolical friends with him. 'And the final condition of that
man is worse than the first.'

It is not enough merely to eliminate a sin from our lives. We
need to have the fulness of the Holy Spirit dwelling within us.
In the final analysis, we are powerless to achieve righteousness.

Only God can bear the fruit of righteousness in us, and that's why, if we would fill the vacuum in our lives, we must flee to Christ, and embrace him.

58. The sign of Jonah for an evil generation (Luke 11:27-36)

The difference between pleasure and happiness (Luke 11:27-28)
Luke begins this section: 'As Jesus was saying these things, a woman in the crowd called out, "Blessed is the mother who gave you birth and nursed you" ' (11:27). Unlike the other members of the crowd who had belittled and criticized Jesus, this woman sees something noble in what Jesus is doing and boldly pronounces a benediction on him. Jesus said, 'Blessed rather are those who hear the word of God and obey it.' Jesus accepted her benediction, but says that the real blessing is held in trust by God for those who hear his word and keep it.

The ultimate form of happiness is what the New Testament calls 'blessedness'. But sometimes we get confused, for there is a similarity between real happiness and pleasure. Now the axiom of Scripture is this: sin can never bring happiness, what it brings is pleasure. That's why we are so much in its power. We wouldn't sin if we didn't think it would make us happy. This is the fundamental tension that man has with God. All of us, as sinners, believe that if we obey God, we are doomed to unhappiness.

But Jesus reinforces the point, for in keeping the word of God comes the happiness or blessedness for which we were created. God has not set his law before us to make us unhappy, but to free and fulfil us, to give us joy, peace and happiness.

The sign of Jonah (Luke 11:29-32)
Then Luke recounts how Jesus said to the crowd: 'This is a wicked generation. It asks for a miraculous sign, but none will be given it except the sign of Jonah' (11:29).

In Luke 11:16 we saw that the people wanted a sign, and Jesus rebukes them for it. They had just seen Jesus heal a demon-possessed man. They had watched Jesus through his ministry; raising the dead, turning water into wine, stilling the storm. He had given one sign after another, indicating a power that only God could manifest. Yet the people weren't satisfied, they still wanted another sign. Jesus says the only sign they are going to get is the sign of Jonah.

What was the sign of Jonah to which Jesus refers? It was a sign of preaching; the preaching of the certainty of judgment. That is the sign of what is going to be given to the generation of Jesus' day; and it is the sign that is given to the people of our day. Just as Jonah was a sign to the Ninevites, so shall the Son of Man be to this generation.

However, it wasn't merely the preaching of Jonah that was significant, but it was Jonah himself. There was something extraordinary about Jonah that bore witness to the people of Nineveh that he was a messenger sent from God. We often think of Jonah's being swallowed by the great fish as a punishment by God, but it was not. The punishment was being thrown into the sea. Jonah was rescued from the sea by the fish, who then delivered him safely on the dry ground. In one sense, the resurrection of Christ is prefigured by the experience of Jonah, as our Lord himself pointed out: 'For as Jonah was three days and three nights in the belly of a huge fish, so the Son of Man will be three days and three nights in the heart of the earth' (Matt. 12:40). This is obviously an allusion to the resurrection. Jonah was a sign to his generation, and Jesus will perform a sign even greater than Jonah's, for Jesus' sign will be his resurrection. It is the resurrection of Christ that confirms beyond a shadow of a doubt that Jesus was who he said he was.

The narrative then continues:

The Queen of the South will rise at the judgment with the men of this generation and condemn them; for she came from the ends of the earth to listen to Solomon's wisdom, and now one greater

than Solomon is here. The men of Nineveh will stand up at the
judgment with this generation and condemn it; for they repented
at the preaching of Jonah, and now one greater than Jonah is here
(11:31-32).

The Queen of Sheba travelled across the world to be instructed
by Solomon, but the Pharisees, who were supposed to be
majoring in the quest for truth, would not go across the street to
hear the Son of God. The Ninevites repented at the preaching
of Jonah. But now one who is greater than Solomon, one who
is greater than Jonah, is here. How can you refuse to hear his
message?

The light of the body is the eye (Luke 11:33-36)
At first glance, Jesus' next words seem detached from this
encounter over signs. However, I think Luke includes them here
to illustrate this issue of the sign that people require.

> No-one lights a lamp and puts it in a place where it will be hidden,
> or under a bowl. Instead he puts it on its stand, so that those who
> come in may see the light. Your eye is the lamp of your body.
> When your eyes are good, your whole body also is full of light.
> But when they are bad, your body also is full of darkness. See to
> it, then, that the light within you is not darkness. Therefore, if
> your whole body is full of light, and no part of it dark, it will be
> completely lighted, as when the light of a lamp shines on you.

Jesus links the idea of lighting a candle and putting it in a secret
place, with the problem of the light of the body and the eye. If
you want to have light in the house, you don't hide the lamp in
a cellar or pot. You put it where the light can be used, where it
can illumine the room. Jesus moves from the lamp to the eye,
saying the eye is the light of the body. This illustration is very
simple. A person standing in a dark room with his eyes shut
will not see very much. If the light is turned on and the person
shuts his eyes, he is still in darkness, because the only point of
entry for the light to reach his brain is his eyes.

Jesus uses this point to illustrate the requirements for seeing the sign of the resurrection. It is not that there is insufficient evidence or that God's light is too weak. God has illumined the whole world with the evidence of his own existence and the evidence of the identity of his Son. By breaking the bonds of death in the resurrection of Jesus, God turned on the lights for the whole world.

However, Jesus himself says, 'Light has come into the world, but men loved darkness instead of light, because their deeds were evil' (John 3:19). When God turns on the lights, wicked men and women shut their eyes. When our lives are characterized by sin we become creatures of the darkness. The thing that we fear most is to be exposed, and light lays bare the soul.

In the final analysis, unbelief is not an intellectual problem. It is not because there is a paucity of evidence, or that God has not made himself clear: the problem is a moral problem. We don't want to believe, because we know that if we acknowledge the God-ness of God and the deity of Christ, that means that we must repent, and therein lies our pain and resistance. In spite of a world filled with the light of the majesty of God, we shut our eyes and our body remains in darkness.

59. Jesus pronounces woes on the Pharisees
(Luke 11:37-54)

'When Jesus had finished speaking, a Pharisee invited him to eat with him; so he went in and reclined at the table. But the Pharisee, noticing that Jesus did not first wash before the meal, was surprised. Then the Lord said to him, "Now then, you Pharisees clean the outside of the cup and dish, but inside you are full of greed and wickedness" ' (11:37-39).

The Bible teaches us that Jesus was scrupulous, to every point of the law. But, in addition to the laws that God had set before his people in Holy Scripture, a body of legislation had been added to the biblical law by the religious authorities of

Israel. One of those was an elaborate law of ceremonial cleansing and purification which was required before the eating of any meal. These laws were passed on to the people as if they were sanctioned by God, and binding on the consciences of the people. Reading between the lines, it is clear that Jesus deliberately broke the laws of the Pharisees, in order to teach them a very important lesson. This Pharisee could not believe that Jesus had not washed before dinner. But Jesus confronts him with the words, 'You clean the outside of the cup and dish, but inside you are full of greed and wickedness.' Jesus warns against the tendency to allow religion to degenerate into dead and empty forms and rituals.

Now, I do believe there is value to ritual in the church, particularly in worship services. We are not just verbal creatures, and doing activities that involve non-verbal communication – kneeling, raising our hands, going through certain other exercises of the liturgy of the church – recognizes that. In the Old Testament God established rituals as a very important part of the religion of Israel; and in the New Testament, Jesus also established rituals and made them into sacraments. However, ritual can be a dangerous thing because it is very easy for people to go through the motions of the liturgy without ever really coming to grips with what the liturgy is designed to teach. The liturgy is a symbol and the symbol points beyond itself to Christ. These Pharisees who had mastered the external forms missed the very thing the forms were drawing their attention to. Jesus is showing that to them, for he says, 'You foolish people! Did not the one who made the outside make the inside also?' How foolish it is to consider only the externals.

Jesus follows this indictment with a list of six woes, six curses, that he pronounces upon the Pharisees. The first woe is found in verse 42: 'Woe to you Pharisees, because you give God a tenth of your mint, rue and all other kinds of garden herbs, but you neglect justice and the love of God. You should have practised the latter without leaving the former undone.' This first woe is because the Pharisees majored in minors. They paid their tithes to the last detail, but they passed over judgment and love. Elsewhere Jesus said: 'But you have neglected the more important matters of the law – justice, mercy and faithfulness' (Matt. 23:23).

One of the most scary things that Jesus ever said was: 'For I tell you that unless your righteousness surpasses that of the Pharisees and the teachers of the law, you will certainly not enter the kingdom of heaven' (Matt. 5:20). It is easy to dismiss that statement glibly – surely it can't be difficult to be more righteous than the Pharisees! Yet, the Pharisees were very dedicated and did much that was commendable. But in the end, it was self-righteousness that disqualified them from entering into the kingdom of God. Notice that Jesus does not say, 'You should not have tithed ...' No, they were right to tithe, but they should not have left undone the weightier matters of justice and mercy. But at least they did the lesser matters. Statistics show that in the USA today only 4% of Christians tithe their income. My fear is that we are ignoring the minor as well as the major matters. We are not concerned with justice and mercy, neither are we bothering to tithe. At this point at least, the righteousness of the Pharisees exceeds our righteousness, and their righteousness was not enough to receive the benediction of Christ. Christ, the Lord of this church, gives us this mandate – we are to do both: tithe and be concerned with the deeper things of justice and mercy.

The second woe is announced in verse 43: 'Woe to you Pharisees, because you love the most important seats in the synagogues and greetings in the marketplaces.' The synagogue was arranged so that there was a semicircular table at the front at which the dignitaries among the religious leaders were seated and they were given due respect and honour by the people. However, many of the teachers were more interested in the honour than in being honourable. They were less concerned about advancing the kingdom of God, than advancing their place in the synagogue. That is a temptation that church leaders have to face and are as vulnerable to it as the Pharisees were. It is nice to be greeted in the marketplace, but if our heart is captured by a desire for recognition, more than a desire for the recognition of Christ, then we are in trouble and are liable to the chastisement of Christ.

The third woe is in verse 44: 'Woe to you, because you are like unmarked graves, which men walk over without knowing it.' If anything was likely to provoke the wrath of Christ the most, it was this. The Pharisees were a snare for the people. The people looked to them in matters of religion; they were dependent on them for their growth and knowledge. People assumed their leaders were holy and righteous, and that they could trust them. But Jesus likened them to unmarked tombs. On another occasion he describes the Pharisees as whitewashed sepulchres, outside bright and clean, but inside filled with dead men's bones. Here, however, his point is rather different. It was common practice to whitewash the tombs, not simply for appearance's sake, but for the more practical reason of making them visible.

In the laws of the Pentateuch, to step on someone's grave made a person ceremonially unclean. If you inadvertently stepped upon a grave, you had to go through a week-long purification ceremony. So, as a precaution, it was a matter of common courtesy to whitewash the tombs. Some tombs, however, did fall into neglect, and were not apparent, and so a stranger would step on them by accident.

Jesus looked at the Pharisees and told them they were like unmarked graves. People walk over them unwittingly, not knowing that death is under their feet. They are disseminating death, teaching falsehood. But the people don't recognize it; they don't realise the outward show of religion is only hypocrisy. And so the people are deceived and led astray. Those who presume to preach and to teach in the name of Christ are responsible, not to set traps for the people of God, but to guide them into the arms of Christ in the kingdom of heaven.

Jesus' discourse of judgment is interrupted at this point by a lawyer, an expert in matters of theological law. He said,

'Teacher, when you say these things, you insult us also.' It is obvious that the man didn't like being included in the indictment of Jesus. So Jesus makes explicit what he had only implied till now: 'And you experts in the law, woe to you, because you load people down with burdens they can hardly carry, and you yourselves will not lift one finger to help them' (11:46). These men were not concerned with ministering to the needs of the people of the congregation, but rather they devised new forms of legislation, passing them off as the law of God. This is still happening in the Christian church today: we can become burdened with rules and regulations that have nothing to do with the word of God. That type of legalism comes under the indictment of Christ, because it doesn't bear witness that the true law of God is a light to our feet. The true law of God drives us to Jesus, but the laws of men crush the spirit and retard the kingdom of God.

Jesus continues with the woes: 'Woe to you, because you build tombs for the prophets, and it was your forefathers who killed them. So you testify that you approve of what your forefathers did; they killed the prophets, and you build their tombs' (11:47-48). In Palestine today you can still see some of the tombs of the prophets that were there in Jesus' time; huge, ornate memorials to the great men of God of antiquity. But Jesus tells the Pharisees they are hypocrites in their memorial projects, for these were the very men their fathers killed. The attitude that was prevalent in their fathers, that led them to destroy the prophets who came speaking the word of God, is present now, because the greatest prophet that ever lived is in their presence and they are prepared to kill him. Jesus discerns their hearts and attacks them for their hypocrisy:

'Because of this, God in his wisdom said, "I will send them prophets and apostles, some of whom they will kill and others they will persecute." Therefore this generation will be held responsible for the blood of all the prophets that has been shed since the beginning of the world, from the blood of Abel to the

blood of Zechariah, who was killed between the altar and the
sanctuary. Yes, I tell you, this generation will be held responsible
for it all' (11:49-51).

The blood of all the prophets and all of the martyrs from Abel
down to the present day in which Jesus was speaking, was shed
as testimony to the truth which was now embodied in the person
of Jesus. In a sense, what Jesus is saying is that if you take all
of the murders of the prophets throughout the whole of history
and add them together, that doesn't add up to the heinousness
of the crime they are about to commit in murdering him. They
had the Son of God standing before them and they despised him.

The last woe is in verse 52: 'Woe to you experts in the law,
because you have taken away the key to knowledge. You
yourselves have not entered, and you have hindered those who
were entering.' Theologians are commissioned and ordained to
be servants of the church to teach the people the theology that
God has delivered in sacred Scripture, not to twist or conceal or
deny that theology. The Holy Spirit has given the key of knowledge, and Jesus accuses the theologians of his day of having
taken away that key. Not only will they not enter in themselves,
but what is worse, they are hindering those who are entering.
That terrifies me. I can't think of a worse indictment than for
Jesus to say to me, 'You are a teacher and you have taken away
the key of knowledge.' I pray to God that I never do that.

Luke finishes his account of the six woes Jesus pronounces
against the Pharisees, thus: 'When Jesus left there, the Pharisees
and the teachers of the law began to oppose him fiercely and to
besiege him with questions, waiting to catch him in something
he might say' (11:53-54).

60. A warning against hypocrisy (Luke 12:1-7)

Having pronounced woes on the teachers of religion who were
superficial in their faith and led many astray, Jesus then goes
on to expand this warning: 'Meanwhile, when a crowd of many
thousands had gathered, so that they were trampling on one

another, Jesus began to speak first to his disciples, saying: "Be on your guard against the yeast of the Pharisees, which is hypocrisy'" (12:1). Jesus gives this warning to his disciples in the midst of a vast thronging multitude, who must surely have overheard what Jesus was saying. 'Be on your guard against the yeast of the Pharisees.'

Jesus uses the metaphor of yeast or leaven on more than one occasion. Sometimes he uses it in a positive way, where he speaks of the leaven of the kingdom of God that has the ability to spread and to swell and to grow to great proportions, but here he uses it in a negative sense, warning them to watch out for a destructive kind of leaven that poisons the entire loaf; the leaven of the Pharisees, which is hypocrisy.

Jesus concludes with a warning: the sure promise of the ultimate exposure of all hypocrisy: 'There is nothing concealed that will not be disclosed, or hidden that will not be made known. What you have said in the dark will be heard in the daylight, and what you have whispered in the ear in the inner rooms will be proclaimed from the roofs' (12:2-3). Ultimately, every mask of hypocrisy will be ripped off. At the judgment seat of God he will separate the real from the counterfeit, the genuine from the hypocritical.

We all have secrets that would be profoundly embarrassing for others to be aware of. To have our secret sins exposed, our weaknesses manifested publicly is terrifying. But there is a day established, where God says that the truth will be revealed. Not only will our secret sins be manifested, but also our secret virtues. But, if I did not know that on that day my nakedness will be covered by the righteousness of Christ, it would destroy me to have to face it. But this is what God promises for his people: in that day of judgment those who are in Christ will be hidden. His righteousness conceals our corruption. That's why we cling to Christ.

Jesus continues: 'I tell you, my friends, do not be afraid of those who kill the body and after that can do no more. But I will show you whom you should fear: Fear him who, after the killing

The word translated 'hypocrite' is borrowed from an ancient term taken from the theatre. A hypocrite, basically, is an actor. He wears a mask and performs a role which does not correspond to his real self. So what Jesus is saying about the Pharisees is that they were role-players, wearing an outward mask of piety and religiosity, but the true stuff, the real essence of godliness, was absent from their hearts. They were play-actors of religion, pretending to be something they were not.

It is not unusual to hear the charge that the church today is full of hypocrites. How do we respond to that charge? No church is perfect and hypocrisy is a problem that every church must face and deal with. But one of the reasons why people think the church is filled with hypocrites is due to a misunderstanding of what the church is, and what people are who are members of the church. We expect the church to be filled with saints, with people who are devoutly righteous. It is right that we should have some expectations about the standard of righteousness that characterizes the church of Christ. Christian people are supposed to be committed to righteousness, to godliness and to obedience, but at the same time we need to realize that these are sinners, and all of the devotion that they achieve, all the righteousness they acquire in this life, will never eradicate the power of sin in their lives. So it should not surprise us to find sin in the church.

However, there is some confusion at this point. Hypocrisy is a sin, but there are many different kinds of sin, and when people say that the church is filled with hypocrites because they see people sinning, that's an unfair indictment. Now if they pretended that they did not commit the sins, then they would be guilty not only of sin in general, but of the particular sin of hypocrisy. It was this sin of fraud in the church that particularly grieved Jesus because he recognized how devastating it is to people when they see the actor unmasked, when an apparently righteous person is discovered to be fraudulent. It causes disillusionment, anger, a sense of betrayal and disappointment. Sometimes all we can do in this situation is point people to Christ, for he will never disappoint us. He will never be exposed as a fraud. Christ will always be true to his own profession. There is no play acting in Jesus.

of the body, has power to throw you into hell. Yes, I tell you, fear him' (12:4-5). Some say that Jesus is saying that the one whom we should fear most is Satan because he has the power to destroy us. But I don't think that is what Jesus is speaking of here. Satan doesn't have the power to kill us; he doesn't have the authority to send anybody to hell. The authority to send the soul to hell rests with God alone. So Jesus is saying here something that is said throughout Holy Scripture, that we ought to fear God. This does not mean that we should be quaking for fear of the presence of God, or think that he is out to get us. The fear that we are to have for God is a fear of offending him, a fear born of awe, reverence and humility before his majesty. But there is another side to this; we should fear the power of God also, fear the punishment at his hands. Repentance, however, that is born of the fear of punishment alone, is not true repentance, it is what is called *attrition*. Godly repentance, or *contrition*, comes from a genuine sorrow for having violated the law of God.

Notice that when Jesus gives this warning he doesn't do it in a harsh or destructive way, but he addresses his disciples as 'my friends'. He is pleading with his friends to have a healthy fear of God. The fool is the one who does not fear the destructive powers that surround him.

Jesus then turns his attention to the positive dimension of God's knowing everything about us, lest we despair at the awesome prospect of final judgment. 'Are not five sparrows sold for two cents? And yet not one of them is forgotten before God. Indeed, the very hairs of your head are all numbered. Do not fear; you are of more value than many sparrows' (12:6-7, NASB).

In some ways these verses sound like a contradiction of verse 5 where he tells the disciples, 'Fear him, who ... has the authority to cast into hell', for he now says, 'Do not fear.' A healthy fear and respect for God should always be balanced by our confidence that in God's sight we are of exceedingly great value. Yes, God knows us intimately, knows the secrets that we harbour in our hearts, yet we should not allow our fear of divine disclosure to drive us to despair. Rather it should drive us to embrace the redemption that is ours in Christ.

61. A warning against blasphemy (Luke 12:8-12)

'I tell you, whoever acknowledges me before men, the Son of Man will also acknowledge him before the angels of God. But he who disowns me before men will be disowned before the angels of God' (12:8-9). Imagine, if you will, the divine tribunal where every secret sin is manifest. You are called to stand before the judgment seat, and God makes public every sin you have ever committed. But then you say, 'I have embraced Christ'. At that moment Christ steps forward as your advocate and confesses before the throne of God, and in the presence of the angels, that you belong to him. The threat of divine judgment is removed by divine redemption.

However, there is a flip-side to this; Jesus warns that those who refuse to confess him, he will refuse to confess before the Father. He will say, 'I don't know him.' That person will have to stand alone before God.

Verse 10 is perhaps the most fearful admonition ever to come from the lips of Jesus. It is the warning concerning the sin that cannot and will not be forgiven. 'And everyone who speaks a word against the Son of Man will be forgiven, but anyone who blasphemes against the Holy Spirit will not be forgiven.' In the other gospels this same warning is set in the context of the Pharisees accusing Jesus of performing his miracles by the power of Satan. This context is the key to understanding precisely what Jesus has in mind. Elsewhere he says that blasphemy of the Holy Spirit is a sin that will not be forgiven in this world or in the world to come. God simply refuses to forgive it. If this sin is committed, it is the end of hope of divine forgiveness.

Many people have lived in mortal terror that they have committed, or might commit, the unforgivable sin and consign themselves thereby to an eternity of the absence of forgiveness.

This is so troublesome because it seems to fly in the face of the spirit of the teaching of Jesus, who again and again makes the free offer of forgiveness.

Well, we have to face the reality that Jesus did say that there is a sin that will not and cannot be forgiven. We need to know what that sin is, because we had better avoid it with all of our might. There has been much speculation about what is meant by the blasphemy against the Holy Spirit. Some say it is murder, some that it is adultery, some say it is using God's name in vain. But nowhere are these sins defined in the Bible as unforgivable. Many of the great theologians in history have identified the blasphemy against the Holy Spirit as being the final and ultimate rejection of Christ. The Bible commands that people come to Jesus, and what happens to a person who steadfastly refuses to come to Christ, even in his last gasping breath? Is that not the thing that will keep a person out of the kingdom of God? We need Christ to get into the kingdom of God, and certainly the rejection of Jesus is linked to blasphemy of the Holy Spirit. But what makes this statement of Jesus' so difficult is that he distinguishes between sinning against him and sinning against the Holy Spirit. Sin against the Son of Man can be forgiven, and what more gross sin could be committed than to kill the Son of Man, and yet on the very cross where Jesus hung he pleaded with the Father to forgive those who were killing him. To help us understand what Jesus meant we need to remind ourselves of the context of these words. This lengthy body of teaching follows the incident in Luke 11:15, where the Pharisees accused him of being in league with Satan. It is in that setting that Jesus warns the Pharisees to be careful not to blaspheme against the Holy Spirit. Blasphemy against the Holy Spirit is a verbal sin. Many theologians link blasphemy against the Holy Spirit with blasphemy against Christ in this way: when a person has become aware of the true identity of Jesus through the revelation of the Holy Spirit, if that person then calls Jesus the devil, that is the unforgivable sin.

When the Pharisees accused Jesus of working miracles by

the power of Satan, Jesus, knowing they didn't have the Holy Spirit in their hearts, warns them that they should have recognized him by now. They are perilously close to the unforgivable sin, and if they continue to make those statements after the Holy Spirit reveals to them that Jesus is the Christ, there will be no forgiveness. I have never witnessed a professing Christian actually call Christ the devil. In fact, it is inconceivable to me that a Christian ever would commit the unforgivable sin. I have heard Christians blaspheme and take the name of God in vain, and that is a very serious offence against his holiness. But what Jesus is defining here is a specific type of blasphemy: a calling of Jesus the devil, as the worst and most gross form of blasphemy we can think of.

One of the most terrifying things I have ever seen was when I was a young man. I, along with others, watched a high school fellow who was very angry at God, shake his fist at heaven and call Jesus every abusive name that he could think of. Although I wasn't a Christian then, I was overcome with a sense of terror for the well-being of the young man. I really expected to see him get hit by a lightning bolt that day. He didn't, but the next afternoon, I saw two medics carrying a stretcher towards an ambulance. There on that stretcher was the young man with a self-inflicted gun-shot wound in his chest. An hour later he died. I was doubly scared, and couldn't help wondering if there was a link between his blasphemous outburst the night before and his act of suicide less than twenty-four hours later.

It was a grim experience, but theologically I would say that it was not blasphemy against the Holy Spirit. Even that young man could have been forgiven in his dying moments, had he repented and come to Christ. If a person knows who Jesus is, has had it revealed to him by the Holy Spirit, and then accuses Christ of being the devil, then I am afraid that for that person there is no hope. Jesus gives the warning, so that our level of respect would be jealously guarded less we arrogantly or flippantly cross the line to the ultimate act of sacrilege. Perhaps those who are involved in devil worship are coming very close to this, particularly if they have had previous revelation of who Christ is. But any other sin, no matter how gross, violent, or blasphemous, may be forgiven, but it requires confession and repentance and embracing the mercy of Christ. Then from that day forth we confess that Christ is Lord, and have done with the utterance of all forms of blasphemy.

Jesus concludes this section with a promise that relates to the Holy Spirit: 'When you are brought before synagogues, rulers and authorities, do not worry about how you will defend yourselves or what you will say, for the Holy Spirit will teach you at that time what you should say' (12:11-12). Whilst we should fear blaspheming against the Holy Spirit, we should also rejoice that in the moment of our trials before men, the Holy Spirit will be there to give us the words that we need. If you are a Christian, the Holy Spirit is with you and he is with your mouth, not only to help you say what needs to be said, but also to guard your lips from saying that which is unforgivable.

62. A warning against covetousness (Luke 12:13-32)

In the middle of the very weighty discourse that Jesus is giving the multitude about the danger of committing the sin of blasphemy against the Holy Spirit, somebody from the crowd interrupts him with a crass and selfish concern. He rushes up to Jesus, and says, 'Teacher, tell my brother to divide the inheritance with me.' Obviously these two men were embroiled in some kind of family squabble over inheritances. In the ancient world, rabbis were frequently called in to act as judges in such disputes within the family, and so the request we have here is, in itself, not altogether unreasonable. But the man's timing couldn't have been worse, and it was obvious to Jesus that the man hadn't been listening at all to the spiritual lesson that Jesus was giving. All he could think about was his finances. His whole being was preoccupied with money. Jesus sounds exasperated: 'Man, who appointed me a judge or an arbiter between you?', but then he takes the opportunity this affords to speak to the whole crowd about covetousness. He tells them the story that has become known as the parable of the rich fool.

He begins with a solemn warning to be on their guard against any form of greed, for 'a man's life does not consist in the abundance of his possessions' (12:15). Jesus is not talking about the evils of having wealth, neither is he denying the validity of earning income, or possessing worldly goods. What he is warning them against, rather, is covetousness, that attitude of the heart that causes a person to be utterly preoccupied with money. He tells us that a man's life does not consist in the abundance of one's personal possessions. This is a lesson not against material things, but against materialism. Materialism is that worldview which sees the essence of life to be found in the possession of wealth. Then to illustrate his warning, he speaks a parable.

> The ground of a certain rich man produced a good crop. He thought to himself, 'What shall I do? I have no place to store my crops.' Then he said, 'This is what I'll do. I will tear down my barns and build bigger ones, and there I will store all my grain and my goods. And I'll say to myself, "You have plenty of good things laid up for many years. Take life easy; eat, drink and be merry" ' (12:16-19).

Now, this is not a man who is struggling to survive or to build up a farming business. He is already rich and on top of his richness he has a bumper crop, a crop that obviously exceeds his own expectations because he didn't have enough space to store the harvest. He could have sold them at the market, but this man isn't thinking about selling, he wants to hoard it all. So he decided to pull down his barns and build bigger ones. He is not interested in adding to his fields and growing more crops for the material well-being of the whole community. No. He wants to build barns to store, so that he can stop working and live a life of wasteful consumption. Now, it is perfectly legitimate to retire at the appropriate age, but this man, created in God's image and called to fulfil the sanctity of labour that God gives in creation, wants to live a life of ease and indulgence long before the appropriate time.

In verse 19 the man speaks to himself words of indolence and greed, but suddenly the tone changes, for in verse 20 God speaks to him: 'You fool! This very night your life will be demanded from you. Then who will get what you have prepared for yourself?' The man had it all figured out. He didn't have a worry in the world. But the verdict of God is that he is a fool, because he really believed that life consists in the abundance of the things which a person possesses. This man had spent a lot of time considering how he was going to enjoy his material possessions, but he never considered the state of his soul. He was thinking of the future, but he didn't know the future. His was the concern for today and for tomorrow that had no room for the consideration of eternity. He neglected his own soul.

Jesus deals with this question many times. Perhaps his most famous statement on this subject is found in the Sermon on the Mount: 'What good is it for a man to gain the whole world, and yet lose or forfeit his very self?' (Luke 9:25). Only a fool neglects to consider the state of his soul. Jesus said, 'This is how it will be with anyone who stores up things for himself but is not rich toward God' (12:21).

Do not worry about your life (Luke 12:22-32)
Anyone who lays up treasure for himself without any consideration towards the things of God is a fool. It is in this context that Jesus then says to his disciples: 'Therefore I tell you, do not worry about your life, what you will eat; or about your body, what you will wear. Life is more than food, and the body more than clothes' (12:22-23). Jesus is speaking passionately here, because he is communicating a vital lesson to his disciples. He is not saying that Christians should be utterly irresponsible with respect to taking care of family matters, clothing, housing, and so on. The rest of the parable makes it clear that it is our responsibility to think of the future, and make provision for our families and for our children's education. But Jesus, here, is using hyperbole to get through to those people who are paralysed by anxiety. All they think about is their bank

account, and in so doing they are missing the most important dimensions of human experience. If we think food or clothing are the essence of life, we have missed the kingdom of God.

So Jesus says, 'Consider the ravens: They do not sow or reap, they have no storeroom or barn; yet God feeds them. And how much more valuable you are than birds!' (12:24). It is interesting that he chooses the ravens for they were considered unclean by the Jews. Jesus doesn't say, 'Consider the dove,' but rather asks them to consider this ugly, unclean bird. It is a scavenger, it doesn't work or have storerooms and yet God takes care of it. You are much more valuable in God's sight than a raven.

Then Jesus adds: 'Who of you by worrying can add a single hour to his life? Since you cannot do this very little thing, why do you worry about the rest? Consider how the lilies grow. They do not labour or spin. Yet I tell you, not even Solomon in all his splendour was dressed like one of these' (12:25-27). No amount of worrying will lengthen our lives by even a day, so why, Jesus asks, do we get so preoccupied with all these lesser things?

In verses 28-30 Jesus again commands us not to worry about clothing or food. He does not deny that we need them, in fact he says 'Your Father knows that you need them' (12.30). In other words, we are to let God worry about them and we are to be wise and take thought of our souls and eternity. He says, 'But seek his kingdom, and these things will be given to you as well' (12:31).

Then he makes a very beautiful and tender statement: 'Do not be afraid, little flock, for your Father has been pleased to give you the kingdom' (12:32). This is the only example in the whole of Scripture of this expression 'little flock'. This is the Good Shepherd speaking to his beloved disciples and urging them not to be afraid, for God wants to give them his inheritance, the riches of his kingdom.

63. The importance of being found ready
(Luke 12:33-50)

Jesus' lengthy discourse against covetousness is drawing to a close. He makes this summary statement: 'Sell your possessions and give to the poor. Provide purses for yourselves that will not wear out, a treasure in heaven that will not be exhausted, where no thief comes near and no moth destroys. For where your treasure is, there your heart will be also' (12:33-34). This text has been very controversial through the ages. Some interpret it as the Christian's mandate to turn over all his material goods to the poor. However, when considered in the light of Jesus' teaching elsewhere, it is clear that is not what he meant. Jesus here is speaking to people who were completely preoccupied with the pursuit of wealth. He weaves into this discussion a sense of urgency: 'Where your treasure is, there will your heart be also.' Immediately he goes on to talk about the preparedness that he expects from his people whose priorities are set in the right order. This point then leads in to a discourse about the importance of being found by God always in a state of readiness for the manifestation of Christ.

> Be dressed ready for service and keep your lamps burning, like men waiting for their master to return from a wedding banquet, so that when he comes and knocks they can immediately open the door for him. It will be good for those servants whose master finds them watching when he comes. I tell you the truth, he will dress himself to serve, will have them recline at the table and will come and wait on them (12:35-37).

The Authorized Version reads, 'Let your loins be girded.' In the ancient Near East the servants in a wealthy man's house usually wore long, flowing robes. These robes, although ornate and beautiful, weren't particularly functional. If a person wanted to ready himself for action, he would put a belt around his robe, freeing his legs. In telling the people that now is the time to put on their belts, to gird their loins, to be prepared and to keep their lamps burning, Jesus is calling for vigilance, for a state of readiness.

Using a brief parable, Jesus tells the story of a master who goes to a wedding feast. He will be gone for several days, and his servants don't know when he will return. These servants could easily slip into a slovenly state and take a rather cavalier attitude towards their responsibilities. Jesus says that when the master returns, if he finds his servants prepared and alert, so that they immediately open the door when he knocks, then those servants will be blessed. However, at this point Jesus departs radically from the customs of the ancient world. To this simple story, drawn from the everyday experience of the people, he adds a consequence that is utterly uncommon. The master on his return gives an unprecedented reward to his workers. He himself, puts on the uniform of service, invites his servants to recline at the table, and waits on them himself. Jesus is obviously applying this to himself; when he comes, those who are found ready, who are busily engaged in their work, having set their hearts on the kingdom of God, and not to the acquisition of material possessions, will be rewarded. When the King comes, the King will serve his faithful people.

Jesus adds to this: 'It will be good for those servants whose master finds them ready, even if he comes in the second or third watch of the night' (12:38). The Romans divided the day into four six-hour periods for guard-duty. The Jews, however, divided the day into three eight-hour periods, or watches. Have you noticed what happens when people expect something of crisis proportions to happen at a given moment, but it doesn't? As time passes, people begin to think that it isn't going to happen at all. It has been almost two thousand years since Jesus said that he would return to this world, and as the time passes a spirit of scepticism emerges in many people. If he hasn't come now, he will probably never come. Perhaps it was only a fairy tale in the first place.

We don't know the appointed day or hour of his return, but we know two things with certainty. One, that he is coming, and two, that his coming is closer today than it was yesterday. With each passing moment, human history moves closer to the return of Jesus. It may be another two thousand years before Jesus returns, although frankly I doubt it. But whether he comes in our lifetime or not, it does not change the fact that we have a sober obligation to be ready at whatever time he comes. That is the call of the New Testament, to be found awake and involved in fulfilling the duties that Christ has given to his people.

Jesus then gives a more serious warning about what will happen to those who are not ready when he comes. 'But understand this: If the owner of the house had known at what hour the thief was coming, he would not have let his house be broken into' (12:39). Burglars generally are very careful not to be caught in the act. No sensible thief would notify the owner of the details of a forthcoming burglary. If he did, there would be a reception committee there to greet him. As Jesus said, 'If the owner of the house had known at what hour the thief was coming, he would not have let his house be broken into.' Jesus applies this to his hearers, 'You also must be ready, because the Son of Man will come at an hour when you do not expect him.'

And Peter said, 'Lord, are you telling this parable to us, or to everyone?' (12:41). Jesus answers the question with another parable.

The Lord answered, 'Who then is the faithful and wise manager, whom the master puts in charge of his servants to give them their food allowance at the proper time? It will be good for that servant whom the master finds doing so when he returns. I tell you the truth, he will put him in charge of all his possessions. But suppose the servant says to himself, "My master is taking a long time in coming," and he then begins to beat the menservants and maidservants and to eat and drink and get drunk. The master of that servant will come on a day when he does not expect him and at an hour he is not aware of. He will cut him to pieces and assign him a place with the unbelievers.

'That servant who knows his master's will and does not get

ready or does not do what his master wants will be beaten with many blows. But the one who does not know and does things deserving punishment will be beaten with few blows. From everyone who has been given much, much will be demanded; and from the one who has been entrusted with much, much more will be asked' (12:42-48).

That passage terrifies me, for the sense of this parable is that Jesus is speaking to Peter, to the disciples, the ones whom he has made responsible over the multitudes, the leaders of his church. For they are the ones who know the Master's will, and if they don't communicate it to the rest of the people, they are like the wicked servant who uses his master's absence to exploit and oppress those he is responsible for. When the master comes back, that steward will be cut in pieces, and assigned a place with the unbelievers. It is interesting that Jesus doesn't say here that those who were ignorant will get off scot-free. They will still be punished for their deeds of wickedness, but those who should have known better, will receive a more severe punishment.

This text is very important to the broader question of the degree of punishment that we will receive at the hands of God. God's justice will be perfect: to whom much knowledge is given a commensurate responsibility is attached to it. That principle still applies today. Those who have been trained and equipped to understand the things of God have, with that greater blessing and greater benefit, a greater responsibility. In James we read a warning to teachers: 'Not many of you should presume to be teachers, my brothers, because you know that we who teach will be judged more strictly' (Jas. 3:1). Isn't it sad, that when Christ appeared, his most outspoken enemies were the religious leaders of his day, those leaders who should have known better.

This sober warning is given both to the rank and file and to the leaders of the church: be ready when Jesus comes. His coming will be a crisis. He said, 'I have come to bring fire on the earth, and how I wish it were already kindled!' (12:49).

Some commentators interpret this as the fire of his spiritual power. Other look at it as the fire of purification; or the fire of judgment. Frequently when the Bible uses the image of fire, it uses it in one of two ways: either, the refiner's fire that purifies, or the fire of judgment which destroys. Jesus is obviously calling attention here to that crisis of final judgment that will come with the consummation of his kingdom. He said, 'How I wish it were already kindled!' How frightening that the Son of Man has a passion in his heart to bring the judgment to conclusion; to bring blessing and redemption to those whom he finds ready, and judgment to those who exploit the absence of the visible presence of God.

But he says, 'I have a baptism to undergo, and how distressed I am until it is completed!' He had already been baptised by John in the river Jordan, but he still had to undergo his own baptism of fire on the cross, when he personally faced the unmitigated judgment of God.

He has accomplished it now, but in a sense this has added to the crisis that you and I face, because we look at the ministry of Christ from this side of the cross, which makes the urgency of our day all the more severe. If you have given your life to the pursuit of wealth and have taken your ease and assumed that you will never be called into account, then hear the words of Jesus. He will come when he is least expected and those who are ready he will bless and he will serve, but those who have ignored him, he will cut to pieces. Therefore, be ready, for he will surely come.

64. Bringing division not peace (12:51-59)

Jesus is identified with peace. His birth was heralded by the angels who spoke of peace on earth. In the Beatitudes he gives his blessing to the peacemakers. But here, Luke records the Prince of Peace saying: 'Do you think I came to bring peace on earth? No, I tell you, but division' (12:51).

At the beginning of the twentieth century, the world of theology was shaken by the work of scholars who called themselves, 'Crisis Theologians'. They called attention to the sense of urgency that surrounds the crisis that befalls the earth at the appearance of Jesus. It was a time of division, a time of judgment. In fact, the New Testament word for judgment is the Greek word, *krisis*. Jesus' appearance in the flesh brought a crisis to mankind, for everyone who encounters Christ is called upon either to stand with him or against him. That crisis will reach its final culmination with his return. Until that moment comes, however, there is still the present crisis of division, the division that comes about because of Jesus. It is true that Jesus brought to this world and to his people a kind of unity and community that the world has never known. Yet, Christ himself was an instrument of division.

There is something of a paradox here, for the New Testament tells us to live at peace with all men, as far as it is possible. God speaks harshly against the spirit of contentiousness that divides people unnecessarily, and Jesus himself was anything but a contentious person. He was not argumentative: he was patient and kind. Yet he was the most divisive person in human history. History itself is divided by his appearance, for we speak of AD and BC. Verses 52-53 describe how families will be divided because of him. He is not advocating a spirit of dissension and disunity, but predicting the inevitable, because Christ is a person of passion. Christ does not invite neutrality, and our commitment to him has and will cause strife, even within one's own family.

This text should not be seen as a licence for obnoxious behaviour on the part of zealous Christians. We are called to a ministry of reconciliation and the virtue of patience. But it is inevitable that with commitment to Christ, divisions will occur. And division over his person and over where he stands in our lives is the ultimate point of division for the human race.

'He said to the crowd: "When you see a cloud rising in the west, immediately you say, 'It's going to rain,' and it does. And when the south wind blows, you say, 'It's going to be hot,' and it is" ' (12:54-55). It doesn't take a genius or a crystal ball to be able to predict the weather. But Jesus then says:

'Hypocrites! You know how to interpret the appearance of the earth and the sky. How is it that you don't know how to interpret this present time? Why don't you judge for yourselves what is right?' (12:56-57). Scholars differ as to what Jesus has in view when he speaks of the imminent danger for first century Palestine. Is he talking about the failure of the theologians of Jesus' own time to recognize him? Or is there a broader application that speaks of his return at the end of the age when people will be able to predict all manner of things; political turmoil, stock market falls, and so on, and yet miss the obvious signs of Jesus' return? In his own day they missed all of the signs that the Old Testament prophets had talked about; every pious Jew should have been able to see that Jesus was the fulfilment of the Old Testament prophets. But they missed it. The Son of Man was standing in their midst, but they missed it. They could read the signs of the weather, the externals, but the things that mattered, ultimately and eternally, they were not able to grasp.

Jesus then uses another illustration from everyday life: 'As you are going with your adversary to the magistrate, try hard to be reconciled to him on the way, or he may drag you off to the judge, and the judge turn you over to the officer, and the officer throw you into prison' (12:58). Jesus takes a very ordinary situation and applies it to his situation with the people. The judge is obviously God, and the adversaries are obviously Jesus and those who are standing in opposition to Jesus. Jesus' message to his contemporaries, is this: 'Look, I am here. We are discussing my identity, your allegiance. Let's settle this issue now. We are opponents, and we are headed for the court. But my Father is the Judge and if you don't settle with me outside of the court, then the Judge is going to throw the book at you. He will turn you over to the constable, and the constable will throw you into prison.'

Jesus pleads with them to make their peace with him before it is too late, before that last judgment comes, and the sentence is brought down. He says: 'I tell you, you will not get out until you have paid the last penny.' Some have taken comfort from these words. At least, they say, those who are thrown into prison, presumably the prison of hell, don't have to stay there for ever, because after they have paid for all of their crimes, they will be released. I take little comfort from the idea of a second chance, because we are debtors who can never pay our debts. In offending a holy, infinite and eternal God, our sin itself is infinite and eternal. That is why we require a sacrifice that is of infinite worth, that is why the cross is our only hope, because on the cross Christ paid that debt. The only possible means of redemption for us is by grace.

Christ has paid that debt, and if you despise his payment, then all you have left is to pay it yourself. His payment, however, is perfect and gracious and will cover every last cent of your indebtedness. Everything that we owe can be settled out of court. Therefore, the judgment is a moment of triumph for Christ and for his people.

65. Why does God allow suffering? (Luke 13:1-5)

Jesus was also asked this question, and Luke records how he dealt with it. Jesus had been speaking and warning people of the urgency of the kingdom of God, and it is in this context that we read: 'Now there were some present at that time who told Jesus about the Galileans whose blood Pilate had mixed with their sacrifices' (13:1).

It is not clear exactly what episode in history the people were referring to. There is no record in the writings of other Jewish historians of Pilate's mingling someone's blood with the sacrifices. However, there is information apart from the New Testament to verify that Pontius Pilate could be cruel and ruthless in the wielding of the power of Rome against the Jews. In fact, some time after the crucifixion of Jesus he was dismissed from his post, presumably for the abuses of his office that had antagonized even the imperial government in Rome.

We can guess, however, what happened. Some Galilean pilgrims, in Jerusalem to offer their sacred sacrifices at the altar, were killed by Pilate, either directly or through his soldiers. The narrative includes the ghastly detail that their own blood was mixed with the blood from the animal sacrifices. This was a particularly heinous offence, indeed it was sacrilege. So the question is understandable.

Jesus answered, 'Do you think that these Galileans were worse sinners than all the other Galileans because they suffered this way?' (13:2). In other words, was this dreadful suffering an indication that these particular Galileans were more wicked than other Galileans? Many people in the ancient world, and even today, believe that a person's suffering is directly proportionate to their sin. The more you sin, the more you suffer. Jesus, on more than one occasion, puts that error to rest. The Old Testament book of Job was written to teach, among other things, that in this world there is not a one-to-one correlation between a person's sin and their suffering. To be sure, there is a link between sin and suffering. Were it not for the presence of sin in this world, there would be no suffering. Sin brought death, pain and suffering into the world, and because the world is under the power of sin, suffering is a daily reality within it. But the fact that a person suffers, does not indicate a direct relationship to his particular sin.

So Jesus dismisses the idea that the murdered Galileans were worse sinners than any others, but he takes the opportunity to say, 'But unless you repent, you too will all perish' (13:3). And then he continues, 'Or those eighteen who died when the tower in Siloam fell on them – do you think they were more guilty than all the others living in Jerusalem? I tell you, no! But unless you repent, you too will all perish' (13:4-5). Now I would have expected Jesus to handle that differently. In his place, I would have offered apologetic excuses, or promised to try to do better next time. But not Jesus. What he said shocks us. 'But unless you repent, you too will all perish.' With this abrupt and difficult answer, Jesus is telling the people that they are asking the wrong question. The question is not why did that tower fall on those eighteen innocent people, but, 'Why didn't it fall on my head?'

They have located their astonishment at the wrong point.

Jonathan Edwards once asked his congregation to give him one reason why God hadn't destroyed them since they got up that morning. He asked them to consider that every moment that we live, every luxury that we enjoy, every blessing that we participate in, is a matter of receiving the grace of God, that it represents God's willingness to be patient with a race of people who have rebelled against him. God has called every human being to perfection. We are not allowed to sin. The penalty for sin is death, and yet we continue to sin and become astonished and offended when God allows suffering.

One of the biggest problems that we have in understanding the Christian faith is that we have not understood two of the most fundamental concepts of the Bible: If we think that God is obliged to be kind to us, that he owes us mercy, then we are confusing mercy and justice. There is an obligatory sense to justice. Justice describes what ought to be done to reward those who have been righteous and to punish those who have been wicked. But mercy, by definition, is never an obligation to God. Again and again God says, 'I will have mercy upon whom I will have mercy.' If grace is owed, it is not grace, it is debt. That's the point of the New Testament.

Every human being walks in this world under the sentence of death. Every human being has violated God and his holiness. The very fact that we are allowed to live from moment to moment is because of his grace. But God's grace and mercy and patience are designed to lead us to repentance. However, they can lead instead to a hardened heart, whereby we begin to presume upon his grace and take it for granted.

We lose our capacity to be surprised by him. So when a tragedy befalls us, we turn in anger to the Lord God of glory, who fills our lives with grace and mercy every day. Jesus detected that kind of hardness of heart in those asking this question, and found it necessary to give a severe warning: 'But unless you repent, you too will all perish.' Oh that we might understand the difference between justice and mercy.

66. The parable of the fig tree (Luke 13:6-17)

In Luke 13:6-9 Jesus tells another parable. In it he describes the frustration of the owner of a vineyard, who had invested in a fig tree, had nurtured and cared for it, but for three consecutive years it had failed to bear fruit. The owner had been patient. He had waited three full seasons, and had had no return on his investment. Eventually he had enough. The tree was using up space and soil that could have been used for another plant, so he decided it should be cut down.

However, the man who tended the vineyard pleaded that this tree may have one more chance to bring forth fruit. There are a couple of things that we need to learn from this story. In the first place, we have to face the fact that God calls his people to bear fruit. We live in a highly competitive, results-oriented society, and there has been a backlash in the Christian community; as a reaction to this preoccupation with results and achievement, many Christians have taken the position that God really doesn't care whether we ever produce fruit. However, this position can't be justified from Scripture, for one of the central themes of the teaching of Jesus is the call to bear fruit. He calls us to make our lives count; to make our ministries count; to make our labour fruitful. The patience of the farmer with the fig tree underscores God's patience with us. He expects us to be productive, but if we are not in the first or second year, God is patient.

But, secondly, there is a limit to God's patience, there is a limit to God's grace. God will not strive with men for ever. The Holy Spirit does not endure patiently for ever. God is long-suffering; God is slow to anger, but he does get angry, and there will be a time when that unproductive plant will be ripped up. The implications of this for us are many, both in the spiritual realm, and also in the realm of the world in which we live. In the spiritual realm the point is obvious: we do not have for ever to repent; we do not have for ever to come before God and bear fruit in our lives. We must take this call seriously.

The call for fruit bearing, for production, both in the spiritual and the material realms, is not a bad thing. We are each called to use the gifts and talents that God has given us, and to be productive people, and if we are not producing where we are at the present time, it may well be an indication that we are in the wrong place. We find a helpful example of this in the New Testament. Mark was accompanying Barnabas and Paul on one of their missionary journeys. However, Mark was not able to do the job that was expected of him, and, in a moment of obvious agony, it became necessary for Paul to ask Mark to leave (Acts 13:13). Yet later Mark wrote one of the greatest books ever written; the gospel of Mark. In the providence of God, a change had to be made. Mark had to lose one job so that he could be set free to go and be replanted in a place where he could bear fruit.

On the other hand, lack of productivity may simply indicate that we need more fertilizer, or a bit of pruning or whatever. But the primary point that Jesus is making in this parable is that the time of the coming of the kingdom is at hand, and God's patience has limits. Produce, or be cut down and replaced by another.

Healing on the Sabbath

Luke's narrative then moves on: 'On a Sabbath Jesus was teaching in one of the synagogues, and a woman was there who had been crippled by a spirit for eighteen years. She was bent over and could not straighten up at all' (13:10-11). Have you ever seen anyone with a disease of the spine, that makes them unable to straighten up? Imagine what it would be like to go through life, in agonizing pain, unable even to lift your eyes to have a conversation. But for eighteen years this poor woman was bent double and could not straighten up. 'When Jesus saw her, he called her forward and said to her, "Woman, you are set free from your infirmity"' (13:12). We see something quite different in Jesus' style of ministry here. Under ordinary circumstances it is the people that come to Jesus, to touch him, to get his attention, to ask him for help and to deliver them from their diseases. But Jesus goes out of his way to help this woman. We read that he even laid hands on her. Again, that was unusual. 'And immediately she straightened up and praised God.' For the first time in eighteen years, this woman could stand up, and when she stood up the first thing that she did was to glorify God. She recognized that this could only be God's doing.

As she was glorifying God, the official from the synagogue became very angry. 'Indignant because Jesus had healed on the Sabbath, the synagogue ruler said to the people, "There are six days for work. So come and be healed on those days, not on the Sabbath"' (13:14). Jesus' ministry is interrupted by an indignant official who has the presumption to rebuke the Lord of glory for carrying out his ministry on a day that God had made for the welfare of humans. He used his distorted moralism as an excuse for attacking the ministry of Jesus Christ.

Jesus rebukes him for his hypocrisy, and points out that each of them tends his ox or his ass on the Sabbath, and 'should not this woman, a daughter of Abraham, whom Satan has kept bound for eighteen long years, be set free on the Sabbath day from what bound her?' (13:16). Jesus reminds them of allowances in the law for animals to be unloosed from their burdens on the Sabbath day. This is what the Sabbath day is for, for works of mercy. Yet they complain when a human being, a daughter of Abraham, is redeemed from eighteen years of misery on the Sabbath day.

What hypocrisy from people who claim to be pious, but who put more value on their livestock than on human beings. 'When he said this, all his opponents were humiliated, but the people were delighted with all the wonderful things he was doing' (13:17). When Jesus taught or healed, the reaction was mixed. Many people were thrilled and praised God, but some became angry and indignant. This should be a lesson to all who seek to minister in the name of Christ. We will never please everyone, but we must continue to do what Christ has called us to. We must seek to be productive and bear fruit in our Christian walk. When opposition arises, we look to Christ, who understands.

67. Jesus talks about the kingdom of God
(Luke 13:18-30)

The theme of the kingdom of God is central to the teaching of Jesus. But it is a difficult theme for many people to grasp, particularly in the age in which we live. Many countries have moved to other forms of government, such as democracies, constitutional or otherwise, and to socialistic or communistic types of government, and so we have to use our imagination to understand the significance of a kingdom.

When Jesus speaks of the kingdom of God, he speaks of a place where God reigns absolutely, and that absolute rule is carried out according to justice, mercy and righteousness. And Jesus is announcing the breakthrough of the kingdom of God on earth. Here the King gives us insight into the nature of the kingdom of God in two short statements, or similes.

First he says: 'It is like a mustard seed, which a man took and planted in his garden. It grew and became a tree, and the birds of the air perched in its branches' (13:19). There is a point of similarity between the mustard seed and its growth into a tree, and the kingdom of God. Out of this tiny seed, growth begins to take place. It germinates, sprouts and eventually grows not just simply to a little bush, but into a tree that is ten to twelve feet high, with enough foliage and branches for birds to nest in. What Jesus is saying is that the kingdom of God starts small, but out of small beginnings comes exceedingly great growth, growth that produces strong and abiding fruit.

It is helpful to remember that Jesus is talking to a handful of people, whom he will commission to go into all the world to spread the gospel. How easy it would have been for the disciples of Jesus to surrender to the pressures of the multitudes. What can so few people do? But the kingdom of God has the power to grow and to enlarge into great proportions. In two thousand years of growth, the kingdom of God has spread throughout the world, and the church is established. Yet in every generation we need new mustard trees, we need new Christian missions.

Every time that we begin something new we begin small, and it is so easy to surrender to that overwhelming sense of powerlessness. But the growth capacity of the things of God is enormous.

Jesus then uses another simile to describe the kingdom of God: ' It is like yeast [leaven] that a woman took and mixed into a large amount of flour until it worked all through the dough' (13:21). Mostly, the Bible's metaphorical or figurative use of the word 'leaven' is negative. Leaven is seen as a disruptive or corrupting element, as in Jesus' warning in Luke 12:1 to guard against the leaven of the Pharisees, which is hypocrisy. Here, however, the metaphor of leaven is used in a positive way. Not many of us bake bread these days, but if you have, you will know that without yeast, or leaven, the bread will not rise. On the other hand, if you put too much yeast in the dough, the bread will rise and engulf the kitchen. It takes just a small amount of yeast to produce the necessary rising influence.

If we consider these two similitudes side by side, on the one hand we have the mustard seed that is tiny and grows to the large tree, and on the other we have the small amount of leaven that causes the bread to rise. Both are growth parables, and Jesus throws these similitudes next to each other, saying that's what the kingdom of God is like. Its power for growth and change is so strong that we ought never to despair about our own feeble efforts.

How many are in the kingdom?
Luke reminds us that Jesus is still making his journey from Galilee to Jerusalem (verse 22). As he travelled someone said to him, 'Lord, are only a few people going to be saved?' The question is one that is still debated by theologians: will only a small percentage of people who have ever lived be saved, or will the majority of people at the last enter into the kingdom of God? Jesus replied: 'Make every effort to enter through the narrow door, because many, I tell you, will try to enter and will not be able to.' We are very critical in our society of people who we consider to be narrow-minded. There is a sense in which

we are called to be broad-minded, to be tolerant, loving and kind; but at the same time, we have to remember that the gate to heaven is a narrow one, and we must strive to enter by it. The word translated 'striving' here is the Greek word from which the English word 'agony' comes. What Jesus is saying is that there must be passion, real effort in striving, not that human effort would ever get anybody into the kingdom of God, but the person who has been quickened by the Holy Spirit, who has caught a glimpse of the reality of Jesus, must make the seeking of the kingdom of God the main business of his life. This whole section of Luke's gospel underscores the urgency of getting your relationship with God settled now. There is no time to postpone it, for the kingdom of God is breaking through and there will be a time when the door will be slammed shut and it will be too late. People will say, 'Sir, open the door for us.' But he will answer, 'I don't know you or where you come from.' The quote continues: 'Then you will say, "We ate and drank with you, and you taught in our streets." But he will reply, "I don't know you or where you come from. Away from me, all you evildoers!"' (13:25-27). For the second time in Luke's gospel, we find this chilling warning. People will come and say, 'Lord, Lord,' and the Lord's response will be, 'Please leave. I don't know who you are.'

Jesus then describes the scene of the final judgment, once the doors have been shut:

> There will be weeping there, and gnashing of teeth, when you see Abraham, Isaac and Jacob and all the prophets in the kingdom of God, but you yourselves thrown out. People will come from east and west and north and south, and will take their places at the feast in the kingdom of God. Indeed there are those who are last who will be first, and first who will be last (13:28-30).

What a strange mixture of human emotions Jesus describes here. At the same time as they are wailing in grief, they will be gnashing their teeth. This latter expression is used in the Bible to depict fury. There is a close relationship between disappointment and anger. There are people who expect to be allowed into the kingdom, but when they get there, they will find that the door is locked, and that they cannot get in, no matter how loudly they cry and gnash their teeth in fury. To add to their misery, they will be able to look in and see Abraham, Isaac and the prophets on the inside.

Jesus then returns to the question, 'Are there just a few who are being saved?' and says, 'People will come from east and west and north and south, and will take their places at the feast in the kingdom of God' (13:29). To the first century Jew these words were scandalous. They thought they had a lock on the kingdom of God, but Jesus tells them that some of them will be left out and Gentiles from all over the world will be let in.

There will be many surprises as to who will be there, but also as to who will be first, and who will be last. Some of us are going to get into the kingdom of God by the skin of our teeth. Others will be given greater rewards for their use of gifts and talents in this world. But remember that God's distributing of rewards in heaven will be according to his perfect wisdom and righteousness. There are many who receive honours now, who will barely make it into the kingdom. And there are those who are completely unknown in this world, but who, with dedication and devotion, serve Christ day in and day out, and when the gates of heaven open we will see them sitting at the honoured seats at the banquet table of God.

We all should earnestly desire the kingdom of God, and strive to enter in, so that we can sit down with Abraham, Isaac, Jacob and the prophets at the banquet table of Christ. That's the promise he holds for those who love him.

68. Jesus laments over Jerusalem (Luke 13:31-35)

In verse 31, we read that Jesus was warned by some Pharisees to leave, because Herod wanted to kill him. In light of the conflict between Jesus and the Pharisees, we may surmise that their warning was a dishonest one, that perhaps they simply wanted him off their territory. It is possible, however, that some of the

Pharisees did have some genuine concern for the safety of Jesus, and they didn't want his blood on their hands.

Jesus' response is rather strange: 'Go tell that fox, "I will drive out demons and heal people today and tomorrow, and on the third day I will reach my goal."' To call somebody a fox was not to compliment them. Today, we use the term 'fox' to describe a kind of cunning or slyness that is surreptitious and not to be trusted. Similarly in the ancient world a fox was considered to be an animal without dignity or honour. And so Jesus' response is meant as an insult. But why does Jesus send this message to Herod? What is the significance of the 'third day' he talks of? It is tempting to read into this expression a cryptic allusion to the resurrection, but Jesus is not giving us a veiled prediction of the resurrection, rather he is making use of a very common Semitic expression. To reach the third day was a symbol, or a metaphor, of completion.

So in effect Jesus is telling Herod that he doesn't have the power to interrupt Jesus' ministry. When he is ready to lay down his life, he will do so. And that is the message that is despatched to Herod. It is interesting that later, after Jesus is arrested and goes on trial before Herod, Jesus refused to answer Herod's questions. So there is a sense in which Jesus doubly insulted Herod. Not only did he call him a fox, but when he was in his presence he refused to speak to him or to acknowledge his presence, which is the supreme insult to a monarch.

Jesus then turns his remarks to the Pharisees and announces: 'In any case, I must keep going today and tomorrow and the next day – for surely no prophet can die outside Jerusalem!' (13:33). This statement of Jesus has a very tragic note. He is acknowledging Herod wants to kill him, but it won't happen there in trans-Jordan. He must press on to Jerusalem, because that is the place where the prophets perished. 'It cannot be that a prophet should perish outside of Jerusalem.'

As a parenthesis, he then utters his lament of tenderness and pathos about the Holy City, saying: 'O Jerusalem, Jerusalem, you who kill the prophets and stone those sent to you, how often I have longed to gather your children together, as a hen gathers her chicks under her wings, but you were not willing!' His heart breaks as he considers the history of Jerusalem. The city that was supposed to be consecrated to the service of the kingdom of God, was the place where the prophets of the kingdom of God were slaughtered.

Following his lament for Jerusalem, he then pronounces a dreadful judgment upon the city: 'Look, your house is left to you desolate. I tell you, you will not see me again until you say, "Blessed is he who comes in the name of the Lord" ' (13:35). In Scripture the house of Jerusalem is the temple, and on more than one occasion Jesus utters specific prophecies about the destruction of Jerusalem. In fact, one of the most powerful indicators of the identity of Jesus is found in the accuracy with which Jesus' recorded predictions were fulfilled.

The rest of the prophecy Jesus utters in verse 35 is perhaps a short-term prediction. It may be that Jesus was saying, 'You are not going to see me, Jerusalem, until I enter the city on Palm Sunday, not that long away. Then the crowds will come out and sing, "Hosanna!" and say, "Blessed is he who comes in the name of the Lord!" ' Most commentators, however, do not think that is what Jesus had in view here, but rather he was speaking eschatologically of the last days, of the consummation of his kingdom, when he would return to this world in clouds of glory. And those who would be saying, 'Blessed is he who comes in the name of the Lord', would be saying it too late. At the last judgment those who have been cut off from the kingdom of God, will try to feign belief and hypocritically declare their allegiance to Jesus. It will be too late, however, for they have already resisted the call to discipleship that Jesus had given on this earth.

69. Jesus dines with the Pharisees (Luke 14:1-24)

In chapter 14, Luke continues to narrate incidents from this last journey of Jesus, and we see him here still locked in combat with the Pharisees. Luke tells us that he went into the house of one of the leading Pharisees, in order to take a meal on the Sabbath. Luke comments: 'he was being carefully watched.'

The circumstances for the invitation are not spelled out by Luke. However, it was customary to invite a visiting rabbi to the principal Sabbath meal following the service of worship in the synagogue. And so, perhaps Jesus was invited not because they were trying to be hospitable, but simply to be consistent with the custom. The language of the text suggests, however, that they were again setting a trap for Jesus. He had stirred up the Pharisees just days before by healing on the Sabbath day, and so perhaps they wanted to see what he was going to do about this growing controversy. When Jesus arrives for the meal, we read, 'There in front of him was a man suffering from dropsy.' This looks very much like a set-up job. The man who was sick from dropsy was invited to be there presumably so the Pharisees could see whether or not Jesus would repeat the offensive action of the previous Sabbath.

Jesus, however, didn't immediately set about healing the dropsical man, but rather he spoke to the lawyers and the Pharisees, asking, 'Is it lawful to heal on the Sabbath or not?' He is there to be put on trial, and instead he turns the tables on the Pharisees. Verse 4 is very telling. We read, 'But they remained silent.' Jesus had put them in an embarrassing no-win situation. If they replied positively that it is lawful to heal on the Sabbath, then they can't complain if he heals this man. If they reply negatively, however, then they look bad in front of this man who is suffering. So they kept silent. And with their silence Jesus went into action. He healed the man suffering from dropsy, and then sent him away. Sending the man away was an act of mercy on Jesus' part, for he didn't want this poor man to become the focal point of a controversy. So Jesus dismissed him and stood alone to deal with the hostility of the Pharisees.

Jesus was aware of the intricate nuances of rabbinic law and knew that it was perfectly appropriate within the oral tradition and the standards set by the Pharisees to bring relief to a suffering farm animal on the Sabbath day. And so Jesus says, 'If one of you has a son or an ox that falls into a well on the Sabbath day, will you not immediately pull him out?' The point is obvious: is the well-being of their animals of greater value to them than the welfare of this poor man? Jesus exposes the hypocrisy of these religious leaders who hid behind their rigid code of moralism and pretended to be righteous men, yet cared little for human dignity.

The law was not intended to inhibit the redemption of suffering humanity. The Son of God came to this earth, had compassion on a man who was suffering, and, having the means to heal him, he exercised that healing.

Jesus then noticed that the Pharisees 'picked the places of honour at the table', and so he used this opportunity to teach them some very heavy truths.

> 'When someone invites you to a wedding feast, do not take the place of honour, for a person more distinguished than you may have been invited. If so, the host who invited both of you will come and say to you, "Give this man your seat." Then, humiliated, you will have to take the least important place. But when you are invited, take the lowest place, so that when your host comes, he will say to you, "Friend, move up to a better place." Then you will be honoured in the presence of all your fellow guests' (14:8-10).

This parable is not to be seen as some clever political strategy for winning the highest place for ourselves. Rather Jesus' point is that honour cannot be grasped by ruthless men, and certainly it cannot be snatched from the hands of God. Not only is it futile to seek a higher position than one deserves in the kingdom of God, but the very act of ruthless presumption will add insult to your own injury when you must face the dreadful embarrassment of demotion in the kingdom of God. God may have reserved the place for someone who is far more worthy than you. So if you don't know what your place is in this roll call of honour, don't grasp for something that doesn't belong to you. Be humble, and if you are situated beneath your dignity, let the owner of the feast, God, say 'Friend, move up to a better place.'

Jesus' conclusion is this: 'For everyone who exalts himself will be humbled, and he who humbles himself will be exalted' (14:11). Honour and exaltation are very rich and meaningful human experiences. The Bible commands us to give honour to various people: the king, our elders, our parents, Christian brothers, and ultimately, and pre-eminently, of course, to give honour to God, and to his Son. God promises the exaltation of his own Son, and not only that, but he promises the people of God that they too shall participate in the exaltation of Christ. But if you seek exaltation for yourself, then you will be humiliated, for the exaltation and honour that we experience is to be given *to* us, not grasped *by* us. This was a heavy truth for the Pharisees to grasp, because they were professionals at exalting themselves.

Jesus then went on to say to the one who had invited him:

'When you give a luncheon or dinner, do not invite your friends, your brothers or relatives, or your rich neighbours; if you do, they may invite you back and so you will be repaid. But when you give a banquet, invite the poor, the crippled, the lame, the blind, and you will be blessed. Although they cannot repay you, you will be repaid at the resurrection of the righteous' (14:12-14).

Jesus is questioning the sincerity of their hospitality. They were not interested in just being friendly, rather they were scheming to advance their own goals. However, Jesus explains that if they really want a return on their investment, then when they give a reception, they should invite the poor, the crippled, the lame, and the blind. In doing so, they will be blessed, because such as these don't have the means to repay a favour. And because they can't repay a kindness, God himself will make the repayment, and his repayment will far exceed anything that the richest man in this world can give.

Somebody then speaks to Jesus using an expression that was common among the Pharisees. 'When one of those at the table with him heard this, he said to Jesus, "Blessed is the man who will eat at the feast in the kingdom of God." ' The Pharisees believed in life after death, and spoke of the future resurrection as sitting at the table in the banquet feast in heaven. And of course every Pharisee tacitly assumed that he would be numbered among the distinguished guests. But the biblical banquet feast is the banquet feast of the Lamb and the one to be honoured is the man who, right at that moment, was under attack by the Pharisees. And so, here's someone who dares to say these words to Jesus, assuming that he himself would eat of it, but also assuming that Jesus would be absent.

Jesus responds to this by telling another parable, beginning in verse 16. This time it concerned a man who was giving a big dinner and had invited many to join him. At the dinner hour he sent his slave to say to those who had been invited, 'Come, for everything is ready now.' In antiquity an invitation had to be given twice. First, the preliminary invitation was given, announcing the event and requesting the presence of those chosen. But protocol also demanded that just before the meal was served, a second announcement was to come by messenger. If a person accepted the first invitation, but, when the second invitation was given, then declined, this was considered to be a grave insult. Grave enough to be grounds for waging war.

Jesus' story is to do with people's response to this second invitation. All alike began to make excuses. 'The first said, "I have just bought a field, and I must go and see it. Please excuse me." Another said, "I have just bought five yoke of oxen, and I'm on my way to try them out. Please excuse me." Still another said, "I just got married, so I can't come" ' (14:18-20). Jesus chooses the flimsiest excuses that people can think of. Imagine somebody declining an invitation to this great feast because he has just bought a piece of land and needs to look at it. The first question that springs to mind is why didn't this person look at it before he bought it? The second excuse is similar: he has bought five yoke of oxen, and needs to try them out. What farmer would buy five yoke of oxen without trying them out first?

When the slave in Jesus' story reported all these excuses to his master, he became angry and said to his slave, 'Go out quickly into the streets and alleys of the town and bring in the poor, the crippled, the blind and the lame.' 'Sir,' the servant said, 'what you ordered has been done, but there is still room.' Then the master told his servant, 'Go out to the roads and country lanes and make them come in, so that my house will be full. I tell you, not one of those men who were invited will get a taste of my banquet' (14:21-24).

Jesus isn't just talking about oriental protocol or about invitations to feasts. He is talking to the leaders of the Jewish nation, who have just rejected him. God had been pleading with Israel for centuries. The first invitation had gone out years previously to enter into the feast of heaven. And now the servant of God, God's Son himself, comes with that second invitation to say that the feast is ready and it is time to attend. But the response of the Pharisees was to make flimsy excuses as to why they could not embrace the kingdom of God. They rejected the invitation of the Son of God to come to the banquet feast. Jesus warns them that God is angry, that he is going to bring destruction upon Jerusalem and the Jewish nation, and instead he is going to turn to the Gentiles. He is going out to the highways and the byways to bring those people into the kingdom of God, who at this point are no-people. This is what the prophet Hosea predicted: those who were not God's people would be called his people. Gentiles were invited to the kingdom of God only after those who were kinsmen according to the flesh of Israel refused the invitation. Gentiles were not children of Abraham, they were strangers to the kingdom of God. But then God found them in their blindness, crippledness and lameness, and invited them to come to his feast. Those to whom the invitation was originally given are shut out. Jesus gives this sober warning to that presumptuous Pharisee who glibly assumed he had a seat reserved in heaven.

No wonder the Pharisees plotted Jesus' death. No wonder he was killed. He had just told them, face to face, that they were not going to make it to the banquet feast. Not only would they not be in the highest seats, but they would not be at the feast at all, because they had rejected the second invitation; the invitation that was given by the Son of God himself.

Where are you with respect to the banquet feast in heaven? You have heard the invitation: what's the excuse that you give to stay away from the table of God?

70. The cost of being a disciple (Luke 14:25-35)

It is hardly conceivable that Jesus, who is so identified with the message of love, would advocate a kind of hate relationship to one's closest family. So these next words recorded by Luke strike us with surprising force:

> 'Large crowds were travelling with Jesus, and turning to them he said: "If anyone comes to me and does not hate his father and mother, his wife and children, his brothers and sisters – yes, even his own life – he cannot be my disciple" ' (14:25-26).

We must remember however that Jesus was an oriental teacher, and used figures of speech in order to communicate emphasis. On more than one occasion, he made use of hyperbole, that literary form that we identify as an intentional exaggeration in order to communicate a crucial point. Jesus here is not advocating a posture of antithesis or hatred, but is saying that if one is going to follow him and be his disciple, that in comparison to the love and devotion that one must have for Christ, the love for our parents or our dearest friends could be seen, hyper-bolically at least, as hate. Jesus' popular ministry had provoked a vast crowd of followers, many of whom were just along for an exciting ride. They clearly did not understand what the ministry of Jesus was about, nor what it meant to dedicate yourself to following after him.

Jesus clarifies his statement in verse 27 where he says, 'And anyone who does not carry his cross and follow me cannot be my disciple.' Now we sometimes turn this into a figure of speech and think that a Christian's cross has to do with the burdens of daily life. But Jesus is not talking about a general participation in suffering, or in bearing the problems and anxieties of daily experience. Instead he is making a clear reference to martyrdom. Unless people were prepared to become martyrs they couldn't be his disciples.

And he amplifies this teaching with some similitudes.

'Suppose one of you wants to build a tower. Will he not first sit down and estimate the cost to see if he has enough money to complete it? For if he lays the foundation and is not able to finish it, everyone who sees it will ridicule him, saying, "This fellow began to build and was not able to finish."

'Or suppose a king is about to go to war against another king. Will he not first sit down and consider whether he is able with ten thousand men to oppose the one coming against him with twenty thousand? If he is not able, he will send a delegation while the other is still a long way off and will ask for terms of peace. In the same way, any of you who does not give up everything he has cannot be my disciple.

'Salt is good, but if it loses its saltiness, how can it be made salty again? It is fit neither for the soil nor for the manure pile; it is thrown out.

'He who has ears to hear, let him hear' (14:28-35).

Jesus is saying that to be his disciple means to participate in his death and humiliation. He warned on other occasions that we would be hated in this world, and that those who were serious about Christ would face daily trials. He had no time for superficial professions of faith. How important it is for us to understand the warning of Jesus, for often we are so eager to increase our memberships that we do everything in our power to make a commitment to Christianity as painless as possible. We become peddlers of cheap grace, obscuring and hiding the message of Jesus which was a call to sacrifice, to steadfast devotion, even to the point of martyrdom.

Jesus was not in a hurry to add numbers to his evangelistic campaign by oversimplifying the demands of discipleship. His message here is very simple: 'If you want to follow me, before you make loud professions of faith and declare your conversion to the world, you had better first count the cost. You must be prepared, if necessary, to be alienated from your household.' And he tells the story of the embarrassment that is suffered by the man who impulsively sets out to build a tower without first sitting down and estimating the cost. If you have started to build the kingdom of God you must count the cost to see whether you are able to finish what you started. The good news to the Christian is that God promises that he is not like the builder who hastily begins a project only to abandon it midway. We are told that having begun a good work in us, he will bring it to completion (Phil. 1:6). We are also told that we are the craftsmanship of God (Eph. 2:10). So

> I am reminded of the words of Dietrich Bonhoffer, the German Christian who was imprisoned for his outspoken ethical criticisms of the Third Reich, and was finally executed. In one of his books he expresses his profound concern over the theology of 'cheap grace' that pervades the Christian world. It is an imitation Christianity that is summed up by the phrase 'rice Christians', which goes back to the early days on the mission field when people professing to be Christian would be given an extra bowl of rice. The implication of the phrase is that their Christian faith was only as strong as the benefits they received from it. When pressure or persecution came, people renounced their faith.

if God has begun to work in you, you can be sure that he will bring that project to completion.

Jesus reinforces his point by another similitude, this time of the king who is about to go to war with another king. Most leaders in this situation would examine the information from military intelligence and take counsel whether his army is strong enough for the encounter. If not, then he may send a delegation and sue for peace. Judicious leaders and wise military generals are careful to count the cost. And we are asked to count the cost.

No-one can be a disciple of Christ who does not give up all his possessions. Now obviously Jesus is not speaking literally here, although some have understood it that way. Jesus rather is talking about abandoning one's dependence on the things of this world and resolutely placing one's future in the hands of Christ.

Jesus then adds: 'Salt is good, but if it loses its saltiness, how can it be made salty again? It is fit neither for the soil nor for the manure pile; it is thrown out. He who has ears to hear, let him hear.' References to salt in Jesus' teaching are fairly numerous. Salt not only adds taste and pungency to food, but primarily it was used as a preservative to keep food from spoiling.

But the salt of antiquity was inferior to the salt today. It was capable of losing its saltiness and its power of preservation, thus becoming useless, not even fit for the soil or the manure heap. These are strange references to us, but they point to additional uses for salt in the ancient world. Sometimes salt was added to dung piles to increase the value of the manure pile as fertiliser. However, salt was also used to destroy the nutritional level of soil, and sometimes heavy dosages of salt were spread secretly upon the enemy's fields to spoil their soil, so that crops could not be cultivated and their armies could not be fed.

Again, Jesus ends with a military reference, talking about the need for Christians to have the kind of commitment and devotion that lasts over the long haul. The authentic discipleship that Jesus is looking for, is a reckless abandonment in personal commitment that some would regard as fanaticism. The difference, however, between Christian discipleship and fanaticism is at the point of sobriety. Jesus calls people to a sober commitment that is based upon a clear perception of what lies ahead. He asks people to consider strongly what it means to be a Christian. It means taking up your cross for the long haul. He did it for us, and he requires it from us.

71: The parables of the lost sheep, the lost coin, and the lost son (Luke 15:1-19)

At the beginning of Luke 15, we read: 'Now the tax collectors and "sinners" were all gathering around to hear him. But the Pharisees and the teachers of the law muttered, "This man welcomes sinners and eats with them." ' Three of the most important parables of Jesus were told by him in response to these words. But before we can have a full understanding of these parables we have to look at their context.

What had happened was that the religious leaders had reacted against Jesus' practice of mixing with tax collectors and sinners. Keep in mind that the Pharisees were separatist, and advocated a doctrine of salvation through segregation. And so, Jesus' behaviour scandalised them.

Luke's aim, of course, is to drive home the point that the gospel of Christ is for the Gentiles as well as for the Jews; that it is for everyone. And so we see Luke reacting strongly to this doctrine of salvation by separation and segregation that was utterly contrary to the teaching of God in the Old Testament.

Parable of the lost sheep (Luke 15:3-7)
Jesus tells, in response to this criticism of him, a parable:

> Suppose one of you has a hundred sheep and loses one of them. Does he not leave the ninety-nine in the open country and go after the lost sheep until he finds it? And when he finds it, he joyfully puts it on his shoulders and goes home. Then he calls his friends and neighbours together and says, 'Rejoice with me; I have found my lost sheep.'

This theme is not an uncommon one in the teaching of Jesus. He went out into the world into the marketplace, to the dregs of society, searching for the lost.

Through this parable he challenges the Pharisees to rethink their values. None would think twice about moving heaven and earth to find a lost sheep, yet they object when Jesus goes searching for lost people. He said, ' I tell you that in the same way there will be more rejoicing in heaven over one sinner who repents than over ninety-nine righteous persons who do not need to repent.' When a lost sinner is found there is a party in heaven. The angels of God rejoice; the heavenly host celebrates that a human being has been redeemed.

The parable of the lost coin (Luke 15:8-10)
Jesus then tells another parable:

> Or suppose a woman has ten silver coins and loses one. Does she not light a lamp, sweep the house and search carefully until she finds it? And when she finds it, she calls her friends and neighbours together and says, 'Rejoice with me; I have found my lost coin.' In the same way, I tell you, there is rejoicing in the presence of the angels of God over one sinner who repents.

This story is not about silver coins, however, it is about people. How far do we have to look in order to find people who are lost? They are all around us. There are millions of people in this world who know nothing of Jesus Christ. And yet the Lord of the church has commanded us to go into all the world. Some have yet to go into all of their communities, because they have fallen for the lie that evangelism is no longer necessary. In fact, not only is it not necessary, it is a negative social activity; some adopt the viewpoint that no-one has the right to seek to proselytize other people to their religious viewpoint. If that is true, then Jesus Christ was the chief violator of human rights because he made that kind of activity the central business of his life and he commanded his people to do the same.

When God commands us to preach the gospel and we refuse to do it, or demean the vocation, we are being arrogant to the extreme. To deny the validity of evangelism, as some within the Christian church do, is treason. It is the mandate of Christ and it is the example of Christ to seek and to save the lost. For when even one is redeemed, the angels rejoice.

The parable of the lost son (Luke 15:11-19)

'There was a man who had two sons. The younger one said to his father, "Father, give me my share of the estate." So he divided his property between them.' This was an unusual request by the younger son, but not altogether unheard of in the ancient world. Normally, sons would inherit their father's estate upon his death, but there was a provision in the ancient Jewish law for a son to request the gift of his inheritance during his father's lifetime. He did not have the authority to dispose of that property, but was entitled to the income from it.

The Deuteronomic laws also had certain instructions regarding inheritance. Deuteronomy 21 required that the elder son receive twice as much as the rest of the sons. Since there were only two sons in this story, the younger son would receive a third of the total property of the father. The father grants his request and turns over a third of the estate to this adolescent boy. Not only does the young man ask for his future inheritance prematurely, but on receiving it, we read in verse 13 that he took his portion and went off with it to a far country. Perhaps it was a sense of wanderlust that prompted this action. Sometimes, we like to travel to distant places where we know no-one, and where no-one knows us, where we can do whatever we please, without fear of being recognized or caught. At this point, the resemblance becomes apparent between this parable and the other two that Jesus had spoken of, particularly with the parable of the lost sheep. Both the younger son and the sheep wandered off and became lost in a far country. And there, we are told the young man wasted his substance. In a very short period of time all that was given him by the father was utterly wasted on riotous living. The details are not given, but we know how easy it is for people to spend a fortune when they are caught up in the revelry of a wild and undisciplined style of life. So this young man's inheritance slipped through his fingers like quicksilver, and suddenly it was gone.

In verse 14, we learn that a mighty famine that afflicted the whole countryside came at the same time as this man's fortune ran out. In order to survive he was driven by his need to take employment wherever he could find it. And so Jesus continues the story: 'So he went and hired himself out to a citizen of that country, who sent him to his fields to feed pigs.' Jesus makes it clear that the man descended to the dregs of society. In the rabbinic laws that governed employment, the occupation of swine-herder was considered so debased that anyone working with swine was seen as being cursed. His work brought the prodigal into daily contact with animals that the Old Testament had declared to be unclean, which meant that under Jewish law he would not be permitted to observe the Sabbath day, because he himself was unclean. He was forced for all practical purposes to renounce his Judaism. His life was at the lowest point of dereliction a Jew could reach. In fact we read in verse 16, that 'he longed to fill his stomach with the pods that the pigs were eating, but no-one gave him anything'.

The story takes a dramatic turn, however. 'When he came to his senses, he said, "How many of my father's hired men have food to spare, and here I am starving to death!" ' Notice that Jesus doesn't say, 'when he came to the end of his resources', or 'when he came to the city limits', but, 'When he came to his senses'. Jesus was aware that there are people who are lost, not only in terms of the kingdom of God, but in personal terms: they don't even know themselves. A person can get so caught up in a kind of activity that he doesn't even know who he is any more.

One of the greatest abilities we have as humans is the ability to deceive ourselves, to rationalize, to make up excuses. Some of us continue to delude ourselves, postponing that painful moment of honest self-evaluation. But this young man woke up to the reality of what he was doing. That awakening is, of course, the most critical point in his life.

He came to himself and asked, 'What am I doing? Even my father's servants have bread enough to eat, yet here am I perishing with hunger.' So he decided to return to his father. 'I will set out and go back to my father and say to him: Father, I have sinned against heaven and against you.' Here we have the essence of conversion. That moment in a human being's life when they come to themselves and realise that they have sinned. Not that they have made a mistake, or been guilty of error in judgment, but that they have sinned. In true repentance, contrition breaks through. The illusions are shattered, the games are over, and the man said, 'I will go and tell the truth.'

The prodigal is going to go home to tell his father what he did. Remember he had gone to a far country, to escape the eye of his father, to do those things that he knew his father would never approve of. In the beginning, when he was having a good time, he said, 'I am glad my father can't see me! He wouldn't understand!' But now, in his brokenness, he resolved to go to his father to confess that he has sinned against him, and isn't worthy to be called his son.

Before this man could ever go to his father, he first had to come to himself. And if you are lost yourself, it is time to take stock, and it is time to get up and go to your father's house.

72. The father's welcome (Luke 15:20-32)

The young man decided to go back to his father. Think for a moment how you would feel if you were in this young man's shoes. Not that long ago you had left the security of your family. You had badgered your father to give you your inheritance in advance. Your father advised against it, but you persisted, and he finally gave in. And here you are, penniless, filthy, coming back to tell your father what you have done

We might expect the young man to time his homecoming so that the household would be asleep. That way he could creep in under cover of darkness. But this man is in a state of total brokenness; considerations like these are not in his mind. He has suffered the laughter of the swineherders and those who had exploited him and taken his money. He has no shame left, and so he returns in the brightness of the day.

'But,' says the text, 'while he was still a long way off, his father saw him.' That in itself is an astonishing part of the story.

Imagine the anxiety of that father as he went to work every day in the fields. Imagine how much time he spent peering into the distance, hoping for a glimpse of his son returning home. There had been no messages, no news, of how his boy was faring.

We are living in an age where much distress has been caused by the children who have rebelled against their family. In many cases they have run away. And one of the most difficult things for a parent to do, is to allow a child to go. But this father had paid that price and allowed the boy to leave the house; however, he had not left his heart. He was always on the look out for him, which is why he saw him when he was still a long way off. How did he recognize him? His appearance doubtless would be very different to when he left, but something in the movement of this figure in the distance told the father this was his boy coming home.

The father didn't sit down and plan what he would say to his son, he didn't rehearse a rebuke or practise an air of casual detachment. No, as soon as he saw his son, he felt compassion for him, and ran and embraced him. In the ancient world a man of his social stature would wear great robes and be careful to follow the customs and protocol of the time. So to see such a man as he was running down the dusty roads, with his robes girded at the waist, was unthinkable. But he didn't care who saw him, he just wanted to get to his son. And when he does, he falls upon his neck and kisses him. In the Orient, to kiss someone in this way is not merely a sign of affection, or recognition, but is also a sign of forgiveness.

The boy had planned his confession speech, but before he even had a chance to open his mouth, his father had already fallen upon his neck and kissed him. He was forgiven before he uttered a word. The father didn't need to hear the words; he could see the brokenness of his son, and his heart was moved to compassion, and he showed that compassion with a kiss. And then the son spoke: 'Father, I have sinned against heaven and against you. I am no longer worthy to be called your son' (15:21). The young man confessed that not only had he disgraced himself, but he had brought shame on his father's house, and didn't deserve to be called his son any more.

The father doesn't answer the son immediately, but instead issues some commands to his servants: 'Quick! Bring the best robe and put it on him. Put a ring on his finger and sandals on his feet.' Now it may seem that the father is making a comment here about his son's dishevelled state, but that's not what is going on. Each one of the items that the father commands be given to the son has special significance.

First of all, there is the best robe. In the ancient Near East the ceremonial robe, the best robe, was a mark of honour. When a king sought to give honour to a visiting dignitary, he would present him with a costly robe. So the father's command carried this implication: Treat this son of mine as the guest of honour in my house.

Then there is the ring, obviously a signet ring. When it was given from father to son, or from king to prime minister, it signified the granting, or the transfer, of authority. The young man says he isn't worthy to be called a son, all he asks is to be made a servant, a person of no authority. But the father, by calling for a ring to be placed on his finger, is restoring to him the authority of sonship in his father's house.

And then the third command to put sandals on his feet. Shoes or sandals were a luxury. They were worn by free men, never worn by slaves. The young son had appeared at his father's house in bare feet, looking like a slave, but the father ordered that shoes be put on his feet.

After these instructions to do with his son's attire, the father then gives the command: 'Bring the fattened calf and kill it. Let's have a feast and celebrate' (15:23). Now meat was rarely eaten, and so to take the fatted calf was a sign that this was an extremely special occasion, a time of feasting for the family and the servants, in honour of the return of the lost son to the family table.

Suddenly a discordant note sounds:

'Meanwhile, the older son was in the field. When he came near the house, he heard music and dancing. So he called one of the servants and asked him what was going on. "Your brother has come," he replied, "and your father has killed the fattened calf because he has him back safe and sound."

'The older brother became angry and refused to go in. So his father went out and pleaded with him. But he answered his father, "Look! All these years I've been slaving for you and never disobeyed your orders. Yet you never gave me even a young goat so I could celebrate with my friends. But when this son of yours who has squandered your property with prostitutes comes home, you kill the fattened calf for him!" ' (15:25-30).

He just could not understand his father's delight at the return of this son who had wasted all his money.

But the father answered: 'My son, you are always with me, and everything I have is yours. But we had to celebrate and be glad, because this brother of yours was dead and is alive again; he was lost and is found' (15:31-32). His brother, whom they had given up for dead, had returned to them, but, instead of being filled with joy, he was consumed with jealousy.

Now this rebuke, of course, is meant for the ears of the Pharisees, who were disgusted by the fact that Jesus was seeking the lost and eating with sinners. They felt no compassion for the lost, in fact, they were disgusted by them, and even when one was converted they didn't want that new convert in their company.

Every Christian has lived this wonderful story of the prodigal son in one way or another. The essence of conversion is the experience of forgiveness, the experience of the grace of God. The great tragedy is that there are so many people still wandering in a far country, afraid to come home. But our God is like this father, who, when he sees us in the distance, runs towards us, and falls upon our necks and hugs us and kisses us. He doesn't make us go over all the lurid details of our lostness and wastefulness, but he welcomes us into his family and forgives us. That's grace. No-one will ever get into the Father's house

by pleading their own worthiness. Only those who acknowledge
their unworthiness will get there.

73. The parable of the unjust steward
(Luke 16:1-18)

Jesus told another parable to his disciples. It begins: 'There
was a rich man whose manager was accused of wasting his
possessions.' Right at the beginning certain similarities are
noticeable between this parable and that of the prodigal son.
The prodigal son had wasted the inheritance that he had claimed
from his father, and in this parable we read of another man, a
steward, who wasted his employer's property,

The point of this parable is not to give us a lesson in
stewardship, but it does serve to remind us that every human
being is a steward on this earth. God owns the world. He owns
us, and what we do with our lives, our money and the earth are
matters of stewardship. We have an indication here of divine
displeasure when stewards waste the goods in their trust. The
main point, however, becomes clear as we read on: 'So he called
him in and asked him, "What is this I hear about you? Give an
account of your management, because you cannot be manager
any longer." ' What the owner does, in effect, is to call for an
audit. 'I want to see the books; you are finished as a steward.'
Before releasing the steward he wants to know exactly what
the balance sheet shows. The steward, who is in big trouble,
'said to himself, "What shall I do now? My master is taking
away my job. I'm not strong enough to dig, and I'm ashamed to
beg" ' (16:3). He was not an accomplished craftsman, and so
was not easily employable. What was he to do?

What happens next shows the extent of his dishonesty and
deceitfulness. He says: 'I know what I'll do so that, when I lose
my job here, people will welcome me into their houses.' And
he summoned each one of his master's debtors, and said to the
first, 'How much do you owe my master?' 'Eight hundred
gallons of olive oil,' he replied. The manager told him, 'Take

your bill, sit down quickly, and make it four hundred.' Then he asked the second, 'And how much do you owe?' 'A thousand bushels of wheat,' he replied. He told him, 'Take your bill and make it eight hundred' (16:4-7). This unscrupulous steward changes the accounts of all of those who owe his master money. Now that is not going to endear him to his master, but it does endear him to the debtors.

So he called every one of his master's debtors to him and told them to change their bills, and we read: 'The master commended the dishonest manager because he had acted shrewdly. For the people of this world are more shrewd in dealing with their own kind than are the people of the light' (16:8). By implication, Jesus himself commends the unjust steward for his action, not that he is putting his blessing upon this kind of deceitfulness, but acknowledges that at least this man had the good sense to look out for his future.

Again, Jesus says to his disciples, 'I tell you, use worldly wealth to gain friends for yourselves, so that when it is gone, you will be welcomed into eternal dwellings.' You had better stick together because the friendships that you develop of unrighteous men will be laughing, but that's not good news, but bad news. But again the steward's owner commended his steward at least for having some kind of business sense as unscrupulous as it was.

Jesus then says: 'Whoever can be trusted with very little can also be trusted with much, and whoever is dishonest with very little will also be dishonest with much. So if you have not been trustworthy in handling worldly wealth, who will trust you with true riches?' (16:10-11). Although these words were obviously aimed at the Pharisees, there is also a broader application. What God is looking for from his people is not success, but fidelity. He doesn't measure us by our bank balance or the degree of our authority. Maybe your task seems insignificant, but God has given it to you and wants to see that you are faithful in it, before he will promote you in his kingdom.

The one who can be trusted with the little things can also be trusted with the big things. But the converse is also true; Jesus said: 'So if you have not been trustworthy in handling worldly wealth, who will trust you with true riches?' If you are a bad steward of material things, don't expect God to trust you with spiritual things. 'And if you have not been trustworthy with someone else's property, who will give you property of your own?' If you can't be trusted with somebody else's property, don't expect God to trust you with great property of your own.

'No servant,' said Jesus, 'can serve two masters. Either he will hate the one and love the other, or he will be devoted to the one and despise the other. You cannot serve both God and Money' (16:13). Where is your heart? What are you serving? It is impossible for a slave to serve two masters, because the desires of the two masters are not always the same. If you are going to be a faithful servant to Christ, he must be your supreme Lord. You cannot try to serve him and at the same time try to serve the forces of this world.

Luke's narrative continues: 'The Pharisees, who loved money, heard all this and were sneering at Jesus' (16:14). But Jesus responded, 'You are the ones who justify yourselves in the eyes of men, but God knows your hearts. What is highly valued among men is detestable in God's sight.' The Pharisees thought that because they had power, wealth and authority in the community, they could use their success to justify their sinful lifestyle. People were willing to be blinded to the evils of the Pharisees, but Jesus reminded them that God knows the heart. He reminds them that we live in a topsy-turvy world, where those things that are highly esteemed among men, are detestable in the sight of God. Power and success, if achieved at the expense of human beings, by the exploitation of the weak and poor, are despicable to God.

Then Jesus said, 'The Law and the Prophets were proclaimed until John. Since that time (that is, since John's appearance) the good news of the kingdom of God is being preached, and everyone is forcing his way into it.' This parallels statements that are made elsewhere in the gospels where Jesus talks about those who take the kingdom of God by force. In other words, what he is saying to the Pharisees is this: in the old days the law and the prophets predicted in a nebulous way the coming of the kingdom of God. But the coming of John signalled a new dimension of urgency. The kingdom of God has broken through, the gates are open, and people are pressing into it, but the Pharisees, who are supposed to be the leaders of righteousness, stand outside the gates and resist it.

'It is easier for heaven and earth to disappear than for the least stroke of a pen to drop out of the Law. Anyone who divorces his wife and marries another woman commits adultery, and the man who marries a divorced woman commits adultery' (16:17-18). This is not Jesus' fullest teaching on marriage and divorce. His intention here is to remind the Pharisees of the importance of the law. These men, who claimed to be pillars of the Old Testament law, were violating that law every day, and nowhere more noticeably than in their utter disregard for Old Testament legislation about marriage. They were quick to grant divorces. Why? Because that is what the people wanted. These men were more concerned to receive the applause of the people than to receive the blessing of God.

Think again of the parable of the unjust steward. The Pharisees were stewards of the law, but they wasted it by reinterpreting it and so compromised it. Although they were highly esteemed by the people, in God's sight they were an abomination.

God looks on the heart and he expects his people to be responsible, just and righteous stewards of the riches and privileges that he has given to them. We must listen to the warnings that Christ gave to the Pharisees, for we know that no-one can ever justify himself in the sight of God. But we are called to be faithful in little and faithful in much, so that the Lord of the house will grant us his everlasting blessing.

74. The rich man and Lazarus (Luke 16:19-31)

In this section we come to another well-known parable of Jesus. He describes a rich man who was clothed in purple. The colour of his clothes is significant, for purple was the most highly esteemed dye of all. It was the colour of kings. This rich man, who was clothed in purple and fine linen, lived in splendour every day. So the picture that Jesus paints is one of a man who is enormously wealthy.

Immediately, however, he is contrasted with another individual, a poor man called Lazarus, who was laid at his gate and covered in sores. We don't know the exact nature of these sores, but presumably they were open wounds that oozed. The man was miserable, he couldn't work and was reduced to begging. Every day he was laid at the gate of the rich man, and we read that he was 'longing to eat what fell from the rich man's table' (verse 21). He had no means of employment, and so he lived off the left-overs of this fabulously wealthy man.

Then Luke writes: 'Even the dogs came and licked his sores.' Now we could take this picture of the dogs licking his sores in two different ways. On the one hand it could be seen as reflecting the depths of his misery and wretchedness, but on the other hand, it is possible that Jesus wanted to show that the only creatures concerned to alleviate the suffering of this wretched beggar were the dogs. Obviously the rich man was not providing ointment for Lazarus' sores; his only ministrations came from the dogs.

'The time came when the beggar died and the angels carried him to Abraham's side' (16:22a). Notice that Jesus says nothing about the burial of the beggar, and some have taken this to mean he was translated directly into heaven, like Enoch, because of the reference to angels carrying him into the bosom of Abraham. It is more likely, however, that Jesus doesn't mention Lazarus' burial because, being a beggar, his body would have been dumped unceremoniously in an unmarked grave. The phrase, the bosom of Abraham, was a common one to the Jew. It was a metaphor for heaven, because Abraham was the father of the faithful, the one with whom God had made his everlasting covenant. To be close to Abraham, to be nestled on Abraham's bosom, is to be in the very presence of heaven. Lazarus was not justified by poverty as some believe. He was obviously a man of God who accepted his suffering without bitterness, complaint or hostility. He was a godly man who had been faithful in little things. Now he is carried by the angels to the bosom of Abraham.

'The rich man also died and was buried. In hell, where he was in torment, he looked up and saw Abraham far away, with Lazarus by his side.' He shut his eyes in death and opened them again in torment, and part of his torment was that he saw Abraham afar off. Now when Lazarus opened his eyes, he saw Abraham too, but he had to adjust his eyes to see him because he was so close to him, being nestled on his bosom. The rich man, however, saw Abraham from a great distance, remote and far removed. Not only did he see Abraham, but there in Abraham's bosom he saw the same person that he had seen every day when he walked out his gates. No doubt when he left the opulence of his palace, he would turn his eyes aside, not wanting to look at that miserable beggar. Now here he is waking up in Hades, and there in the distance he sees Abraham with Lazarus. So the rich man called to Abraham, one whom he would obviously regard as a peer, 'Father Abraham, have pity on me and send Lazarus to dip the tip of his finger in water and cool my tongue, because I am in agony in this fire' (16:24). Talk about wretchedness! This wealthy man was not asking to have restored to him his palace and power. He was asking only that the miserable beggar, Lazarus, would dip his finger in water, and just touch the tip of his tongue. He was in such torment that he would have given everything or done anything he could, just to be at the gates of his own house, having dogs lick his wounds.

'But Abraham replied, "Son, remember that in your lifetime you received your good things, while Lazarus received bad things, but now he is comforted here and you are in agony" ' (16:25). Our topsy-turvy world has been set aright. 'You had your chance,' Abraham said to the rich man, 'and you had no

compassion or mercy, so how can you cry for mercy now?'
The rich man could have had compassion on Lazarus, but he
wouldn't. Now this man who was the prince has become the
beggar. He is begging Abraham to send Lazarus, but Abraham
says he can't for 'between us and you a great chasm has been
fixed, so that those who want to go from here to you cannot,
nor can anyone cross over from there to us' (16:26). In effect
Abraham is saying that it is too late. This is the situation of
ultimate separation. Not only is there a great, unbridgeable
chasm, but it is fixed. Nothing can change it.

So, the rich man, realizing there is no hope for himself, makes
another request. He begs Abraham to send Lazarus back to earth
to warn his brothers of this terrible place of torment. But
Abraham said to him, 'They have Moses and the prophets, let
them listen to them.' The implication is that they had the same
messengers that Lazarus had; and Lazarus had heard Moses,
Lazarus had listened to the prophets. Now Lazarus is in heaven.
Abraham questions why the man's brothers needed a special
messenger to warn them of this place. God had provided a wealth
of information. He had spoken through Moses, Isaiah, Jeremiah,
Amos, Micah, Joel, Nahum, and all the prophets, and the
message had been substantially the same. Mankind has been
warned about these things for centuries.

But the rich man thought there had to be another, better way
to warn them. They're not going to believe Moses or the
prophets: they lived too long ago. But if somebody went back
from the dead, somebody they recognize, somebody like
Lazarus, and tells them what it's like, then they will repent. But
Abraham's response is, 'If they do not listen to Moses and the
Prophets, they will not be convinced even if someone rises from
the dead' (16:31).

The prevailing idea in our society is that entrance into heaven
comes automatically with death. We like to believe in heaven;
we hate to think of hell. But now is the time to think about it. If
we will not believe Moses, and we will not believe the prophets,
and we will not believe Jesus who has come down from heaven,

what will persuade us? What will prepare us for that moment
when we will be placed on one side of that gulf or the other?
My prayer is that you will press into the kingdom of God, now,
before it is too late.

75. Jesus instructs his disciples (Luke 17:1-10)

Chapter 17 comprises a series of very short sayings, sometimes
described as aphorisms, little vignettes of wisdom or admonition.
Some scholars believe that Luke brought together some of the
more poignant sayings of Jesus, with no particular desire for
coherency. That is one possibility, but I am not convinced. These
sayings do seem to hang together and may have been given to
the disciples following Jesus' debate with the Pharisees.

Sin and forgiveness (Luke 17:1-4)

'Jesus said to his disciples: "Things that cause people to sin are
bound to come, but woe to that person through whom they come.
It would be better for him to be thrown into the sea with a
millstone tied round his neck than for him to cause one of these
little ones to sin" ' (17:1-2). It is sobering to contemplate the
words of Jesus. They contain an awesome warning, a warning
to professors, to teachers, to pastors, that God will hold them
responsible for what they teach. James tells us that not many
ought to become teachers, for with teaching comes the greater
judgment (Jas. 3:1). Teachers are responsible for what they teach
and Jesus pronounces the prophetic oracle of doom on any who
cause his little ones to stumble.

In verses 3-4, Jesus gives another warning: 'So watch yourselves. If your brother sins, rebuke him, and if he repents, forgive
him. If he sins against you seven times in a day, and seven times
comes back to you and says, "I repent," forgive him.' The New
Testament has much to say about forgiveness, but often we can
be very confused in our thinking on this subject. This passage
is a mini-lesson on forgiveness and has much to teach us.

The appropriate response if a brother sins against you is to
forgive him. Peter tells us that there is a love which covers a

multitude of sins (1 Peter 4:8). We are not to keep accounts of people's minor indiscretions, but if somebody seriously violates us, we are called to bring that to the person's attention. People's words or actions can injure us severely, and they may not be aware of it, but they should want to know the effect they have had on us. So we are told to rebuke our brother, if he trespasses against us.

Jesus, however, is quick to add that if the erring brother repents, then he is to be forgiven. But what if he doesn't repent? Are you then under obligation to forgive him? Christians sometimes think that they are required to forgive all people, whether they repent or not. But I cannot find that teaching in the New Testament. There are places where Jesus and others convey that kind of forgiveness before there is repentance; for example when Jesus pleads with his Father from the cross to forgive those who have crucified him; or when Stephen cried out to God in the midst of his execution, 'Lay not this sin to their charge.' We are permitted to grant forgiveness where repentance is not present, but forgiveness is not automatically required. The Bible makes provision for disciplinary action to be taken within a church, or to take one's case before the civil magistrate. Similarly if somebody steals your property and refuses to repent, within the context of the biblical ethic it is permissible to involve the law to seek restitution.

All this may sound shocking or surprising, for forgiveness is so central to the New Testament, but notice that Jesus said that it was when the person repented that he was to be forgiven. But if repentance is there, we don't have an option – we must forgive.

But how do we know whether the repentance is genuine? It is easy to say we are sorry, and Jesus obviously has that in view because he said, 'If he sins against you seven times in a day, and seven times comes back to you and says, "I repent," forgive him.' If a person says he is sorry, even if he is insincere, we are required to forgive him. If his apology is not genuine, that is for God to deal with, but our duty is to forgive.

Where there is no repentance we don't *have* to forgive; but where there is repentance we *must* forgive. But if we are going to understand what this text is getting at, we have to ask what it means to forgive someone? Forgiveness in biblical terms means to hold a sin against a person no more. We are called to forgive and forget, because that is how God deals with us. The Bible teaches that when God forgives us, he casts our sins into the sea of forgetfulness and remembers them no more. It would be absurd to interpret this to mean that the omniscient God suddenly suffers from amnesia, and can no longer recall that we had transgressed his law. God does not forget in that sense, but in a legal sense he forgets. He never brings charges against us again. Authentic forgiveness means that if I say to you, 'I forgive you', I can never hold that against you again, nor mention it again to you or to anyone else. Now that is not so much an attitude of the heart as a pattern of behaviour. We are not to keep a record of past offences. That is one of the hardest things in the world to do. What Jesus is saying is, if a person sins against you, seven times in one day, but each time turns and says, 'I am sorry', you must forgive him.

Faith (Luke 17:5-6)

Jesus' lesson on moral behaviour is exceedingly difficult to implement. Few of us have the ability to forgive to this degree. The disciples knew that themselves, as their response indicates. 'Increase our faith!' they said to Jesus. They knew they would only be able to do what Jesus asked if he increased their faith. And Jesus said, 'If you have faith as small as a mustard seed, you can say to this mulberry tree, "Be uprooted and planted in the sea," and it will obey you.'

Jesus is telling them that they have enough faith already to implement this. He is not asking them to command trees to be uprooted and planted in the middle of the sea, although if they had just a tiny amount of real faith they could do that. What he asked of them may well be difficult, but it is not as difficult as moving trees. The slightest bit of faith is all that is required to forgive people, because if we understand anything about

Christianity, we should understand forgiveness, because we are by definition forgiven people.

Duty (Luke 17:7-10)
Jesus then goes on to illustrate his point about forgiveness:

> Suppose one of you had a servant ploughing or looking after the sheep. Would he say to the servant when he comes in from the field, 'Come along now and sit down to eat'? Would he not rather say, 'Prepare my supper, get yourself ready and wait on me while I eat and drink; after that you may eat and drink'? Would he thank the servant because he did what he was told to do? So you also, when you have done everything you were told to do, should say, 'We are unworthy servants; we have only done our duty.'

Before a slave can attend to his own needs, he has to do his duty. He will not expect his master to be grateful, for he is doing no more than he has been commanded to do.

Jesus' lesson is this: if God commands us to do something and we don't do it, we are in trouble. However, if we do do what he commands, that is not an occasion for boasting, for we have done no more than what was expected of us. The King James' Version expresses it thus, 'We are *unprofitable* servants; we have done that which was our duty to do.'

There is no way that we can save up merits for ourselves. There is nothing more demeaning to the biblical ethic than the doctrine that emerged in the Middle Ages of works of supererogation, the gaining of excess merit by doing works that were defined by the church as being above and beyond the call of duty.

This was one of the great issues of the Protestant Reformation. Nobody can ever have excess merits, because we are commanded to be perfect, and nobody can be better than perfect. If we are perfect, we are only doing what God has commanded us to do. There is no surplus of profit beyond that, that would place God under some kind of indebtedness or obligation to thank us.

However, God does crown our works with rewards, but he even does that graciously, not because he is obligated to. All that we have and all that we do is received as a gift from God. The very essence of that gift is found in the free forgiveness that he has bestowed upon us. Therefore, we in turn, are to bestow forgiveness freely on those who repent. It is required, therefore we must be willing to forgive.

76. Ten men healed of leprosy (Luke 17:11-19)

Jesus is still making his final journey to Jerusalem, the capital city of Israel, where the cross awaits him. He is travelling through Samaria and Galilee, and enters a village that is not named, and there he sees ten lepers. Lepers were required to keep themselves at a distance from other people. They were banished from involvement in local society, and the law prescribed that when they came near a town or a village, they had to cry out, 'Unclean! Unclean!', lest anyone inadvertently came in contact with this dreadful disease. They were social outcasts.

When Jesus encountered these ten lepers, they 'called out in a loud voice, "Jesus, Master, have pity on us!"' Obviously there was no corner of Palestine untouched by the reputation of Jesus and his wondrous powers of healing. So when these lepers learnt that Jesus was coming to their neighbourhood, they rushed to the edge of the city to await his presence, and when they saw him in the distance, they lifted up their voices to ask for mercy.

When he saw them, he said, 'Go, show yourselves to the priests.' And as they went, they were cleansed. One of them, when he saw he was healed, came back, praising God in a loud voice. He threw himself at Jesus' feet and thanked him – and he was a Samaritan. Jesus asked, 'Were not all ten cleansed? Where are the other nine? Was no-one found to return and give praise to God except this foreigner?' Then he said to him, 'Rise, and go; your faith has made you well' (17:14-19).

The interpretation that I have heard again and again is that although Jesus healed ten lepers, only one of them was grateful. I don't believe that for one moment, and it seems to me that this interpretation obscures the point. To understand all that is involved, we need to examine the legislation in Leviticus concerning the principles of purification. It was the job of the priests to diagnose various illnesses and in the case of skin ailments this involved a lengthy monitoring process. At the end of this observation period the priest would then pronounce the person clean or unclean (See Lev. 13–14). If the pronouncement was leprosy, in a sense the person's life came apart at the seams, and that had happened for every one of the ten Jesus encountered. Their only hope was Jesus, and so they cried out to him. Jesus' response was an immediate command: 'Go, show yourselves to the priests.' Only the priest could lift the ban that would restore the leper to the fulness of fellowship in the community. If a leper thought that his leprosy was getting better, he would go to the priest for a check up.

Luke continues his narrative with these words: 'And as they went, they were cleansed.' If we have any understanding what a leper went through, we would know that now even the most corrupt and crass sinner could fail to be grateful for healing. When these lepers saw that their flesh had been restored, that this marvellous healer, Jesus, had done his work, no doubt they began leaping for joy and couldn't wait to go home to be reunited with their families. Very probably they would have got down on their knees to thank God. That would be the normal thing to do. So nine out of ten went straight home.

The tenth one too may well have started out for home, but he paused, and then decided to take the time not only to be grateful, but to express that gratitude. Luke notes, that the one who came back was a Samaritan.

Now Jews and Samaritans never associated with each other, yet this band of lepers Jesus encountered clearly were a mixed group. Jesus said in verse 18, 'Was no-one found to return and give praise to God except this foreigner?' the implication being that the others were not strangers: they were Jews. In a leper colony social and ethnic divisions fell away.

Only one returned to give glory, and Jesus said to him, 'Rise and go.' Go on home. Celebrate! 'Your faith has made you well.' It is not sufficient to be grateful: we are required to give thanks to God personally.

77. The coming of the kingdom of God
(Luke 17:20-37)

The focus of attention shifts again, and once more we find Jesus being questioned by the Pharisees, as to 'when the kingdom of God would come'. Jesus answered, 'The kingdom of God does not come with your careful observation, nor will people say, "Here it is," or "There it is," because the kingdom of God is within you' (17:20-21).

Here is the King of kings standing in their midst; here is the One who reigns over heaven and earth, who has power over the hopeless disease of leprosy, and the Pharisees are saying, 'When will the kingdom of God come?' And Jesus said, '... the kingdom of God is within you.' Now that verse is one of the most frequently misunderstood verses in the New Testament. People have read it to mean that the kingdom of God is something that takes places simply in the hearts of men: an internal, psychological matter. But Jesus is not talking to the Pharisees about psychology. He is talking about history. Jesus is saying that they are looking at the kingdom of God, for it has come in the sense that their king has come.

> Then he said to his disciples, 'The time is coming when you will long to see one of the days of the Son of Man, but you will not see it. Men will tell you, "There he is!" or "Here he is!" Do not go running off after them. For the Son of Man in his day will be like the lightning, which flashes and lights up the sky from one end to the other' (17:22-24).

In the glory of the final consummation and manifestation of the Kingship of Christ, when the veil will be removed from his identity and every eye shall behold his glory as the King of kings, we won't need a press report. The lightning will light up the whole sky. The blaze of glory that will attend his return will be so great that not even the Pharisees will be able to miss it.

'But,' said Jesus, 'first he must suffer many things and be rejected by this generation.' The leadership of the present generation had rejected him; they had missed the coming of their king, and Jesus likens their situation to how it was in the days of Noah: 'Just as it was in the days of Noah, so also will it be in the days of the Son of Man. People were eating, drinking, marrying and being given in marriage up to the day Noah entered the ark. Then the flood came and destroyed them all' (17:26-27). The flood that destroyed the world in the days of Noah was not without warning. God had told Noah that the Holy Spirit would not always strive with men, and Noah had warned his neighbours of the impending judgment, but nobody took him seriously. Everybody carried on with the daily business of life, right up until Noah entered the ark, and suddenly the flood came and destroyed them all. That's the analogy that Jesus is drawing here. Christ will return to this world, but for the most part people will go about their daily business without giving a second thought to the possibility of his sudden return. And when it is not expected, the skies will be illumined with the majesty of the return of Christ.

Jesus draws another analogy in verses 28-29: 'It was the same in the days of Lot. People were eating and drinking, buying and selling, planting and building. But the day Lot left Sodom, fire and sulphur rained down from heaven and destroyed them all.' In the midst of daily activity, the volcanic eruption, or the fire and brimstone, engulfed Sodom so unexpectedly that people were buried alive. Jesus reminds them of this catastrophic event and then says, 'It will be just like this on the day the Son of Man is revealed' (17:30). Then he goes on to elaborate: 'On that day no-one who is on the roof of his house, with his goods inside, should go down to get them. Likewise, no-one in the field should go back for anything' (17:31). There will not be time to gather up your belongings, or check your fields. It will be the supreme moment of truth for all mankind, and it will happen in an instant.

Then Jesus admonishes them to: 'Remember Lot's wife!' If anyone ever had a possibility of escaping from a calamity, it was her. Lot and his family had been warned to flee from the city. So, while everyone was going about their daily business, Lot and his wife and two daughters fled the city. They were already safely outside the city, but at the last second, Lot's wife hesitated and looked back. In that moment she was caught in the storm and turned into a pillar of salt. Jesus then goes on to say, 'Whoever tries to keep his life will lose it, and whoever loses his life will preserve it' (17:33). Some people are so tied to the things of this world that their commitment to Christ is not certain. The time to get that settled is now, not at the last second.

Jesus continues: 'I tell you, on that night two people will be in one bed; one will be taken and the other left. Two women will be grinding grain together; one will be taken and the other left' (17:34-35). At that moment when Christ comes for his people, there will be some committed to Christ and some who are not. They may be in the most intimate relationship, husband and wife, best friends, or co-labourers, but one will leave to join Christ and the other will be left. One will be spared, one will be destroyed.

If that were to happen tonight, what would happen to you? Would you be spared or would you be destroyed? That's the issue that confronts every human being, at present only as a theoretical question, but at the moment of truth, theory will disappear as all will be brought before the judgment of the appearing Lord of glory.

When the Pharisees asked, 'Where, Lord?' they wanted to know where the judgment would fall, or where the people would be taken to be joined with Christ. Jesus' replied, 'Where there is a dead body, there the vultures will gather' (17:37). This text has been interpreted in two different ways historically. On the one hand, the view favoured by most commentators is that Jesus gives a negative answer – the judgment will fall where Christ appears and finds people who are opposed to his kingdom. Those who are in a state of spiritual death will be like those exposed to the vultures.

The other interpretation is more positive. Where the body is, or, where Christ appears, there the vultures will gather around him. That is, people will fly up to meet him. This may be a cryptic allusion to what the New Testament elsewhere describes as the 'rapture', when Christians will be caught up to meet Christ in the air when he returns.

But whichever interpretation is correct, we must not miss the note of earnestness and urgency in Jesus' words as he points to a future crisis, and pleads with people to be ready when the Son of Man appears.

78. The parable of the importunate widow (Luke 18:1-8)

Chapter 18 begins with another parable of Jesus, a parable of great importance for the future.

> Then Jesus told his disciples a parable to show them that they should always pray and not give up. He said: 'In a certain town there was a judge who neither feared God nor cared about men. And there was a widow in that town who kept coming to him with the plea, "Grant me justice against my adversary."
>
> 'For some time he refused. But finally he said to himself, "Even though I don't fear God or care about men, yet because this widow keeps bothering me, I will see that she gets justice, so that she won't eventually wear me out with her coming!"
>
> 'And the Lord said, "Listen to what the unjust judge says. And will not God bring about justice for his chosen ones, who cry out to him day and night? Will he keep putting them off? I tell you, he will see that they get justice, and quickly. However, when the Son of Man comes, will he find faith on the earth?" '

This fascinating parable tells the story of a widow who did not have the advantage of a husband to protect her interests in the law courts of the day. The Old Testament had special provisions for justice to be dealt out on behalf of widows and orphans and those who were in some way handicapped in the ruthless competition of the marketplace. A just judge was as scrupulous to hear of the case of the poor, helpless and needy as he was to hear the case of the more affluent. The judge of Jesus' parable, however, was unjust; he had no particular regard for justice, but was involved in his enterprise strictly for financial gain. He was a godless man who had no respect for God, neither did he consider God in the judgments that he made. He was an utterly ruthless scoundrel.

Having painted this negative portrait, Jesus then tells of the poor widow who pleads with him repeatedly for legal protection from her opponent. The judge was unwilling, but after a while he gave in and yielded to her request because of her persistence.

Jesus uses contrast and comparison in this parable to make his point. If an unscrupulous, unjust judge with no regard for men or God will heed the pleas of this pestering woman, how much more will the heavenly Father, who is just and caring, hear the cries of his people. The point of the parable is that 'they should always pray and not give up' (18:1). We are not to give in to despair, or hopelessness, thinking that because God has delayed giving us the total fulfilment of his promises, ultimately he is going to forget about us. No, he tells us to keep praying and not to give up.

Many times Christ tells his disciples that if they are faithful to him, they will suffer injustice at the hands of unscrupulous men; they will be persecuted and falsely accused and slandered. But when Christians have been victims of injustice and slander, if they cry day and night to their God, God promises to vindicate them. Jesus said, 'I tell you, he will see that they get justice, and quickly.' We are prohibited by sacred Scripture to seek vengeance for ourselves. We are not to be vengeful, rather we are to suffer in patience. For God says, 'Vengeance is mine. I will repay' (Lev. 19:18; Deut. 32:35; Rom. 12:19). We have a divine pledge that we will be vindicated for every injustice we have to suffer.

The point of the parable comes home. In the midst of this teaching of the future, Jesus tells his disciples they will have to wait. They will have to go through a period of suffering before the manifestation of the Son of God. But Jesus encourages them not to despair, but to pray, in season and out of season, and not lose heart.

At the end of this conversation, however, Jesus asks a rather unexpected question: 'However, when the Son of Man comes, will he find faith on the earth?' Here Jesus is talking to the Pharisees, within earshot of his own disciples, yet he queries whether he will be able to find people who have faith when he returns. Or will he find a generation like these godless, faithless Pharisees? Jesus does hint, however, that when he comes, it will not be at a time of great fidelity. Elsewhere we are told that he will appear at a time when the strength and faith of his people will be at a low ebb. Some historians have noted that our day is one of the most difficult periods in church history, in terms of the vitality of the church itself. It is marked not so much by faithfulness, as by faithlessness. Therefore, we should pray without ceasing, not only for the vindication of the people of God, but that when our Lord appears he will find faith in us.

79. The parable of the Pharisee and the tax collector (Luke 18:9-17)

This parable of Jesus was addressed to 'some who were confident of their own righteousness and looked down on everybody else.' This general section includes some direct discourse between Jesus and the Pharisees, so we can assume that his comments here were directed towards them. The Pharisees were the ones who trusted in their own righteousness and viewed others with contempt. So Jesus tells them the story of two men who went to the temple to pray, one a Pharisee, the other a tax collector. That alone would be enough to kindle the wrath of the listening Pharisees, that a fellow Pharisee would ever be caught in the same section of the temple praying in the presence of a tax collector. If there was any class of people who were held in utter contempt by the Pharisees, it was the class of tax collectors. Thus, in this parable Jesus draws a stark contrast between these two character types: a Pharisee, the paragon of righteousness in the community, respected by all for their morality, and the hated figure of the tax collector.

Jesus continues the story: 'The Pharisee stood up and prayed about himself: "God, I thank you that I am not like all other men – robbers, evildoers, adulterers – or even like this tax collector." ' This is a prayer of thanksgiving. He does not take total credit for his own achievements of righteousness, but nods in the direction of heaven and gives some credit to God. He thanks God that he is not like other people, and his words make us wonder whether his prayer was directed to God or was meant for the ears of the tax-gatherer standing in the corner.

The Pharisee then goes on to list his moral credentials. He said, 'I fast twice a week and give a tenth of all I get.' He claims to be involved in spiritual exercises and religious acts of charity and devotion, which were extraordinary. There were occasions in the Jewish religion where fasting was required – in preparation for the day of atonement, during periods of national calamity, and so on – but certainly Jewish law did not require to fast twice every week. But this man said he did. Now this is no mean feat. And again, in the matter of tithing the Pharisee went beyond the requirements of the law, for certain types of income were exempt. But the Pharisee claims to tithe ten per cent of all that he makes.

However, this Pharisee not only performed these acts of devotion, but he was proud of them; and not only that, he was trusting in them for his redemption. He was a man who trusted in his own good deeds to get him into the kingdom of God. He never considered for a moment the possibility that any righteousness he might possess was a result of the grace of God.

He took full credit for all of his good deeds.

In verse 13 we read the prayer of the tax collector: 'But the tax collector stood at a distance. He would not even look up to heaven, but beat his breast and said, "God, have mercy on me, a sinner." ' It is not clear how we should interpret the words 'stood at a distance', but perhaps it means that the tax-collector was so smitten by his conscience that he didn't dare come close to the presence of God but stayed in the outer court. He couldn't even lift his eyes to heaven, but was beating his breast, overcome with a sense of contrition. And he cried out, 'God, have mercy on me, a sinner.'

Jesus brings the parable to its point in verse 14: 'I tell you that this man, rather than the other, went home justified before God. For everyone who exalts himself will be humbled, and he who humbles himself will be exalted.' No-one enters the kingdom of God on the basis of his own righteousness, because apart from Jesus no human being has ever acquired enough righteousness to fulfil the absolute and perfect demands of the holy law of God. It is by grace and grace alone that we can ever have access into his presence. All of us stand guilty before the righteousness of God, Pharisee and tax-collector alike. The difference, however, between these two men was not that one was righteous and the other a sinner. They were both sinners. The difference was that the tax-collector knew that he was a sinner, and he repented of his sin.

Now many people in this world are willing to acknowledge that they are sinners. It is commonplace to hear people say, 'Well, no-one's perfect and that includes me.' But so often that is the end of our confession. But it is not enough to admit that one is a sinner. One *has* to repent of that. In fact, to acknowledge that we are sinners and not repent of it, is to blaspheme God. This tax-collector here not only recognized that he was a sinner, he also confessed it before God and begged God for mercy. He came into the presence of God in humility. And Jesus said he went home justified. So although the Pharisee was a religious man, he was not a justified man.

Let us abandon the hope of gaining access to God on the basis of our own righteousness and cling instead to the righteousness of Christ. When we come into the presence of God, let us come not with an attitude of self-justification, but with an attitude of dependence upon his mercy. For the point at issue here was not the track-record of the Pharisee or tax-collector, but the present attitude of their minds towards God.

Following this parable, Jesus turns his attention to children: 'People were also bringing babies to Jesus to have him touch them. When the disciples saw this, they rebuked them.' The people who were eager to follow Jesus and hear his words were bringing their babies and little children to him so he might touch them, and pronounce a benediction upon them, in keeping with the Jewish tradition. But the disciples were annoyed that people were bothering Jesus in this way, presumably because they thought he had more important things to worry about. 'But Jesus called the children to him and said, "Let the little children come to me, and do not hinder them, for the kingdom of God belongs to such as these. I tell you the truth, anyone who will not receive the kingdom of God like a little child will never enter it" ' (18:16-17). How fitting that Luke places this incident after the parable of the Pharisee and the tax-collector, for the Pharisee thanked God that he was so mature, whereas the tax-collector became as a child.

Jesus, here, lays down a condition for entering the kingdom of God. This should make our ears perk up, lest we overlook that prerequisite. He says that unless each of us enters the kingdom of God as a child, we will not enter it at all. So often this passage is interpreted to mean that Christians are always to have a child-like faith, in the sense that we ought always to keep our faith very simple, and not allow it to be encumbered by diligent study of the word of God. However, there is a difference between a childlike faith and a childish faith. A childish faith chooses to remain immature, but a childlike faith, the kind that Jesus calls for, is a simple, confident trust in, and dependence on, our heavenly Father, a trust born of humility rather than arrogance. The difference is crucial. The apostle Paul exhorts us 'in evil be babes, but in your thinking be mature' (1 Cor. 14:20). When it comes to our salvation, we must have a childlike trust in God's mercy and grace or we will miss the kingdom of God.

80. The rich young ruler (Luke 18:18-30)

Luke describes an encounter between Jesus and a man who was a ruler. This man approached him and said: 'Good teacher, what must I do to inherit eternal life?' Here is a man who is not looking for healing or for a handout, rather he raises a profound theological question. Jesus' immediate response, however, is quite surprising: 'Why do you call me good? No-one is good – except God alone.' This text has prompted some debate, for the Bible is filled with reference to the sinlessness of Jesus Christ, but some interpret this passage as a personal denial of his own sinlessness. However, others interpret it differently. Jesus is not denying either his sinlessness or his deity at this point. He understands that as far as the rich young ruler is concerned, he is just a good teacher. Perhaps the man may also suspect that Jesus is a prophet, but it is quite obvious that he is not aware that he is talking to God incarnate. He is only looking for answers to his theological questions. Jesus is aware that the man doesn't recognize his full identity, but he also sees that the man has a defective understanding of what goodness is. So Jesus wants to get this straight first. No-one is good compared to God.

When we use the term, good, we use it in a relative way. According to the general pattern of behaviour among mankind, some people are relatively better than others. But we make a fatal mistake here: the standard by which our goodness will ultimately be judged is not the standard of run-of-the-mill human morality. The ultimate standard by which we will be judged will be the standard of God's goodness. Viewed from that perspective, none of us measures up, for our deeds are measured not only by their mere external forms, but also by their inward motivations. For a deed to be ultimately good in the biblical sense, not only must it do what the law requires, but it must be motivated by a heart that loves God completely. No human being is good in that ultimate sense, and Jesus is reminding this young man of a deeper understanding of the nature of goodness, lest his superficial understanding of goodness be the very thing that keeps him out of the kingdom of God.

Jesus then begins to answer the man's question: 'What must I do to inherit eternal life?' Jesus said, 'You know the commandments: "Do not commit adultery, do not murder, do not steal, do not give false testimony, honour your father and mother" ' (18:20). How surprising that Jesus should answer like this, in view of the teaching contained in the previous nine verses. In the parable of the tax collector and the Pharisee and the incident of Jesus calling little children to himself, the emphasis is that the only way we will ever get into the kingdom of God is by grace, not by doing good works. But Jesus tells this man that if he wants to get into heaven he must keep the law. It is a puzzling answer and we need to read on to get a clue as to why Jesus answered the way he did.

The rich man said, 'All these I have kept since I was a boy' (18:21). What an arrogant answer. But perhaps he didn't mean to be arrogant, maybe he was just impatient and expected something different from Jesus.

Obviously, the rich young ruler was not present when Jesus in his Sermon on the Mount exploded the current misunderstanding of the full ramifications of the ten commandments. The Pharisees held the simplistic view that even if they were consumed by lust, so long as they refrained from actual adultery, they had kept the law. Similarly they could be eaten up by hatred for someone, but so long as they didn't murder that person they hadn't sinned. Jesus taught, however, that looking at someone lustfully or hating someone without just cause is itself a breach of the law. His teaching probed deeply into the implications of authentic righteousness contained in the ten commandments. Anyone with an in-depth understanding of the ten commandments would not claim to have kept the law for five minutes, let alone since his youth. If

we had to keep the ten commandments perfectly to enter into
the kingdom of God, we wouldn't have a chance of getting there.

So, why did Jesus tell this man that that was the way to
heaven? He is trying to get this young man to see the
fundamental mistake that he has made.

'When Jesus heard this, he said to him, "You still lack one
thing. Sell everything you have and give to the poor, and you
will have treasure in heaven. Then come, follow me" ' (18:22).
We will not find in the ten commandments a demand that people
dispossess themselves of all of their wealth and distribute it to
the poor. In fact, the ten commandments protect personal
property by prohibiting stealing and coveting. Private property
is a right, given to man by God, so why is Jesus telling this man
to liquidate all of his assets and give them to the poor?

The man had just claimed in the presence of Jesus Christ
that he had kept the ten commandments from his youth. The
very first commandment prohibits any kind of idolatry.
Obviously Jesus detected in this rich man, someone who not
only enjoyed his wealth, but was so hung up on money that
virtually he worshipped it. He had turned his money into an
idol.

So Jesus puts the man to the test to see if he has any other
gods before God. That is why he asks him to give all he has to
the poor. When I read this text, I have to ask myself, how I
would react if Jesus were to ask the same of me? Fortunately he
doesn't make it a universal command, but he will ask it of me if
my money becomes an idol.

The story has an unhappy ending. We read in verse 23: 'When
he heard this, he became very sad, because he was a man of
great wealth.' He shook his head and walked away from Christ.
He could not give up his idol. He made a choice between his
money and the kingdom of God. Five minutes earlier he was
the most excited man in the world about gaining entrance into
the kingdom of God, but when he saw the price tag, he was no
longer interested.

'Jesus looked at him and said, "How hard it is for the rich to enter the kingdom of God! Indeed, it is easier for a camel to go through the eye of a needle than for a rich man to enter the kingdom of God" ' (18:24-25).

Many times Scripture warns those who are blessed with prosperity, that they face a peculiar temptation. So often wealth is accompanied by a certain measure of power, and power is often accompanied by a sense of self-sufficiency; people begin to put their confidence and trust in their power and wealth, making them poverty-stricken with respect to the things of God.

Jesus' warning on this occasion is couched in radical terms. He doesn't say that people who have riches cannot enter the kingdom of God, but he says it is particularly difficult for them. In fact, he says it is easier for a camel to go through the eye of a needle, than for a rich man to enter into the kingdom of God. Through the years this saying has been the subject of much scrutiny by scholars, because it is such a bizarre image. It is difficult enough to get a thin piece of thread through the eye of a needle, but to push a camel through such a small aperture, would of course be a feat that even the best magician could not perform. That is, if we take the text literally.

Some commentators have argued that as the word for camel is very close to the Semitic word for rope, we could be looking at a scribal error here, and what Jesus actually said was that it is easier to pass a rope through the eye of a needle, than it is for a rich man to get into the kingdom of God. However, the word that appears in the best Greek manuscripts is camel. Another possible interpretation offered by scholars is that 'the Eye of the Needle' was in fact the name for a particularly narrow gate in the walls of Jerusalem. The only way a camel could get through such a small opening, would be for its master to get it to kneel down and sort of shimmy along the ground, scraping its knees and back as it tried to squeeze through the gate. I am not sure how accurate that information is, but it is a possibility. If it were the case, then what Jesus was saying was that although a camel could pass through the Eye of the Needle, it was only with great difficulty. So it is not impossible for the rich to get into the kingdom of God, but it is very hard.

It is helpful, however, to take into consideration the response of Jesus' hearers. They took his words to indicate not only something that would be very difficult, but something that was manifestly impossible, because we read in verse 26: 'Those who heard this asked, "Who then can be saved?" Jesus replied, "What is impossible with men is possible with God." '

Naturally speaking, it would be impossible for a rich man to enter the kingdom of God, but the impossibility would be based on the fact that he would lack the necessary righteousness that God requires, for God demands the righteousness of perfection. However, at that point, the rich man is not in any particularly special category, for a poor man is as deficient in perfect righteousness. So, in one sense, it is impossible for anybody to enter the kingdom of God. Only an act of God can get us in. So that which is impossible for us, is indeed possible for God.

'Peter said to him, "We have left all we had to follow you!" "I tell you the truth," Jesus said to them, "no-one who has left home or wife or brothers or parents or children for the sake of the kingdom of God will fail to receive many times as much in this age and, in the age to come, eternal life." ' Anyone who, out of a spirit of real devotion and commitment to the kingdom of God, has made a significant sacrifice, will receive the certain blessing of God, both in this world and in the world to come.

81. Jesus predicts the future
and heals a blind man (Luke 18:31-43)

Jesus took the Twelve aside and told them, 'We are going up to Jerusalem, and everything that is written by the prophets about the Son of Man will be fulfilled. He will be turned over to the Gentiles. They will mock him, insult him, spit on him, flog him and kill him. On the third day he will rise again.' The disciples did not understand any of this. Its meaning was hidden from them, and they did not know what he was talking about.

Following the discourse on riches prompted by Jesus' encounter with the rich young ruler, Jesus now withdraws from the multitude and speaks privately with the Twelve. The message he gives them is brief but ominous; all things written by the prophets concerning the Son of Man shall be accomplished.

This is the fourth time since Luke 9 that Jesus has told his disciples candidly that he is going to suffer. Again Luke makes an editorial aside to the effect that they didn't understand it. It was unthinkable to these men that if Jesus indeed was the Messiah, that he should suffer, or be delivered over to Gentiles and subjected to the indignation of which Jesus speaks in this passage. So, although he tells them these things, they ignore it because their expectations are quite different. Maybe they just write it off as a melancholy mood of their Teacher. But Jesus again points to Jerusalem, where all the things that are written through the prophets concerning the Son of Man shall be accomplished. Jesus says that his destiny is tied to what was prophesied in the Old Testament by the prophets. If we look at the language here, we see that it's not that the prophets themselves advanced the theory that the Messiah must suffer, and be raised again, but rather those things were written *through* the prophets, the word here has to do with the instrumentation of the prophets. Jesus clearly sees the prophets as instruments of divine revelation with respect to the mission and the destiny of the Messiah.

Jesus fills in some details with regard to his coming suffering; how he would be delivered to the Gentiles, that he would be mocked, spat on and mistreated, and then put to death, and after that he would rise again. But they did not understand him, perhaps because of their own expectations of the Messiah. However, Luke also adds that 'its meaning was hidden from them' (18:34). God, for some reason, kept them from understanding until the appropriate time.

Verse 35 moves away from this discourse, to carry on the narrative of the journey.

As Jesus approached Jericho, a blind man was sitting by the
roadside begging. When he heard the crowd going by, he asked
what was happening. They told him, 'Jesus of Nazareth is passing
by.' He called out, 'Jesus, Son of David, have mercy on me!'
Those who led the way rebuked him and told him to be quiet, but
he shouted all the more, 'Son of David, have mercy on me!' Jesus
stopped and ordered the man to be brought to him. When he came
near, Jesus asked him, 'What do you want me to do for you?'
'Lord, I want to see,' he replied. Jesus said to him, 'Receive your
sight; your faith has healed you.' Immediately he received his
sight and followed Jesus, praising God. When all the people saw
it, they also praised God (18:35-43).

There are certain questions about the location of this incident
and whether, in fact, it is the same incident that other gospel
writers record of the healing of a blind man named Bartimaeus.
But what is important is that once more Jesus acts in compassion.
If Christ ever had a legitimate reason to ignore the entreaties of
a needy person, it was at this point in his life. This event takes
place just a few days before the crucifixion. Jesus is moving
steadfastly towards Jerusalem. His disciples don't want Jesus
to be interrupted, as he nears his destination. This is the setting
for Jesus' encounter with this blind man who was sitting by the
road begging.

The blind man obviously couldn't see what was going on,
but he was aware of the commotion caused by the entrance of
Jesus. So he enquired what it all meant. As soon as he heard
that Jesus of Nazareth was passing by, the blind man cried out
for Jesus, the son of David, to have mercy on him. The advance
group of Jesus' disciples rebuked him and told him to be quiet,
for Jesus was in a hurry. But he ignored them, and cried out all
the louder.

Once again Jesus stops in the midst of a crowd. He did it in
the case of Jairus, and the case of the woman with the issue of
blood. Jesus takes time to extend his compassion to the
individual. He asked what he could do for him, and the man got
right to the point: 'Lord, I want to see.' His heart's desire was

to be able to see, and Jesus said very simply, 'Receive your sight.' It was a command, a divine imperative. Then he said, 'Your faith has healed you', and instantly the man received his sight, and followed Jesus, and glorified God. All the people who witnessed this event, joined in and gave praise unto God. Just a few days before his death, Jesus makes a blind man see, and the crowd cheers.

82. Salvation for Zaccheus (Luke 19:1-10)

Jesus entered Jericho and was passing through. A man was there by the name of Zaccheus; he was a chief tax collector and was wealthy. He wanted to see who Jesus was, but being a short man he could not, because of the crowd. So he ran ahead and climbed a sycamore-fig tree to see him, since Jesus was coming that way. When Jesus reached the spot, he looked up and said to him, 'Zaccheus, come down immediately. I must stay at your house today.' So he came down at once and welcomed him gladly (19:1-6).

There is a sense of childlike delight and even humour attending the well-known story of Jesus' meeting with Zaccheus. There is something comic about this man who had distinguished himself as chief among the tax-gatherers, climbing up a tree to see what was going on. There is something ironic about this description of Zaccheus, because his name means 'the righteous one'. But he was curious, and he has obviously heard some of the advance reports of Jesus.

As the thronging multitude moved through the streets of Jericho, a beautiful city in the ancient world, a city of lush palm trees and flowing springs, Zaccheus had a problem – he was too small to see what was going on. But he is enterprising because we read that he ran on ahead down the street. This was an unusual thing for a member of the wealthy class to do, but he ran anyway, and climbed up into a sycamore tree to see Jesus, for he was to pass that way.

A sycamore tree was a very beautiful tree. It did not grow

tall, but rather was squat and very heavily branched, and so made a wonderful shade tree. It was into one of these shade trees that Zaccheus climbed so that he could get a better look at Jesus. When Jesus came to the place, he looked up and saw him, and immediately spoke to him with words of recognition, saying, 'Zacchaeus, come down immediately. I must stay at your house today.' Well Zaccheus was beside himself with joy. Here was this celebrity who was passing through the town, who had not only taken notice of him, and spoken to him, but had actually asked to come and be his guest. This would be exciting for anybody in the city of Jericho, but for a tax-collector to be singled out in this way was all the more remarkable.

We read that Zaccheus scrambled down out of that tree as fast as he could, 'and welcomed him gladly. All the people saw this and began to mutter, "He has gone to be the guest of a 'sinner'." ' Again, Jesus does what he has done consistently throughout his ministry, he violates the established traditions of the Pharisees.

Then Zaccheus said, 'Look, Lord! Here and now I give half of my possessions to the poor, and if I have cheated anybody out of anything, I will pay back four times the amount.' Here, in capsule form, is a bold and moving confession of sin, an act of repentance and a confession of faith, by Zaccheus. He recognises Christ and calls him 'Lord'. To demonstrate his repentance, he vows to give away half of his goods, but not only that, he is going to make restitution to all the people he has cheated. However, he is not merely going to return what he had taken, but says he will give back four times as much.

A radical change has taken place in this man's value-system. He realizes he is talking to the Pearl of Great Price, and so is willing to give away his possessions as an act of love and devotion and repentance in the presence of Christ. Zaccheus does not divest himself of all his possessions, and Jesus does not rebuke him for keeping the other half, but rather pronounces his blessing and benediction upon him: 'Today salvation has come to this house, because this man, too, is a son of Abraham.'

For his whole adult career, presumably, Zaccheus had been a traitor to the household of Israel, but in this moment of confession of faith, he becomes a son of Abraham.

It is a story of inspiration and example for all of us, for it demonstrates that Jesus has the power to transform lives. Jesus himself adds this comment: 'For the Son of Man came to seek and to save what was lost' (19:10). This is not the first time that we have heard Jesus define his own mission in terms of seeking and saving those who are lost. Zaccheus was a man of enormous wealth, yet he was lost, and there are people like that all over this world. People of influence, authority and wealth, who are lost. Well, Jesus came to find people who were lost. Everybody in Jericho knew where Zaccheus lived; they knew him by name, but they didn't realize that he was lost. But even while the man was concealed in the dense foliage of the sycamore tree, Jesus found him, and redeemed him. That's the ministry of Christ.

Scripture is silent about the future of Zaccheus, but church history is not. The Bishop of Alexandria, Clement, whose writings exist to this day, mentions in one of his homilies that Zaccheus continued faithfully in the growth and nurture of the Lord, and served Christ to the end of his life with distinction, being elevated ultimately to the role of bishop of Caesarea. So this little man, who climbed the tree to see Jesus, left the lucrative money-changing tables at the crossroads leading to Jerusalem, and became a spiritual leader in the church.

83. The parable of the ten minas (Luke 19:11-27)

The parable told in this section has two underlying concerns. It begins: 'While they were listening to this, he went on to tell them a parable, because he was near Jerusalem and the people thought that the kingdom of God was going to appear at once.' This introduction is very important if we are going to understand what Jesus is teaching. The closer Jesus draws to Jerusalem and the more excitement that is generated by the crowds that are following him, the greater is the sense of expectation of his disciples. Because he was near Jerusalem, the disciples supposed that the kingdom of God was going to appear immediately. They believed that history was on the threshold of the breakthrough of the kingdom of God, where Jesus would no longer conceal the fulness of his power, but would let it burst forth for all to see. It is in the midst of that spirit of eager expectation that Jesus teaches this parable.

'A man of noble birth went to a distant country to have himself appointed king and then to return. So he called ten of his servants and gave them ten minas [the equivalent of a hundred days' wages]. 'Put this money to work," he said, "until I come back." But his subjects hated him and sent a delegation after him to say, "We don't want this man to be our king." ' The whole concept of this strange story seems unrealistic. Jesus' contemporaries would remember a similar event that took place: when Archeleus, son of Herod the Great, was appointed king of Judaea, the Jewish leaders sent a delegation to the Roman emperor beseeching him not to make Archeleus king.

So perhaps Jesus is building on this memory, by telling this parable of the nobleman who goes to a far country to receive a kingdom and the people send a delegation to say that they do not want him to rule over them. Obviously, however, Jesus is not telling the parable simply to remind people of Archeleus. He has a far more significant point. Jesus is coming to Jerusalem and his disciples are expecting that now he will bring in the kingdom of God. But what they don't understand is that, although he is only hours away from his triumphal entry into Jerusalem, he is only a week away from this death and only a few weeks away from his ascension to heaven. His departure into a far country is where he will be invested by God the Father with his crown as King of the kingdom of God. So Jesus is hinting here at his imminent departure, when he goes to receive his kingdom, where he will reign until some future moment when he will return in triumph. Once again, Jesus is teaching them about the future manifestation of the kingdom of God, which will come only after a period of visible absence of Jesus.

Obviously Jesus has a reference here to his people, his disciples, whom he leaves with certain gifts and responsibilities that they are to use well, so that when he returns he will find fruitful servants.

In the parable, two of the servants invested their master's money and made him a profit, but the third came, saying, 'Sir, here is your mina; I have kept it laid away in a piece of cloth. I was afraid of you, because you are a hard man. You take out what you did not put in and reap what you did not sow.' This servant was afraid to risk the loss of his gift by investing it, or by using it, or by putting it to work. Here Jesus is borrowing from the principle of capitalism, not to teach us how to play the stock market, but rather to talk about the investment of our lives, the investment of the gifts that he gives to us. We are to put them to good use, that they may bear fruit. Every member of the body of Christ is given a gift by God the Holy Spirit, but we have a tendency to allow our gifts to atrophy. For fear of competition, or fear of failure, or for fear of loss, we can choose not to use our gift.

But Jesus gives a sharp rebuke to the man who played it safe and refused to take risks. He said, ' "Why then didn't you put my money on deposit, so that when I came back, I could have collected it with interest?" Then he said to those standing by, "Take his mina away from him and give it to the one who has ten minas" ' (19:23-24). Here is a case of the rich getting richer and the poor getting poorer. But Jesus says there will be a penalty for a failure to try to produce fruit. The gift or the talent will not stay in the drawer for ever, but will be given to those who are committed to the Lord, to the degree that they are willing to take risks necessary to put that talent to work.

At the outset of this study we said that there were two points to this parable. One is the responsibility of the servants to make use of the gifts that the Master leaves behind. But the second has to do with the enemies of the Master who sent the delegation,

saying they didn't want the nobleman to rule over them. From
the first day of Jesus' public ministry there had been people
who protested against the idea that he was the Messiah. When
Jesus returned to sit at the right hand of God, to be the Lord of
the universe, the number that worshipped him increased. But
wherever the church has spread and Christ's influence has gone,
there have been persistent delegations of those who hate him
and hate his reign, and who still conspire saying, 'We will not
have him to rule over us.' In certain sections of the world, this
attitude has intensified in its fury against God and his anointed,
so that those who seek to be faithful, those who seek to serve
Christ, are subjected not only to hatred but the physical
expression of that hatred – persecution, imprisonment, physical
torture.

The parable ends soberly: 'But those enemies of mine who
did not want me to be a king over them – bring them here and
kill them in front of me.' This seems so out of character with
his usual teaching. But occasionally he warned his people that
at the time of his second advent, every knee would bow before
him. Some would bow before him willingly, but those who
remained hostile would also kneel, for we are told that the
Messiah will come with a rod of iron in his hand and will break
the knees of those who despise him. They too will bow, not
willingly, but because they will have no choice.

Our King will return and he will ask each of us for an
accounting.

84. Jesus' triumphal entry into Jerusalem
(Luke 19:28-44)

Jesus has made his way from Galilee to Jerusalem and at last is
about to enter the Holy City. In order to get to Jerusalem, he
had to pass over the Mount of Olives.

'As he approached Bethphage and Bethany at the hill called
the Mount of Olives, he sent two of his disciples, saying to
them, "Go to the village ahead of you, and as you enter it, you

will find a colt tied there, which no-one has ever ridden. Untie it and bring it here"' (19:29-30). We are reminded of the Old Testament prophecy in the book of Zechariah, in which he speaks of the king of the Jews entering the Holy City riding on a donkey. Every Pharisee would have been aware of that Messianic prophecy and certainly Jesus was, and he was making a self-conscious move. No longer was he going to keep his identity a secret, and so he orders his disciples to fetch him a carefully designated donkey upon which he would ride triumphally into the city of Jerusalem.

'And he said, "If anyone asks you, 'Why are you untying it?' tell him, 'The Lord needs it.' " ' He is obviously sending his disciples to the home of someone whom he knows in Bethany, perhaps even that of Mary and Martha. In the context of teachers and their disciples, whenever the question was raised why something was to be done, the statement that would end all discussion was, 'The Lord needs it.' It was not using the word, Lord, in its ultimate sense of the sovereign God, but in the sense of one who is a ruler or a master over a servant. If the master needs it, then it is up to the servant to provide it. It is that simple. Jesus tells his disciples to use this formula should anybody raise an objection.

'They brought it to Jesus, threw their cloaks on the colt and put Jesus on it. As he went along, people spread their cloaks on the road. When he came near the place where the road goes down the Mount of Olives, the whole crowd of disciples began joyfully to praise God in loud voices for all the miracles they had seen: "Blessed is the king who comes in the name of the Lord! Peace in heaven and glory in the highest!" ' Luke's description is brief, but Matthew and the other gospel writers describe how they waved palm branches and shouted words like, 'Hallelujah' or 'Hosanna'.

This was a festive occasion to beat all festive occasions. This is the moment the Jewish people had longed for for centuries. This was the public reception of the long-awaited Messiah. They were so excited they even took off their garments and threw them in his path, so this donkey, bearing the burden of the King of kings, could step on them.

As Jesus enters the town, the people wave the branches and cry, 'Hosanna, Blessed is the *king* who comes in the name of the Lord.' In so doing, they are acknowledging that the kingship of Jesus is designated by God himself. They cry out, 'Peace in heaven and glory in the highest.' The song of the people on Palm Sunday is almost identical to the song of the angels at the nativity of Jesus: 'Glory to God in the highest, and on earth peace to men on whom his favour rests' (Luke 2:14).

The reaction of some of the Pharisees was one of fury: 'Teacher, rebuke your disciples!' But Jesus answered, 'I tell you, if they keep quiet, the stones will cry out!' It is not clear to what stones Jesus was referring. Perhaps it was simply the vast array of stones that covered the environs of Jerusalem, or perhaps the stones for which Jerusalem was famous, the stones of Herod that made up the temple and dwarfed everything else. Was it those stones that Jesus said would cry out? Those stones that Jesus said would not be left one upon another? Those stones that would come crashing down in protest at the rejection of the King of kings in the destruction of Jerusalem in AD 70, in fulfilment of prophecy. We can only speculate what was in his mind at that point.

'As he approached Jerusalem and saw the city, he wept over it and said, "If you, even you, had only known on this day what would bring you peace!"' The crowds were crying 'Peace!', but the people of Jerusalem knew no peace. In his lament he says, 'But now it is hidden from your eyes. The days will come upon you when your enemies will build an embankment against you and encircle you and hem you in on every side. They will dash you to the ground, you and the children within your walls. They will not leave one stone on another, because you did not recognize the time of God's coming to you' (19:42-44). Jesus is saying, 'God himself has visited this town, but you didn't recognize him. And because of that, O Jerusalem, your enemies will come and they will destroy you.' And with these words of lamentation, Luke ends his account of Jesus' entry into Jerusalem.

85. Jesus in the temple (Luke 19:45–20:8)

Soon after Jesus entered into the City of Jerusalem he went to the temple. The chronology is not clear, but it is very likely that that was the first place he went after entering the city for it would be the natural place to conclude his triumphal entry.

Jesus drives the traders out of the temple (Luke 19:45-48)
'Then he entered the temple area and began driving out those who were selling. "It is written," he said to them, " 'My house will be a house of prayer'; but you have made it 'a den of robbers'." ' We know from John 2:12-22 that on another occasion Jesus also cleansed the temple, much earlier in his ministry. The similarity of these events, however, has led some critics to suppose that Luke's chronology is out of order here, but there is no reason whatsoever to assume that Jesus did not act in a similar way on more than one occasion. Obviously he was greatly upset the first time he came across the traders in the temple courtyard, and so it would not be inconsistent for him to show the same anger when he sees the same practices repeated. Pilgrims came from all over Palestine and beyond for the annual feast days, and it was required of these visitors to the temple to offer certain sacrifices, according to the customs of the feasts. It was very inconvenient for many pilgrims to carry livestock with them on a long and arduous journey and so they would wait until they arrived in Jerusalem to purchase the necessary sacrificial animals. The religious officials in charge of the maintenance of the temple found it very lucrative to make available these necessary provisions for sacrifice, presumably in the court of the Gentiles or in the outer court of the temple. Because of the high demand, they could charge exorbitant fees for these animals, and they took advantage of the pilgrims' need to acquire the appropriate local coinage by charging very high rates of exchange. Some scholars think that there were also

booths selling religious trinkets or souvenirs, just as you would find in present day Jerusalem. No doubt these transactions were accompanied by loud discussions or arguments creating an atmosphere that was a far cry from the sense of peace appropriate for acts of worship and prayer. When Jesus saw this going on he was furious, and took action immediately to cleanse the temple.

After this incident, we read that 'every day he was teaching at the temple. But the chief priests, the teachers of the law and the leaders among the people were trying to kill him. Yet they could not find any way to do it, because all the people hung on his words' (19:47-48). The astonishing thing is that having infuriated the religious leaders by his entry into Jerusalem and his disruption of the traders in the temple grounds, Jesus was allowed to get away with it, at least for the time being. You would think that the merchants would have gathered together and killed him, or that the religious officials would have had him arrested. So what was it that restrained them? Humanly speaking, Jesus was surrounded by a thronging multitude, cheering him on; public support was so overwhelmingly in his favour that nobody dared raise a finger against him. They wanted to stop him, however, and conspired together to plan his downfall. Then one day they seized their opportunity.

'One day as he was teaching the people in the temple courts and preaching the gospel, the chief priests and the teachers of the law, together with the elders, came up to him' (20:1). Luke notes that the chief priests and the scribes come with the elders. This is a specific reference to men of particular authority in the Jewish community. The religious community of Israel was ruled over by the Sanhedrin. Each member of the Sanhedrin was called an elder, but in the local jargon there was an elite core within the elite, an inner circle of those who held the most influence, and these men were known collectively as 'the elders'. Luke's use of the term 'the elders' suggest that it wasn't the rank and file members of the Sanhedrin that came to confront Jesus, rather it was the highest officials of the Sanhedrin. They had obviously spent quite some time plotting how to trap him, for the question they ask was cleverly thought out: 'Tell us by what authority you are doing these things,' they said. 'Who gave you this authority?' (20:2).

Jesus was a Rabbi, but not having been ordained by the Jewish Sanhedrin, he was not recognized as an official of Judaism by the officials themselves, and so by asking this question they hope to trap him. If he claimed to operate by his own authority then he could be charged with blasphemy; if he said by no authority, he would show himself to be a maverick. So they have placed Jesus in a dilemma and are obviously trying to discredit him.

In characteristic fashion, Jesus answers their question, 'I will also ask you a question. Tell me, John's baptism – was it from heaven, or from men?' Jesus knew what they were trying to do and so he moves the focus of attention from himself to John the Baptist, and asks them about the source of his authority. 'They discussed it among themselves and said, "If we say, 'From heaven,' he will ask, 'Why didn't you believe him?' But if we say, 'From men,' all the people will stone us, because they are persuaded that John was a prophet." So they answered, "We don't know where it was from" ' (20:5-7).

I would have loved to have seen the faces of these men as they fumbled about for an answer to answer Jesus' question. John was immensely popular among the people, a thing that we often overlook today. In terms of Christian history, John is nothing more than a footnote to the central importance of Jesus, because we are reading a New Testament that was written after the death, resurrection and ascension of Jesus and of course John didn't rise from the dead or ascend into heaven. But in the first century, John was more famous than Jesus, and it is interesting to note that the Jewish historian, Josephus, in writing the history of Israel in the first century, gives much more to John the Baptist's ministry than he does to Jesus.

So Jesus questions them about John the Baptist. They knew that if they said he was from heaven then Jesus would say they had better repent because that was John's message, and Jesus would go on to ask why they didn't listen to him when he testified of Jesus. So they cannot say that John was from heaven without incriminating themselves, but neither could they say he was not of heaven for they were afraid of inciting the rage and fury of the mob. So what do they do?

They set out to trap Jesus, but instead Jesus does to them what they were trying to do to him. You can almost hear the ripple of laughter as the crowd watches these arrogant men admitting shamefully that they don't know the answer. So Jesus said to them, 'Neither will I tell you by what authority I am doing these things.' The confrontation is over and for the moment at least the leaders of the Sanhedrin must leave in humiliation.

86. The parable of the vine-growers
(Luke 20:9-18)

After the incident in the temple where the religious leaders tried to discredit Jesus, Luke writes:

> He went on to tell the people this parable: 'A man planted a vineyard, rented it to some farmers and went away for a long time. At harvest time he sent a servant to the tenants so they would give him some of the fruit of the vineyard. But the tenants beat him and sent him away empty-handed. He sent another servant, but that one also they beat and treated shamefully, and sent away empty-handed. He sent still a third; and they wounded him and threw him out. Then the owner of the vineyard said, "What shall I do? I will send my son, whom I love; perhaps they will respect him." But when the tenants saw him, they talked the matter over. "This is the heir," they said. "Let's kill him, and the inheritance will be ours." So they threw him out of the vineyard and killed him. "What then will the owner of the vineyard do to them? He will come and kill those tenants and give the vineyard to others." When the people heard this, they said, "May this never be!"' (20:9-16).

This parable has certain similarities to the one Luke records in 19:11-27 of the nobleman who went into a far country to receive a kingdom. However, this parable has a deeper, more important meaning. Before we look at it, it is helpful to note that it, perhaps more than any other parable with the exception of the parable of the sower, benefits from an almost allegorical method of interpretation. Normally we would seek to draw out only one or two points from a parable, but there are occasions when the various characters and events within a parable have a symbolic meaning.

The parable we are looking at in this section is one of the easiest to understand, and it is plain that his contemporaries grasped the point right away. The image of a vineyard was commonly used by Old Testament people to refer to the nation of Israel itself; God had planted a vineyard by creating for himself a covenant people, a people consecrated and sanctified to him for his purposes. And so, in this parable, God is obviously the one who planted the vineyard, which is the household of Israel, and he rented it out to vine-growers, obviously meaning the religious leaders. Jesus, by way of parable, was summarizing the history of Israel, where for generation after generation, the people of God were led by dishonest leaders, false prophets and priests who didn't bring forth the fruit that God had required from the nation, his personal vineyard. And so, from time to time, God would send prophets to bring about change and repentance so that the fruit would be produced just as God intended. But the prophets were despised and persecuted.

Finally, Jesus tells how the owner of the vineyard decided to send his beloved son. It would have been clear to anyone standing there that Jesus was talking about himself – he is the Son of the owner of the vineyard, the Son that the vine-growers plotted to kill that the inheritance may be theirs.

One of the reasons why Jesus provoked so much jealousy and hatred among the religious leaders was that he was a threat to their power. They were accustomed to public adulation and respect, but when Jesus comes, his righteousness exposes their lack of righteousness, his truth dwarfs their falsehood. Instead of repenting and falling on their knees before him, they conspire to rid themselves of him. In the parable Jesus says they cast him out of the vineyard, before killing him. Jesus is predicting that he will be killed not by the Jewish nation but that they will send him out of the temple, out of the city to Golgotha, to be judged and condemned by Gentiles.

Jesus attaches to the end of the narrative this question, 'What then will the owner of the vineyard do to them?' Any sober man, no matter how angry or hostile towards Jesus, should have been able to face this question. Jesus was challenging them to think about the consequences of what they were planning to do. Then he answers his own question: 'He will come and kill those tenants and give the vineyard to others.' The New Testament tells how after Israel rejected their own Messiah, the gospel then went to the Gentiles, in part as a judgment upon Israel.

When the people heard these words they said, 'May this never be!' Jesus looked directly at them and asked, 'Then what is the meaning of that which is written: "The stone the builders rejected has become the capstone"?' This quotation from Psalm 118 is a cryptic reference to the Messiah himself. The image is of a stonemason carefully examining the raw materials in order to select only the best stones for their building. They find one piece of stone that they consider marred and unworthy of the beautiful edifice they are creating and so they consign it to the reject pile, yet that stone becomes the very cornerstone of the building. Jesus is himself the cornerstone, the builders who reject him are the religious leaders of Israel, but God chooses him to be the cornerstone of his new building, his church.

Jesus then says, 'Everyone who falls on that stone will be broken to pieces, but he on whom it falls will be crushed' (20:18). This cornerstone was also a stumbling block to the Jews: they looked at Jesus and rejected him, they tripped over him, and their fall was disaster for they were broken to pieces and scattered like dust. This was the fate of Jerusalem in the year 70.

87. Paying taxes to Caesar (Luke 20:19-26)

When the scribes and the chief priests heard the parable of the vine-growers that Jesus told, their rage intensified greatly, and we read in verse 19, 'The teachers of the law and the chief priests looked for a way to arrest him immediately, because they knew he had spoken this parable against them. But they were afraid of the people.' For a moment they abandoned their attempt to discredit Jesus and instead tried to grab him themselves and kill him, for their fear of the multitudes was overwhelmed by the intensity of their fury at these words he spoke. They understood that he spoke this parable against them, and the people understood that too – it was clear that the wicked wine-growers represented the chief priests and the scribes themselves.

But, once again, as furious as the leaders are, they manage to contain their anger for the moment and withdraw in order to devise another way to trap him: 'Keeping a close watch on him, they sent spies, who pretended to be honest. They hoped to catch Jesus in something he said so that they might hand him over to the power and authority of the governor' (20:20). This time their idea is more devious – they decide that as they cannot stir up problems for Jesus from the multitudes, maybe they could try to trap him into doing or saying something that would get him into trouble with the Roman governors. That way, the Jewish religious leaders would not be at fault in the eyes of the people, rather it will be the Romans. So they ask Jesus another trick question designed to trap him: 'So the spies questioned him, "Teacher, we know that you speak and teach what is right, and that you do not show partiality but teach the way of God in accordance with the truth"' (20:21). The words of flattery fall from the lips of these devious spies that are pretending to be righteous, pretending to be devout followers of Jesus. Then comes the punch line, the question designed to catch him out, 'Is it right for us to pay taxes to Caesar or not?' These people had learnt their lesson the last time they had tackled Jesus with a question – he had responded with another question, and so this time they were not going to allow him to evade the answer.

So they said basically, 'What's your answer: Yes or No? Is it lawful for us to pay taxes to Caesar or not?'

But again Jesus detected their trickery and so he asked them to get him a coin, a denarius. They see that he is going to answer their question, but they also detect that once again Jesus is master of the situation. So while they are fetching a denarius, the anticipation and awe of the crowd were growing to a climax – they wait to see what Jesus is going to do with this coin. Jesus 'said to them, "Show me a denarius. Whose portrait and inscription are on it?" "Caesar's," they replied. He said to them, "Then give to Caesar what is Caesar's, and to God what is God's"' (20:24-25). What an answer!

Out of deference to their religious beliefs, the Roman occupiers allowed the Jews to mint their own coins without images of people on them. It is still possible to come across coins from ancient Israel decorated with emblems from nature: ears of corn, vine leaves, palm branches and so on. But the one thing they didn't have was portraits because that was considered an offence against the Ten Commandments. However, there were also many Roman coins in circulation, the most basic of which was the silver coin, the common monetary unit called the denarius which bore the likeness of Caesar. This coin indicated the reach and extent of the rule of Rome. Coinage bearing the image of the ruler of a nation was used as a sign of that nation's authority over subject nations, so in a sense the rule of a nation extended as far as their coinage was in circulation. These coins, however, also carried with them the notion of the divinity of the Emperor, something which was utterly repugnant to the Jew.

But Jesus pointed to the coin and asked whose image it bore. When they answered 'Caesar's', he said: 'Render to Caesar the things that are Caesar's.' Caesar's image on the coin signified that they were under Caesar's legal political authority. They might not like it or enjoy it, but they couldn't deny it. They were under the authority of the Roman Empire and so were obliged to obey the civil magistrates where possible according to divine law, and as Caesar's picture was on the coin then they had also to pay the tax.

What was not appropriate, however, was the granting of worship to Caesar. If Jesus were to say that they should obey Caesar at every point, again he would be guilty of speaking blasphemy, for he would be suggesting that the Jewish people should worship Caesar. If, however, he were to tell the people not to pay the tribute, then the chief priests and the scribes could report him to the Roman authorities. But again Jesus outwitted them by dividing the question up very neatly: 'render to Caesar the things that are Caesar's, and to God the things that are God's', in other words, worship, devotion, obedience – those things belong to God alone.

So yet again they were unable to catch him out before the people, and marvelling at his answer they became silent.

88. Marriage and the resurrection (Luke 20:27-40)

Luke's narrative continues with the account of yet another attempt to discredit Jesus, this time by the Sadducees. The Sadducees are not mentioned very frequently in the New Testament, for they were a very small group, a much smaller party than the Pharisees. It is thought they derived their name from the Old Testament high priest Zadok, and were members of the Israeli aristocracy, the chief priests. They were very wealthy and were not particularly beloved by the people, because in order to protect their wealth they had collaborated with the Roman conquerors. They were distinct from the Pharisees and one point of perpetual dispute and debate between these two groups was to do with whether or not there was life after death. The Pharisees affirmed a belief in life after death but the Sadducees did not. There is also evidence to indicate that the Sadducees, although they accepted the whole Old Testament, gave special weight to the five books of Moses.

So it is this group that now sought to trap Jesus with an impossible question: 'Teacher,' they said, 'Moses wrote for us that if a man's brother dies and leaves a wife but no children,

the man must marry the widow and have children for his brother'
(20:28). The first thing to note is that they appeal to a very
obscure point of Old Testament law, and, as far as we can tell,
the actual practice of this law had been dormant for centuries.
This law was called the Law of Leverite Marriage, and required
that if a man married a woman and then died childless, lest his
line should be cut off, his unmarried brother was required by
law to marry the widowed woman to ensure that his brother
would have descendants.

So the Sadducees present Jesus with a hypothetical case
regarding this Levite stipulation: 'Now there were seven
brothers. The first one married a woman and died childless.
The second and then the third married her, and in the same way
the seven died, leaving no children. Finally, the woman died
too. Now then, at the resurrection whose wife will she be, since
the seven were married to her?' (20:29-33).

In response to this thorny question Jesus says some very
strange and puzzling things: 'The people of this age marry and
are given in marriage. But those who are considered worthy of
taking part in that age and in the resurrection from the dead will
neither marry nor be given in marriage, and they can no longer
die; for they are like the angels. They are God's children, since
they are children of the resurrection' (20:34-36). To understand
what Jesus is driving at, we need to understand certain of the
expressions he uses.

Firstly, when he speaks of 'the people of this age' he is simply
referring to anybody who is alive. Then he uses the phrase 'to
marry and are given in marriage'. This expression also occurs
earlier in Luke's gospel and is used frequently in Scripture to
indicate a very loose view of marriage and divorce, but in this
context such an interpretation does not fit. It would seem that
Jesus is simply saying that here on earth, people get married,
but those who are considered worthy to attain to that age, that
is, those who are able to enter into the kingdom of God, and the
resurrection, neither marry nor are given in marriage. Jesus'
words suggest, therefore, that in heaven there is no such thing

as marriage. Now that comes as a profound disappointment to a lot of people, particularly those who are looking forward to a joyous reunion with their spouses in heaven.

What Jesus is showing, however, is that people wrongly assumed that life would go on after death without any significant change in quality. The New Testament, especially in 1 Corinthians 15, does teach a continuity of existence from this world to the next, but there will be significant changes in the kind of life that we will enjoy in heaven. However, very little is said about what changes will take place, but we know that whatever the change, it will bring with it an improvement. Our joy will be augmented far beyond what we can imagine. Part of the reason why marriage means so much to us, is the companionship it brings – we have one person on whom we can depend for their loyalty, love and affection. In heaven I think we are going to have that kind of close relationship with everybody, because once sin is removed from human relationships, we will be able to enjoy a closeness with others that would transcend what we enjoy with our own marriage partners now. Jesus is not saying that when I get to heaven I will not know my wife, but I can only assume that when we get to heaven we will be able to have an even deeper love relationship there than we ever could here.

Another phrase in Jesus' reply that would have been significant for a Jew was 'they can no longer die'. He is not simply saying that once we go to heaven we will not die anymore, but we will not *be able* to die anymore. One of the reasons that marriage was so important in the Jewish context was its role in bearing children. This was seen as a way of keeping one's name alive, to live on through one's children. Jesus understands the thinking of his contemporaries here and points out that this will not be an issue in heaven, because, once there, we are free from death: 'they can no longer die; for they are like the angels.' Jesus does not spell out what he means by 'they are like the angels', but notice he does not say that they *are* angels. When we die, we will not suddenly become angels, as some have supposed. Others have argued that this means we will lose our sexual identity, because angels are thought to be genderless. All this is utter speculation, however. I suspect that Jesus uses this phrase simply to emphasize the immortality of the redeemed – like the angels they cannot die.

Then Jesus goes on to say, 'They are God's children, since they are children of the resurrection' (20:36b). The trap the Sadducees were seeking to lay for Jesus was to do with one's earthly family, but Jesus points out that when we get to heaven the family that we will be a member of will be the family of God, we will be children of God, even as we are now, by virtue of our regeneration. Jesus' answer confounds those who are trying to trick him, but he doesn't stop there. He faces head on the belief that provoked the question in the first place, namely that the Sadducees were convinced that there was not life after death. He turns their attention back to Moses: 'But in the account of the bush, even Moses showed that the dead rise, for he calls the Lord "the God of Abraham, and the God of Isaac, and the God of Jacob." He is not the God of the dead, but of the living, for to him all are alive' (20:37-38). He reminds the Sadducees of the encounter of Moses with the bush that burned but was not consumed, in which God revealed himself by name as the God of Abraham, Isaac and Jacob. The inference that our Lord himself draws from the Old Testament text is that God is the God of the living, and so, though Abraham and Isaac and Jacob died according to the mortality of the flesh, nevertheless with respect to God they are alive with him.

Again Jesus answered successfully the tricky question posed to him. Luke comments: 'Some of the teachers of the law responded, "Well said, teacher!" ' The scribes were used to this kind of debate and were impressed with the profundity of Jesus' answer. The Sadducees had to admit defeat at this point. Then Luke adds, 'And no one dared to ask him any more questions' (20:40). They recognized that the more questions they asked, the better they made Jesus look.

We should take comfort from this incident not simply because it demonstrates Jesus' great ability in public debate, but because he shows his desire to provide assurance for his people of the reality of heaven and of life beyond the grave.

89. David's Son and David's Lord (Luke 20:41-44)

Having dealt with the Sadducees' difficult question about marriage and heaven, Jesus, himself, then raises an even more complex question. It is almost as if he has saved the most difficult question for last and raises it before they can ask it of him. 'Then Jesus said to them, "How is it that they say the Christ is the Son of David?" ' (20:41).

Jesus knew of the Jewish expectation that the coming Messiah would be someone from the lineage of David. They were dreaming of the day when the Messiah would restore the golden age of the monarchy that David had established, and so the hopes for the Messiah were all tied up with the hero character of David. Now, of course, Jesus is not discounting the fact that he is of the lineage of David. On numerous occasions the Scriptures make it very clear that Jesus was the Lion of Judah, that he came from David's tribe and that the genealogies of Mary and Joseph, found in the New Testament, show he is from that direct line of descendancy from David. So, with that in mind, we can dismiss the view that Jesus was telling them here that they were wrong to expect the Messiah to come from the line of David. That's not Jesus' point at all. Rather he is seeking to highlight an apparent contradiction: how is it that Christ is David's Son, but David himself refers to Christ as 'the Lord'? Verses 42-43 read:

> David himself declares in the Book of Psalms:
>
> > ' "The Lord said to my Lord:
> > 'Sit at my right hand
> > until I make your enemies
> > a footstool for your feet.' " '

This question may not seem all that difficult to us in the West but to Jesus' contemporaries it was very baffling. They operated under the belief that the father is always greater than the son, and the grandfather greater than the grandson. This semitic belief was very strong with respect to the honour that was accorded to one's parents and grandparents, so it would have been unthinkable to a Jew that Isaac could be greater than Abraham, since Abraham was the father of Isaac and Isaac depended upon Abraham for his very existence. Similarly, it would have been unthinkable that Jacob would be greater than Isaac, and so on down the line. So how could one who was a descendant of David be at the same time the Lord of David, the one who stood over David? To answer the question Jesus quotes David himself from Psalm 110. Here is David himself, who is considered the greatest king of Israel, the father of the house of David, speaking of the Messiah who is to come as being his own Lord. David himself acknowledges that there is at least one exception to the Jewish rule of greatness; there will be one descendant who is greater than his father and that is the one to whom God assigns the anointed office of Messiah, the son who is greater than David because David himself confesses that he is Lord.

Of all the wonderful passages in the Old Testament, this one is the most frequently quoted in the New Testament. The words of the psalm are so majestic and so important it is no wonder that the early church fathers and the biblical writers made so much of it.

Often in the Old Testament when the word 'Lord' is used it is printed in capital letters, 'LORD'. When printed in this way it represents the Hebrew word 'Yahweh'. At other times, however, it is printed in lower-case letters. If we were to look at the Hebrew text of Psalm 110 we see that it says: 'Yahweh says to my Adonai', not 'Yahweh says to Yahweh'. In the Old Testament, Yahweh is the name of God, but his supreme title is 'Adonai' or 'Sovereign One'. And so in this extraordinary passage we find David describing a conversation between God and the one who is David's Lord. David is saying 'God said to my Sovereign', or 'Yahweh said to my Adonai' – he is recognizing that there is one who has the name of God, *Adonai*, yet somehow must be distinguished from God, *Yahweh*. It is impossible to make any sense of this apart from the concept of the trinity and the concept of the incarnation, because here David is speaking about the Lord that God himself appoints to Lordship. The title *Adonai* is that which Paul calls 'the name that is above every name' – the Messiah.

David is saying that the one who is the Messiah is the one who is his Lord. He must prostrate himself before the one whom God designates as the Messiah, regardless of whether he is David's son or grandson. If God gives him the role of Messiah then he is my Lord, says David, even though he is my son.

Even Mary his mother and Joseph his legal father accepted Jesus' greatness and worshipped him. Mary herself confesses that Jesus is her Lord, again reversing the patriarchal and matriarchal lines of authority of the semitic people.

Jesus' question is a rhetorical one: 'David therefore calls him 'Lord', and how is he his son?' He is his son according to earthly genealogy, but by heavenly descent Jesus is greater than David. Jesus is not denying that he is the son of David, but he is saying that he is that, but also far much more: he is David's son and he is David's Lord. And so, in this text we have a demonstrative and clear claim by Jesus that he is indeed the promised Messiah.

90. The hypocrisy of the scribes and a widow's gift (Luke 20:45–21:4)

Following the difficult words of Jesus, recorded in 20:41-44, Luke then writes how Jesus turned and addressed some words of warning to the disciples.

The hypocrisy of the scribes (Luke 20:45-47)

'While all the people were listening, Jesus said to his disciples, "Beware of the teachers of the law. They like to walk around in flowing robes and love to be greeted in the marketplaces and have the most important seats in the synagogues and the places of honour at banquets. They devour widows' houses and for a show make lengthy prayers. Such men will be punished most severely." '

Jesus says these provocative things to his disciples in the presence of the scribes. He is not at pains to tell them these things in secret, but rather warns of the hypocrisy of the scribes in such a way that the scribes themselves had no choice but to hear. This is not the first time Jesus had accused the scribes of hypocrisy, describing how they loved public adulation and honour, but on this occasion he adds a further significant accusation. In verse 47 he accuses them of devouring widows' houses. In other words, he charges them with the crime of exploiting some of the most defenceless people in society. In the ancient world, the plight of the widows was desperate; economically and legally. They were at the mercy of state and, for the most part, had little or no income and no power in the courts. It is no accident that the Bible singles out widows as the particular object of concern and compassion for the Christian community. In fact, James tells us that the essence of true religion is to take care of widows and orphans: ' Religion that God our Father accepts as pure and faultless is this: to look after orphans and widows in their distress ...' (Jas. 1:27). They are not to be neglected, but are to be honoured, respected and helped whenever help is needed.

The widows looked to their scribes, as the ones who would speak comforting words of God, who would be advocates of justice and apostles of mercy. They invested a lot of trust and hope in their religious leaders. However, not only did these scribes fail to help the widows as God had ordained, but they, in fact, became some of their main exploiters.

There was a rule among the Rabbis that the scribes were not allowed to receive financial remuneration for their teaching, and in order to get round those rules they solicited donations. Often, however, they did it by taking advantage of the desperate plight of the widows. They would befriend them and then defraud them of their income. Jesus uses the word 'devour':

they 'devour widows' houses and for a show make lengthy prayers'. The prayers that they gave on behalf of the widows were in themselves nothing more than a camouflage of their real intentions which was to separate the widows from their money. Jesus utters a dreadful warning: 'Such men will be punished most severely.'

The widow's gift (Luke 21:1-4)

After delivering this warning about the hypocrisy of the scribes, Jesus looked up and 'saw the rich putting their gifts into the temple treasury. He also saw a poor widow put in two very small copper coins. "I tell you the truth," he said, "this poor widow has put in more than all the others. All these people gave their gifts out of their wealth; but she out of her poverty put in all she had to live on."'

Scholars tell us that the treasury in the temple was not the place where money was stored, but rather where money was given. There were approximately thirteen trumpet-shaped chests where people made their offerings on behalf of the poor, and also to help with some of the temple expenses. It was situated in the portion of the temple known as the Women's Court. This area was not restricted exclusively to women, but was a place where women could come without restrictions.

Most of us at one time or another have heard of the 'widow's mite', and here is the story as Jesus tells it. As he was standing in the temple he saw some wealthy people depositing gifts into the treasury. They were giving out of their abundance, but then Jesus saw 'a certain poor widow'. This poverty stricken widow was voluntarily putting in two small copper coins. These coins were the smallest unit of coinage in the Jewish currency, and were of very little value. In Rabbinic law a person was not allowed to put into the box less than two of these mites, because it was more trouble to handle one of these tiny coins than it was worth. And so this woman complies with this rule and puts in two small copper coins.

Jesus was obviously moved by her act and comments: 'I tell

you the truth, this poor widow has put in more than all the others.' Clearly Jesus was not speaking in a financial sense, but this widow put in something that was worth more than money; her heart was in that gift. The point that Jesus is making is that this woman gave sacrificially.

The New Testament equivalent of the Old Testament method of tithing does not spell out in detail what percentage we are to give, but rather that we are to give cheerfully, and as the Lord prospers us, so we are to give. This woman, in spite of her unspeakable poverty, was still so thankful for the blessings that she enjoyed from God that she gave proportionally so much more than the wealthy man, for they 'gave their gifts out of their wealth'. Hers was a sacrifice of love and though she was poverty stricken economically she was fabulously wealthy spiritually. She did not expect to be noticed for her tiny act of sacrifice, but she was noticed by the King of Heaven who pronounced his benediction upon her for her charity, compassion and sacrificial love.

91. Jesus predicts destruction of Jerusalem (Luke 21:5-22)

In this section, Luke records a conversation that Jesus had with his disciples that is known as the Olivet Discourse. It took place as Jesus and his disciples were going from the temple to the Mount of Olives where they were spending the night during Holy Week, and is recorded in all three of the synoptic gospels. In it Jesus predicts the destruction of Jerusalem and talks of his own second coming. Because of the imagery that is used and the difficulty of the passage, theologians have been severely divided on how we are to understand Jesus' words. Jesus is talking about two clearly different events separated by many centuries, so there has been much debate over what portions of the text apply to the events of AD 70 and what portion apply to Jesus's return.

The discourse begins in Luke 21:5, following the story of

the generous widow. 'Some of his disciples were remarking about how the temple was adorned with beautiful stones and with gifts dedicated to God. But Jesus said, "As for what you see here, the time will come when not one stone will be left on another; every one of them will be thrown down."' We have already noted in previous studies that the temple of Jerusalem was one of the wonders of the ancient world. The people of Palestine were aware of the longevity of buildings made out of stone and it was inconceivable that something as huge, stable and impregnable as the temple of Herod could ever be destroyed. But Jesus predicts that 'the time will come when not one stone will be left on another; every one of them will be thrown down.' The disciples by now knew better than to ask, 'How can that be?' They had seen Jesus do the remarkable, the miraculous and so, instead of questioning the possibility of this event, they asked: 'Teacher, when will these things happen? And what will be the sign that they are about to take place?' (21:7).

He replied: 'Watch out that you are not deceived. For many will come in my name, claiming, "I am he," and, "The time is near.' Do not follow them. When you hear of wars and revolutions, do not be frightened. These things must happen first, but the end will not come right away.' Then he said to them: 'Nation will rise against nation, and kingdom against kingdom. There will be great earthquakes, famines and pestilences in various places, and fearful events and great signs from heaven' (21:8-11).

The first thing Jesus says in answer to their question is a warning to be on their guard about false Messiahs. Many fraudsters appeared, as early as twenty years after Jesus' ascension, claiming to be the returning Messiah. So Jesus warns them not to be misled.

Then Jesus describes some of the other signs: rumours of wars and disturbances, international disputes, earthquakes, plagues and famines. From the writings of historians from the first century AD we know that many of these things did in fact happen before the fall of Jerusalem. And so it is not necessary to take these signs and apply them to his return at the end of the age.

Jesus then says: 'But before all this, they will lay hands on you and persecute you. They will deliver you to synagogues and prisons, and you will be brought before kings and governors, and all on account of my name' (21:12). The book of Acts in its account of the early Christian community shows the accuracy of this prediction. We read of persecutions and imprisonment and of men like Paul and Silas being brought before kings and governors because of their commitment to Christ. Of the eleven disciples, ten suffered a martyr's death, and the eleventh, John, died of old age in exile. Paul, himself, was eventually beheaded in Rome. Many early Christians were subjected to persecution and their martyrdom added magnificent testimony to the truth of the claim of Christ. As Jesus said:

> 'This will result in your being witnesses to them. But make up your mind not to worry beforehand how you will defend yourselves. For I will give you words and wisdom that none of your adversaries will be able to resist or contradict. You will be betrayed even by parents, brothers, relatives and friends, and they will put some of you to death. All men will hate you because of me. But not a hair of your head will perish. By standing firm you will gain life' (21:13-19).

It may seem strange that Jesus said this, because the hair on their head did perish; they suffered unbelievable physical pain and death. Jesus' point, however, is that their eternal reward was not jeopardised by these things. Nothing could happen to them that was outside the sovereign protection of God, so, ultimately, although the hair on their head was hurt for a moment, they were not destroyed, because Christ had promised the final triumph of his kingdom even over death, and with it the resurrection of the body.

Jesus then tells them of more signs: 'When you see Jerusalem being surrounded by armies, you will know that its desolation is near. Then let those who are in Judea flee to the mountains, let those in the city get out, and let those in the country not enter the city. For this is the time of punishment in fulfilment of all that has been written' (21:20-22). Jesus' warning and instructions here run counter to established practices in the ancient world. He tells them that when they see Jerusalem being surrounded by armies, they are to flee the city. This instruction is opposite to the normal practice of the ancient world. Whenever enemy armies began to invade a country, the people who lived in the desert or countryside would always make their way to the strongest fortress or walled city in order to seek refuge from the ravages of war. But Jesus warns his followers not to go into the city, but instead to flee to the mountains. And this is precisely what many Christians did. They recalled the teaching of Jesus, and when the Roman armies marched towards Jerusalem, instead of seeking refuge in the city, large numbers fled to Pella, across the Jordan to the east, and so were spared from destruction.

92. Predictions concerning Jerusalem and the Gentiles (Luke 21:23-24)

Luke's narrative then continues with Jesus' solemn lament:

> 'How dreadful it will be in those days for pregnant women and nursing mothers! There will be great distress in the land and wrath against this people. They will fall by the sword and will be taken as prisoners to all the nations. Jerusalem will be trampled on by the Gentiles until the times of the Gentiles are fulfilled' (21:23-24).

Pregnant or nursing women are some of the most vulnerable members of society and the conditions of deprivation caused by a siege would be particularly distressing and dangerous for them. Jesus laments for them in their distress, then goes on to predict the fate of the Jewish people.

Various early historians, recounting the events of the fall of Jerusalem, show how accurate Jesus' predictions were. Not a single Jew was left alive in Jerusalem, and those who survived were, in fact, taken captive and sent all over the world. They lost their homeland, they lost their capital city, but they never lost their ethnic identity. It has been 1,900 years since the Jews were expelled from Jerusalem and to this day it is the dream of every Jew to see Jerusalem, to celebrate the Passover there.

The first Jews who were allowed to return to the destroyed city of Jerusalem were numbered among those Christians who had fled to Pella. After the conclusion of the Roman-Jewish war they were given permission to inhabit a portion of the ruined city, which they did, under the leadership of a man called Simeon, who, according to church history, was the successor to James as the leader of the Jerusalem Church. The only other inhabitants of the city at this time were the famous Tenth Legion of the Roman soldiers.

In 132 Jerusalem again became a centre of warfare. Certain Jews, who were not living in Jerusalem, staged a revolt against Roman authority under the leadership of a man called Bar Kochba who claimed to be the Messiah. Hadrian, the emperor of Rome at that time, determined to make Jerusalem a pagan city and so he re-established it as a Roman Colony and renamed it Alia Capitalina. A new shrine was built right on the place of the temple, a shrine to the pagan god Jupiter.

In the fourth century, the Roman empire was Christianized and the city came under Christian control, but three centuries later the Muslims, led by Omar, conquered the city. To this day, one of the most important Islamic sites in the world is the Dome of the Rock, built on the site of the Herodian temple to commemorate Abraham and Ishmael, from whom some of the Islamic peoples are descended. And so, even though Jerusalem has once again come under the control of the Jewish people, the sacred temple area is still in the hands of Gentiles.

Much speculation has been made concerning Jesus' words in verse 24, 'until the times of the Gentiles be fulfilled'. Since the 1948 mandate that established the state of Israel, the Christian community has seen a revival of frenzied eschatological expectations. Some Christians and theologians are convinced that the events that have taken place in Palestine and Jerusalem in the twentieth century have no eschatological significance whatsoever, while others are reading the Bibles and the newspapers together everyday. There is by no means agreement on the significance of modern Israel to biblical prophesies about the future of the Jews. But verse 24 of this chapter, 'Jerusalem will be trampled on by the Gentiles until the times of the Gentiles are fulfilled', is taken very seriously by many people because elsewhere, most significantly in the letter to the Romans (11:25), Paul hints that after the gospel has spread to the Gentiles that God will deal once more with ethnic Israel.

Remember that Jesus described the destruction of Jerusalem as the vengeance of God against his people for rejecting their Messiah, and because of that, Jesus teaches that the promises of salvation will be given to strangers. The first generation of Christians were largely of Jewish descent but all that changed and, for the most part, Christianity has emerged as a Gentile religion. But Paul seems to suggest that there will come a time when another chapter will be written for the Jews, 'after the times of the Gentiles are fulfilled'. The word in verse 24 that is translated 'until' suggests a terminus – once the moment comes in redemptive history when the days of the Gentiles are fulfilled, then one expects a great work of God to bring Jews into his kingdom.

Another phenomenon is the unbelievable increase of Jewish Evangelism over the last twenty years or so. Some people see in this the converging of eschatological signs, but on the other hand it could be said that Jerusalem is still being trampled under foot by the Gentiles and some argue that until the Dome of the Rock is removed and the Jewish temple is restored, the end of the ages hasn't yet arrived.

I don't know much about those things. But I think it is important that we understand why there is so much concern about present day Israel and Jerusalem with respect to the prophesies of Jesus.

93. Signs of the return of Christ (Luke 21:25-38)

Jesus then goes on to talk about other signs, which most scholars agree represent the signs not of the destruction of Jerusalem, but rather of his coming at the end of the age: 'There will be signs in the sun, moon and stars. On the earth, nations will be in anguish and perplexity at the roaring and tossing of the sea. Men will faint from terror, apprehensive of what is coming on the world, for the heavenly bodies will be shaken' (21:25-26).

The language is not nearly as specific as that relating to the destruction of Jerusalem. Instead Jesus now gives general characteristics and signs. Many of these signs take place in nearly every generation; there is always perplexity and people fainting from fear. For these things to have any significance, therefore, they must take place in significant proportion. Because of the great threat of nuclear war and the fact that we are now involved in space travel and space-age technology, some people are convinced that we are living in the last hours of the last days.

I have never been one to speculate on the timing of the return of Jesus, but I do know that we have an absolute guarantee that he is coming. There are reasons in our own day for us to be alert to the very real possibility that in the not too distant future the end of history as we know it will be upon us. We must be prepared, for Jesus said, 'At that time they will see the Son of Man coming in a cloud with power and great glory. When these things begin to take place, stand up and lift up your heads, because your redemption is drawing near' (21:27-28). Most people are terrified by the thought of the end of the world, but for the Christian, it is the greatest hope that he has. Therefore when these things take place, the Christian is called to look up and rejoice in the knowledge that his Redeemer is coming.

Jesus concludes this discourse with a very short parable that is included in the other synoptic gospels also.

> And he told them a parable: 'Behold the fig tree and all the trees; as soon as they put forth leaves, you see it and know for yourselves that summer

is now near. Even so you, too, when you see these things happening, recognize that the kingdom of God is near at hand. Truly I say to you, this generation will not pass away until all things take place. Heaven and earth will pass away, but my words will not pass away' (21:29-33, NASB).

The primary meaning of this parable is not difficult to discern; Jesus is drawing an obvious parallel with nature. Just as we can tell the changing of the seasons by observing the leaves of the trees, so also when we see certain things coming to pass, these things that he has just explained, we must be prepared for the fulfilment of these things – for the kingdom of God is about to break in.

Verse 32, however, has caused no small amount of problems: 'I tell you the truth, this generation will certainly not pass away until all these things have happened.' This statement has been interpreted by some to mean that Jesus was predicting his own return within the lifetime of his disciples; obviously, as he did not return, many have doubted the accuracy of his words. However, the predictions Jesus made with regard to the destruction of Jerusalem and the dispersal of the Jews have been fulfilled with such a degree of accuracy and so it would seem strange that he could be so inaccurate with regard to such an important event. So there have been various attempts to resolve this difficulty.

Some have pointed to the fact that the word that is translated 'generation' does not necessarily refer to a particular age group of people, but rather to a kind of people. They interpret the phrase to mean that this unbelieving world will be with us until the end, or, conversely, that there may be true believers such as the disciples are, right up until the time of Jesus' appearance.

Others have sought to find the solution in a more technical approach to the structure of this entire discourse and the key meaning of the phrase, 'these things'. If 'these things' refers specifically to the events surrounding the destruction of Jerusalem, then of course 'these things' did take place before the death of the disciples.

Others say that we have an allusion to the coming of the

kingdom of God, not in its final consummation with the
appearance of Jesus at the end of the age, but with Jesus'
manifestation of his kingly power and glory at the ascension;
still others point to the outpouring of the Holy Spirit on the Day
of Pentecost.

But the point that Jesus is making is that every single promise
that he has made will surely come to pass. The interpretation I
favour is that by 'this generation' he means the believers who
form this new generation of hope that stretches from Christ's
ascension to his return. This interim period of history will
continue until the kingdom is consummated; everything else
may perish, but the word of Christ will remain intact.

Jesus then ends with an exhortation to vigilance and to prayer:
'Be careful, or your hearts will be weighed down with
dissipation, drunkenness and the anxieties of life, and that day
will close on you unexpectedly like a trap. For it will come
upon all those who live on the face of the whole earth' (21:34-
35). Jesus is warning his followers not to allow themselves to
be so enamoured by the frivolous activities of this world that
they give themselves up to drunkenness. The word translated
as 'dissipation' is the Greek term for a hangover, for somebody
who has been out carousing all night and wakes up with a
headache. Such ones are missing the spiritual experience of the
things of God and are the ones who will be trapped unexpectedly
when the kingdom of God comes. This, of course, is an allusion
to a hunter who sets his trap in order to catch the unsuspecting
game. However, God is not fiendishly setting traps to catch
people unaware; the very reason our Lord is giving this discourse
is so that we will *not* be caught off guard. But Christ understood
how it is difficult for humans to keep their thoughts focused on
heavenly matters, becoming instead preoccupied with the cares
of this world.

His conclusion is simple: 'Be always on the watch, and pray
that you may be able to escape all that is about to happen, and
that you may be able to stand before the Son of Man' (21:36).
There is a two-edged admonition here; on the one hand, there is

a very sober warning of certain destruction that will befall people who have taken the teaching of Christ lightly and who have ignored the mandates of God himself. On the other hand, however, there is a glorious note here. The Authorized Version puts it this way: 'Watch ye therefore, and pray always, that ye may *be accounted worthy* to escape all these things ... and to stand before the Son of Man' (21:36).

The goal of the Christian life may be summarized in what the theologians call the Beatific Vision, which means the privilege to stand face to face before God. No-one has seen God at any time; his face is veiled to human eyes, and yet we look forward to that day when, as John promises, we will see him as he is (1 John 3:2). We are also reminded of Jesus' statements in the Sermon on the Mount: 'Blessed are the pure in heart, for they shall see God' (Matt. 5:8). So watch and pray always that you may be worthy to stand in the presence of Christ.

The chapter concludes with these words: 'Each day Jesus was teaching at the temple, and each evening he went out to spend the night on the hill called the Mount of Olives, and all the people came early in the morning to hear him at the temple' (21:37-38). The words used for 'spend the night' is the specific word for camping out. So the suggestion of the text is that Jesus did not retire to the comfortable headquarters in Bethany, perhaps at the home of Mary and Martha, but he actually went into the groves by the olive presses to spend the night. This, of course, is consistent with how he would spend the next night of his life, pouring out his heart in agony beneath the twisted and gnarled branches of the olive trees in Gethsemane.

94. Preparing for the Passover (Luke 22:1-14)

The twenty-second chapter of Luke's gospel marks a change from recording the teaching of Jesus to a more straightforward narrative form, detailing the events as they move rapidly towards their culmination in the passion of Jesus at Golgotha. Chapter 22 begins as follows:

> Now the Feast of Unleavened Bread, called the Passover, was
> approaching, and the chief priests and the teachers of the law were looking
> for some way to get rid of Jesus, for they were afraid of the people. Then
> Satan entered Judas, called Iscariot, one of the Twelve. And Judas went
> to the chief priests and the officers of the temple guard and discussed
> with them how he might betray Jesus. They were delighted and agreed
> to give him money. He consented, and watched for an opportunity to
> hand Jesus over to them when no crowd was present (22:1-6).

Luke refers to the Feast of Unleavened Bread and comments
that it is also called the Passover. Critics have drawn attention
to this particular statement because according to Deuteronomic
law the Feast of Unleavened Bread is a separate celebration
from the Passover. However, from a reading of the works of
Josephus, the Jewish historian, it is clear that he treats them as
if they were synonyms. It would seem that at this point in Jewish
history the Passover was more or less incorporated into the longer
celebration of the Feast of the Unleavened Bread. So Luke is
quite correct in what he says. It was at this time that the chief
priests and scribes continued their attempts to set a snare for Jesus.

Whereas the other gospel writers mention the treachery of
Judas, Luke is the only one to mention Satan, commenting that
'Satan entered Judas'. Luke isn't excusing Judas' act as the act
of a demon-possessed man, but to what extent Satan enters into
Judas, Luke leaves unanswered. It is not clear whether he simply
means to imply that Satan was making good use of the evil
intent of Judas' already diabolical heart, or whether there was a
conspiracy between the prince of darkness and Judas. But the
scriptures in no way diminish Judas' personal responsibility
for his role in this act of treachery.

Luke's kindness towards Judas is striking. He is giving an
account of the most insidious act of betrayal in all of human
history, and if he were writing according to the flesh doubtless
he would fill pages with vitriolic and vituperative attacks against
the character of this one who had betrayed the whole company.
Luke writes with great restraint, simply telling the facts with
very little comment.

The text of the Authorized Version reads: 'And he went his way, and communed with the chief priests ... and they were glad and covenanted to give him money.' Normally we think of words such as 'communed' and 'covenanted' in a holy context. But men make covenants of an unholy kind too, and this covenant between Judas and the chief priests was the most unholy covenant of all; the life of the Son of God was traded for money.

Luke then begins his account of the Last Supper that Jesus celebrated with his disciples on the eve of his death.

> Then came the day of Unleavened Bread on which the Passover lamb had to be sacrificed. Jesus sent Peter and John, saying, 'Go and make preparations for us to eat the Passover.'
> 'Where do you want us to prepare for it?' they asked.
> He replied, 'As you enter the city, a man carrying a jar of water will meet you. Follow him to the house that he enters, and say to the owner of the house, "The Teacher asks: Where is the guest room, where I may eat the Passover with my disciples?" He will show you a large upper room, all furnished. Make preparations there' (22:7-12).

There is something rather mysterious and secretive about this section of the narrative. Why did Jesus send Peter and John with such strange instructions about finding the place to celebrate the meal? I don't think that it requires a great deal of speculation to figure it out. Jesus had made no secret of the fact that he had come to Jerusalem to die, and he also predicted that he would be betrayed to the Gentiles. At the feast itself, on the eve of the Passover, Jesus declared that one who would eat with him was indeed going to betray him, so we can safely assume that Jesus was well aware that he had been betrayed by Judas, and that the conspiracy was already in motion. However, we also know that Jesus had a profound desire to celebrate the Passover and was not going to allow himself to fall into the hands of his captors until the hour he determined.

Now obviously an ideal place for Judas to arrange an arrest away from the multitude would be at this meal. There was never a better time for a secret betrayal, a secret arrest, than on that particular evening when the streets of Jerusalem would be virtually deserted, when people would be gathered in small groups in their homes or, in the case of pilgrims, in borrowed rooms, to observe the Passover. So Jesus arranges for this meal not by announcing the site to all of the twelve, but rather by sending Peter and John, his two closest disciples, to a location not even they know about.

Jesus said 'a man carrying a jar of water will meet you'. How were they to know which man they were to follow – wouldn't there be thousands of people walking around with pitchers of water? Well, in the ancient world only women carried water in pitchers, whereas men customarily carried water in water skins, so Jesus is telling them to look out for something unusual. When they meet this man they are to follow him into the house that he enters. Clearly Jesus had already made arrangements with the person whose home this was, and tradition has it that it was the home of Mark. We don't know that for certain, but in any case it was a house that belonged to someone who followed Jesus and recognized him as the Master.

And so, in obedience to the directive of Jesus, Peter and John went and found it all just as he had said it would be. And they made ready the Passover. 'When the hour came, Jesus and his apostles reclined at the table' (22:14). One of those twelve must have been very frustrated indeed. Jesus obviously kept near to Judas, not giving him an opportunity to slip away and betray the site of the Passover meal, for he wouldn't know it until he got there himself. Jesus wanted to share this special meal with his disciples, and we are reminded of those words he spoke in John 10:18, 'No-one takes it [his life] from me, but I lay it down of my own accord.' So Judas has to delay his treachery until the appointed time.

95. The Last Supper (Luke 22:15-23)
Jesus and the twelve were reclining at the table, as was the custom, when Jesus said to them: 'I have eagerly desired to eat this Passover with you before I suffer.' The affection that he

has for his disciples is partly the reason for this desire, but so
also is the significance of the Passover. The Passover involved
the sacrifice of the Pascal Lamb, that lamb who is now perfectly
embodied in the person of Jesus. Jesus is the meaning of the
Passover, the essence of the Passover, and before he dies as the
sacrificial lamb he has an earnest desire once more to celebrate
the passing over of the angel of death and the exodus of the
people of God from bondage. Our Lord betrays great emotion
in his next words: 'For I tell you, I will not eat it again until it
finds fulfilment in the kingdom of God' (22:16). He has
celebrated this grand feast every year since he was a small child
but this would be the last time he would eat it until it is totally
fulfilled in the kingdom of God.

> After taking the cup, he gave thanks and said, 'Take this and divide it
> among you. For I tell you I will not drink again of the fruit of the vine
> until the kingdom of God comes.' And he took bread, gave thanks and
> broke it, and gave it to them, saying, 'This is my body given for you; do
> this in remembrance of me.' In the same way, after the supper he took
> the cup, saying, 'This cup is the new covenant in my blood, which is
> poured out for you' (22:17-20).

The order of the ceremony in Luke's narrative is not exactly
like that recorded in other gospels. Luke gives us less of a
detailed account, but also the other gospel writers stress the
sequence of the bread first and then the cup. Here, however, we
have Jesus taking a cup, giving thanks and telling them to divide
it, and then breaking bread and then again the cup.

Luke, like the other synoptic writers, does not define exactly
how Jesus ties in the Lord's Supper with the actual celebration
of the Passover. In the Passover feast bitter herbs are consumed,
the meal is eaten, hymns are sung, passages of Old Testament
history are recited, and, in the course of the whole meal, wine is
taken on four distinct occasions. It is not clear on which of these
occasions Jesus gave new meaning and significance to the act
and from a theological perspective the order is unimportant – it
is the significance of the act that is important. Twice in this

passage he refers to the coming of the kingdom of God, so that, in the celebration of the Passover, Jesus not only looks back into history to the works that God had done in bringing Israel out of bondage, but he also looks ahead to the future, to the celebration of the banquet feast of the Lamb in Heaven.

The church today, when celebrating holy communion, the Lord's Supper, in a sense looks at the things of God from these three perspectives: the past, the present, and the future. All Christians agree that one of the reasons for the Lord's Supper is to remember what Jesus did for them on the Cross. 'Do this in remembrance of me'; this is a command from our Lord not to forget. In the Old Testament, apostasy, falling away from fidelity, was associated with the concept of forgetting. So Jesus is urging his disciples, no matter what else they forget of all they have seen in his company, not to forget the significance of this event. Every time they break bread and drink the cup, they are to do it in remembrance of him.

Thus when the church follows that mandate in its celebration of the Lord's Supper, it looks to the past, but, as Jesus stresses, there is also a sense in which the celebration of the Lord's Supper is a foretaste of the future feast that God has promised for his people in heaven. Then we will sit down with our Lord and celebrate the great wedding of Christ and his bride, the Church.

So we look to the past and we look to the future, but what about now? Controversy abounds among Christians with respect to how Jesus is present in the Lord's Supper. Many regard it simply as a symbol, but the majority of Christians do believe in the real presence of Christ at the Lord's Supper, though they dispute over the mode of Christ's presence. As the people of God come together, looking back to the past and looking ahead to the future promises of our King, there is also the present enjoyment and blessing of being in the presence of Christ.

Jesus referred to the new covenant in his blood (22:20). He was bringing new significance to an element of this meal and he does so using the terminology of covenant. He talks about a new covenant that he is inaugurating, a new covenant that he will ratify with the pouring out of his own blood. This is the moment of transition from the Old Testament people of God to the New Testament Church; there, around that table, the Church of Jesus Christ was born.

Jesus talks of his betrayer (Luke 22:21-23)
Jesus then said, 'But the hand of him who is going to betray me is with mine on the table. The Son of Man will go as it has been decreed, but woe to that man who betrays him' (22:21-22). Jesus announces the dreadful news that the one who would commit the ultimate act of treason in betraying the Son of God himself had the audacity to sit at this holy feast of celebration with the rest of his comrades and with the Lord. Some people have felt sorry for Judas, seeing him as merely a pawn in a divine chess game, forced against his will to enact this drama, Jesus clarifies that point for us; this *is* something that has to take place in the determinate counsel of God, but God did not force Judas to an uncharacteristic act of evil, rather God works through Judas' evil intentions. This does not excuse Judas in any way, rather he hears the oracle of doom pronounced by the Prophet of prophets, Jesus himself.

Then the disciples began to ask which of them would do this thing. Luke's account ends there, but Matthew records how even Judas asked the question, 'Surely not I, Rabbi?' and Jesus looked at him and said, 'Yes, it is you' (Matt. 26:25). Then John writes that Jesus dismissed Judas, saying, 'What you are about to do, do quickly' (John 13:27). And then he writes: 'he went out. And it was night' (John 13:30).

96. The disciples argue who is the greatest
(Luke 22:24-38)

Even as the disciples were arguing over which of them would betray Jesus, their minds quickly revert to themselves. Luke writes: 'Also a dispute arose among them as to which of them was considered to be greatest' (22:24). One of the greatest burdens of leadership is the propensity for people to compete with one another rather than co-operating as a team, and Jesus' disciples were no different in this respect. But to have this take place in the very last hours before his death and in the midst of a holy celebration of deliverance by God, reveals the corruption present even in the hearts of the disciples.

So Jesus said to them, 'The kings of the Gentiles lord it over them; and those who exercise authority over them call themselves "Benefactors".' Jesus, thus saying, is showing them that whilst the kings of the Gentiles like to exercise their lordship over the people, they are careful to ensure they are called 'benefactors' in order to dupe people into believing that all they care about are the interests of the people themselves.

Jesus' negative judgment on this activity becomes clear in his next statement: 'But you are not to be like that. Instead, the greatest among you should be like the youngest, and the one who rules like the one who serves. For who is greater, the one who is at the table or the one who serves? Is it not the one who is at the table? But I am among you as one who serves' (22:26-27). John in his account broadens the story and tells how Jesus performed the unbelievable act of washing his disciples' feet and how Peter rebelled at the thought of Jesus humbling himself in that way. But Jesus said, 'Unless I wash you, you have no part with me' (John 13:8). To which Peter replied, 'Then, Lord, not just my feet but my hands and my head as well!'

Jesus is willingly embracing his own humiliation, and while he is preparing himself for the darkest act of humiliation in the history of the world, his disciples are arguing about their own glory. So he rebukes them and teaches them at the same time: 'You are those who have stood by me in my trials. And I confer on you a kingdom, just as my Father conferred one on me, so that you may eat and drink at my table in my kingdom and sit on thrones, judging the twelve tribes of Israel' (22:28-30). Jesus, in making this promise, is also giving them a rebuke: 'How many times do I have to tell you that the Father has prepared a kingdom for you, that you all are going to sit in judgment on

the twelve tribes of Israel, that you are going to participate in
my glory? When I sit down in my Father's kingdom, you are
all going to sit with me at the King's table, so why are you
arguing over who is going to be in the place of greatest honour?'
There is plenty of glory to go around, but the message that has
to be repeated, even after his death, is that unless we are prepared
to participate in the humiliation of Christ we cannot participate
in his exaltation.

Jesus then turns to Peter, and tells him some dreadful news:
'Simon, Simon, Satan has asked to sift you as wheat. But I
have prayed for you, Simon, that your faith may not fail. And
when you have turned back, strengthen your brothers' (22:31-
32). When Jesus addressed Peter here, he repeated his name,
which as we have noted previously, indicated affection and
intimacy. We can almost feel the pain in his voice as he says,
'Simon, Simon'. It is interesting that Jesus reverts back to Peter's
old name. Perhaps this is to indicate that Peter is showing his
characteristic instability and impetuosity. Jesus saw that at this
stage Peter was very weak. But notice what Jesus said, 'But I
have prayed for you, that your faith may not fail. And when
you have turned again, strengthen your brothers.'

Jesus had defined Judas as one who was diabolical from the
beginning; there was no spark of faith in his heart, he was never
a converted man. Peter, on the other hand, was a man who was
truly born again, and yet he denies Jesus. I don't believe we can
lose our salvation, not because we are able to keep it, but because
Christ himself preserves us. He will not allow us to be snatched
out of his hand; he intercedes for us continually as our high
priest. The great difference between Peter and Judas is not their
intrinsic character but that Jesus says to Peter, 'I have prayed
for you.' It was a foregone conclusion, as far as Jesus was
concerned; that is why he did not say 'If you turn again', but
'When you have turned again, strengthen your brothers.'

Peter, however, protests vigorously that he will never
abandon Jesus: 'Lord, I am ready to go with you to prison and
to death.' He makes this bold declaration of his fidelity, but

Jesus says, 'I tell you, Peter, before the rooster crows today, you will deny three times that you know me' (22:34). Jesus' prediction of Peter's denial was accurate to the last detail.

Before concluding this last dinner with his disciples, Jesus has some further words to say:

> Then Jesus asked them, 'When I sent you without purse, bag or sandals, did you lack anything?'
>
> 'Nothing,' they answered.
>
> He said to them, 'But now if you have a purse, take it, and also a bag; and if you don't have a sword, sell your cloak and buy one. It is written: "And he was numbered with the transgressors"; and I tell you that this must be fulfilled in me. Yes, what is written about me is reaching its fulfilment.'
>
> The disciples said, 'See, Lord, here are two swords.'
>
> 'That is enough,' he replied (22:35-38).

Jesus is warning them that everything is about to change. Whereas they were once welcomed because of him everywhere they went, all that has changed – the world is about to turn on them in hatred because of him.

97. In the Garden of Gethsemane (Luke 22:39-53)

After celebrating the Last Supper with his disciples, Jesus left the upper room. Luke's narrative continues: 'Jesus went out as usual to the Mount of Olives, and his disciples followed him. On reaching the place, he said to them, "Pray that you will not fall into temptation" ' (22:39-40). Jesus' words here are capable of two meanings. On the one hand, Jesus could have been telling his disciples that they need to pray, perhaps as never before, that they won't be tempted to sin or to falter in their loyalty to him. On the other hand, he may be exhorting them to pray that they do not have to participate in the same trial to which Jesus himself is being subjected at that very moment.

Jesus withdrew from them about a stone's throw and knelt down to pray. When we read this today we don't notice anything unusual for it is customary for us to kneel down to pray, but in the ancient world the Jews would pray standing up and looking to heaven. Jesus on this occasion broke with that tradition; the burden of his prayer was so heavy and it bore down on him so much so that he sank to his knees to pray. And he said, 'Father, if you are willing, take this cup from me; yet not my will, but yours be done.'

From the moment of his birth, Jesus lived in the shadow of the cross. From the moment when the prophet Simeon declared to Mary that a sword would pierce her own soul it was clearly established that Jesus was destined to die a horrible death, not simply in terms of human pain, but because he would die as a sacrifice, under the wrath of God. Jesus, even in his perfect humanity, shrank back at the utter horror of it and so he cries out to his Father to remove this cup from him. Jesus was not referring to a cup containing a toxin that would bring about a speedy death, he was using the Jewish image of the cup filled with the wrath of God. So he wrestles with the Father, pleading that he might find some other way to satisfy his justice and fulfil his plans for the redemption of this fallen race. But for all that Jesus desired not to take the cup, there was something that he desired more fervently, and that was to do his Father's will.

'An angel from heaven appeared to him and strengthened him' (22:43). Some think that stories of angels are merely products of mythological or legendary background, but angels, as we have noted before in this study of Luke, are a very important part of the history of the life of Jesus. His birth was announced by angels; after resisting the temptations of the devil in the wilderness angels came and ministered to him; and here again we read of an angel strengthening him. One function of an angel is to announce very important messages. The word *angelos* from which we get the English word 'angel' means 'messenger'. But this is not the only function of the angels. The book of Hebrews tells us that the angels are sent by God to minister to the needs of his elect, and here, of course, the supreme chosen one of the Father becomes the object of the ministry of the angels.

Jesus in his agony prays ever more earnestly, to the point

that 'his sweat was like drops of blood falling to the ground.' Luke is clearly using a simile here; Jesus did not actually sweat blood, but his struggle was so great that he was perspiring to the degree that sweat was dripping from him, as blood would drip from a wound.

'When he rose from prayer and went back to the disciples, he found them asleep, exhausted from sorrow' (22:45). The hearts of the disciples were so laden with sorrow that they fell asleep. It is not unusual for a person who is sad or troubled to be lethargic. Sleep provides a welcome relief from the things that weigh us down and so perhaps that is why the disciples fell asleep. Jesus said to them, 'Why are you sleeping? Get up and pray so that you will not fall into temptation.' There will be plenty of time for sleeping, but right now a crisis is at hand and they need to stay awake and pray.

Just as he was rousing them from their sleep, 'a crowd came up, and the man who was called Judas, one of the Twelve, was leading them. He approached Jesus to kiss him' (22:47). Judas at the front of the crowd marches straight for Jesus and makes as if to kiss him. This was a common form of greeting in the ancient world, but it is obvious from the text that Judas had arranged with his accomplices that the one he kissed would be the one he was marking for arrest and betrayal. As he makes his move, Jesus stops him and says to him, 'Judas, are you betraying the Son of Man with a kiss?' Of all the ways to betray someone, Judas used a kiss, the symbol of friendship or love.

'When Jesus' followers saw what was going to happen, they said, "Lord, should we strike with our swords?" And one of them struck the servant of the high priest, cutting off his right ear' (22:49-50). Luke does not identify who it was that cut off the ear, but the other gospels tell us it was Peter, the impetuous one, who grabbed his sword and sliced off the man's ear. Jesus' response was to give the command, 'No more of this!' and then he touched the man's ear and healed him. At the very moment that Christ was being arrested, he still has enough mercy and compassion to stop and heal one of his own captors.

'Then Jesus said to the chief priests, the officers of the temple guard, and the elders, who had come for him, "Am I leading a rebellion, that you have come with swords and clubs? Every day I was with you in the temple courts, and you did not lay a hand on me. But this is your hour – when darkness reigns' (22:52-53). Jesus is calling attention to the fact that these men, for the most part men of power and authority from the Sanhedrin itself, did not have the courage to arrest him in view of the public, and so they sneak into the garden under cover of darkness. But Jesus went along with their plan.

98. The arrest of Jesus (Luke 22:54-65)

Luke now turns his attention to the arrest of Jesus and the denials of Peter. His narrative continues: 'Then seizing him, they led him away and took him into the house of the high priest. Peter followed at a distance. But when they had kindled a fire in the middle of the courtyard and had sat down together, Peter sat down with them.' When Jesus was arrested, Peter followed, keeping at a safe distance, but at least he didn't run away – he is anxious to follow Jesus. Earlier that evening Jesus had announced that Peter would deny him three times before the cock crowed at dawn. Now Peter follows, confused and frightened, staying out of sight but witnessing the procession that took Jesus to the hall of judgment.

At the high priest's house Peter joined a group of people sitting round the fire. Presumably some of them had been part of the group that had invaded the Garden of Gethsemane, perhaps some were just onlookers, and perhaps even some of the officials were there, warming themselves. Peter was obviously trying to blend into the crowd but a servant girl saw him 'seated there in the firelight. She looked closely at him and said, "This man was with him." ' While Jesus was on trial before the high priests of the land, and would soon stand before the imperial authority of Rome vested in the person of Pontius Pilate, Peter is simply confronted by a servant girl, a person with no legal powers whatsoever, who recognizes him as having been with Jesus. There was nothing illegal about being in Jesus' company; if there was, then the authorities would have made more arrests in Gethsemane. But they didn't. This woman simply observes that Peter was with him, and he denied it, saying, 'Woman, I don't know him' (22:57).

Peter was afraid, and embarrassed; he didn't want this particular group of people to know of his association with Jesus. Before we judge Peter harshly for this act, we should remember that each of us at times has been inclined to down play our commitment to Christ, for various reasons. Shortly after this another person spotted him and again said to Peter, 'You are one of them too', and Peter again denied it. Luke gives us a very concise account of this story. The other gospel accounts are more detailed and it is obvious that these people were all talking amongst themselves. Peter responds to the questions three times and Luke records that for us.

The third time, Luke writes, 'About an hour later another asserted, 'Certainly this fellow was with him, for he is a Galilean" ' (22:59). Peter's Galilean accent would have been immediately recognizable to those in Jerusalem, and this man knew that Jesus' disciples, for the most part, were Galileans and so he makes the connection. Peter for the third time denies being a follower of Jesus. From the extra information in the other gospels, we know that Peter's third denial was accompanied by cursing, and while he was still speaking, the cock crew.

We don't know exactly where Jesus was at this moment, he may have been crossing the courtyard itself, perhaps being moved to another building by his captors. We don't know, but Luke writes: 'The Lord turned and looked straight at Peter. Then Peter remembered the word the Lord had spoken to him: "Before the rooster crows today, you will disown me three times" ' (22:61). Jesus' gaze brought home to Peter what he had just done. I don't think it is possible for us to conceive how deeply Peter felt the glance of Christ at that moment. Luke simply tells us that Peter went out and wept bitterly. These were tears of remorse, provoked by Jesus' gaze into the very soul of Peter.

Luke's attention moves now to the trial of Christ. It is interesting that Luke and in fact most of the gospel writers give more space to the trial of Jesus than the actual crucifixion. The reason must be that the Bible wants to make very clear something of the meaning of the death of Christ, that here is a man who is innocent of human crime, yet nevertheless is delivered to be crucified.

'The men who were guarding Jesus began mocking and beating him.' While the officials and the high priests are waiting to interview Jesus, he was being detained by the guards who decided to have some cruel fun with him, beating him and mocking him. 'They blindfolded him and demanded, "Prophesy! Who hit you?" And they said many other insulting things to him' (22:63-65). The men guarding Jesus tormented and mocked him, playing a kind of blindman's bluff with him, asking him to guess which one of them struck him. This episode takes up only a couple of verses, but it is worth remembering, because it has significance later on in the narrative.

99. The trial of Jesus (Luke 22:66–23:12)

Before the Sanhedrin (Luke 22:66-71)
'At daybreak the council of the elders of the people, both the chief priests and teachers of the law, met together, and Jesus was led before them' (22:66). The Sanhedrin, the ruling body of the Jews, could not legally hold a trial at night, but it is obvious that Jesus was interviewed immediately by the high priest as soon as he was arrested. It would seem that a kangaroo court was in session. But they made it official by assembling together in a formal group when it was day. They lead Jesus into their council and begin to ask him some very telling questions. The first question is: 'If you are the Christ, tell us.' Jesus answered, 'If I tell you, you will not believe me, and if I asked you, you would not answer.' So the question they are all eager to ask is, 'Jesus, are you claiming to be the Messiah?'

Jesus, however, becomes evasive because he knows that they have a defective concept of what the Messiah is. So he says in verse 69, 'But from now on, the Son of Man will be seated at the right hand of the mighty God.' Here is his answer, for he knew that if they understood the Old Testament prophesies about the Messiah, then they would know that the Son of Man would be seated on the right hand of the power of God. So although his answer is cryptic, its meaning would not be hidden to anyone who knew the Scriptures. He was indeed claiming to be the Messiah.

The Sanhedrin was a council of seventy-one members that had supreme power over the Jewish faith and behaviour, within limits imposed by Rome. Tradition places the Sanhedrin in the body of seventy elders appointed by Moses. The Romans retained the authority to overrule any decision taken by the Sanhedrin, in particular, the right to impose the death penalty. The Sanhedrin was dominated by the Sadducees, although Pharisees and scribes were also members. The high priest functioned as president of the council. Jesus, Peter, John, Stephen and Paul all appeared before the Sanhedrin.

Then they asked him a question that was crucial to the trial: 'Are you then the Son of God?' Jews, on occasion, would refer to human beings as sons of God, but always with the indefinite sense. In this question, however, they used the definite article; 'Are you *the* Son of God?' In other words they wanted to know if he professed a more intimate relationship with God – it is one thing to claim to be the Messiah, it's quite another thing to claim to be divine. Jesus answered this second question with the words 'You are right in saying I am', and that was good enough for his accusers: 'Why do we need any more testimony? We have heard it from his own lips' (22:71). The trial didn't have to go any further, because Jesus, in their eyes, had committed a capital offence.

The trial of Jesus was made up of several sections, but basically two different trials were running side by side. There is a trial before the Jewish authorities and the trial before the Roman authorities. The first of these focuses on Jesus' claims to deity. Blasphemy under Jewish law is a capital offence. And so now they have heard his confession, in their minds there is no question that Jesus is a blasphemer and is, therefore, worthy of the death penalty. The problem, however, is that the Jews were governed by the Roman authority, and had no power of their own to carry out an execution without the permission of the Roman authorities. Although blasphemy was a capital offence in Jewish law, in Roman law it was not. The Sanhedrin, therefore, had to accuse Jesus of a crime that the Romans *would* consider worthy of the death penalty.

Before Pilate (Luke 23:1-7)

'Then the whole assembly rose and led him off to Pilate. And they began to accuse him, saying, "We have found this man subverting our nation. He opposes payment of taxes to Caesar and claims to be Christ, a king"' (23:1-2). The Jewish authorities try to translate Jesus' claim to messiahship and deity into categories that would make him guilty of civil crimes punishable by death by Rome. They accuse him of sedition, of misleading the nation, and then, in a direct lie, accuse him of forbidding people to pay their taxes. Then, to crown it all, they tell Pilate of Jesus' claim to be the Christ, which they explain to him, means that Jesus is claiming to be King. Jesus is presented as a political revolutionary with kingly aspirations.

Pilate hears the accusations, and senses the great hostility of the Jewish leaders, but before things proceed further he has to ask Jesus questions himself. So he asks: 'Are you the King of the Jews?' and Jesus answers, 'Yes, it is as you say.' Again Jesus gives a cryptic answer, because obviously Pilate didn't understand the meaning of Jesus' kingship any more than the Sanhedrin did.

Pilate then said, 'I find no basis for a charge against this man.' This was very important because Pilate embodied earthly authority and justice, and he pronounced the faultlessness of

Jesus. The trial should have ended right there, but the Jewish authorities insisted on pursuing it, and in effect lodged an appeal against Pilate's verdict.

'But they insisted, "He stirs up the people all over Judea by his teaching. He started in Galilee and has come all the way here."' On hearing this, Pilate asked if the man was a Galilean. When he learned that Jesus was under Herod's jurisdiction, he sent him to Herod, who was also in Jerusalem at that time' (23:5-7).

Before Herod (Luke 23:8-12)

Pilate saw a way out of his own difficult situation. He knew that Herod the Tetrarch, the ruler of that section of Galilee, was presently in Jerusalem. Herod, although appointed by the Romans, was himself a Jew, and Luke records that when he saw Jesus, 'he was greatly pleased, because for a long time he had been wanting to see him' (23:8). It would seem that Herod's enthusiasm was not that justice should be done, but rather that he wanted to see for himself some of the miraculous feats he had heard about.

So 'he plied him with many questions, but Jesus gave him no answer'. In Luke's account this is the only time during Jesus' whole trial that he remains absolutely silent. All we can assume is that Jesus did not find anything in Herod's questions that made them worthy of a response. The chief priests and scribes, however, continued to accuse him vehemently, and Herod, it would seem, takes this opportunity to play to the crowd. 'Then Herod and his soldiers ridiculed and mocked him. Dressing him in an elegant robe, they sent him back to Pilate' (23:11).

Jesus is sent back to Pilate with this symbolic investiture of Christ in the robes of the king, and Luke comments: 'That day Herod and Pilate became friends – before this they had been enemies' (23:12). That enmity went back many years and was profoundly deep. Yet the friendship between Herod and Pontius Pilate was kindled over something they had in common; they were both called upon to sit in judgment at the execution of the Son of God.

100. Jesus is sentenced to death (Luke 23:13-31)

Jesus was taken back to Pilate: 'Pilate called together the chief priests, the rulers and the people, and said to them, "You brought me this man as one who was inciting the people to rebellion. I have examined him in your presence and have found no basis for your charges against him."'

Pilate is acting in a very admirable fashion at this point. It takes courage to resist a howling mob, thirsty for blood. He had gone through the process of a civil trial and could not find any evidence to support their allegations; neither could Herod (23:15). Then Pilate comes to a decision: 'Therefore, I will punish him and then release him' (23:16). Why, if a man is exonerated, should he be subject to any form of punishment? In Roman times, however, it was not uncommon when a man was exonerated, for him to receive a very mild whipping, presumably as a reminder to be more careful about his conduct.

In verse 17 Luke comments that Pilate was obliged to release one prisoner at the feast. Presumably Pilate intended this to be Jesus, but the narrative goes on, 'With one voice they cried out, "Away with this man! Release Barabbas to us!"' (23:18). This prisoner that the crowd wanted released in preference over Jesus 'had been thrown into prison for an insurrection in the city, and for murder'. Barabbas was a man who had been judged worthy of the death penalty, but the people demanded that the one who was truly guilty of the charges be released, and the one proven innocent be killed instead. There is a certain significance here: Christ, the innocent dies in the place of the guilty, in terms far exceeding that of a mere substitution for Barabbas.

Pilate tried to persuade the crowd, but they kept on calling out, 'Crucify him!' This is the first time that the word crucifixion is mentioned in the narrative of the trial. It wasn't Pilate's idea to crucify Jesus, but the crowd is screaming for it to happen. It would be wrong to assume that everybody was screaming against Jesus, as we shall see shortly, but those who were opposed to Jesus were well organized and vocal. There was unbelievable pressure on Pilate, to the point that his career was in jeopardy because the last thing he could afford was a popular insurrection. In many ways Palestine was a testing place for up and coming government officials in the Roman empire. It was one of the most difficult outposts of the whole empire, and if one could do well there, then he was assured of a lucrative and successful future in the Roman Government system. If on the other hand he failed there, it could mean the end of the line careerwise. Pilate's career, which had been meteoric in its rise, reached a turning point that night, and within a very short time he was finished as a Roman Governor.

Once again, in response to the crowd, Pilate tried to reason with them for Jesus' release: 'For the third time he spoke to them: "Why? What crime has this man committed? I have found in him no grounds for the death penalty. Therefore I will have him punished and then release him"' (23:22). For a third time the figure representing the highest authority in the world at that time pronounced Jesus Christ innocent. But the crowd were insistent and, writes Luke, 'their shouts prevailed'. What a comment; it was not the voice of truth, or the voice of authority that prevailed, but the howl of hatred.

We read of the end of Pilate's integrity as a leader, for he caves in to their demands: 'Pilate decided to grant their demand' (23:24). The governor is governed by the people. 'He released the man who had been thrown into prison for insurrection and murder, the one they asked for, and surrendered Jesus to their will.' He turned over an innocent man to a vicious mob.

Simon the Cyrene carries the cross (Luke 23:26-31)
We now reach the actual events surrounding the crucifixion. 'As they led him away, they seized Simon from Cyrene, who was on his way in from the country, and put the cross on him and made him carry it behind Jesus' (23:26). From the other gospel accounts we learn that the reason Simon was called in to carry the cross for Jesus was that Jesus collapsed under the weight of it and was unable to carry it. Why should a presumably fit man – after all you needed to be strong to be a carpenter in

those days – not be able to carry at least the cross piece to the execution site, as was the custom? Evidence of Jesus' physical weakness is also seen in the speed with which he died. Usually the victim of crucifixion took up to three days to die, but Jesus was dead within hours.

How do we account for this? One eminent specialist recently wrote an essay in which he claims that the condition of Jesus, as described by the gospel writers, fits the pattern of one suffering from a bruised heart muscle. Sometimes, when the heart muscle is subject to a direct blow it becomes bruised and severely weakened. The person's breathing becomes laboured, he experiences a great lack of energy and severe weakness. Usually this condition is fatal. So, in the opinion of that specialist, Jesus died from a broken heart, not from the vigours of crucifixion itself. Perhaps such an injury was the result of a blow sustained during the mocking games of the guards, we don't know. What we do know, however, is that by this stage Jesus was so weak that he could not even carry his own cross.

As they progressed to the place of execution a multitude of women followed, mourning and wailing. But Jesus turning to them said:

> 'Daughters of Jerusalem, do not weep for me; weep for yourselves and for your children. For the time will come when you will say, "Blessed are the barren women, the wombs that never bore and the breasts that never nursed!" Then they will say to the mountains, "Fall on us!" and to the hills, "Cover us!" For if men do these things when the tree is green, what will happen when it is dry?' (23:28-31).

Jesus is not angry at these women for showing compassion and sympathy, but he stops and looks at them and he tells them that if they understood at all what had been going on, they would not be weeping for him but for themselves, because of the judgment about to come upon their nation. Jesus, of course, was referring to the destruction of Jerusalem in AD 70, which has been called the first Jewish Holocaust. Over a million people were slaughtered by the Romans. More seriously, however,

Jesus' words are a reminder of the last judgment. We must all stand before the judgment seat of God on that day of great fear and mourning.

101. The crucifixion (Luke 23:32-43)

The narrative is now building up speed, moving inexorably towards the hill called 'The Skull': 'Two other men, both criminals, were also led out with him to be executed. When they came to the place called the Skull, there they crucified him, along with the criminals – one on his right, the other on his left' (23:32-33).

Each of the gospel writers places emphasis on different elements from this event and Luke, although his account is less detailed than some of the others, is at pains to highlight the fact that Jesus was crucified between two criminals. Perhaps Luke wishes to remind us of the significance of this with regard to Isaiah's prophecy that the Messiah would be numbered among the transgressors in his death (Isa. 53:12).

Then Jesus spoke and said, 'Father, forgive them, for they do not know what they are doing' (23:34). Jesus utters a prayer

---

Crucifixion was a method of execution originally practised in the East but adopted by the Romans to punish serious crimes. It was not inflicted on Roman citizens, but was reserved for slaves, pirates, and religious and political rebels.

The cross was generally a pole placed in the ground, and topped by a portable crossbar. Prior to being crucified, the victim was beaten with a leather whip containing pieces of metal or bone that tore the flesh. He was then forced to carry the crossbar to the place of execution. The crossbar was fixed to the top of the pole, and the victim was either tied or nailed with his arms stretched along it. Death was a slow process and could take up to several days. Sometimes, in order to hasten death, the Romans increased the strain on the body by breaking the leg bones of the victim; without the ability to support their body the victim's lungs collapsed causing suffocation.

from the cross asking the Father to bestow his grace, mercy and forgiveness on those who at that very moment were killing him. He asks God to take into account their ignorance, and his words have raised some important theological and ethical questions. Is ignorance an excuse for sin? Roman Catholic moral theology makes a distinction that has been both helpful and important to all theology. It is the distinction between evincible ignorance and invincible ignorance. In other words it highlights two forms of ignorance; on the one hand is ignorance that can be overcome and on the other is ignorance that we could not possibly overcome. Obviously if God is just and righteous he will not hold us accountable for not knowing things that we have no possibility of ever finding out, for example. Therefore invincible ignorance is excusable. But in a situation where we should know better, ignorance doesn't excuse us from our guilt. The people crucifying Jesus could not be excused on the grounds of invincible ignorance for they should have known better. They had the Scriptures and the prophets and the signs and miracles that Jesus performed. They had no excuse, but Jesus is pleading with his Father to take their ignorance into consideration and be merciful to them and forgive them. He doesn't ask for them to be exonerated – he acknowledges their guilt and asks that they be forgiven. The same statement is made later on in Paul's writings when he talks about the people who delivered up the Lord of Glory out of ignorance; they should have known, but they did not understand fully. Jesus is concerned about the eternal destiny of his tormentors even though he is close to death.

Luke then goes on to record that his captors 'divided up his clothes by casting lots' (23:34b). As far as we know the only material legacy that Jesus left was his carefully home-spun single-pieced robe that was considered to be of some value. This passage indicates that Jesus was crucified naked, which to the Jewish person was dreadfully humiliating and an insult to human dignity. Christ's punishments far exceed the physical pain of crucifixion, for he experienced the outer darkness of the forsakenness of God. He became a public spectacle.

'The people stood watching, and the rulers even sneered at him. They said, "He saved others; let him save himself if he is the Christ of God, the Chosen One" ' (23:35). Luke is careful to point out that although Jesus was subjected to ridicule and mockery, it was not at the hands of the crowd in general. We must not assume that five days after hailing him as the Messiah, the whole city was screaming for his blood: it was the rulers primarily that were concerned to destroy Jesus, but many of the crowd were horrified and grief stricken by what was happening.

'The soldiers also came up and mocked him. They offered him wine vinegar and said, "If you are the king of the Jews, save yourself!" ' (23:36-37). Crucifixion was an agonizing and slow death, and the sour wine that Luke mentions was offered to those being crucified as a form of pain killer, as an act of mercy. The soldiers, however, were far from merciful in their taunts, but there was an unconscious irony in their words, 'If you are the King of the Jews, save yourself!' There is irony in these words. He was the king of the Jews, but more significantly he was the saviour of the Jews and he was interested not in saving himself, but in saving the people of Israel and all who believe in him. He could have saved himself, but in so doing he would not have been able to save anybody else.

Above his head Pilate had placed the inscription, 'This is the King of the Jews'. These words, although intended as mockery, announced the ultimate truth.

Luke now draws our attention to the criminals that were being crucified with Jesus. 'One of the criminals who hung there hurled insults at him: "Aren't you the Christ? Save yourself and us!" ' (23:39). Even one of the thieves hanging with him gets in on the act, but with one difference – 'Save yourself *and us*!' It was his last hope, but was obviously done in a disbelieving, sneering way, for the other thief rebuked him and said, 'Don't you fear God, since you are under the same sentence? We are punished justly, for we are getting what our deeds deserve. But this man has done nothing wrong' (23:40-41).

It is very rare for a guilty person not only to admit his guilt but to go that very important step beyond and acknowledge that his punishment is just. This is a remarkable man who rebukes his fellow criminal with the words, 'Don't you fear God?' I wonder if God is going to ask each one of us this question some day: Did you not have any fear, any respect for me? Then this thief makes an admission: 'We are punished justly, for we are getting what our deeds deserve. But this man has done nothing wrong.' That is authentic repentance.

Then he said to Jesus, 'Jesus, remember me when you come into your kingdom' (23:42). This man was being crucified as a criminal, but as he looked at Christ, through the Holy Spirit, he saw more than a fellow sufferer; he recognized his Redeemer and he made a confession of faith. He has recognized in Jesus his own King and he submits himself to him, calling him Lord.

Jesus' answer is significant, 'I tell you the truth, today you will be with me in paradise' (23:43). This passage has been the cause of much controversy as there are many different theories

---

Seven Sayings on the Cross

The four gospels record seven sayings of Jesus when he was on the cross.

The first was addressed to God and was a prayer on behalf of those who were crucifying him: 'Father, forgive them, for they do not know what they are doing' (Luke 23:34).

The second was said to the penitent criminal, dying on a cross beside him: 'I tell you the truth, today you will be with me in paradise' (Luke 23:43).

The third was spoken to his mother, Mary, and the disciple John: 'Dear woman, here is your son,' and to the disciple, 'Here is your mother' (John 19:26, 27).

The fourth was a cry to God: 'My God, my God, why have you forsaken me?' (Matt. 27:46; Mark 15:34).

The fifth was an exclamation: 'I am thirsty' (John 19:28).

The sixth was a cry of triumph: 'It is finished!' (John 19:30).

The seventh was his committing himself to God as he died: 'Father, into your hands I commit my spirit' (Luke 23:46).

about what happens when we die. Some believe we go into a state of suspended animation; this is called the doctrine of soul sleep, where we stay unconscious until the end of the age. Others, however, believe our souls go immediately and consciously to the presence of Christ. One of the most important texts in support of this second theory is this verse, '*Today* you will be with me in paradise.' There is a further consideration also. When Jesus begins a saying with the word 'I tell you the truth', what follows immediately is a matter of emphasis, so really Jesus is saying to this thief, 'I tell you the truth, *today* you shall be with me in paradise.' 'As soon as we pass through this pain into death,' Jesus was saying, 'we're going together to paradise.' And so this text, along with others in the New Testament, teaches that when we die, immediately our souls go to be with the Lord, to know his presence, and to wait for the resurrection of the body. We cross the valley of death into something far more wonderful than anything we can possibly enjoy here. In Paul's words: 'For to me, to live is Christ, and to die is gain' (Phil. 1:21). Our Lord, in speaking to this thief, speaks also to all who put their trust in him, and promises his presence with them in paradise the moment that they die.

102. Jesus' death and burial (Luke 23:44-56)

In Luke 23:44 we read, 'It was now about the sixth hour, and darkness came over the whole land until the ninth hour, for the sun stopped shining.' According to Jewish time, that means that these events took place between noon and 3 pm. The 'darkness' that Luke refers to has puzzled some. There is no record of an eclipse around this time, so we don't know whether this phenomenon was natural or supernatural. But Luke calls attention to a tangible darkness, like God had turned off the lights of his glory. But Luke also mentions that 'the curtain of the temple was torn in two'. The curtain of the temple was not some delicate piece of fabric but was a very heavy item with layer upon layer of folded fabric. It would have been next to impossible to tear by natural means, but God obviously had torn the curtain in the temple. Matthew links this event to an earthquake that befell the city of Jerusalem at this moment and left the inner sanctum, the holy of holies, open to all to look into. The function of the curtain was to keep people out of the holy of holies, but the atonement having been made by Jesus, they now had access to the presence of God. The veil that symbolized the barrier between God's inner sanctuary and a polluted human race had been torn apart.

'Jesus called out with a loud voice, "Father, into your hands I commit my spirit." When he had said this, he breathed his last' (23:46). The other gospels record some of the most well-known words of Jesus from the cross, particularly his excruciating cry of agony of soul and heart, 'My God, my God, why have you forsaken me?' He was forsaken for a time, but then he followed that anguished exclamation with the statement, 'It is finished.' Presumably the forsakenness was over, the atonement had been made, it was finished and God gazed once more at his Son and Jesus could say, 'Father, into your hands I commit my spirit.' The Father had just put the Son through hell, had just poured out the wrath of absolute righteousness upon him; yet the Son in saying, 'Father, I put my spirit in your hands,' vindicated not only the holiness of God but his own sinlessness.

'The centurion [the man in charge of the soldiers who did the actual crucifixion], seeing what had happened, praised God and said, "Surely this was a righteous man."' Throughout the narrative Jesus is vindicated by official witnesses; Pilate four times stated 'I find no guilt in the man', and now the captain of the guard declares Jesus' innocence.

'When all the people who had gathered to witness this sight saw what took place, they beat their breasts and went away. But all those who knew him, including the women who had followed him from Galilee, stood at a distance, watching these things' (23:48-49). People were there straining to get a glimpse of the spectacle, but those who were loyal to Christ, those whose hopes were pinned on him, began to wail and publicly mourn.

Jesus is buried (Luke 23:50-56)

' Now there was a man named Joseph, a member of the Council, a good and upright man, who had not consented to their decision and action. He came from the Judean town of Arimathea and he was waiting for the kingdom of God. Going to Pilate, he asked for Jesus' body' (23:50-52). This man who was a member of the Sanhedrin, had not consented to their plan and played no part in the conspiracy. He was obviously already a believer, and is described as 'waiting for the kingdom of God'. He had held on to the Old Testament prophecies about the coming King and obviously recognized that the King had indeed come in the person of Jesus. We also know that Joseph of Arimathea was a noble man, a man of great wealth and influence, for he went to Pilate and asked for the body of Jesus.

Then Joseph took the body down, wrapped it in linen cloth and placed it in a tomb cut in the rock, one in which no-one had yet been laid (23:52-53). Long before, Isaiah prophesied that the suffering servant would die with the wicked and would make his grave with the rich (Isa. 53:9). It was customary for the Jews to bury executed criminals in the rubbish dump outside of Jerusalem known as Gehenna. Joseph of Arimathea went against common procedure, and buried Jesus' body with dignity. We read in Acts 2:31 that this was in fulfilment of another prophecy, for God had promised that he would not allow his Holy One to suffer decay (Psalm 16:10).

As Jesus' body was placed in a grave, all the rituals and prescriptions of an honourable burial were accorded to him. Grave plots were expensive, but stone caves were the most expensive, and so it was common to find a number of niches in it where bodies would be placed. It was a rare thing for a man to be wealthy enough to have his own private mausoleum, but obviously Joseph of Arimathea was and he donates his own sepulchre for the burial place of Christ.

We read in verse 54, 'It was Preparation Day, and the Sabbath was about to begin.' When Jesus died it was very close to the beginning of the Sabbath day and no burial provision could be made once the Sabbath started. So they had to move quickly to get Jesus' body to the tomb and properly prepared. My guess is that Joseph oversaw this stage of the procedure and was able to anoint the body with spices he already had in store, and then the women went to the tomb days later to complete the act of anointing since it was interrupted by the Sabbath day. They went with Joseph to the tomb and saw where he placed the body. Then, writes Luke, 'they went home and prepared spices and perfumes. But they rested on the Sabbath in obedience to the commandment' (23:56). They were obedient to the law, but obviously were anxious to finish the proper ministrations of the body. But before the final act of anointing of his shrouded body could be completed, death surrendered to his power.

103. The resurrection (Luke 24:1-34)

This is the last chapter in the gospel of Luke, and is the culmination of the life and work of Jesus of Nazareth. This is the resurrection chapter, the record of an event that turned the world upside down. The earliest creed of the Christian Church was simply 'He is Risen,' and there is a sense in which the entire impact of Christianity stands or falls with the truth of this message.

Very early, after dawn, the women came to the tomb to complete their tender act of anointing Jesus' body with spices. However, when they got there 'they found the stone rolled away from the tomb, but when they entered, they did not find the body of the Lord Jesus.' Now, if all we had in the Bible was the record of an empty tomb, then that would not be proof that Jesus had risen. An empty tomb could be explained in a number of ways: the disciples could have taken away the body or Jesus' enemies could have stolen it. But the testimony of the empty tomb is backed up by the resurrection appearances.

When the women first entered the tomb, they did not find Jesus' body. They were puzzled by this and didn't immediately conclude that Jesus had risen. 'While they were wondering about this, suddenly two men in clothes that gleamed like lightning stood beside them. In their fright the women bowed down with their faces to the ground, but the men said to them, "Why do you look for the living among the dead?"' (24:4-5). Here we have an angelic announcement that Christ is no longer to be found in the tomb among the dead but he is to be found among the living, for 'He is not here; he has risen!'

Here we find the first announcement of the resurrection of Christ in the New Testament, and it is proclaimed not by men but by angels, the messengers of God: 'Remember how he told you, while he was still with you in Galilee: "The Son of Man must be delivered into the hands of sinful men, be crucified and on the third day be raised again." Then they remembered his words.' Jesus had prophesied his return from the grave and the women couldn't wait to tell the others: 'When they came back from the tomb, they told all these things to the Eleven and to all the others. It was Mary Magdalene, Joanna, Mary the mother of James, and the others with them who told this to the apostles' (24:8-10).

It is significant, I think, that the first witnesses of the resurrection were the women who had stood by him when the men fled out of fear. There is a sense in which their loyalty and devotion to Christ was uniquely honoured by their being the first to get the message of the resurrection. However, when they first passed on the news to the disciples, Luke writes, 'But they did not believe the women, because their words seemed to them like nonsense' (24:11). When we first discover Christ and have the scales removed from our eyes, we can't understand why everybody around us doesn't share our excitement. We can't understand the attitude of scepticism and cynicism, but think of it, Jesus' own disciples rejected the news of his resurrection as nonsense. Peter was prepared to check it out, and ran to the tomb to see for himself. 'And he went away, wondering to himself what had happened' (24:12).

Jesus' followers had seen the empty tomb for themselves, and had heard the message from the angels that he had risen, but still Christ had not appeared to them.

The road to Emmaus (Luke 24:13-34)

The narrative that follows is one of the most moving of the entire New Testament, and is recorded only in Luke's gospel. It tells of the appearance of Jesus to two people walking on the road to Emmaus. 'Now that same day two of them were going to a village called Emmaus, about seven miles from Jerusalem. They were talking with each other about everything that had happened. As they talked and discussed these things with each other, Jesus himself came up and walked along with them; but they were kept from recognizing him' (24:13-16). For some reason Christ kept his identity a secret for the moment and fell in with them as they were walking and eavesdropped on their conversation.

Then he interrupted their conversation to ask: '"What are you discussing together as you walk along?' They stood still, their faces downcast. One of them, named Cleopas, asked him, "Are you only a visitor to Jerusalem and do not know the things that have happened there in these days?" ' (24:17-18). Their response is one of consternation mixed with sadness: 'What's the matter with you, how could you possibly not know the things that have happened?'

But Jesus probes further: 'What things?' he asked. Even in the resurrection Jesus has a sense of humour.

'About Jesus of Nazareth,' they replied. 'He was a prophet, powerful in word and deed before God and all the people. The chief priests and our rulers handed him over to be sentenced to death, and they crucified him' (24:19-20). They were speaking to a total stranger as far as they were aware, and yet they openly speak of their feelings about events and lay the blame squarely at the feet of the religious leaders. For all they knew, this man could have been a spy from the Sanhedrin, but it would seem they didn't care, they were so full with the emotion of recent events.

They continued to pour out their hearts to him:

'But we had hoped that he was the one who was going to redeem Israel. And what is more, it is the third day since all this took place. In addition, some of our women amazed us. They went to the tomb early this morning but didn't find his body. They came and told us that they had seen a vision of angels, who said he was alive. Then some of our companions went to the tomb and found it just as the women had said, but him they did not see' (24:21-24).

They hadn't embraced the message of the women – it was hearsay, as far as they were concerned, even though some of the men had been to check for themselves. The tomb was empty, but no-one had seen the risen Jesus.

Jesus then rebukes them: 'How foolish you are, and how slow of heart to believe all that the prophets have spoken!' Jesus' words are crucial; notice he doesn't rebuke them for not believing the testimony of the women, but for not believing all that the prophets had foretold. When he calls them foolish he doesn't mean that they were slow in their minds or unable to reason properly due to insufficient evidence, rather he was making a moral judgment. The problem was not their rationality, but their hearts; they were still cold to the truth of God. And so he asks, 'Did not the Christ have to suffer these things and then enter his glory?' This was no accident, it was an absolute necessity. 'And beginning with Moses and all the Prophets, he explained to them what was said in all the Scriptures concerning himself.' How I would love to have listened in on that sermon!

It was customary among the Jews at that time to cease one's travel when darkness fell. Jesus acted as if he intended to go on, but they pleaded with him to stay with them because they were enjoying this conversation with this man who knew the Old Testament so well. And so Jesus stayed with them.

The narrative goes on: 'When he was at the table with them, he took bread, gave thanks, broke it and began to give it to them' (24:30). Jesus engaged in the usual procedure of breaking bread for the evening meal. But at that moment of intimacy, God removed the veil from their faces, 'Then their eyes were opened and they recognized him, and he disappeared from their sight. They asked each other, "Were not our hearts burning within us while he talked with us on the road and opened the Scriptures to us?" ' How can we hear the story of the resurrection of Christ with a cold heart? These disciples' hearts were almost consumed as they listened to Christ expound the scriptures about himself.

'They got up and returned at once to Jerusalem.' They rushed back to Jerusalem, they didn't care that it was dark, they didn't care that it was seven miles away, they were so thrilled by what had happened. 'There they found the Eleven and those with them, assembled together and saying, "It is true! The Lord has risen and has appeared to Simon" ' (24:33-34).

104. Resurrection appearances and the ascension (Luke 24:35-53)

The two men rushed back to Jerusalem and found the eleven and began to tell them that they had proof that Christ was indeed risen and they had seen him for themselves. While they were all talking excitedly, Jesus himself appeared to them. Their excitement suddenly turned to fear for they thought they were seeing a ghost. But Jesus spoke to them, and asked, 'Why are you troubled, and why do doubts rise in your minds?' Then he takes the trouble to reassure them that he is not in fact a spirit: 'Look at my hands and my feet. It is I myself! Touch me and see; a ghost does not have flesh and bones, as you see I have' (24:38-39).

When we say we believe in the resurrection of Jesus we are not proclaiming the eternal significance of an idea – nor are we saying that Jesus lives on in somebody's memory or that his reappearances were simply visionary experiences. The confession of the Church of Christ for two thousand years has been, and must continue to be, an unequivocal conviction of the bodily resurrection of Jesus Christ. Anything less is at complete variance with the testimony of the New Testament.

This was no vision confronting the disciples: it was a resurrected body. To be sure it was a glorified body and changes had taken place in it that we do not understand, but the text declares unequivocally that it was a bodily resurrection.

Yet 'they still did not believe it because of joy and amazement' (24:41). It just seemed too good to be true and they couldn't believe it for joy. While they were still marvelling he said to them, 'Do you have anything here to eat?' Ghosts don't have appetites, visions don't sit down and break bread with people. Luke, with a preciseness that characterizes his writing, notes, 'he took it and ate it in their presence.'

Jesus then speaks to the group in the same way that he spoke to the two men on the road to Emmaus, calling attention to the whole testimony of sacred Scripture, saying that it is necessary these things must be fulfilled (24:44). 'Then he opened their minds so they could understand the Scriptures. He told them, "This is what is written: The Christ will suffer and rise from the dead on the third day, and repentance and forgiveness of sins will be preached in his name to all nations, beginning at Jerusalem. You are witnesses of these things"' (24:45-48).

The promised Holy Spirit

The gospel of Luke is coming to an end, but Luke, of course, writes a second volume, the book of Acts, in which he bears testimony to the fidelity of these disciples to the mandate delivered to them in this room by the risen Christ, even unto death. If the Church is to be the Church, it must embrace the resurrected Christ and obey his mandate that repentance for the forgiveness of sins should be proclaimed in his name to all the nations.

Jesus said, 'I am going to send you what my Father has promised; but stay in the city until you have been clothed with power from on high.' Here Jesus was telling them about the gift of the Holy Spirit that would soon be bestowed on them.

On his last day on earth Jesus led them out as far as Bethany on the hillside across the valley from Jerusalem. Luke writes:

'He lifted up his hands and blessed them. While he was blessing them, he left them and was taken up into heaven. Then they worshipped him and returned to Jerusalem with great joy. And they stayed continually at the temple, praising God' (24:50-53). What a way for Luke to end this narration of the life and work of Jesus of Nazareth! With the blessing of the risen Christ ringing in their ears, these disciples were overflowing with joy and praise to God.

At first, the disciples' joy on parting with Jesus seems a bit strange. Surely it would have been more natural for them to feel sad or reflective at a time like that. When we part from the one we love it is usually a sad moment. So can you imagine how you would feel if having walked, talked and lived with Jesus for three years and witnessed his miracles, his death and resurrection, he then left you, saying 'I go where you cannot come'. Would you not be devastated? Instead, however, Luke tells us that they returned to Jerusalem filled with joy. Why? Because they understood that it was better for Jesus to leave than for him to stay, for he went to take up his seat at the right hand of God, where all authority is given unto him.

He is the King right now of the universe. Here was the culmination of the Old Testament prophecies about the Messiah. Not only would he save the people from their sins and conquer death, but he would be elevated to the right hand of God. So it was not the fact that he had gone that was important, but *where* he went that filled his followers with joy. The resurrection was not Christ's ultimate act of glory, it was his penultimate, for in biblical history, his ascension must be ultimate. Jesus' ascension included his elevation to the throne of the universe, to rule as King of kings.

The ascension of Jesus, however, will not be the last event, for he has declared that he will come again at the end of the age when his rule will become visible to all. In the meantime we are called to the fact that right now he is the King.

A few days after he had gone up he fulfilled his promise and poured out his Spirit upon the church at Pentecost and sent them out into the world to every nation, to every people, fulfilling the great commission. And so Luke's fascinating story about the greatest life ever lived ends on a note of joy.

INDEX

IRC UK
College farm
Church Road
Denham Eye
Suffolk
IP21 5DE.   01 379 68937 S

Books
by
R. C. Sproul
published
by
Christian Focus

The Gospel of God

256 pages   ISBN 1 85792 077 5   large hardback

An exposition of the Book of Romans

Mighty Christ

144 pages   ISBN 1 85792 148 8   paperback

A study of the person and work of Jesus.

The Mystery of the Holy Spirit

192 pages   ISBN 1 871676 63 0   paperback

Examines the role of the Spirit in creation,
salvation and in strengthening the believer.

Ephesians

160 pages   ISBN 1 85792 078 3   paperback

Focus on the Bible Commentary, useful for
devotional study of this important New Testament book.